Foundations for Research
Methods of Inquiry in Education
and the Social Sciences

INQUIRY AND PEDAGOGY ACROSS DIVERSE CONTEXTS

Kathleen deMarrais, Series Editor

deMarrais and Lapan • Foundations for Research: Methods of Inquiry in Education and the Social Sciences

Foundations for Research
Methods of Inquiry in Education and the Social Sciences

Edited by

Kathleen deMarrais
University of Georgia

Stephen D. Lapan
Northern Arizona University

 LAWRENCE ERLBAUM ASSOCIATES, PUBLISHERS

2004   **Mahwah, New Jersey**   **London**

Editor: Naomi Silverman
Cover Design: Kathryn Houghtaling Lacey
Production Editor: Eileen Alanna Engel
Full-Service Compositor: TechBooks

This book was typeset in 10/12 pt. Goudy, Italic, Bold, Bold Italic.
The heads were typeset in ITC Officina Sans, Italic and Bold.

Lawrence Erlbaum Associates, Inc., Publishers
10 Industrial Avenue
Mahwah, NJ 07430
www.erlbaum.com

Library of Congress Cataloging-in-Publication Data

Foundations for research : methods of inquiry in education and the social
    sciences/edited by Kathleen deMarrais, Stephen D. Lapan.
        p.   cm.
    Includes bibliographical references and index.
    ISBN 0-8058-3650-0 (pbk. : alk. paper)
        1. Education—Research—Methodology.   2. Social sciences—Research—Methodology.
    I. deMarrais, Kathleen.   II. Lapan, Stephen D.

LB1028.F64   2004
370′.7′2—dc21   2003011807

Books published by Lawrence Erlbaum Associates are printed on
acid-free paper, and their bindings are chosen for strength and
durability.

Printed in the United States of America
10 9 8 7 6 5 4 3

To my brother (1951–2000)
Always a smile.   kpd

To my brother David (1944–2001)
The consummate mentor, he selflessly supported all he
touched—so many needed him to stay.   sdl

Contents

Preface

This text is designed for use in introductory research courses in the professional fields and social sciences. The major goal of the book is to acquaint students and beginning researchers with a broad view of research methodologies, as well as an understanding of the assumptions that inform each of these approaches. Because the book presents such diverse approaches to research, more experienced researchers will also find the book useful in acquainting them with research methodologies and theoretical frameworks that are new to them. In designing this book, the editors invited research methodologists from diverse theoretical and methodological locations to write essays that would invite novice researchers to examine both the perspective underlying differing research traditions, as well as the specific methods utilized in particular research approaches.

FOCUS POINTS

One of the strengths of this volume is its focus on **research ethics**. The volume begins with a chapter detailing multiple ways of approaching ethical principles and the roles of researchers and participants within research projects. Subsequently, these ethical considerations are addressed explicitly or implicitly in each of the following chapters within specific research methodologies. Readers leave the volume with an understanding of the controversies and complexities of creating ethical research to address social problems across a variety of sociopolitical contexts.

Another strength of the book is the consistent focus throughout on the **intertwined relationship of theory and research design**. Epistemological stances and theoretical frameworks inform the research process no matter what design and methods are selected for use in a particular study. The authors emphasize the necessity for researchers to clearly articulate their assumptions, beliefs, and values about the nature of reality, knowledge, and research. Each of the chapters engages readers in the sociohistorical context of a specific research methodology, presents key concepts and issues within that design, and concludes the chapter with a discussion of the methods of data collection, interpretation, and representation.

In addition, the book **systematically examines ways to design and implement high-quality, trustworthy research across varying research designs**. The authors discuss issues of validity and credibility as they illustrate ways to plan for research that results in trustworthy findings. Across the research designs presented here is a consistent emphasis on the need for high-quality, trustworthy research. Specific strategies are suggested throughout for readers to use in their own work as they seek to improve the quality of their research.

Finally, each author provides **specific methods for implementing research** within that framework. Thus, readers are not only engaged in the ethical, theoretical, and methodological issues, but are learning the practical tools employed by each of these researchers. Examples and illustrations abound throughout the volume ensuring a clear, articulate presentation by experienced researchers and teachers of research methods.

The editors include a series of **pedagogical strategies** designed to engage readers in the text, including a "Meet the Author" feature, which introduces the author through both text and photographs, **questions throughout each chapter** designed to encourage readers to apply key chapter concepts to their own thinking and research, and **extensive bibliographies** for each research approach to encourage further exploration of the various research methodologies in more depth.

OVERVIEW

Unlike more traditional introductory research texts, this volume avoids organizing the chapters into the discreet categories of qualitative and quantitative approaches. Although some chapters rely more heavily on qualitative approaches and others are more quantitative, many employ multiple research methods to investigate particular research problems and questions. In addition, the book is not organized into single, contradictory positivist–interpretivist categories of research. The authors often situate methodologies within a variety of, and sometimes multiple, theoretical positions particularly as these approaches are shaped within the historical context of social science research. For example, Hutchinson describes both positivist and constructivist assumptions underlying survey research, and Preissle and Grant review objectivist foundations for participant observation fieldwork.

The book begins with a chapter on research ethics to emphasize the crucial issues related to ethical practice across research methodologies. Following a chapter on historical research are chapters that utilize interview approaches in their research designs (qualitative interview studies, critical incident technique, focus group research, and narrative inquiry). The next several chapters

present methodologies that rest primarily on observational approaches to research (ethnomethodology, ethnography and participant observation, and critical
and postcritical ethnography). Next are chapters that utilize multiple research
approaches, both qualitative and quantitative (case study research, evaluation
studies, participatory evaluation, and multimethods research). The subsequent
chapters examine survey and experimental research approaches (survey research,
single-subject design, and experimental research). The final chapter of the book
illustrates the need for multiple approaches to research to critique and inform
public policy issues.

ACKNOWLEDGMENTS

We wish to acknowledge the high-quality work of the book's authors and the insightful comments of reviewers who were crucial to the development of the book.
We are indebted to the students we teach in our research courses for their many
questions about the research process. These questions led to the conception and
organization of this book. It is our hope that the book will assist in answering
some of those questions but, more importantly, raise new questions in our thinking about doing research and teaching research methods. In addition, we wish to
thank Yali Zhao and Rachel Foster for their fine assistance with the preparation
of the final manuscript and the staff at Lawrence Erlbaum Associates for their
work in preparing this book for publication. We acknowledge the thorough and
thoughtful contributions of the Lawrence Erlbaum Associates reviewers throughout the construction of this book, especially Patricia Hays, Kathy Farber, Pamela
Bettis, Jamie Lewis, and Naomi Silverman, for their insightful comments and support throughout the development of this project.

Foundations for Research
Methods of Inquiry in Education and the Social Sciences

1

Introduction

Kathleen deMarrais and Stephen D. Lapan

Research: the systematic investigation into and study of materials and sources in order to establish facts and reach new conclusions; from Old French (late 16th century), *re* (expressing intensive force) + *cerchier*, "to search" (*The New Oxford American Dictionary*, 2001, p. 1448).

As teachers of research methods courses, we may begin by engaging students in thinking about the concept of research. What is research? What is the purpose of research? What are the assumptions that underlie research methodologies? What is the difference between research methodologies and research methods? The above definition of research is typical of most dictionaries and research methods texts in that it emphasizes the systematic and careful nature of the work, and the goal of the work—to discover new understandings or knowledge about a problem. The origins in Old French turn our attention to both the focus on the word *search*, as well as the intensity of the enterprise. Our work is a thorough and systematic search—we expect an intensive one—to understand a phenomena or a problem and to contribute our learning to an already existing knowledge base in a particular discipline or across disciplines.

We find it helpful to understand students' conceptions of research to facilitate their processes in developing their own research questions and designs. To assess students' notions of research, we often ask them to draw a picture of their notions of research. A student may draw a picture of a library setting with piles of books in front of a lone scholar, indicating their notions of research as a search of existing literature. Another depicts a researcher in a white lab coat in front of test tubes and a microscope, where research takes place in the form of scientific experimentation. Students with more extensive research experience may draw pictures in which research is illustrated with people filling in survey forms, a researcher in front of a computer, or a researcher interviewing people or groups of people. Occasionally, a student presents a researcher with notepad taking notes in a setting. We can see in each of these illustrations that one's previous experience with the research and assumptions about the process shape, and often limit, the way we view research. This book is intended to entice novice researchers into a world of research that is rich with multiple possibilities for systematically exploring problems in education and the social sciences. We anticipate that the research methodologies presented in the following chapters will provide readers with new ways of viewing research, as well as intriguing ways of thinking about the nature of reality, the nature of knowledge, and the complicated role of the researcher in the practice of ethically responsible research with human participants.

Research in education and the social sciences has changed dramatically over the past few decades. With few exceptions, until the 1980s, the typical research training in universities focused on statistics, measurement, and experimental methods, with little or no attention to other approaches to research. As Eisner and Peshkin (1990) reminded us

> the psychometric model long dominated educational research, as it has generally dominated the social and behavioral sciences. If professors and their students departed from it, they invited scorn, if not rejection. To conduct experiments and surveys was to be scientific; to do otherwise—and otherwise covered considerable territory—was to be soft-, wrong-, or muddle-headed. (p. 1)

As qualitative research gained more prominence throughout the 1980s, the "paradigm wars" took place, in which scholars heatedly debated the virtues and limitations of quantitative versus qualitative methodologies (see Schutz, Chambless, & DeCuir, Chap. 16, this volume, for more detail and references). These debates are largely over, with researchers in both camps recognizing the value of multiple views and approaches to research practice. Students in professions such as education, business, nursing, and social work, as well as in the social sciences, have access to courses and programs in both qualitative and quantitative approaches to research. Although quantitative courses may dominate in some fields and departments in universities, students do not have to search far for opportunities to study qualitative methodologies and use them in their graduate research. An examination of conference proceedings and journals across the disciplines illustrates a wide range of research methodologies used to contribute new knowledge around human problems. The decade of the 1990s raised new challenges to research practice, with scholarly debates around the power differentials in researcher–participant relationships, ethical issues in the conduct of research, and in ways in which researchers represent participants in written accounts, particularly when participants are women and people of color. Much of this debate was of a philosophical nature based on postmodern challenges to traditional modernist notions of research assumptions and practice (see Lather, Chap. 12; Noblit, Chap. 11; and Preissle and Grant, Chap. 10, in this volume). As we begin the 21st century, these theoretical and methodological debates continue as scholars critique and rethink what has been and explore what might be in social science research. Researchers today are keenly aware of the multiple methodologies available for contributing new knowledge to the disciplines and the challenges entailed in the use of each of those approaches. As Lather (1994) reminded us, "There are many ways to do science" (p. 105).

In designing this book, we wanted to represent the discussions in both theory and method in the research literature today. We believe that in order to prepare new scholars for the multiple paradigmatic perspectives of research, they must be knowledgeable about the historical, philosophical, and moral foundations of inquiry. Paul and Marfo (2001) argued:

> Vigorous debates about the dominance of the quantitative tradition in educational research have substantially opened up the conversation regarding what constitutes

legitimate research. The debates have taken the discourse about research to a deeper level where topics range from technical issues of representation to the moral force of voice.

It is in this context that we have made the case for expanding the research education curriculum to include an emphasis on the nature of inquiry, including the epistemological, moral, and aesthetic foundations of knowledge and knowing. The narrow focus on methods in traditional research education programs does not prepare researchers for critical understandings of their own research orientation. Furthermore, the continued socialization of students in the view that *good science* is necessarily *quantitative science* leaves these future researchers ill-prepared to participate in informed critique or collaborative inquiry with other researchers who work within different paradigms of knowledge. (Emphasis in original, p. 543)

This volume attempts to do what Paul and Marfo assert is necessary for research training in today's context of graduate education. We invited research methodologists, many of whom are teachers of research, from diverse research orientations to write essays to encourage novice researchers to examine both the perspectives underlying differing research traditions, as well as the specific methods utilized in particular research approaches. Our goal was to challenge readers to think about their own values and assumptions about the nature of reality, knowledge, and research in relation to those presented in each of the chapters.

A NOTE ABOUT METHODOLOGY AND METHOD

In our own teaching, we have found that students new to research are sometimes unfamiliar with the language of research. New to them are words such as paradigm, theoretical framework, conceptual framework, epistemology, positivism, postpositivism, constructionism, subjectivism, and so forth. Words in research are used to convey specific meanings, but these meanings are not always shared across authors or across disciplines and theoretical perspectives. Readers will encounter these words in the following chapters in ways that will enable them to clearly understand these concepts.

For purposes of clarity as we begin the text, we turn the readers' attention to two words used throughout these discussions: *method* and *methodology*. Although the terms are often used synonymously, it is helpful for novice researchers to understand that the terms carry different meanings. A method is a particular research technique or way to gather evidence about a phenomenon. Methods are the specific research tools we use in research projects to gain fuller understanding of phenomena. Examples of methods include surveys, interviews, and participant observation. These methods or tools can be used in many different approaches to research.

We use methodology to describe "the theory of how inquiry should proceed" that "involves analysis of the principles and procedures in a particular field of inquiry" (Schwandt, 1997, p. 93). Much more than just methods or tools of research, methodology involves the researchers' assumptions about the nature of reality and the nature of knowing and knowledge. Tuchman (1994) compared the terms *method* and *methodology*:

> I do not use the term *methodology* in its current sense of "application of a specific method," such as analysis of documents or participant observation. Rather, I use *methodology* in its classic sense: the study of the epistemological assumptions implicit in specific methods. I thus assume that a methodology includes a way of looking at phenomena that specifies how a method "captures" the "object" of study. (p. 306)

Using another approach to the definition, Harding (1987) defined methodology as "a theory and analysis of how research does or should proceed" (p. 3). Methodology encompasses our entire approach to research. Our assumptions about what we believe knowledge is are embedded in methodological discussions and therefore have consequences for how we design and implement research studies. For example, ethnography is a research methodology that is informed by particular theoretical frameworks (such as symbolic interactionism or critical theory). Ethnography also uses particular theoretical assumptions about its core concept of culture. By contrast, the methods used in ethnography are typically participant observation, ethnographic interviews, and document analysis. It will be helpful for readers to keep these distinctions in mind as they move through the text. It is our goal to engage students in the methodologies first and the method in a secondary way. Each of the methodologies presented here is supported by a rich history of scholarship cited by the authors. We urge readers to pursue these readings in more depth as they begin to identify their own research questions and approaches.

KEY THEMES AND CONCEPTS OF THE BOOK

There are several consistent themes evident throughout the chapters, including the following: (1) ethical issues and responsibilities of researchers, (2) researcher–participant relationships, (3) the intertwined nature of theory and research design, (4) the sociohistorical context of particular research methodologies, (5) explanations of research methods used within each methodological approach, and (6) designing high-quality, trustworthy research. Although authors vary in their approaches to these topics, readers will leave the book with a complex understanding of the current issues and controversies within each theme. We have articulated the key concepts and issues raised by each of the authors in Table 1.1.

TABLE 1.1
Key Concepts in Chapters

Author	Research Approach	Key Concepts and Issues
Kirsten Crowder Tisdale	Ethics in research	Ethical responsibilities of researcher Philosophical perspectives on ethics Ethical principles and power in research Participant and researcher vulnerabilities Designing ethical research
Kate Rousmaniere	Historical research	Personal histories of education Past and present in educational history Differing theoretical perspectives in historical interpretation (consensus, revisionist, neo-revisionist, and postmodern) Primary and secondary sources Validity in historical research
Kathleen deMarrais	Qualitative interview studies	Types of qualitative interviews Definitions of interviews Phenomenological interview studies Bracketing interviews Methods for selecting participants Designing interview guides Power issues in researcher–participant relationships
Dan Kain	Critical incident technique	Historical perspectives on critical incident research components of a critical incident study Advantages and disadvantages of critical incident research Positivist roots of critical incident technique Interpretivist perspectives
Pamela Kleiber	Focus group research	Historical background of focus group research Role of the moderator in focus group research Variety of uses for focus group research Participants' perspectives on focus groups Strengths and limitations of focus group research Purposeful sampling for focus groups Suggestions for focus group procedures

Author	Research Approach	Key Concepts and Issues
Mary Kay Kramp	Narrative inquiry	Definitions of narrative
		Paradigmatic vs. narrative ways of knowing
		Elements of narratives
		Interpretation of narrative interviews
		Personal nature of narrative research
		Analysis of narrative and narrative analysis
Juanita Johnson-Bailey	Positionality/power in narrative work	Narratives in feminist research
		Use of narratives to portray women's lives
		Use of narratives to address power disparities
		Concept of the "Other" in feminist research
		Negotiating power in narrative inquiry
		Problematizing notion of the "insider"
		Researching within and across cultural boundaries
		Reconciling power and positional statuses in research
		Issues of ownership and representational in narrative research
Kathryn Roulston	Ethnomethodology (EM)	Membership categorization
	Conversational analytic (CA) studies	Indexicality and reflexivity
		"Straight-ahead" and applied EM and CA research
		Ethnomethodology as multidisciplinary
		Features of ethnomethodological research
		Local logic and emic rationality
		Using CA procedures
		CA transcription conventions
Judith Preissle and Linda Grant	Ethnography and participant observation	Fieldwork
		Ethnography and participant observation
		Participant observer roles
		Ethnographic research in anthropology and sociology
		Culture concept
		"Going native"
		Nature of reality
		Realism–dealism continuum

(continued)

TABLE 1.1
Key Concepts in Chapters (*continued*)

Author	Research Approach	Key Concepts and Issues
George Noblit	Critical and postcritical ethnography	Objectivism, constructionism, and subjectivism in fieldwork Evaluating the quality of fieldwork Synthesis of ethnography and critical theory A research method is theory Methods are historically situated Historical overview of critical ethnography Defining critical ethnography Crisis of representation and objectification Postmodernity and poststructuralism Antifoundationalism and postfoundationalism Representation in postcritical ethnography
Patti Lather	Feminist and poststructural perspectives	Critical social science as both understanding and changing Postpositivism Distinguishing method and methodology Role of ideology in research Crisis of representation Decentering the researcher as the master of truth Realist, critical, and deconstructive representations of research Discrepant data Researcher–researched relations and "othering"

Patricia A. Hays	Case study research	Purposes of case studies:
		  Selecting a site and bounding the study
		  Unit of analysis
		  Purpose of a literature review
		  Case study data sources
		  Triangulation
		  Construct validity
		  Data analysis and member checking

Stephen D. Lapan	Evaluation studies	Criteria of merit Standards for measuring performance Focus of evaluation studies compared with other forms of social science research

Author	Research Approach	Key Concepts and Issues
Gila Garaway	Participatory evaluation	Role of stakeholders in evaluation
		Data sources for evaluation research
		Purposeful and random sampling techniques
		Validating results through member checking and triangulation
		Defining participatory research
		Action research and participatory action research
		Rationales for participatory evaluation (utilization, empowerment, decision making)
		Validity and credibility of findings
		Characteristics of professional evaluators
		Methods for participatory evaluation
		Emotional and psychological costs of conflicting perspectives in evaluation
Paul A. Schutz, Courtney B. Chambless, and Jessica T. DeCuir	Multimethod research	Method and methodology
		Epistemologies
		External and objective realities
		Socially constructed realities
		Knowledge as fallible and changeable
		Sociohistorical contexts
		Triangulation
		Complementarity
Susan R. Hutchinson	Survey research	Definition of survey research
		Situating survey research within research design frameworks
		Varying uses for survey data
		Assumptions underlying survey research
		Developing surveys for trustworthiness
		Planning stages in survey research design
		Sample selection
		Types of survey items

(continued)

9

Table 1.1
Key Concepts in Chapters (*continued*)

Author	Research Approach	Key Concepts and Issues
Karen Sealander	Single-subject experimental research	Reliability and validity issues in survey research
		Electronic and Web-based survey research
		Aims of single-subject experimental research
		Casual and functional relationships between variables
		Procedures in single-subject experimental design
		Selecting target behaviors
		Establishing baseline conditions
		Operationalizing constructs
		Repeated measurement
		Basic forms of design
		Analysis and interpretation of results
Lawrence Cross and Gabriella Belli	Experimental research	Definition of experiment
		Types of variables (independent, dependent, and extraneous)
		Theories, hypotheses, and proof
		Casual inferences and relationships
		Correlation
		Internal and external validity
		Threats to validity
		Random sampling and random assignment
		Quasi-experimental designs
		Ethics of educational experiments
Ernest R. House	Using multiple methodologies: the case of retention in Chicago retention and social promotion	Independent evaluation of public policies
		Misuse of testing data
		Effective research-based strategies for alternative to retention and social promotion

Following the methodological chapters, we conclude the book with House's chapter, focused on the issue of retention in Chicago's city schools to illustrate the use of multiple research methodologies to evaluate and critique the use of retention programs in schools. This chapter provides a practical example of ways researchers might inform public policy to provide appropriate research-based practices and solutions to critical educational problems.

We began this introduction with a definition of the word *research*, with an emphasis on an intense, systematic search for understanding and knowledge. Another dictionary entry suggests that research is "to travel through" (*Webster's New World College Dictionary*, 1997, p. 1141). We invite you to employ this metaphor of traveling through as you begin to explore the methodologies and methods of research presented in the following chapters and expect that you will begin to envision ways to travel through your own research endeavors.

2

Being Vulnerable and Being Ethical With/in Research

Kit Tisdale
University of Georgia

MEET THE AUTHOR

Formerly a professional horseback rider, **Kit Tisdale** is currently a doctoral candidate in educational psychology at the University of Georgia. Born in New Orleans, she grew up in Jackson, Mississippi, and later moved to Florence, Alabama, to train 3-day event horses and to finish high school. Living in the horse country of Lexington, Tisdale was graduated from the University of Kentucky with a bachelor's degree in psychology in 1995. The impetus to enroll in graduate school came from a year of studies in psychology at University College, London, in England. After partly analyzing her thesis data from the back of her horse, Tisdale earned a master's degree in educational psychology from the University of Georgia in 1999.

Tisdale spent 2 years working with emotionally disturbed adolescents at a residential treatment facility in Versailles, Kentucky. She credits her past work as a youth counselor for her current research interests in emotions, disability studies, and qualitative research methods. She has published studies in the journals *Educational Psychologist*, *Journal of Educational Psychology*, and *Reading Research and Instruction*. In her dissertation, Tisdale examined the sense of self of emotionally disturbed adolescents within a Foucaultian archaeology of emotional disturbance. When not working on her research, Tisdale can be found outdoors—hiking with her family, playing Frisbee with her dog, or riding a horse.

Watching other people live their lives, asking people about their experiences, and using words to tell others' stories are hallmarks of social science research methods. Because of the close relationship of the researcher to the researched forged with these methods, the power of research to both help and harm is often felt acutely by researchers. Ethical responsibilities permeate our lives and implicate us in all sorts of unsavory situations. Even with the best of intentions, we can be blindsided by our carelessness and violence. We strive to do good and to do no harm, but being ethical, it turns out, is not as easy as following the guidelines of one's profession or institutional review board (IRB). Our diverse ways of conceptualizing protection and goodness leave us without the foundations we may have once believed grounded our ethical decisions. Although the presence of IRBs and professional codes of ethics give the appearance of a common basis to resolve ethical dilemmas, the ground becomes shaky indeed under the feet of social science researchers.

This chapter is about becoming comfortable with that uncomfortable, shaky ground. As researchers, we must do our work—it would be unconscionable to turn our backs on the world just to save our ethical skins. Getting on with it means we must negotiate ethics; we must ask difficult questions of ourselves and of our work. In this chapter, I ask the difficult questions of whether we have different responsibilities to different people and whether we have the potential to harm some people more than others. First, in a brief discussion of various theories of ethics, multiple ways of conceiving of our duties toward one another and of ethical actions are outlined. In the second section, I delineate two ways of conceptualizing what it means to be vulnerable in research. Finally, the diverse ways researchers have used their conceptions of duty and ethical actions within social science research with vulnerable people are discussed.

CONSIDERING ETHICS

Consider the following scenario:

> Dr. Patin is studying a group of boys at a juvenile justice facility in a midsized city. After spending 6 months interviewing the boys and observing their interactions in classrooms and during recreational time, Dr. Patin feels that he knows the boys well. He has learned about their family histories, the crimes they committed, their group dynamics, and their hopes for the future. Dr. Patin is planning on using the data for a tradebook on juvenile justice issues and for a series of scholarly articles on peer relationships in institutional settings. Before a 9 a.m. scheduled interview with Jason, one of the participants, Dr. Patin receives a phone call from the facility. He is told that another resident and friend of Jason's committed suicide in the early morning hours. Jason has been clearly upset since hearing the news. The director of the facility inquires if Dr. Patin wants to proceed with the scheduled interview.

What is the right thing for Dr. Patin to do? What are his duties in this situation? Because there are many ways to understand ethics, there are many ways to answer these questions. The main work in the philosophy of ethics is divided into the general study of goodness and the general study of right action (Deigh, 1995). This chapter will consider both right action and the determiner of right action, goodness. The principles of right and wrong "govern our choices and pursuits" and make up the moral code that "defines the duties of men and women who live together in fellowship" (Deigh, p. 246). But, as I will show, the principle of right and wrong and moral code that defines our duties toward one another is not a monolithic entity; there are various theories to explain what it means to be moral and virtuous. For example, Jacobs (1980) delineated four types or theories of ethics important to social research: utilitarian, Kantian, covenantal, and situational. These theories overlap somewhat with May's (1980) five types of ethics: teleological, utilitarian, deontological, critical philosophy, and covenantal. An understanding of these diverse and sometimes conflicting ethical theories is necessary for social science researchers who must all negotiate ethics in their work. In an effort to parse out these various theories, I'll use the delineations made by May and Jacobs to examine various answers to two questions of morality: (1) What are our duties toward one another? and (2) what is right action?

According to teleological, or consequentialist, ethics, we have a responsibility to pursue certain good ends. Alleviating human suffering by curing cancer could be an example of a good end. Right actions are defined as the best way to pursue good ends—simply stated, the ends justify the means. If Dr. Patin in the above scenario subscribed to this belief system, he might decide that collecting this important data is the good end that he must pursue. Because of his interest in peer relationships, Dr. Patin is especially interested in understanding Jason's reaction to his friend's death. Thus, Dr. Patin would do what was necessary to meet with Jason this morning. Dr. Patin would not worry much about the immediate distress the interview might cause as long as the outcome of the research was good.

A type of teleological ethics, utilitarianism, focuses the good or harm that human action produces. To determine the rightness of an action under utilitarianism, a cost–benefit analysis is useful. For example, following this philosophy, a researcher aiming to cure cancer would need to determine if a specific treatment would provide greater human benefits with less human cost before using it in a research trial. As another example, philanthropists might use a utilitarianism philosophy to decide how their gifts of money might bring the greatest good to the greatest number of people. Dr. Patin might consider the benefits his reports of the research could bring to a large number of boys even though the research interview may further distress Jason.

Deontological, or nonconsequentialist, ethics focus on the principle of obligation that restrains human action. Under this philosophy, we have a duty to act in certain ways toward others regardless of the consequences resulting from our actions. If following this code of ethics, Dr. Patin might decide to cancel the morning interview. He may believe that he has a duty not to inflict more distress on Jason. Even if the outcome of the data collection could help many other boys, Dr. Patin may consider himself restrained from collecting the data because of his obligation of respecting Jason's time of grief. He may write a note to Jason expressing his condolences and telling Jason that he'll see him the following week.

The Ten Commandments in the Judeo-Christian religious tradition provide examples of specific duties that are considered right actions in and of themselves and require no further justification, such as a good outcome. Kant's formalism, which is based on the rational abilities of humans rather than the command of a divine being, is another example of this type of ethics. According to Kant, reason makes it possible for us to determine moral principles, which, in turn, "regulate our conduct insofar as we engage each other's rational nature" (Deigh, 1995, p. 246). Thus, we must respect others as rational, autonomous persons "regardless of how their values or interests may conflict with one's own" (Jacobs, 1980, p. 373). Another example of deontological ethics is rights theory. Our duties toward one another are to equally acknowledge the natural, inalienable rights of every individual. From this theoretical perspective, right actions follow Thomas Jefferson's call to respect each other's life, liberty, and pursuit of happiness.

Kant's philosophy, in particular, concerns how to treat people universally and does not leave room for the special obligations we might have to others, such as our family members (May, 1980). Covenantal ethics is more about these special relationships. The reciprocal nature of covenants is reflected in its biblical origins, which tell of the covenants between God and the Israelites. Covenantal ethics involves "making a pact with a group, subscribing to their ideals, for example, and establishing categorical obligations to or with them" (Jacobs, 1980, p. 373). These ethics "rest on a deeper footing than contract [ethics, which are more about buying and selling than giving and receiving], on a lower pedestal than philanthropy, and on a more concrete foundation that Kant's universal principle of respect" (May, 1980, p. 368). If Dr. Patin was guided by covenantal ethics, he might feel a duty toward the group of boys who have trusted him with their stories. The boys are sharing their lives with Dr. Patin, and Dr. Patin might see himself as obligated to respect and affirm the special relationship he has developed with the boys. In this scenario, he may meet with Jason at 9 a.m. but suggest that they spend their time "off the record." Based on what he knows about Jason's interests, Dr. Patin might suggest they spend the time playing basketball, sketching with new pencils and a field book Dr. Patin brought, or cowriting a letter to the friend's parents. Their time together would not be for Dr. Patin to collect data. Rather, the time would be an opportunity for Dr. Patin to honor the special relationship he has developed with Jason.

In comparing the strengths and weaknesses of teleological and deontological ethics, why do you think it is necessary to make this distinction between the two classifications?

Ethics arising from critical theory (e.g., Habermas, 1975) are another category defined by May (1980). Critical philosophy focuses ethics on special obligations to oppressed populations; actions of advocacy are considered right actions. In a research setting, this ethical orientation reminds researchers that "in allowing themselves to be studied, a subject population has a right to expect from the field researcher something more substantial than bourgeois respect, courtesy and honesty; they have a right to the social power that comes from knowledge" (p. 365). A researcher may act as an advocate for the oppressed population, an adversary to the powerful, and/or as a facilitator, or collaborator. Within these roles, the researcher's commitments to the discipline, the truth, and other people set limits on what the researcher will do on behalf of the subject community. If working within this philosophical framework, Dr. Patin might cancel the interview and spend the morning investigating the inadequate funding for mental health professionals at the facility. He may write an op-ed column for the local newspaper, bringing this issue to public attention. By taking political action on the event causing distress to his participant, Dr. Patin would be trying to meet his duties toward Jason and his other participants.

Jacobs (1980) outlined situational ethics as another type of ethics. To determine the right action, "one examines the ethical problem in context of situations, as they occur" (p. 373). It is a "kind of anti-theoretical, case-by-case applied ethics" (Becker, 1995, p. 738). Using situational ethics, Dr. Patin would not have a simple answer to this or any question of ethics. Even if he had previously canceled an interview after a distressing event, he would consider Jason's case on its own. He might consider his personal relationship to Jason, previous conversations with Jason about death or this friend, his own knowledge of the counseling services available to Jason, his obligation to his professional organizations, his skills at interviewing, and so forth.

Postfoundational theorists would take issue with Becker's (1995) contention that situation ethics are antitheoretical. These types of ethical actions are, in fact, situated within theories such as poststructuralism. Rather than using decisions based in humanist foundational philosophies, which ground the previously discussed theories, situational ethics "explodes anew in every circumstance . . . and hounds praxis unmercifully" (St. Pierre, 1997, p. 176). A researcher must constantly negotiate right action while simultaneously using ethics under erasure (Derrida, 1997)—knowing that using ethics are both necessary (we want to relate to each other in ethical ways) and problematic (we can never absolutely fix the definition of relating to each other in ethical ways). An acknowledgment of the multiplicity of ethical meanings "tears up and multiplies our responsibilities" (Gregoriou, 1995, p. 314) and complicates situational ethics.

> Compare critical philosophy with situational ethics. How do these compare with teleological and deontological approaches? Where do you stand on them?

These theories show divergent beliefs of what it means to act ethically. As the scenario with Dr. Patin illustrated, sometimes a choice of action may be similar across theories, but the underlying reasons for choosing that action over another can be very different. In the governance of research, federal guidelines (later discussed) are based on moral principles that are "generally accepted" in our culture. But the multiplicity of these theories, as I've just discussed, makes the concept of "generally accepted" suspect. Nevertheless, it is vital that, as researchers, we know the acknowledged principles, for those are the ones that we must negotiate in order to legitimate our research in the realm of IRBs. I turn now to a discussion of the legal conceptualization of vulnerability and the ethical principles that ground it before I will consider alternate ways of interpreting vulnerability.

BEING VULNERABLE

The National Commission for the Protection of Human Subjects of Biomedical and Behavioral Research (NCPHS) was created by the U.S. Congress in 1974 to advise the Department of Health, Education and Welfare (DHEW) in its supervision of federally funded research and IRBs. In 1978, the commission submitted to Congress, President Jimmy Carter, and the DHEW The *Belmont Report: Ethical Principles and Guidelines for the Protection of Human Subjects of Research* (BR). This brief document is a "statement of departmental policy" to "provide federal employees, members of Institutional Review Boards and scientific investigators.... [a]n analytical framework that will guide the resolution of ethical problems arising from research involving human subjects" (NCPHS, 1978, excerpt of letter to President Carter).

Vulnerability is used in the BR (NCPHS, 1978) to describe categories of research participants who deserve special protection. The term, however, is not clearly defined in this important document. Rather, the moral principles guiding research with humans are explicated in the BR, thereby giving researchers and IRBs the tools deemed necessary to make ethical decisions related to vulnerable populations. The following section is a response to the question, What does it mean to be vulnerable? I discuss vulnerability in two ways: (1) as an a priori description of peoples' positions in our society (e.g., these people are poor, and therefore they are innately vulnerable) and (2) as an a posteriori interpretation of participants' positions created within the research process (e.g., these participants' identities have become known, and therefore they are now vulnerable).

A Priori Vulnerability

The BR (NCPHS, 1978) provided three basic moral principles "among those generally accepted in our cultural tradition" (p. 4) to guide research involving humans. They are respect for persons, beneficence, and justice. The BR draws researchers' attention toward two of the moral principles—respect for persons and justice—for the consideration of the preexisting vulnerability of potential participants. The first principle, respect for persons, indicates a researcher's "requirement to acknowledge [a person's] autonomy and requirement to protect those with diminished autonomy" (p. 5). The principle of justice directs researchers to fairly distribute the benefits and burdens of research to all people. I will take each of these principles in turn to explicate the preexisting vulnerability of certain potential research participants.

The first principle, respect of persons, directs researchers to respect the autonomy of people and to protect those with diminished autonomy. An autonomous person is defined in the BR (NCPHS, 1978) as "an individual capable of deliberation about personal goals and of acting under the direction of such deliberation"

(p. 8). It is, however, the cases of diminished autonomy that are important when discussing vulnerability. A person is considered to have diminished autonomy if that person is incapable of reasoned deliberation about personal goals, of acting from that deliberation, or both. In essence, he or she lacks self-determination.

Diminished autonomy creates circumstances where a person is easily manipulated and, therefore, is vulnerable (O'Connor, 1979). For example, a mentally ill individual may be unable to think logically and, thus, is easily manipulated. Another person who is institutionalized may be able to think logically but is unable to act on every reasoned decision he or she makes because of the rules of the institution. Thus, an institutionalized person can be manipulated. Further, children are considered easily manipulated because they do not have the ability to think or act on those thoughts from a "mature" position. Each of these three cases creates vulnerability when an individual is disrespected by the act of manipulation.

The BR (NCPHS, 1978) recognized that diminished autonomy can be a permanent or temporary state of affairs. For instance, autonomy may diminish permanently for an individual with a mental disability. In contrast, autonomy can diminish during a temporary period for another individual with a physical illness, but autonomy can return with the individual's improved health. Circumstances such as incarceration can determine the more or less permanently diminished autonomy of people. Finally, in the case of children, diminished autonomy is considered temporary because autonomy is gained through maturation. It is simply the temporary period of childhood that creates the lack of self-determination. Vulnerability, then, can be a permanent or temporary state of affairs as situations that weaken self-determination arise in peoples' lives.

The BR (NCPHS, 1978) used a second principle, justice, to further consider vulnerability. "Who ought to receive the benefits of research and bear its burdens?" (p. 8) is a question of justice. The principle of justice dictates that researchers should not burden an already burdened group of people in society. Because of easy availability and societal prejudice, certain people are considered vulnerable to carrying more than their fair share of the burdens of research. People against whom there exists historical prejudice are just such a burdened group. Thus, researchers may not unjustifiably target poor populations and ethnic or racial minorities as their participants. In addition, the easy availability of certain populations may exacerbate their vulnerability. O'Connor (1979) pointed out that availability does not appear to be a sufficient way to define vulnerability because the BR does not include college students, an ever available and used population in research, in the explanation of the principle of justice. Instead, to be considered vulnerable, the population must be one that, in addition to being easily available, has been historically viewed as less than "desirable." Thus, drawing participants from a prison raises questions of justice, whereas drawing participants from college classrooms does not.

O'Connor (1979) also pointed out that deviant people can be considered vulnerable. Deviant behavior is outside of accepted norms and can put those exhibiting such behavior in the "undesirable" category delineated in the BR (NCPHS, 1978). Researchers are directed by the BR not to "select only 'undesirable' persons for risky research" (p. 18). Because deviants are considered to be burdened by their difference, people such as sexual deviants and illicit drug users can be considered vulnerable if researchers place "further burdens on already burdened persons" (p. 18).

Using the two principles of respect for persons and justice, the BR (NCPHS, 1978) implicitly defined people who are vulnerable to exploitation and harm within research and who are in need of special protection. This special protection leads researchers to carefully consider the following procedures within research studies: informed consent, risk–benefit assessment, and participant selection. These procedures are part of the research plan and require consideration while the participants are still imaginary. This planning is possible because the existence of these categories of vulnerability precede the research.

The ethical principles used to consider vulnerability represent varied ethical theories. Respect for persons reflects Kant's deontological theory, which stresses the goodness of acting with regard for people's rational nature. The principle of justice reflects two theories: a utilitarian, teleological theory of ethics, which stresses our duty to pursue good ends (the benefits of research), and a rights-based deontological theory, which stresses the equitable treatment of people. Although these theories and the BR's (NCPHS, 1978) extraction of vulnerability from these theories are helpful in the planning stages of research, this understanding of vulnerability fails to fully consider the realities of social science research. The realities of research indicate that vulnerability can arise within the research process.

> In your own words, what does the term *a priori vulnerability* mean in relation to the application of ethics in research? In what ways might this encourage ethical behavior?

A Posteriori Vulnerability

To make the point that vulnerability arises during the research process, I now turn the ethical principle of beneficence. Beneficence is widely defined as "doing good" (Mish, 1984). Within the BR (NCPHS, 1978), it is defined as an obligation to two general rules: (1) Do no harm and (2) maximize possible benefits and minimize possible harms (p. 6). O'Connor (1979) pointed out the peculiarity of the commission's use of the two previously discussed ethical principles to consider vulnerability when the principle of beneficence may be what truly guides our duty to protect others and to do no harm. Although the principles of respect for persons and justice allow researchers to understand which populations are deserving of special protection, the principle of beneficence actually reminds researchers of what it means to protect and to do good. Although we must address the vulnerability discussed in the BR in order to gain legitimacy in the eyes of our institutions and the federal government, we must also address this a posteriori vulnerability in order to gain respect in the eyes of our participants and ourselves.

But what does it mean to protect and to do good? I've already written that section, so the reader may see me going in circles. I am, but I have reasons. Because the ethical theories define our duties differently, doing good and doing no harm can be conceived of in various ways. What may seem to be unethical to a person operating with a teleological view of ethics may not seem unethical to a person operating with a deontological view of ethics, and vice versa. When we consider that we do not all believe in similar ethical theories, vulnerability becomes all sorts of things. To make my point, I revisit what it means to protect and do good from the multiple ethical philosophies.

If a researcher knows that the publication of an ethnography of a school will benefit many other schools (but perhaps bring harm to the studied school), the teleologically ethical researcher might decide to publish the manuscript. In contrast, if that researcher operated from a covenantal standpoint, the sense of obligation the researcher has to the studied school might preclude the publication of harmful data. If the researcher used a critical theory notion of ethics, the researcher may be obligated to use the study specifically to advocate for school improvements. Finally, a researcher using situational ethics might repeatedly negotiate the publication with the school community as issues related to publication arose. In each of these examples, protecting and doing good is based on ethical perspectives.

> Can you think of your own example for a teleological versus a covenantal versus a critical theoretical versus a situational approach to research ethics?

We have to use our individual philosophical beliefs to conduct ethical research. In any of the above examples, not doing the right thing from the perspective of a particular theory would produce harm from the perspective of that theory (but not necessarily from the perspective of another theory). We cannot simply rely on the general principles that established the BR (NCPHS, 1978). Although they are useful in some ways, they represent a fairly narrow view of ethics and may not fully represent our own views. Vulnerability arises in so many ways that we are not able to plan for it. We could never plan for all the possibilities. Yet, as researchers, we are responsible for all of the possibilities. As St. Pierre (1997) wrote, "We are always on the hook, responsible, everywhere, all the time" (p. 177). We therefore have to negotiate ethics in situ. It is toward this enactment of ethical research that I now turn.

BEING ETHICAL

Social science researchers have used various methods to protect vulnerable research participants. The BR (NCPHS, 1978) and subsequent IRB protocols suggested methods of protecting those preexisting vulnerabilities previously discussed. Researchers, however, have had less guidance when dealing with the vulnerability created within research projects. I first discuss the ways researchers have designed, implemented, and represented studies with preexisting vulnerable populations. Second, I explore the ways researchers, in the attempt to remain ethical, have adjusted the design, implementation, and representation of studies that have given rise to vulnerability.

A Priori Vulnerability

Selecting participants, making risk–benefit assessments, and obtaining informed consent are applications of ethical principles detailed in the BR (NCPHS, 1978). These procedures "concentrate primarily on the initial review of the experimental protocol" (Cassell, 1978, p. 140). Informed consent in particular has been criticized for potentially creating "meaningless rituals" rather than "improving the ethics of field research" (Thorne, 1980, p. 285) and for being more appropriate for experimental research than qualitative fieldwork (Lincoln & Guba, 1989). Nevertheless, the procedures of IRB approval and the explication of a priori vulnerability in the BR seem to have helped researchers in the design, implementation, and representation of studies with vulnerable populations.

In designing studies, researchers have considered how to respect the diminished autonomy of participants and how to manage the burdens of research on already burdened groups. Recruitment of vulnerable populations can be complicated. Nack (2000) chose to study women who had been diagnosed with sexually transmitted diseases (STDs). The participants could not be actively recruited by Nack but, rather, had to find her after their doctors gave them information of Nack's study. Using previously published information is another approach to finding participants whose vulnerability is apparent. Davis (2000) used stories of alleged child abuse victims and abusers in her study of false memory syndrome. Confidentiality and recruitment of participants were made simpler with Davis' choice to use previously published abuse accounts from books, newsletters, and Internet sites as the data for this article.

Covert participant observation is a design choice some researchers have used with vulnerable populations for both pragmatic and ethical reasons. When beginning research with codependent self-help groups, Irvine (1998) decided it was best for her to approach this population by attending only open-to-the-public meetings. She struggled with the idea of identifying herself and obtaining informed consent. Irvine finally decided not to identify herself or obtain informed consent from the group at large for three reasons: (1) There were no gatekeepers to "allow" her access to the group; (2) there was a culture of anonymity already in place for the 12-step program; and (3) she deemed it most harmful to interrupt the meetings to announce her research agenda (to people seeking help for always putting other's needs before their own). Erickson and Tewksbury (2000) used covert participant observation to record behaviors of male strip-club patrons. The authors made the decision to not identify themselves or obtain informed consent because previous research in sexualized environments indicated to them that patrons tend "to be highly secretive and suspicious of others" (p. 275). The authors of these studies using covert participant observation maintained the anonymity of the vulnerable populations studied.

Researchers have implemented their research projects sensitive to the physical and psychological comfort of vulnerable populations. When working with adolescents, some researchers used collaboration so that the adolescents could have more control over the process and products of the research (e.g., Eicher, Baizerman, & Michelman, 1991; Oldfather & Thomas, 1996a, 1996b). Some researchers interviewing children and adolescents have used strategies such as interviewing at home instead of at school (e.g., Eicher et al., 1991) and creating homogenous focus groups that exclude authorities from attending (e.g., Barker & Loewenstein, 1997) to protect adolescents' confidentiality and to gain trust. Smith (1998) felt it was important for her to validate the participants' feelings by practicing "nonjudgmental listening" when interviewing children whose military parents were deployed to the Bosnian War. When interviewing adolescents about sex, Eyre (1997) recognized the need for the interviewer to establish rapport and help the participant feel comfortable enough to talk about his or her sex life. One aspect of establishing comfort was to pair the interviewer and participant based on gender.

Other researchers who work with poor participants have made it a point to address vulnerabilities by being of benefit to the participants. In *Hard Living on Clay Street*, Howell (1972) discussed his efforts to be of immediate use to his participants: "As a neighbor I did what most neighbors were expected to do. I helped out when I could. Helping out consisted of giving people rides when they needed transportation, lending money, and writing letters to bill collectors, magazine companies, or doctors for people who felt they were being abused" (p. 392).

Behar (1993) a Cuban American researcher, also wrote of the ways she negotiated a mutually beneficial relationship with her poor, socially marginalized participant, Esperanza. Behar wrote that their relationship as "comadres" allowed them "to transcend, to a certain extent, our positions as gringa and Mexicana" (p. 6). Nack (2000) tried to reciprocate with her patients with a diagnosis of STD by providing support and resources from her job as a sexual health educator.

Researchers have also addressed participant vulnerability by being sensitive to issues of representation. To maintain confidentiality of vulnerable participants, some researchers use minimal amounts of information to identify participants' quotes (e.g., Barker & Loewenstein, 1997; Eicher et al., 1991). Though she has a video of young Yup'ik girls "story-knifing" in their natural setting, deMarrais (1998) has chosen not to share the videotape publicly. She reflected, "Asking a 10-year-old for permission to use the tape, even with the permission of the parents, may not be informed consent. I wonder what that child will think of her consent to use the tape when she is an adult" (p. 93). While ethically considering the representation of Esperanza's life story, Behar (1993) discovered that vulnerability was situational. Esperanza was only worried about what the women in her own village would say; she told Behar that she could do as she pleased with her life stories—"Let the gringos read them" (p. 19). Esperanza felt invulnerable as long as the stories were written in English because "only in her original tongue would her confessions be dangerous" (p. 20).

> Do you believe the researchers were being ethical in all of these examples? How do you think they might have been more so?

To a large extent, vulnerabilities such as those previously discussed can be considered in the planning stages of social science research. If a researcher knows that the potential participants have somehow been marginalized or compromised within society, the researcher is ethically (and legally) obligated to take precautions. There are many ways that researchers can recruit participants, collect data, reciprocate benefits, and represent participants when they know about the vulnerabilities. But what about the vulnerabilities that arise during research projects?

A Posteriori Vulnerability

When researchers heed the principle of beneficence, they recognize the need to prepare for vulnerability in ways that go beyond the mandates of federal regulations. When the routines dictated by IRB boards are completed, researchers are left with "generally accepted" ethical principles, the guidelines provided by their professional organizations, their own ethical and paradigmatic stances, and their research. "Ultimately the inquirer must make individual judgments reflecting his or her value structure, the internalized ethical codes of mentors and trainers, and the situation in which the inquiry is conducted. Thus, ethical decisions are basically left to the individual inquirer" (Lincoln & Guba, 1989, p. 223).

Researchers do not always know what makes people vulnerable and how they or the research itself can bring harm to others. For example, Deyhle (1998), a European American woman collecting ethnographic data on a Navajo reservation, was surprised to realize that her "White" presence brought embarrassment to the family of key informants with whom she lived. Further, her unwitting cultural faux pas of transporting a traditional ceremony item brought negative repercussions on the family. Her actions and her presence made the Navajo family vulnerable within their community. Researchers can prepare to address those "obvious" vulnerabilities previously discussed, but sometimes the vulnerability only becomes obvious during the study. The ethical considerations for this vulnerability are not resolvable a priori but, rather, require ongoing reflection and decision during the research process (Bresler, 1996). In this section, I review various circumstances of and decisions regarding vulnerability in research.

Rosenblatt (1995) conducted research with farm families in which there had been a fatal farming accident. To recruit volunteers, Rosenblatt advertised. Although the IRB approved this method of recruitment because it was apparently free of any coercive or deceptive elements, the researcher realized that family members were coercing one another to participate. Further, interviewing families can be an ethically sticky situation. A completely informed consent for an interview can be impossible for researchers to obtain because interviewers do not usually follow strict interview protocols and, thus, surprising interview topics can emerge. It has been argued that this problem is exacerbated in family research because of the "pervasiveness of family life" (LaRossa, Bennett, & Gelles, 1981, p. 305), which connects family life with all other aspects of individual lives. A researcher may plan to talk about career issues, and before he or she knows it, marital problems between the participants become part of the conversation.

Rosenblatt (1995) decided the most ethical action he could take was to allow the (sometimes coercive and sometimes not fully informed) interviews to take place because the results could be catalysts for grieving families to heal. He used a teleological rationale. Rosenblatt realized he often caused pain to surface in his participants by asking them to retell the fatal trauma of a family member. He wrote, "From the perspective of the cost–benefit analysis that is at the heart of most IRB reviews, some reviewers consider the grief that people may experience during a loss interview too high a cost to justify the research" (p. 144). In contrast, he believed that the hurt experienced and expressed in interviews could be part of the healing process. There were times, however, when he did not feel this was the case, and his reaction was "to move the interview away from the painful matters" (p. 145). He reported using "processual consent," as a supplement to traditional informed consent, to repeatedly give participants an opportunity to stop the interview or avoid particular questions.

A critical ethnographer can feel unethical when he or she takes no action to correct social problems (e.g., Velazquez, 1998). For example, Sleeter (1998, p. 55) approached her research with a critical philosophical orientation to research. In her critiques of teachers, she played the role of adversary to the powerful in order to advocate for children. For her, ethical action was defined by the actions that supported the less powerful in society. She wrote the following:

> Much of my work over the last 20 years has been guided by the question of how to make schooling a better experience for children of color and from low-income backgrounds, or both. It has become increasingly clear to me that, whenever faced with conflicting questions of purpose and affiliation, I regard my main clients as children in schools, rather than as teachers (or administrators or pre-service students). (p. 55)

In your opinion, is it a sufficient argument that "Rosenblatt believed that the hurt experienced . . . could be part of the healing process"? And, will you leave it to Sleeter to determine what is in the best interest of children?

A researcher with a different ethical philosophy such as Kant's would not find that compromising others to help "primary clients" was right action.

Cassell (1978) pointed out that it is unethical for researchers to form relationships with participants, act like friends, and then leave the situation when the research project concludes. This reflects an ethical philosophy, such as covenantal ethics, that considers the obligations that form from relationships between people. There is a similar deontological concern arising when the researcher does nothing with the data that the participant has contributed. Altork (1998) reported a participant's concern that she had been brushed aside for more interesting data. Behar (1996) recounted the Italian movie *Il Postino* to make a similar point:

> The scene when this postman, his family, and neighbors pore over a foreign newspaper account of [the poet] Neruda's sojourn in their village, expecting to find some mention of themselves, struck me as especially poignancy in depicting the sense of loss and alienation experienced by those who took the poet-exile into their lives expecting that he, too, would take them into his own life with the same fullness of feeling. (p. 25)

Not using a participant's story may at times be as harmful as researchers believe publishing the story will be.

Participants can lose power in the context of the research. LaRossa et al. (1981) demonstrated the power depletion that arises when interviews are conjoint (as with family research), when the interviewer shifts to an interrogation style to gather information quickly, or when the participant is interviewed in a crisis situation. Neale (2000) reported a study conducted in crisis circumstances. Neale interviewed individuals admitted to emergency rooms for nonfatal suicidal drug overdoses. According to the *BR* (NCPHS, 1978), these individuals would be vulnerable before meeting the researcher. The participants may also have become more vulnerable in the process of research. Although she recognized she was approaching people who were in physical pain, as well as emotional and situational turmoil, Neale interviewed the patients as soon as she could, which was immediately in some situations. However, in other situations "the researcher had to wait several hours until the patient regained consciousness" (p. 87). She concluded that her study revealed that "in the hours following an illicit drug overdose, many drug users are emotionally vulnerable, willing to talk and anxious for assistance" (p. 92). Although she does not talk about ethics in this way, it seems that Neale must have had a strong conviction that the ends of her research would justify the risks she brought to the interview situations.

Not getting the story right can be harmful. Altork (1998) related her distress over unwittingly representing a participant as a drunk, which was an inaccurate portrayal of the woman, by writing about her consumption of alcohol in a misleading fashion. Sometimes the story is right but can be used in the wrong ways (the researcher was ethical in their actions, but was teleologically unethical). Researchers' data and reports have been used in ways that do not benefit the participants (e.g., Deyhle, 1998; Tunnell, 1998). Cassell (1978) stated that this can be particularly problematic with research on deviance, which can be used to "control those who are studied, or to explain differences between them and the majority in terms of 'social pathology'" (p. 139).

All of these situations are unanticipated ethical problems that have emerged during the research process. Often, the researcher makes decisions in situ, relying on his or her personal ethical convictions. At other times, there is not a decision to be made but a lesson to be learned when harm occurs and cannot be ameliorated.

Comparing a priori to a posteriori vulnerability, which do you think is more difficult to apply in practical situations and why?
How might their application make researchers more ethical?

FURTHER IMPLICATIONS OF VULNERABILITY
AND ETHICS IN RESEARCH

Even after planning for vulnerability and addressing vulnerability in situ, there are still participant vulnerabilities to which we, as researchers, remain oblivious. Researchers become preoccupied with some aspects of harm and unaware of others (Bresler, 1996). One researcher may be sensitive to the harm that arises when confidentiality is compromised, but unmindful of the harm that comes from never publishing a research report.

Our lack of awareness of certain aspects of harm may partly be attributed to the fact that, too often, we do not follow up with our participants. The harm emerging from the research process or the research publication can remain unnoticed by the researcher who is busy in the academy. Feminist efforts at maintaining relationships with participants (reflecting covenantal ethical relationships) move closest to capturing the full impact of researcher decisions on participants (e.g., Lather & Smithies, 1997). Further, Schensul (1980) pointed out that "the critics of the traditional field research process have sought their solutions to ethical problems from everyone else but those under study" (p. 310). When working out "our" ethical dilemmas, researchers will consult IRBs, other researchers, and past literature. Do we try to resolve ethical issues with our participants? If not, perhaps it is because we are still trying to resolve our ethical decisions based on the "generally accepted" principles, which do not require us to negotiate goodness and harm with participants. But, as I have demonstrated, sometimes those principles do not offer us the resolutions and understandings we need to ethically act when vulnerability arises during the research process. It is then that we could find it very useful to work with participants to define goodness and harm within the research context.

To complicate the notion of vulnerability, I now consider the researcher as vulnerable. Within the research process, the researcher is often susceptible to harm. Most researchers begin their work with a dissertation, which is

> a solo enterprise with relatively unstructured observation, deep involvement in the setting, and a strong identification with the researched. This can mean that the researcher is unavoidably vulnerable and that there is a considerably larger element of risk and uncertainty than with more formal methods. (Punch, 1994, p. 84)

There is also an emotional type of vulnerability for researchers. Behar (1996) wrote of researchers, like herself, who write "vulnerably" by making their emotions part of their ethnographies, by wearing their hearts on their sleeves. She explained, "Vulnerability doesn't mean that anything personal goes. The exposure of the self who is also a spectator has to take us somewhere we couldn't otherwise get to" (p. 14).

Other writers have talked about the power relationships that create vulnerability in the researcher. Cassell's (1978) example of a researcher trying to live safely in a ghetto reminds researchers that there are times when they are not the powerful players in the field. They may, in fact, have little of the power that matters most in the setting. May (1980) wrote of researchers being vulnerable to the "sweet talk of outside money" (p. 359), which often makes use of a teleological ethical position to decide who and what gets studied—the greatest good to the greatest number. When a sponsor is responsible for funding a researcher's forays into a setting, the funding agency then holds power over the researcher (Trend,

1980). Further, a researcher loses control of the data and the interpretation once it is published (Cassell, 1978; Deyhle, 1998). Galliher (1973/1991) wrote, "Social scientists are even more vulnerable than journalists because the former do not enjoy the constitutional guarantees of freedom of the press" (p. 350).

> What would you now include in your list of what you must do and reflect on to become a more ethical researcher? What ethical issues have you encountered in your own research? How have the ideas presented in this chapter shaped your thinking on those issues?

CONCLUSIONS

A social science researcher could easily be overwhelmed by all of this vulnerability. The potential for harm is in society and in our research; it affects our participants and ourselves; it is sometimes resolvable and other times irresolvable. As researchers (and as people) we have to acknowledge vulnerabilities without being paralyzed by their possibilities. We must get on with our work.

Being ethical as we get on with our work has several implications. We have to prepare for participants who arrive to our studies with choices limited by the power of societal prejudices and social institutions. We also have to admit (at least to ourselves) the basis of our own ethical convictions because that is what we will use to resolve ethical problems arising during the research. We cannot rely on principles defined by others but must be active in our ethical decisions and must constantly question and define "do no harm." The seemingly firm foundations of "generally accepted" moral principles, IRBs, and federal regulations will not hold us up all the time. The meaning of "do no harm" is in flux and may disappear when we need it most. But, with ongoing intellectual and moral work on our part, this shaky ground holds promise of being a more ethical place for social science researchers to stand.

3

Historical Research

Kate Rousmaniere
Miami University

MEET THE AUTHOR

Kate Rousmaniere is professor in the Department of Educational Leadership at Miami University, Ohio. Her research interests center on the history and politics of American teachers and methodological questions in the social history of education. Her publications include *City Teachers: Teaching and School Reform in Historical Perspective* (1997) and two coedited international volumes, *Discipline, Moral Regulation, and Schooling: A Social History* (1997), with Kari Dehli and Ning de Coninck-Smith, and *Silences and Images: A Social History of the Classroom* (1999), with Ian Grosvenor and Martin Lawn. Kate is currently working on a biography of Margaret Haley, the turn-of-the-century leader of the first teachers' union in the country, the Chicago Teachers' Federation.

Think about your own educational experience. How might you tell the story of your own personal history of education? What questions would you ask? What parts of your education would you consider important? What would you emphasize? Perhaps you would be interested in the way in which your schooling shaped you as an individual, in which case your narrative might emphasize the development of your personality, grade school relationships, experiences at recess or on the sports field, and the influence of certain adults in and outside of school. The historical artifacts that you would draw on for evidence would be social and personal ones—photographs of friends, personal letters, your yearbook, and other memorabilia. In this history, your research question would center on the way in which your education helped to shape the development of your personal identity.

Or you could ask a different question of your educational history. You could be less interested in the development of your personality and more interested in the way in which certain structures of your life gave you some opportunities and not others. What was the effect of your own class, gender, and race in your schooling experience, and what structural limitations were presented by the economic and political position of your school district; the presence or absence of key facilities and systems like bussing or tracking; the role of tests; the pressure, or lack thereof, of college preparation? The historical sources drawn on would be financial records, newspaper articles, interviews with school officials, test results, and college attendance data. Your research questions would be about the impact of certain structural phenomenon and the systemic practices of schooling on you (Rousmaniere, 2000).

What would you include in a presentation of your educational history? What would you omit?

Certainly, there are more than two ways to tell your educational history, but the scenarios presented above are intended to be an example of the work that educational historians do when they set about their task of chronicling and then explaining the past. The example above raises three initial points to know about historical method. First, history is more than the stringing together of facts. Second, historical narrative is driven by the questions asked by the historian, the theory relied on, and the argument created. Third, the nature of the historical data that is used drives the interpretation. In other words, there is not one true historical story out there waiting to be told if only the correct facts are pulled together. Rather, history is interpretation of the past, drawing on available sources, and it is the historian who does the interpretation. In a very real sense, there is no history until historians tell it, and it is the way in which they tell it that becomes what we know of as history. The radical historian Howard Zinn (1989) argued that historians write from their own subjective experience and perspective about the world. It's not that historians make outright lies about the past, but that they omit or deemphasize some data over others, and the definition of what is important depends on each historian's values. Educational historian Barbara Finkelstein (1992) argued further that historians are like mythmakers in that "through their analyses of the past, they reveal meaning and . . . make sense of reality" (p. 255).

HISTORIOGRAPHY

Historiography literally means the study of the techniques of historical research and historical writing. Historians work very much in the context of the contemporary field of history: Their work is as grounded in other historians' work as it is in the research data that is their subject. Historical studies often interlink and cross-reference the research and theories of other historians; subsequently, historians put more emphasis on historiography than they do on specific historical methods. For example, a good historian of rural education needs to be familiar not only with the types of historical data available but also with the historiography of the field, including the different arguments made by other historians about how rural education developed, what forces shaped rural education in certain ways and not others, what politics and social movements were at play, and, ultimately, whose interests were served and whose were ignored and oppressed (Fuller, 1982; Theobald, 1996). These historiographical debates shape the understanding of history as much as any specific historical document or any type of historical method.

How would you explain what historiography is in your own words?
Would you trust the results of this kind of research more or less than other kinds?

The changing nature of the subject of history in school and university curriculum is an excellent example of the shifting nature of historical writing, because it reminds us that history has been rewritten in different ways over the years and that history is, to a great extent, shaped by the historical time period in which it was written and the historian who wrote it. Although we now think of history as a central part of the American curriculum, history as a discreet subject was not adopted into American schooling until the early 20th century. Prior to that time, the limited history that was taught in school intentionally emphasized both religious and ideological values. For example, in the effort to promote a distinct American identity, 19th-century American history textbooks contrasted images of the hardworking sober Protestant American with luxury-loving and deceitful Catholic Europeans (Fitzgerald, 1979, p. 74).

By the early 20th century, professional associations of historians in the United States promoted a more "scientific" history based on the sequencing of what they considered to be objective facts. History texts still held strong ideological positions on prominent issues such as Americanization, the role of immigrants and Native Americans, capitalism, and religion, but the narrative was swathed in a scientific prose that presented this interpretation as objective fact. One notable exception to this was Harold Rugg (1931), whose *Introduction to the Problems of American Culture* indicated by its very title that American history was filled with political conflict, economic disparity, and social inequality. But by World War II, Rugg's texts came under fire by the National Association of Manufacturers and citizens groups that accused such progressive perspective as being anti-American and procommunist. These criticisms continued through the 1950s and 1960s, when history textbooks continued to present an image of a unified America where democracy provided equality and comfort for all.

The debate between what should be part of the history canon continues today in American public school board debates about what kind of history students should learn. Some conservatives argue that the emphasis of contemporary history curricula on the history of women, people of color, and radical groups is the result of left-wing conspiracists who are intent on dismantling the unity of the nation. Others argue that knowledge of the complexities and struggles of American history will make American students both better thinkers and better citizens (Levine, 1996; Nash, Crabtrees, & Dunn, 1997). In terms of what the appropriate subject of study for American school children is, then, the history curriculum has its own contentious and still unresolved history.

The field of the history of education shares similar debates about what is valuable, important, and even "true" history. The field has struggled with its own opposing arguments about whether the history of American education has been a democratic process or one designed by and for a controlling elite. The debates are based on historiographical and methodological issues, as well as political and ideological debates about the role of history in American culture.

THE HISTORY OF EDUCATION AS A FIELD

Historians of education are rooted in the education profession, even though they also identify as historians. Although many historians in the arts and sciences may explore the history of education as part of broad social history research, people who identify as historians of education are overwhelmingly located in education schools and may as likely be attending the American Educational Research Association annual meeting as one of the annual conferences for historians. Yet their methods and modes of research do not always fit with those of other qualitative or quantitative researchers in education, just as the types of questions they ask do not always fit with the general historical field. Historians of education are in many ways strangers in two worlds.

> How are historical methods different from both qualitative and quantitative approaches to research? How are they similar?

The difference between the historian who studies education and the educational historian is not merely one of semantics. To a great extent, historians of education link their historical work with the contemporary educational research that they and their colleagues conduct. Unlike many fields of history that are focused primarily on the past, the history of education is also integrally related to the present. Many historians of education believe that contemporary school reform cannot be effective unless a close analysis of the history of school reform is connected to it; subsequently, educational historians often take on a role of professional advocacy. The educational historian who writes about the history of special education, for example, is inevitably asking contemporary educators to attend to the origin of special education as a holding pen for students who deviated from socially constructed norms, whether by intellectual or physical abilities, or by race, class, gender, and behavior. More recent movements in special education have flipped attention from the socially marginalized student to middle-class children who are not performing well in school. What do these historical lessons tell us about the way that we approach special education today and how we might consider reforming our conception of the field? (Franklin, 1994; Lazerson, 1987).

Another example of the simultaneous historical and contemporary character of the history of education is the study of the cyclical, and often repetitive, history of American school reform, what Tyack and Cuban (1995) referred to as "tinkering toward utopia." Tyack and Cuban argued that Americans have historically devised specific educational prescriptions for broad social and economic problems. Americans' passionate faith in the school to solve all ills began with the Puritan's creation of a public school system so that young Americans would read the Bible and keep the "Olde Deluder Satan" at bay, and has continued through President Ronald Reagan's warning that we are "a nation at risk." This faith in education, Tyack and Cuban argue, is positive because it has led Americans to build the most comprehensive education system in the world, but it is negative because it leads to an overblown faith that adding or subtracting certain elements to education can solve broader social problems. Ultimately, the history of American school reform is one of piecemeal innovations that after a century have left the schoolhouse remarkably unchanged. Tyack and Cuban believe that contemporary reformers need to remember the originating purpose of public education to further democracy for the public good, and to not focus on narrow and piecemeal improvements for only select groups.

Other educational historians are less specific in their comparison of past and present, but the very nature of their work raises profound questions about contemporary educational practices and attitudes. In her examination of the 18th- and 19th-century American school curriculum, Kim Tolley (1996) found that girls studied science and math, whereas boys studied the humanities, because at the time it was Latin and Greek that assured young men of a good job. Only in the early 20th century, when science and math became subjects of economic import, did the emphasis change, so that today we see boys dominating those fields of study. Tolley's work implicitly suggests that the issue of gender inequity in schooling and the economy may not be either gender's inherent talent for math and science, but social pressures and economic expectations. Perlstein's (1997) study of a New Deal reconstruction project in a poverty-stricken mining town in West Virginia shows that even well-intentioned progressive educators can apply undemocratic and exclusionary methods to their reform efforts, a theme that echoes in many of today's school reform initiatives. And Vanessa Siddle Walker's (1996) historical study of a segregated Black school and its community over a 30-year period not only revises the common view that all-Black schools were bad schools, but also suggests that the implementation and legacy of school integration has not always worked well for Black children. In each of these historical projects, there are strong implications of the effect of past practice and policy on current beliefs about schooling.

Thus, the field of the history of education has always stood partly between past and present, and for many educational historians the driving question of their research is simultaneously historical and contemporary. According to Ronald Butchart (1988), who wrote about the history of African American peoples' struggle to obtain schooling, "history must appraise the past to suggest political, social, and economic strategies for the present and future. Like schooling, history is inescapably political" (p. 333). A study of the development of the field of history of education illustrates how, over time, historians of education have constructed their interpretations through different political lenses.

The Origin of the Field and Consensus History

Educational history began as an academic area of study only recently. Between 1900 and 1950, Paul Monroe (1940), Ellwood P. Cubberly (1919), and Thomas Woody (1929) wrote the first general histories of American schooling and promoted the field as a necessary subject for educators. In general, their perspective about education in America was one of a progressive continuum toward improvement. They argued that the American school system had been set up to promote democracy and equality, and it had done so effectively. In addition, they assert that through the study of American educational history, teachers could better understand how schools were "a great national institution evolved by democracy to help it solve its many perplexing problems" (Cubberly, 1919, p. 42). To tell this tale of progress and democracy, these historians relied on public policy documents that chronicled the institutional and political development of the American public school systems from the colonial period through the 19th century. Given this perspective and the types of sources that they used, it is not surprising that these historians rarely asked questions about who was not favored by schooling, who was excluded, or what was lost by the development of state education systems. Even Woody (1929), in his landmark history of the education of American women, still described his subject with utmost optimism, reporting that women went from few opportunities to many, and that equality was (in 1929) achieved.

The early historians' emphasis on inexorable progress in education led them to be called "consensus historians" in later years. (Consensus history is also referred to as the Cubberly tradition, after its most prominent author.) Their story is one of success and improvement with an ending picture of education as advantaging all, as if the entire country was in consensus about who should have the right to go to school, what they should learn, how they should be taught, and how schools should be organized and funded. Critiques of the consensus school were that the narratives were parochial and isolated from the main currents of historical and social research, that they relied primarily on the testimonies of White male school leaders, and that by highlighting the development of intellectual ideas, they assumed that educational practice was a result of philosophical choices, not social and political dynamics.

The Social History of American Education

The next major shift in educational historiography changed the scope and method of history, even as it continued the consensus historians' optimism about American education. For Bernard Bailyn and Lawrence Cremin, who first wrote in the 1950s and 1960s, the critical question for educational historians was what counted as education. Bailyn (1960) called for a complete redefinition of education from the narrow focus on schools, policy, and institutions to include "the entire process by which a culture transmits itself across generations" (p. 14). For Cremin, too, education as a historical (and contemporary) phenomenon was only partly occurring in schools, but also in social and cultural agencies. Cremin (1977) defined education as any "deliberate, systematic, and sustained effort to transmit, evoke, or acquire knowledge, attitudes, values, skills, or sensibilities, as well as any outcome to that effort" (p. viii). The task of historians was to analyze the impact of education on society and to draw a link between educational ideas and social behavior. These new historians examined a broad range of institutions that served educational functions, including libraries, charity and community organizations, vocational institutions, and newspapers and film, and they expanded the types of sources used as historical data to include biography, census material, lectures and sermons, personal and professional papers, and oral history. This breadth of the subject and diversity of sources opened up new areas for inquiry in the history of education, such as the growth of higher education and the professions, the development of public media, and the role of popular culture in creating and shaping national ideologies (Veysey, 1965; Webber, 1978; Welter, 1962).

Still, the questions remained primarily intellectual and for the most part positive. According to these historical arguments, education in both schools and in the broader arena had progressed steadily over time to inform an increasing number of people in positive ways. Consensus was still the guiding perspective, and the voices and experiences of certain groups were still absent from the narrative.

Revisionist Interpretations in the History of Education

More radical perspectives on the history of American education emerged in the 1960s. In part, modern historians realized that political critiques of contemporary schools made the optimistic view of educational history seem absurd. In light of the continued struggles for racial integration in schools, and government and local efforts to address poverty, the shocking reports from inside schools such as Jonathan Kozol's *Death at an Early Age* (1967) and new academic explorations of race, class, and gender problems, historians began to question the consensus argument of continued progression. Michael Katz led what was to be called the revisionist school of history of education, with his neo-Marxist interpretation of the school reform movement in the early republic. Turning his attention to specific school funding and authority issues in 19th-century Massachusetts, Katz (1968) argued that rather than being democratic, humanitarian, and rational enterprises, early public schools were "hand maidens of corporate capitalism—the product of self-interested, status-seeking middle-class elites seeking to conserve their advantages and extend them for their children" (p. 218). The development of American public schooling, then, was a story of systemic oppression and greed, exclusion, institutional marginalization, and the use of power of one class over another. Samuel Bowles' and Herbert Gintis' *Schooling in Capitalist America* (1976) furthered this perspective by arguing that the development of public schooling in all time periods closely followed from and reflected the expansion of capitalist industrial economy. Schools were set up by the ruling class to reproduce social inequality and to act as the primary agent of social control.

The revisionist argument was a powerful impetus in the history of education, in part because it opened up the field from the history of intellectual ideas to questions about power relations, economics, social struggle, and politics. Ironically, the subject matter remained where the consensus school has established it—in schools as institutions—but the depth of analysis and critique was far more creative.

Historical work that was influenced by the revisionist perspective explored the nature of those who wielded power in the development of American education, often arguing that power struggles and ideological conflict existed among those who designed state school systems. Carl Kaestle (1983) argued that the eventual acceptance of state common school systems in the late 18th and early 19th centuries was furthered by school leaders' translation of republican, Protestant, and capitalist values into educational policy. David Tyack's influential *The One Best System* (1974) examined the specific development of urban school bureaucracies over the 19th and early 20th centuries, and proposed that organizational change and professionalization had as much a role to play in educational development as did class interests per se. Herbart Kliebard (1987) turned his analysis to curriculum and argued that the evolution of modern American curriculum was the result of a struggle between interest groups that upheld distinct intellectual and ideological positions about learning. James Anderson (1988) explored the depths of control in his study of African American education in the South after the Civil War, finding that white Northerners and Southerners used the education of freed African Americans as a strategy for social and economic stability and reconstruction of the South. Their differing views over the form and extent of African American education reflect not only different levels of racism but also conflicting conceptions of education and political economy.

Neorevisionist Histories of Education

Later historians took the revisionist argument outside of schools, to explore the relationship of schooling to work and family; gender, class, and race relations; labor issues; the history of childhood; and other social history topics. The focus here was on education as one of many social forces, institutional structures, and ideological patterns that shaped American people. Often this shaping was forceful, as in the school structures and curricula set up to enculturate Native American and immigrant children in Anglo-American values. But education also shaped more subtly by creating and reinforcing social norms that were intricately bound up with the broader economic and political agendas of dominant social groups.

The original revisionist historians had presented schooling as an all-oppressive force, allowing its subjects little voice or agency. Later neorevisionist historians began to ask more nuanced questions about how power worked, positing a more complicated relationship between the powerful and the oppressed. Often inspired by theorists like Antonio Gramsci and Michel Foucault, these historians argued that educational inequity was never as systemically planned as some might think, nor as effective as educators might have wished: New social historians found that there was often resistance, adaptation, and accommodation to the oppressive structures of schools. Historians mined new sources to uncover individual lives, experiences, and relationships in schools, and to investigate evidence of resistance to powerful structures of schooling. Drawing on oral history, family manuscripts, contemporary media, and other cultural sources, historians developed new theories about relations within schools. For example, a study of missionary education revealed moments of resistance when native students both fought back and worked with their Anglo teachers, and when teachers, too, adopted some of their work practices to their students' culture (Yohn, 1991). Julia Wrigley's (1982) study of schooling in early-20th-century Chicago showed that business groups, progressive educators, teacher unions, and industrial labor all negotiated school reform in terms of their own class interests. A study of teachers in early-20th-century New York City showed how teachers developed their own work culture that served to buffer them from oppressive administrative rule and support them in their own definition of good work, even as it also mired teachers in conservatism, fear of change, and isolation from progressive reforms (Rousmaniere, 1997). In new histories of the lives of children, high school education, vocational education, women's education, and special education, historians found a continuing dialectic between opportunity and constraint that operated in almost all educational institutions and for all players. Formal schooling, however oppressive and however marginalizing its motives, also offered people access to social improvement, and even the most powerless people tried to negotiate their way through those systems to make meaning out of their work in schools and to use that experience to gain power.

Postmodern Histories of Education

The notion of a postmodern historiography of education is relatively new in the field, and initially it strikes many historians as a redundant concept. Historians might argue that if postmodernism challenges the metanarratives of rationalist scientific progress of education, then revisionists and neorevisionists have already done that work. Further, the very nature of historiography teaches us to question the notion of ultimate truths or objective facts. But the deeper significance of postmodernism as a challenge to historical narrative presents a greater challenge to historians because postmodernism is inherently ahistorical: If postmodernism challenges both generalizations and generalized narratives, then the very process by which historians analyze and describe historical change is impossible. Historians' ultimate reliance on historical "facts," however they are determined, as the backbone of their narrative is challenged by postmodernism. By relying on scientific method, an explanatory narrative of cause and effect, and a structural analysis of change, historians are, by definition, modernist (Lowe, 1996).

Nevertheless, some educational historians have taken on postmodernism in the history of education by exploring the way in which postmodern ideas might change the types of questions asked and methods used. At the very least, postmodernism can challenge historians to be more concerned with the process of historical discovery than in "results"; to experiment with new historical methods and models of narrative; to consider writing history from a variety of different viewpoints or perspectives; and to continue the exploration of historical topics that have as of yet been considered unavailable to historians because of the absence of traditional historical sources. Thus, postmodern ideas in history overlap with new social history topics and methods.

Harold Silver (1992), for example, challenged historians to stop focusing on the institutional development of schools and to focus instead on the people who inhabit these structures and "the locations, forms, dimensions, and meanings of their experience" (p. 108). Silver agrees with earlier social historians that structural concepts of gender, race, and class have prevented historians from exploring the experience and meaning of education (Clifford, 1989; Finkelstein, 1989). A close social history of the classroom would uncover histories that have heretofore been silent, such as the history of children's experiences of classroom cultures, routines, activities, and emotions. Writing about these silences involves a creative use of new resources, including oral history, the study of architecture, school photographs, and critical readings of school texts from curricula to student notes. Such readings are inherently interdisciplinary, creative, and imaginary, and necessarily involve the self-conscious presence of the historian in the text (Grosvenor, Lawn, & Rousmaniere, 1999). Such a project draws on postmodern notions that "experience is transitory and ephemeral; reality is fragmentary and unknowable; and history is arbitrary and directionless" (Green, 1994, p. 72).

> How might a researcher undertake a history that examines children's experiences of classroom activities and emotions?

The postmodern concern with relationships between knowledge and power has also helped to develop the work of "life histories" in education. Life history work inherently critiques the notion of an objective and singular biography, both for the purpose of critiquing academic categories of life that do not match with that of real people, and for the purpose of uncovering broader power relations that have shaped educational experiences. Sue Middeton's (1993) feminist study of the life history of teachers takes all adult memories and interpretations, even when contradictory, as valid because the central concern of her study is "not the events themselves but the interpretations the women made of them and the importance the women attached to these interpretations in their becoming feminists and educators" (p. 68). For women, teachers, children, people of color, and other disenfranchised people, life history work does more than simply allow the voiceless to tell their story, it also encourages them to tell it in their own way, using their own categories and identities. As Richard Quantz (1992) argued in his promotion of ethnohistory as an interpretive method of historical research, this type of approach can provide "a mechanism for reconstructing the multiple, contradictory and conflictual cultures of the past in such a manner as to reveal new stories of struggle and complacency, of resistance and acceptance, of domination and mindlessness that characterize the life of teachers, students, and other school participants in our past" (p. 190).

Postmodern approaches in the history of education have also included discourse analysis, and critical studies of the representations of teachers, students, and modernist conceptions of "the child" (Richardson, 1996). In Kathleen Weiler's (1998) study of women educators in late-19th- and early-20th-century rural California, for example, the focus is "the ways in which people construct meaning from the images and assumptions of the culture in which they move" (p. 6). Weiler studies how teachers negotiated the discursive categories of culture and ideology that were embodied in the identity of "the teacher" while simultaneously developing their own independent responses to a developing state education system that marginalized women.

At the very least, historians of education are beginning to acknowledge that postmodern theories help them to rethink how to read and write history, to question how they authorize as valid certain sources and not others, and how to connect history to the present. Postmodern theories have also helped to "loosen up" liberal models of class, race, and gender identity to include more fluid concepts of culture and identity, and to attend more critically to the issue of the context in which historical texts were produced. For historians of education, "postmodernism does not really force us to do anything new: but it does oblige us to do it well and to be seen to be doing it well" (Lowe, 1996 p. 323).

Explain your own education history through the different theoretical perspectives Rousmaniere describes here.

WRITING HISTORY: QUESTIONS, THEORIES,
AND ARGUMENTS

Historians begin their research with a question, usually a simple one such as, What happened? followed by more complex questions such as, why did it happen? or what was the experience or meaning of what happened to a specific group of people? Note how the shaping of the question inevitably guides the rest of the research: an interest in why something happened—for example, the creation of government boarding schools for Native American children in the late 19th century—leads to investigations of power relations in American racial history, and the political, economic, and social ideologies at work in the decision to develop a specific school system. The same topic shifts dramatically when the question posed is: What happened to the Native American children who were forced to attend the schools and the communities that they left behind? This question leads to the examination of completely different sources, which lead to an understanding of native children's experience of boarding school. Both versions tell two different sides of the story of Native American boarding schools, evolving out of two different questions (Adams, 1997). Thus, refining and clarifying a historical question is a key first step in historical writing.

Theory provides the explanatory categories with which historians expand their initial question into an argument. Any historical narrative that is beyond a mere chronicle of dates is one in which the historian sees relationships between events and explains that connection with a theory. Historians often draw on theories from disciplines outside of history. For example, in Thomas Webber's (1978) *Deep Like the Rivers*, a neorevisionist study of the African American slave community, the historian drew on learning theory to develop his question of what slaves learned from the social curriculum that the White slaves' owners delivered to them, taking into account the way that the slave community itself resisted that curriculum and taught their own resistant cultural values. Feminist theory has driven the work of many histories of women's education. For example, historians of women in higher education have found a systematic practice of "expansion and exclusion" whereby women have been gradually admitted to higher education, but simultaneously relegated only to low status and marginalized areas of institutions (Graham, 1978; Rosenberg, 1982). Other feminist historians have argued that women fared better in single-sex schools and institutions where women's community furthered experiences of feminist empowerment (Palmieri, 1995). Other historians have used psychoanalytic theory to explore questions of development and behavior codes in student life (Finkelstein, 1974). Recently, some historians have adopted postmodern theories of identity and representation into their studies of the complicated and often contradictory meanings of teachers' and students' work in schools in the past (Copelman, 1996; Theobald, 1996). The work of Michel Foucault has inspired a new generation of scholars to investigate questions of disciplinary practices and modes of knowledge and control in both student lives and in the organizational structure of schooling (Rousmaniere et al., 1997). Whatever the theory used, and whether or not it is explicitly referred to, historians need to be conscious that their argument and interpretation about what happened in the past is driven by an explanatory theory.

> How might the use of question, theory, and argument be similar or different in your research?

Question and theory lead to argument. A historical argument is the stated proposition of the research. In a sense, the argument is the historian's "results," or response to the question, guided by theory. A study of three different histories of the development of the American high school illustrates a good example of different arguments. Edward A. Krug's (1969, 1972) two-volume history of the shaping of the American high school from 1880 to 1941 argued that the early-20th-century high school developed as part of broader social changes in American society. Krug began his research with a question about the origin of the college preparatory curriculum, and he developed a lively consensus narrative about the often misguided but ultimately well-intentioned development of the American high school as a fledgling academic institution. David Labaree (1988) made a more decisive argument—that the development of the high school had less to do with academic content and more to do with social status: The high school developed as a credentialing agency that furthered status concerns of middle-class Americans. Labaree's argument developed from his revisionist concern with class and market forces in education and his question of how the development of the high school furthered that power dynamic. Finally, David Angus' and Jeffrey Mirel's (1999) study of the 20th-century high school started with the question about the origin of the highly divergent political views about the purpose of high school education today, including the controversy over academic goals and standards. Guided by a neorevisionist understanding of conflicting movements for educational equality and drawing on extensive quantitative data of student coursework, Angus and Mirel argued that the American high school has, since the 1930s, taken on a custodial function that ultimately dominates its role as an academic or vocational institution. Note that these three texts do not necessarily refute each other; rather, they contribute to the variety of arguments and theories, as well as data, regarding the history of the high school.

Historical Sources

Historians do not address questions of methodology in the same way that other qualitative or quantitative researchers do. Historians' main methodological concerns have to do with sources, or the different types of historical data available to them, and the way in which they interpret them. Here again, the types of sources used and the way in which they are interpreted have a lot to do with the types of questions asked, the theory relied on, and the argument.

History is generally divided into four main focus areas: intellectual, political, social, and cultural history. Intellectual history is the history of ideas: the development of intellectual patterns of thought, theories, and ideologies over time. An intellectual history of education might emphasize the emergence of new theories of curriculum, pedagogy, and child development. A study of progressive ideas of classroom practice, from Friedrich Froebel to John Dewey to Paolo Freire, for example, would be a narrative of the development of the intellectual ideas of educators. Note that such an intellectual history would not necessarily be a study of the extent to which those ideas were implemented into actual classroom practice.

Political history studies formal political processes such as government policies, law, and other official treatises. A political history of education might emphasize the development of local, state, or federal policy and law, as well as the political platforms of unions, parent organizations, and other interest groups and the way in which those laws and policies were developed, negotiated, and implemented. The effect of those laws and policies on students and teachers would be only a secondary concern.

Social history is the history of social groups and individuals, and usually this implies groups that did not play an active part of the processes of intellectual or political history, such as women, African American and native peoples, immigrants, children, workers, people with disabilities, the poor, and other disenfranchised or marginalized groups. A social history of education would emphasize the experiences of students, teachers, and parents, and would more likely focus on the classroom and community than on school board policy or on the intellectual ideas of educators.

Finally, cultural history is the study of cultural processes, both in the anthropological sense of culture as a shared system of meaning and in the cultural studies sense of culture as a production of people's work. A cultural historian of education might study not only the educative forces of cultural agencies like Americanization programs for immigrants, the Girl Scouts, Black churches, and labor colleges, but also the history of youth cultures, girls' culture, and gay and lesbian culture, and the ways in which those communities were formally and informally educational.

Within these broad categories are other types of historical categories or subfields. Historians of education often identify themselves by the specific topic or genre of their research subject, be it women's history of education, the history of higher education, the history of teachers and teacher education, the history of childhood, the history of African American education, or the history of school policy and reform. The biographies of prominent educators is a popular subject, as well as a newer field of "educational biography" that examines the educationally significant influences of a person's life, whether those be through formal schooling or other life experiences (Kridel, 1998). The institutional histories of schools and universities are often written as case studies to explore both the chronological development and significance of a single educative institution. Curriculum historians focus on the development of curricular theories and courses of study, finding in the lens of curriculum a powerful insight into educational ideology, as well as classroom practice (Kliebard, 1986; Schubert, 1980). Each of these areas has its own particular historiographical and theoretical debates.

Intellectual, political, social, and cultural historians not only draw on different sources, but ask different questions of those sources. Intellectual and political historians rely on formal, institutional sources, or on the writings of prominent educators or policy makers, and their questions revolve around the development of ideas and policies. A social historian may refer to those types of sources too, but will rely more heavily on sources conceived by or about common people, including oral history, letters and diaries, local newspaper sources, and other unpublished manuscript material as they try to explain how a political or intellectual change affected common people. Cultural historians may share the same sources, but their question and interpretation will center on the broad development of cultural patterns and practices.

Historians define their sources in one of two groups: primary and secondary. Primary sources are those closest to the topic: either generated at the time of the event or by the subject in question. Primary sources can include letters, diaries, speeches, contemporary newspaper articles, photographs, or other contemporary material. A curriculum plan by a teacher, minutes of a school board meeting, or an academic journal written during the time period in question are all primary sources. Secondary sources are removed from the historical event in time and place, and often interpret the primary sources. The most common secondary source is a history of your topic that a previous historian has written, although later newspaper articles or evaluations of past events are also secondary sources. The two types of sources can overlap—an oral history could be considered a primary source in that the person speaking is the subject under study, but it could also be a secondary source if that subject describes an event as an outsider. There is no set rule on which type of source is most reliable or useful, but historians should know the difference between types of evidence and the assets and disadvantages of each.

The weighing of the value of these different types of sources is an important part of the historians' task, and it is intricately related to common rules of historical methodology. Historians rely on primary sources as the evidence that is literally closest to the topic, although this does not necessarily mean that the source is the most accurate one. Consider, for example, how a principal in Boston in 1870 might describe his school in his own words, but how that description might differ radically from the way that a young pupil described the school. Which of these primary sources would be "more" or "less" authentic? The context in which a primary source is created needs to be taken into account. Is the principal's text a fund-raising broadside? Is the pupil's observation from a private diary or from an essay submitted to a public competition? So, too, do secondary sources need to be evaluated in terms of the quality of the research (a high school history paper versus a best-selling book on the same topic, versus a very scholarly book on the same topic), and the theoretical perspective and types of sources used for the research. Elwood Cubberly and Michael Katz both wrote about early American schooling, but their historical interpretations differed radically. For the historian, interpretation is intricately related to sources, their trustworthiness, and their type. In the process of writing history, a historian searches for and constantly sifts through sources for the purpose of writing the narrative. Unlike other types of research, the data and the theory evolve simultaneously, and the role of the historian as interpreter is ever present.

Historians are constrained in their work by the availability of sources. One reason why the first histories of education were intellectual and political history was that these types of sources had survived in the form of institutional records and government documents. The common artifacts of daily schooling—teachers' and students' notes, diaries, papers, and letters—are less likely to be preserved, because they have less often been considered important historical data. In part because of the absence of available data, historians are more flexible than other educational researchers about mixing quantitative and qualitative sources. For historians, the use of either type of data does not have to guide the theoretical foundation of the research, or the questions or arguments in the same way that it might in a contemporary study.

For example, historians have made good use of statistical data from census and school board records. These sources can provide important data about changes in racial and gender characteristics in school enrollment and hiring, curriculum registration, and class size over time (Kaestle & Vinovskis, 1980; Perlmann, 1988). In her quest to understand the history of women school superintendents, for example, Jackie Blount collected and analyzed a database of over 50,000 school superintendents in the 20th century. Her analysis of this data revealed new information about the history of women in educational leadership: In the early 20th century, women held a significant number of county superintendencies, but with the centralization of school systems and the decline of these intermediate positions, the percentage of women superintendents dropped drastically, from a high of 11% in 1930 to a low of 3% in 1970. With this quantitative data in hand, Blount proceeded to write a historical study of women in educational administration, developing her argument for why these changes happened, how women were affected and responded, and what this history says about gender relations in formal school systems (Blount, 1998). Similarly, in his study of the development

of girls' education at the turn of the century, John Rury (1991) used a rich combination of census and enrollment statistics, national and regional school surveys,
and student and teacher diaries. Combined in this way, Rury was able to both tell
the narrative of educational change and analyze the meaning that these changes
had for young girls and educators.

Related to the theoretical changes in the history of education in the last
20 years, historians have diversified their research approaches from reliance on
traditional manuscript documentation to creative uses of oral history and memory, biography, architecture, material culture, and film and fiction. As opposed
to earlier histories that were based on the recorded actions of school boards and
administrators, the life of the classroom itself has become more central to many
histories. The use of many of these sources reveals previously unknown histories
of students, teachers, and parents, and uncover stories of joy and pain, frustration, anger, and sorrow inside schools in the past. These new social histories of
schooling are a good example of how different sources and methods of historical research can change the topic of the history and can reshape the historian's
questions.

The increasing use of oral history is a good example of recent changes in both
the method and theory of the social history of education. Oral history allows historians access to historical narratives that are absent from the formal archives, professional publications, and institutional histories (Dougherty, 1999). The voice of
common people, talking about their common work in classrooms, hallways, and
communities, changes both the content and the interpretation of educational
history, revealing "conflict where other historians previously claimed consensus," and introducing "a rich complexity and . . . a gritty narrative" (Altenbaugh,
1997, p. 313). Many oral histories of education have centered on teachers and
their experiences in schools, uncovering histories of classroom practice, informal
employment rules, teachers' professional development, and the rich and often
contentious work culture of the schoolhouse (Gardner & Cunningham, 1997;
Markowitz, 1993; Vaughn-Roberson, 1992).

Some historians of education have also drawn on cultural studies methods of
interpretation of images, cultural themes, and theories of textual production and
reception. One popular topic has been the portrayal of teachers and students in
novels and films as representational sources of cultural norms (Cohen & Scheer,
1997; Joseph & Burnaford, 1994; Perlstein, 2000). Historians have also interro-
gated photographic imagery of schooling in the past both as documentary sources
of schooling and as indicators of cultural norms (Provenzo, 1999). The symbolism of the architectural style of school buildings, the design and production of
textbooks and other school artifacts, and the introduction of media into schools
have also become subjects of interest (Cutler, 1989; Depaepe & Henkens, 2000).
Both postmodern theories and advanced technology have furthered the mixing of
mediums; Alan Wieder's (1997) text *Race in Education* is a collection of historical

essays on race and education, oral histories, and a reflective photo essay on race in contemporary South Carolina.

Some historians have broadened the definition of validity even more by drawing on contemporary art or fiction, interrogating the way in which memory works, linking historical events to cultural metaphors or social mythologies, and making bold suggestions about the social meaning and cultural impact of history. Stretching the boundaries of what is a "valid" interpretation or source is still subject to judgment by other historians, who draw their line of interpretation on what they consider to be more reliable facts. This debate about what is good and bad history, valid and invalid, and fact or fiction is a continuing debate in the professional historical journals.

CONCLUSIONS

To return to your own historical story: How might you tell the story of your own personal history of education? What questions would you ask? What guiding theory would you draw on, and what argument would you ultimately make about the effect of your education on your life? What types of sources would you use, and how would you interpret those sources? What other histories or educational biographies would you read to reflect on how you might interpret the events in your life? What theoretical arguments about key issues in your education would you explore?

All educational researchers can consider how a historical interpretation might enrich their own projects. Perhaps you are conducting an ethnography of a school, and that school itself has a history that will shed light on the current organization and culture of the school. Or you may be doing a study of the effects of an educational policy or specific school reform. What types of historical questions can you ask of those policies that will further your study? What theoretical perspective will you draw on?

Most important, any historical study needs to be well grounded in the historiography of the subject. The best way to write history is to read history, and to pay attention to historical arguments, types of sources used and how they are interpreted, and to theoretical perspectives. History is more than the stringing together of facts; it is the shaping of an argument based on the research and insights of other historians.

A variety of sources are available to help you in your research. There are a number of guides for writing history, such as Jacques Barzun's and Henry F. Graff's *The Modern Researcher* (1985). Other useful sources include Clinton Allison's *Present and Past: Essays for Teachers in the History of Education* (1995), John Hardin Best's *Historical Inquiry in Education: A Research Agenda* (1983), and Donald Warren's *American Teachers: Histories of a Profession at Work* (1989). Three journals publish the best articles in the field, including occasional historiographical essays: *The History of Education Quarterly*, the journal of the American History of Education Society; *Historical Studies in Education*, from the Canadian History of Education Society; and *Paedagogica Historica*, from the International Society for the Study of the History of Education. Division F of the American Educational Research Association sponsors research sessions on the history and historiography of education at every annual meeting. Other education journals often include history essays, thereby showing how the history of education can be integrated into general education research.

> How might you use historical approaches in your research? What interests you most about it? What would you see to be the challenges of this approach to research?

Finally, it's important to keep in mind that history ultimately does more than tell a story about the past. History also helps to make meaning about the present. A good historical study can provide insight into contemporary school reform processes; it can raise significant questions about current assumptions about academic values, levels of achievement, and cultural norms; and it can help to clarify the complex political dynamics of educational leadership and educational policy making. History is the study of change, and as educators we are committed to understanding and interpreting change, whether it be changes in achievement levels of a group of students over a 3-month period, or curriculum change in a local school district during one academic year or in a nation over a decade. Like all educational research, educational history is the study of educational processes at work, the meaning that we can make from understanding those processes, and improvements that we can recommend as a result of our enhanced understanding.

4

Qualitative Interview Studies: Learning Through Experience

Kathleen deMarrais
University of Georgia

MEET THE AUTHOR

Kathleen deMarrais is a professor and the coordinator of the Qualitative Inquiry Program at the University of Georgia. She earned her doctorate at the University of Cincinnati in social foundations of education. She uses sociocultural perspectives in her research to explore school equity issues, particularly as related to social class, gender, and ethnicity. Much of her work deals with the experiences of rural and urban Appalachian students in schools. She is a teacher educator and has worked for years with in-service and preservice teachers in literacy education and in supporting their action research efforts. Prior to her work in higher education, Kathleen was a special education teacher (LD/BD) for 14 years. In addition to numerous articles and chapters, her books include *Inside Stories: Reflections on Qualitative Research, The Way Schools Work: A Sociological Analysis of Education* (with Margaret LeCompte), *Life at the Margins: Profiles of Diverse Adults* (with Juliet Merrifield, David Hemphill, and Beth Bingman), and *Educating Young Adolescent Girls* (with Patricia O'Reilly and Beth Penn).

What is an interview? How does a researcher's theoretical framework inform the interview design and process? Are there different types of interviews? What makes a "good" interview? What strategies do experienced qualitative interviewers use that novice interviewers might use to improve their interview practice?

These are typical questions raised by novice qualitative researchers interested in using interviews in their research studies. In this chapter, I explore the design and implementation of qualitative interview studies incorporating responses to these questions to engage readers in thinking about their own research interview practice. Although there are specific types of interviews based in different theoretical frameworks and academic disciplines, I use the label *qualitative interviews* as an umbrella term for those methods in which researchers learn from participants through long, focused conversations. Qualitative interviews are used when researchers want to gain in-depth knowledge from participants about particular phenomena, experiences, or sets of experiences. Using interview questions and follow-up questions, or *probes*, based on what the participant has already described, the goal is to construct as complete a picture as possible from the words and experiences of the participant. This can only be accomplished when the qualitative interview is open ended enough for the participant to provide a depth of knowledge on the research topic. The intent is to discover that person's view of an experience or phenomenon of study.

What experiences have you had with qualitative interview studies? What types of interviews are used most commonly in your academic discipline?

Qualitative interviews rely on developing rapport with participants and discussing, in detail, aspects of the particular phenomenon being studied. Although researchers develop an interview guide, they do not necessarily use that guide as a standard protocol for each interview. Because each participant is unique, each qualitative interview experience will also be unique. Questions can be tailored to fit comfortably into the experience of each interview. Some types of qualitative interviews enable the participant to guide the discussion more than others.

Qualitative interview studies are known by a variety of labels. In the methodological literature about interviews, the following labels describe interviews that fall into the general category of qualitative interviews: intensive interview, in-depth interview, open-ended interview, unstructured interview, conversational interview, clinical interview, long interview (McCracken, 1988), nondirective interview, focused interview (Merton & Kendall, 1946), the group depth interview (Goldmand & McDonald, 1987), and focus group interviews (Barbour & Kitzinger, 1999; Kreuger, 1994; Morgan, 1988, 1993). Weiss (1994) argued that intensive and in-depth refers to the completeness and detailed nature of the interview. Researchers using terms like *open-ended, unstructured* (Lofland, 1971), and *conversational* are characterizing the informal, conversational style of the interview process, which enables the participants to engage in the process more freely without merely responding to researcher-generated questions. Nondirective and clinical approaches to the interview process come from psychological, therapeutic approaches. A nondirective approach derives from the work of psychologist Carl Rogers, in which the clinician is nonjudgmental and accepting of what the client has to say, pausing only for clarification and reflecting back what has been said. The interviewer role here is more passive than in other types of qualitative interviews (Weiss, 1994).

Some types of interviews specify the nature of the knowledge sought by the researcher. For example, feminist interviews (cf. Oakley, 1981; Reinharz, 1992), phenomenological interviews (cf. Kvale, 1983; Pollio, Henley, & Thompson, 1997; Thompson, Locander, & Pollio, 1989; van Maanen, 1990), and biographical, oral history, and life history interviews (cf. Dollard, 1935; Langness & Frank, 1981) are all types of interviews that are informed by a set of assumptions and use labels that describe the purpose for conducting the interview.

I begin here with an examination of the definition of an interview, followed by a discussion of ways in which theoretical positions and assumptions inform the interview process. I then move more specifically to the design of qualitative interview studies, including discussions focused on participant selection, construction of the interview guide, phases of the interview, relationships between researcher and participant, and elements of a "good" interview. I conclude the chapter with suggestions for high-quality interview practice.

WHAT IS AN INTERVIEW?

An interview is a process in which a researcher and participant engage in a conversation focused on questions related to a research study. These questions usually ask participants for their thoughts, opinions, perspectives, or descriptions of specific experiences. Maccoby and Maccoby (1954) defined the interview as "a face to face verbal interchange in which one person, the interviewer, attempts to elicit information or expressions of opinions or belief from another person or persons" (p. 499). Lofland (1994) described an unstructured interview as a "guided conversation whose goal is to elicit from the interviewee rich, detailed materials that can be used in qualitative analysis" (p. 18). Dexter (1970), Merriam (1998), and many other qualitative methodologists view an interview as a conversation between two people that is focused on the research topic. Although researchers set out to design the interview as a conversation, it is much different from an everyday conversation between two people. Intent on generating data for a research study, the researcher tends to have a greater stake in the whole process. The researcher determines the research purpose, designs the study, selects the participants, and intends to implement it. The participant is asked and has agreed to participate in this "conversation" with the researcher, who may be a stranger. The researcher, rather than the participant, asks questions from an interview guide that was designed prior to the interview. Whereas qualitative interview studies are flexible in that questions are generated in the process of the interview, an interview guide serves as the basis for the conversation. Usually, the interviewer speaks much less than the participant, focusing the conversation on the participants' views and experiences.

> Compare your experiences of interviewing to the conversations you have had with friends or acquaintances. What are the similarities and differences?

Mishler (1986) borrowed the notion of "speech events" from Hymes (1967) and "speech activities" from Gumperz (1982) to describe the nature of interviews. He used Gumperz's definition of a speech activity as "a set of social relationships enacted about a set of schemata in relation to some communicative goal" (Mishler, 1986, p. 35). For Mishler, interviews are not simply exchanges of questions and answers by researchers and participants, but a form of discourse where the researcher and participant engage in coconstructing meaning within a particular type of social relationship. He argued that "even questions that are apparently simple in both structure and topic leave much room for alternative interpretations by both interviewer and respondent" (p. 45). Thus, the interviewer and participants engage in a process where both are working toward shared meanings. Mishler elaborated on this researcher–participant relationship:

> Although I have been focusing on the complexity and ambiguity of the questions
> themselves, it is particularly important to recognize that question form is not the
> determining factor in the process through which ambiguity is manifested and re-
> solved. This is done through the way that interviewers and respondents attempt to
> "fit" their questions and responses to each other and to the developing discourse.
> Presumably "simple" questions are as open and sensitive to this process as are com-
> plex ones. Ambiguities are resolved through the discourse itself and not by efforts to
> give a more precise statement to questions in the interview schedule. (pp. 46–47)

Mishler's notion of the interview as a unique form of speech event or activity,
with the focus on the social construction of meaning, challenges researchers to
view the interview in more complex ways in that the researcher's as well as the
participant's discourse, then, become data within the written transcript of the interview. The work can be examined for how both participated in a social process—
the interview—to construct this data. The interview then becomes a unique
form of discourse between two people where one is an informed learner who is
there to learn more about another's experiences or series of experiences, views,
or perspectives, or reactions to a particular phenomenon or event. Researchers'
theoretical and disciplinary perspectives, life experiences, cultural backgrounds,
genders, ages, physical appearances, and other characteristics influence the way
in which they attend to and respond to the conversation and construct meaning within that interview. Researchers and participants tend to filter each interview experience through unique sets of experiences, beliefs, and assumptions
about the topic of the research. I turn now to a brief discussion of phenomenological interview studies to illustrate one theoretical orientation to qualitative
interviewing.

The Role of Theoretical Perspectives in Shaping Interview Approaches and Practices

As indicated above, different purposes and theoretical perspectives shape qualitative interview approaches. The set of assumptions within a particular theoretical framework inform how the study is conceived, designed, and implemented.
For example, if I am working from a critical theory framework, I may construct
my questions to examine issues of social class and power relations to explore
my research questions. From a feminist stance, I make issues of gender relations
and experiences central to the design of my interviews. For purposes of illustration here, I use phenomenological interviewing to illustrate the extent to which
the theoretical framework informs and shapes the interview itself. In a longer
chapter, one could do the same with other theoretical frameworks, including

other interpretivist theories that seek to understand phenomena, as well as more transformative theories such as feminist theories, critical theory, and critical race theory. My purpose here is to challenge readers to consider ways in which the theories they are using inform, enable, and constrain the qualitative interview studies they conduct.

Phenomenology enables researchers to examine everyday human experience in close, detailed ways. This form of inquiry attempts to discover the meaning people place on their lived experiences. These projects result in contextual, holistic, thematic descriptions of particular experiences. Pollio et al. (1997) argued that Heidegger (1927/1962) combined the existentialism of Kierkegaard (cf. 1844/1936, 1844/1980, 1846/1941) and the phenomenology of Husserl (1913/1931) into a single project—"that of describing everyday human existence in uniquely human ways" (p. 5). Later, Merleau-Ponty (1945/1962) brought these existential phenomenological foundations to the psychological study of human existence. Giorgi (1970, 1975, 1983), Kvale (1996), and Pollio et al. (1997) explored phenomenological methodology and method in the discipline of psychology. Kvale (1983), as well as those mentioned above, described a focus on "lived experience" as one of the central elements of phenomenological work. Thompson et al. (1989) explained this key concept:

> Existential-phenomenology seeks to describe experience as it emerges in some context(s) or, to use phenomenological terms, as it is "lived." The concept of Lebenswelt, or life-world, is one manifestation of existential-phenomenology's focus on lived experience. The world of lived experience does not always correspond with the world of objective description because objectivity often implies trying to explain an event as separate from its contextual setting. . . . Rather than separating and then objectifying aspects of the life-world, the purpose is to describe human experience as it is lived. On this view, the meaning of an experience is always situated in the current experiential context and is coherently related to the ongoing project of the life-world. (pp. 135–136)

Referring to Husserl (1970) and Schutz and Luckman (1973), Max van Maanen (1990) described phenomenology as the

> study of the lifeworld—the world as we immediately experience it pre-reflectively rather than as we conceptualize, categorize, or reflect on it. Phenomenology aims at gaining a deeper understanding of the nature or meaning of our everyday experiences. Phenomenology asks, "What is this or that kind of experience like?" (p. 9)

Phenomenological researchers create contexts in which participants are encouraged to reflect retrospectively on an experience they have already lived through (van Maanen, 1990) and describe this experience in as much detail as possible to the interviewer. Moustakas (1994) explained that the aim of empirical phenomenological research

> is to determine what an experience means for the persons who have had the experience and are able to provide a comprehensive description of it. From the individual descriptions general or universal meanings are derived, in other words the essences or structures of the experience. (p. 13)

The goal for phenomenologists is to learn about the nature, or "essence," of particular, everyday experiences in people's lives. The essence of an experience makes the experience what it is (Husserl, 1913/1931; Merleau-Ponty, 1945/1962). Van Maanen (1990) described the essence of a phenomenon as

> a universal which can be described through a study of the structures that govern the instances or particular manifestations of the essence of that phenomenon. In other words, phenomenology is the systematic attempt to uncover and describe the structures, the internal meaning structures, of lived experience. A universal or essence may only be intuited or grasped through a study of the particulars or instances as they are encountered in lived experience. (p. 10)

The essence of an experience emerges from interview data as participants describe the particular aspects of the experience as they lived it. Researchers seek to "discover" the essence or structure of the experience through an interpretation of the rich, textual data provided by participants describing the particular experience being studied. Thus, the purpose of phenomenological interviews is to "attain a first-person description of some specified domain of experience" (p. 138). To do this, the researcher assumes the role of learner in that the participant is the one who has had the experience, is considered the expert on his or her experience, and can share it with the researcher. The interview is a conversation with the participant, taking the lead in describing the particular experiences in whatever way he or she chooses.

How would you explain this phenomenological framework to a colleague? What are the key components of this work? Do you believe that researchers can get at the essence of an experience in this way? Defend your position.

The interview begins with the open-ended phenomenological question the researcher has developed to best elicit detailed descriptions of the particular experience being studied. For example, the researcher might ask: "Think about a time when you experienced fear and tell me about it." This gets the conversation started, and the participant continues to take the interview in the direction she or he wants related to the experience. The interviewer uses follow-up questions using the participant's own words in the probe. For example, "You mentioned

_____. Tell me more about that" or "What was ____ like for you?" The goal of the researcher is to keep the conversation focused on descriptions of the particular experience rather than abstract discussions about the experience. The participant describes precisely what he or she experiences, how he or she responded, and how he or she reacted within the experience (Kvale, 1983).

The use of "why" questions is worthy of a brief discussion here in that a researcher can turn the discussion away from the particular experience and to a more abstract level through the use of such questions. Because the purpose of the phenomenological interview is to keep the coparticipant focused on a particular experience, a question beginning with "why" turns the focus away from a detailed description of the experience and toward a causal analysis or rationalization about the experience, and this is to be avoided in phenomenological interview studies (Locander et al., 1989). As Kvale (1983) reminded us, the purpose of the interview is to obtain "uninterpreted" descriptions of an experience. In phenomenological interviewing, the researcher assumes the role of a nondirective listener (Locander et al., 1989) who asks short, descriptive questions that lead participants to respond in long, detailed descriptions of the experience being studied. The researcher attempts to establish equality between researcher and participant by privileging the knowledge shared by the participant, sharing researcher interpretations, asking for responses to the interpretations, and sharing the final manuscripts.

Prior to beginning the phenomenological interview process, the researcher engages in a "bracketing interview" (Pollio et al., 1997), in which he or she is interviewed by another researcher often using the same question he or she plans to use in his or her study. This bracketing interview is an attempt to get at the assumptions and beliefs the researcher brings to the study. The bracketing interview is transcribed, thematized, and later used as he or she works through the actual research project from data collection through interpretation. Often, an interpretive research group familiar with phenomenological research analyzes the bracketing interview. This group, already familiar with the researcher's assumptions as reported in the bracketing interview, is used to help with the interpretation of the interview transcripts. The group can serve as a check during the interpretation process to evaluate the extent to which the researcher's beliefs and assumptions interfered with the interpretation. This bracketing interview and research group process can be used in research more generally to increase the trustworthiness of the research findings.

> In thinking about your own work, what might you discuss in a bracketing interview?

Phenomenological interview studies are one way in which qualitative interviews are framed. The phenomenological interview approach is useful in any study where the researchers want to understand specific experiences and/or engage participants in rich, detailed stories about their own experiences (see Kramp, chap. 7, this volume). Researchers will want to be clear on the theoretical position they are assuming in their interview studies to set out how these beliefs and assumptions inform the work. With that understanding in place, I turn to a more general discussion of interview design and implementation that can guide researchers through the remainder of the research process.

DESIGNING A QUALITATIVE INTERVIEW STUDY

The interview study design begins with a clear statement of purpose. What is the purpose of the study? This purpose should be situated in a problem statement that serves as the context for the study. The problem describes the topic of the research and reviews relevant literature for what researchers have learned about that topic. The problem usually describes the gaps in the literature or what is not well understood and, consequently, provides the rationale for the study. Refining a problem and purpose statement will take work, as well as discussions with others to clearly articulate what the study is about. Often with an interview study, the purpose statement will begin with the following phrase: "The purpose of this study is to understand . . . [a particular phenomenon, experience, or set of experiences]."

Sometimes, the purpose statement comes only after researchers think about why they want to engage in the study, the types of people to be interviewed, or the kinds of questions that they want to have answered. Talking with people who have knowledge or experience with the topic may assist researchers in refining the purpose statement. These activities lead to clearer understanding and articulation of the research purpose.

Selecting Participants

The research purpose should lead quickly to the possible participants for the study. Interview researchers select people to talk with who have the knowledge and experience about the particular focus of the study. A primary consideration is to select participants who can talk about the topic or phenomenon under study. It would be fruitless for me to attempt to interview women teachers who said they never experienced anger in classroom or school settings. There may be many people who could be interviewed about a particular research topic, so it is necessary to select from a larger population of participants. Qualitative researchers use the term *criterion-based selection* to refer to the process through which they construct a list of characteristics or attributes the participants in the study must possess (LeCompte & Preissle, 1993). Common criterion-based strategies qualitative researchers use to select participants include the following: comprehension selection, network selection, typical-case selection, unique-case selection, and reputation-based case selection. Comprehensive selection can occur when all cases that fall into a particular category are included in the study (LeCompte & Preissle, 1993). This strategy is used when the population that falls within the criteria is quite small. For example, perhaps a researcher is interested in understanding more about elementary students who bring guns to school in a particular district. If he or she finds that the number in this district is small (10–12), he or she would be able to use a comprehensive selection strategy and interview all students within this group.

It is more likely that a qualitative researcher will use a network selection in which he or she locates one participant who fits into the selection criteria and that person who refers the researcher to others who also fit the criteria. For example, one of my students was interested in understanding the experiences of women who (1) had gone through a divorce after being in long-term marriages (more than 25 years in length) and (2) had been homemakers throughout the marriages. She wanted to talk with these participants about their learning processes after the marriage had ended. She was able to locate one woman who fit the selection criteria, and that person referred her to others she knew personally who had similar experiences. The network selection strategy enables the researcher to use personal contacts to locate other potential participants for the study.

Typical-case selection, unique-case selection, and reputation-based case selection are all strategies that are self-evident. In typical-case selection, the researcher sets out criteria that are typical of a person within a group. Based on demographic information, a "typical" elementary teacher might be European American, female, and middle class, and therefore participants who fit this description could be considered for typical-case selection. Unique-case selection relies on working with participants who are unique in some way. For example, women superintendents in Georgia may constitute a unique-case group. Reputation-case selection researchers rely on the recommendation of others. In my dissertation study of an urban Appalachian first-grade classroom (Bennett, 1986, 1990), I wanted to study a teacher who was considered exemplary by her principal and by other teachers in the school. She had a reputation as being an excellent teacher.

How many participants should be included? Novice researchers (or their dissertation committee members) often wonder how many participants is enough for a qualitative interview study. Or, conversely, how many are too many? Because qualitative studies are so contextually based, the response to this questions is usually, "It depends." It depends on the richness of the interviews, the extent to which the participants are able to respond to the research purpose and questions. Researchers will want to think about the database that is generated with high-quality in-depth interviews so as to consider the amount of data that will need to be analyzed and interpreted. A good interview of approximately $1\frac{1}{2}$ hours will yield a transcript of approximately 25 to 30 pages of text. Returning to the research purpose—to understand a particular phenomena—the researcher needs to interview enough participants to gain this understanding. In qualitative studies, I like to think about the notion that "less is more." Fewer participants interviewed in greater depth usually generates the kinds of understandings qualitative researchers seek. When researchers begin to see similar patterns in the responses from participants or when little new information is received from the interview process, it is probably time to stop the interview portion of the study.

> Like other qualitative methodologists, the author has not provided specific details for the number of participants that would be included in a qualitative interview study. How, then, would you defend to a dissertation committee the number of participants you select for a given study?

Benefits to Participants

One issue to consider in planning an interview study involves the benefits to the participants. Researchers benefit by engaging in the process in the form of a sense of accomplishment or achievement; completion of a project leads to a degree or may result in an article or book. These achievements in turn may result in a new profession, new position, or may be used to evaluate scholarly productivity and can be rewarded with raises and merit pay. How will the participants in the study benefit from their involvement? They, too, may get a sense of satisfaction from participating in a study that leads to increased knowledge. They may also benefit from the experience of having someone listen to and appreciate their views or their experiences. They may also benefit from building a relationship with the researcher. Sometimes, researchers provide cash payments or other forms of remuneration for their participation in the study.

Constructing an Interview Guide

Another design step involves the construction of an interview guide for use in talking with participants. By spending time constructing guiding questions that participants will address, researchers make clear in their own minds what they want to talk about and how best to engage participants in these conversations. I find the following guidelines helpful in constructing interview questions:

1. *Short, clear questions lead to detailed responses from participants.*

Sometimes, researchers new to qualitative interviewing have a tendency to construct long, elaborate questions that can be full of academic jargon. When such questions are posed to participants orally, they usually respond with "What do you mean?" Then, the interviewer takes more time to explain meanings and may steer the interview toward his or her own assumptions about the topic. The more simply and conversationally the questions are stated, the more clear they will be to the participants. A good focused question goes a long way toward encouraging participants to provide a detailed narrative. The phrase "Tell me about . . ." serves as a good lead to a question. In the teachers' anger study mentioned earlier, my first question asked participants to respond to the following: "Think of a time when you experienced anger in the classroom and tell me about it." Invariably this led to a long, detailed narrative of what happened in a particular incident. At appropriate points along the way, I could ask for more details or elaboration.

2. *Questions that ask participants to recall specific events or experiences in detail encourage fuller narratives.*

As seen in the last example, guiding questions that request a retelling of a particular event or experience yield wonderfully detailed stories. These types of narratives enable researchers to more fully understand human phenomena. Some approaches to in-depth interviewing, such as phenomenological interviews, rely on a single, well-constructed question that encourages a participant to recall, in detail, a specific experience. When researcher's questions are requests for generalized information, they move away from particular, real-life experiences. For example, returning to my anger interviews, early in the process I asked women to talk in general about what makes them angry. This line of questioning was unsatisfactory in that it yielded short, even one-word, responses that provided little of their real-life experiences of anger. Women tended to say that they "got angry at unfairness" or "at being disregarded." Although this was a start, it meant that I had to go back to ask for specific examples of unfairness or feeling disregarded to find out what was meant by those phrases. Asking for such generalizations moves the conversation away from specific experiences and events.

3. *A few broad, open-ended questions work better than a long series of closed-ended questions.*

A graduate student was working on a thesis that explored the phenomena of backlash on women in sports. She came to me with an interview guide of 35 questions for each participant to answer. Although the questions were short and clear, they were also closed-ended questions that were framed around her beliefs and assumptions about the topic or from specific findings from previous studies. An example of such a closed, yes-or-no question was "Do you believe there is a backlash on women in sports?" This particular question could be "opened up" and refocused on the participant's experience of backlash in sports. After a process of listing the topics she wanted her participants to talk about as well as combining and opening up the questions, we were able to construct an interview guide of six or seven good open-ended guiding questions for her interviews. The final interview guide encouraged participants to talk in great detail about their experiences and yielded wonderfully rich data.

Whyte (1984) included descriptive and evaluative questions in his discussion of types of interview questions. The descriptive question is a request for a telling of what happened at a particular time, event, or series of events. The evaluative question is a request for an assessment of how the participant feels about that event or happening. These categories can be helpful in considering the design of the questions to use in the study.

The interview guide is just that—a guide. Researchers will not necessarily ask all the questions on the guide. Often, once started, participants will carry the interview and with good researcher prompting and probing, will respond to everything planned on the guide without even asking. Novice interviewers often come back from an interview and report that they did not even have to ask the questions because the interviewee had covered them within the course of the narratives and stories he or she told.

PHASES OF THE INTERVIEW PROCESS

Each interview is a unique experience between two people. To illustrate the phases of the interview process, consider the metaphor of going out to dinner with a close friend who has been away for a long time. Friends plan ahead to go out to dinner, agreeing on the time and place to meet, and making reservations in advance. When both arrive at the restaurant, they've already done some preparation for the evening by thinking about and perhaps anticipating what the experience might be like for them. They greet each other and engage in light conversation. They might be somewhat nervous or tense because of the length of time that has passed since their last visit together. After being seated, they order drinks, peruse the menu and order their meals while continuing the conversation. They relax a bit over appetizers. By the time their meals have arrived, they are fully focused on sharing more intimate details of their lives. If the conversation is flowing smoothly, they linger over dinner without interruptions from the server. As they move into the coffee and dessert phase, they know that time is drawing to a close and begin to change the course of the conversation to perhaps lighter or future-oriented topics. As they pay the bill and begin to take leave of one another, they promise to stay in touch, write, or keep one another posted on their life's journeys. They realize that the experience has brought them together and enabled them to renew and build old friendships.

Although not precisely the same, an in-depth interview has a similar pattern or flow to the dinner described above. The "getting ready phase" begins with the researcher asking a participant to join him or her in an interview. They decide on a time and place that is pleasing to both. The interview begins with greetings, light conversation, a sharing of information about the study, and consent from the participant to proceed with the interview.

The main meal is the actual focused interview, where the researcher begins the exchange with a guiding question and the participant responds. As the researcher and participant begin to build a relationship with one another through talking together about the topic at hand, they relax a bit and concentrate closely on what the other is sharing. The researcher listens more than talks, but offers supportive, encouraging nods, smiles, and verbal expressions. The interviewer asks for more details or explanations when the participant has paused. The interview focuses on particular events and moves from safer, descriptive topics to those that may be more emotionally loaded or difficult for the participant (Whyte, 1984). Asking difficult or emotionally risky questions too soon before trust has been built interrupts process and causes discomfort. When the flow of the interview is good and easy, time passes quickly. What seems like a few minutes might actually be an hour. Both are enthusiastic and inspired by the dialogue.

An essential element in the interview process is that of active listening and probing where appropriate for more elaboration. Sometimes participants will assume shared meanings about a particular word, phrase, or event. Researchers need to be sure to have the participant explain in more detail even those concepts where meaning might be assumed. For example, in an interview study of elite athletes, one of my students (who was also an athlete) missed several opportunities in interviews to probe for more detail because he assumed shared knowledge. The participant described "tightening up" at the end of an event. When I questioned what that meant, the interviewer explained from his viewpoint what that meant, but this may or may not have been the intent of the participant. A good probe at that point would be "You mentioned you tightened up. What was that like for you?" This probe would have produced a more detailed description of the experience. Probes are easily accomplished if the researcher is able to jot down participants' words or phrases to return to at a break in the conversation. Then simply use the word or phrase as a lead-in to the probe: "You mentioned _____. Could you tell me more about that?"

> What other strategies can you think of that might encourage the participant to describe his or her experiences in more detail? What approaches have you found effective in similar situations?

At some point, it will become clear to both participant and interviewer that it is time to bring the interview to a close. Both may be tired from the intensity of the experience; they may have exhausted the topic for the time. They move into the "taking leave phase," where they move to talking about more everyday topics. They may make arrangements to talk together again, the researcher may promise to provide a transcript of the tape for the participant to read and respond to, or the researcher might simply thank the participant for his or her time and participation in the study.

RELATIONSHIPS BETWEEN RESEARCHERS AND PARTICIPANTS

Relationships between the researcher and participants can take many forms, depending on the type of interview study, the length of time researchers and participants spend together, the intensity of the subject matter of the research, and the rapport established within the interviews. The researcher's beliefs about the researcher or participant relationship influence the way in which he or she designs his or her study. Some researchers design studies so that the researcher and participant come together for one long interview with little or no follow-up. Other researchers design interview studies so that a series of interviews are conducted, encouraging the researcher and participant to form closer relationships and more permanent friendships. The more the participants are encouraged to be a partner in the research process, the more intense their relationship is likely to become.

Power issues, whether or not those involved in the study recognize them, are central to relationships between the researcher and the researched. The researcher has the power in studies where participants view him or her as the one who designs and conducts the study, interprets the findings, and publishes the results. The researcher has ownership over the project, with little input from participants except for the initial interview process, where the participants can decide what knowledge they are willing to share with the researcher. At the other end of this researcher–participant power continuum is the collaborative study, where both researcher and participants engage jointly in the construction, implementation, and publication of the study. Collaborative ventures such as these require extensive negotiation and sharing of power throughout the process. They can be fraught with difficulties—often much messier than more traditional forms of interview studies—but can also lead to strong relationships between the participants and the researcher, as well as good quality inquiry. There are many possibilities between these two points on the continuum. Consider the options as you explore ways to be comfortable within researcher–participant relationships.

What do you think about the author's characterization about the power differential within the interview process? What are some ways to diminish power differences? What might you do if the participant controls the interview more than you anticipated or desired?

TABLE 4.1

Researcher and Participant Roles in Qualitative Interview Studies

	Researcher	Participant
Before the interview	Designs study (including research purpose, guiding questions for interview) Selects participants Explains study to participants	Listens to interviewer describe study Asks clarification questions about study Consents to be interviewed
During the interview	Begins interview with initial question Asks additional interview questions Probes participants' responses for more detail explanations Assumes role of active listener, encourager May make some conversation, depending on type of interview Listens more than talks	Responds to questions Elaborates and explains answers more fully in response to interviewer's probes Talks more than listens
After the interview	Listens to tape recording of interview Transcribes tapes (or has them transcribed) Checks transcriptions Analyzes data Checks findings with participants	Possibilities: Reads over transcription Participates in subsequent interviews Responds to transcription Responds to researcher's findings Reads research report
Possible roles	Designer Guide Learner Listener Encourager Supporter Collaborator Analyzer Interpreter	Responder Storyteller Narrator Teacher Learner Collaborator Interpreter
Who holds control or power in the interview process?	Power of social science inquiry; power of scholarly language; power of researcher position Control in the design of the study and guiding of the interview process Control in the interpretation of data Control in where and how research results get disseminated	Power of knowledge and experience sought by researcher Control in what is told and what is omitted from the telling Control in reinterpreting or providing alternative interpretations of data if given the opportunity to review transcriptions, analyses, and research reports Possible collaboration in where and how research results get disseminated based on negotiation with the researcher

ELEMENTS OF A "GOOD" INTERVIEW

Novice and more experienced interviewers come to their craft with differing abilities and experiences, but even the most inexperienced interviewer will be able to talk with participants in a way that will yield quality information for a research project. Researchers can improve the quality of their interviews through a rigorous design process in which the research problem and purpose are carefully articulated. More rigor in design, as well as skill in the interview itself, enhance the credibility and trustworthiness of the study. Carefully constructed interview questions go far in engaging people in qualitative interviews. In my work with students new to qualitative interview studies, I have found the following to be barriers to their success within the interview process:

1. The interviewer uses long, complicated questions so that the participant is lost in the verbal barrage.
2. The interviewer asks yes-or-no or closed questions that can be answered with a word or two.
3. The interviewer asks questions that are vague or deal with generalities rather than specific details of events and experiences.
4. The interviewer asks leading questions based on his or her own theories, beliefs, and assumptions.
5. The interviewer fails to recognize clues or markers, passing references to an important event or feeling (Weiss, 1994), that may signal that there is something more to be shared if the interviewer picks up on it.

Sometimes an interviewer has difficulty finding common ground with the participant because of communication barriers. The interviewer might have difficulty being "present" in the interview, because he or she is thinking ahead to the next question or listening closely to the participant. He or she may interrupt when he or she could have provided additional "wait time" for the participant to elaborate on a point. Sometimes, interviewers asks questions that are on the interview guide but have already been answered within the context of responding to a previous question. This is a signal to the participant that the interviewer is not listening carefully and may result in some frustration on the part of the participant. In a good interview, the researcher will avoid giving advice or making judgments on what the participant has shared. He or she will avoid inserting him- or herself extensively into the interview to the point that it draws attention away from the experiences of the participant.

> What other barriers and problems can you foresee in the interview process? What ways might these problems be avoided? In what ways might poor interviews become good ones?

Participants take cues from interviewers as to how to converse within the context of the interview. If the interviewer asks for elaboration of a story, the participant will know to provide more detailed responses. If the interviewer moves from one question to another without follow-up, the participant will learn to use more succinct, focused responses to the specific question without elaboration. Sometimes a participant is distracted or put off by the interviewer's use of academic language or technical jargon and does not understand the point of the question. The nonverbal interactions within the interview can be distracting. For example, the interviewer might be writing or looking in another direction while the interviewee is talking. She or he may have difficulty establishing and maintaining an attentive listening posture. All of the above behaviors interrupt the flow of the interview, making the interview difficult for both participant and interviewer. A difficult or uncomfortable interview is likely to be a short one.

Novice qualitative interviewers will want to carefully examine their own process in the context of the interview. Through a close analysis of the transcript and listening to the tape, one can see the pattern in the interview style that enabled or constrained a quality interview. Carefully examine the questions that were asked and the ways the participant responded to those questions. Locate the points in the interview when communication was not as clear or smooth as it could have been to determine ways to improve interview practice for subsequent interviews.

CONCLUSIONS

Qualitative interview approaches to research can be stimulating and rewarding experiences for both researchers and participants. This chapter began with a list of questions for researchers new to qualitative interview studies. I have attempted to respond to those questions through a brief introduction to qualitative research interviews that included discussions of major elements of interview design: the role of theoretical perspectives in the shaping of the study, setting a research purpose, considering the selection of participants, designing a quality interview guide, and using interview techniques that yield detailed descriptions from research participants. Although this presentation was designed to introduce and assist researchers new to qualitative interview studies, I emphasize again that there are many different forms of qualitative interviews situated within disciplinary and theoretical traditions. There are differences among these approaches and, consequently, there is no one "right way" to engage in qualitative interview studies. I invite readers to use my words here as a beginning point for their own work. The qualitative methodological literature is rich with detailed accounts of the qualitative interview design and can serve as guideposts for those readers who wish to pursue these approaches to qualitative inquiry.

5

Owning Significance: The Critical Incident Technique in Research

Daniel L. Kain
Northern Arizona University

MEET THE AUTHOR

Daniel L. Kain, professor of instructional leadership, is currently dean of the College of Education at Northern Arizona University, in Flagstaff. He earned degrees from Montana State University, the University of Washington, and the University of British Columbia. He is the author of *Camel-Makers: Building Effective Teacher Teams Together* (1998), *Problem-Based Learning for Teachers, Grades K–8* (2002), and *Problem-Based Learning for Teachers, Grades 6–12* (2003). In addition, he has written a number of book chapters on interdisciplinary teaching, teacher teaming, team leadership, and teacher education. His articles have appeared in *Teachers College Record, the Journal of Curriculum and Supervision, Middle School Journal, Research in Middle Level Education Quarterly, The Journal of Educational Thought*, and other publications. Kain teaches undergraduate courses in secondary education and graduate courses in curriculum and educational research.

Imagine an across-the-fence conversation between two neighbors. Leaning through the white pickets (why not?), Elwood starts it off:

"My your yard is green, Harvey."

"Thank you, Elwood. Always nice to have a compliment. And may I say that yours also looks fine."

"I appreciate the thought, Harvey. But as you can see, my lawn is not nearly so carpetlike, so tightly woven with thatch, never a dandelion poking through. How do you do it?"

"Usual stuff, Elwood. I water regularly, mow occasionally, and chase away the rabbits."

"Right, but there's more to this than meets the eye, Harvey. There must be something else."

"Now that you mention it, I suppose there was a turning point for me. About two months ago, having just heard a speaker at Charlie's Place, I decided to try a mixture of flat beer and tobacco juice on the grass. I sprayed it once a week, and I guess the turf has never looked better."

"Hmm. Makes sense, Harvey. I've used the same mixture on myself for years, and I'm pretty fit."

Was the conversation between Elwood and Harvey an example of research? Here we have an inquirer (Elwood) facing a real and important question (what makes the lawn green?). He engages a respondent (Harvey) in his seeking for evidence and explanation. Yet, instead of the usual approaches to inquiry (experimentation, surveying, and so on), Elwood simply asks Harvey for the significance he sees in some event. Harvey reflects on his experience, finds a point of significance, and interprets this for the inquirer. In brief, and with a nod to metaphor, this is the critical incident technique for research.

> What are the research topics that might lend themselves to this technique?

DEVELOPMENT OF THE CRITICAL INCIDENT TECHNIQUE

The critical incident technique essentially involves asking a number of respondents to identify events or experiences that were "critical" for some purpose. These incidents are then pooled together for analysis, and generalizations about the event or activity are drawn from the commonalities of the incidents. If Elwood made his way around the neighborhood, asking everyone he could find about turning points (good or bad) in their lawn-tending experience, he could analyze the responses and conduct a sort of critical incident study.

The critical incident technique originated in studies of aviators in World War II (Flanagan, 1954). This research technique has seen waves of popularity and a wide variety of applications, including studies of the following occupations and issues: airline pilots, research personnel, air traffic controllers (Flanagan, 1954), store managers (Andersson & Nilsson, 1964), growth group leaders (Cohen & Smith, 1976), teachers (Engelking, 1986; Tripp, 1993; Wodlinger, 1990), principals (Fris, 1992), speech professionals (Stano, 1983), women's self-actualization (Woolsey, 1986), team skills (Morgan, Glickman, Woodard, Blaiwes, & Salas, 1986), and computer programmers (Freeman, Weitzenfeld, Klein, Riedl, & Musa, 1991).

Before proceeding with a description of this research approach, it is worth pausing to consider the label, *critical incident technique*. When Flanagan (1954) originally articulated this research approach, he was operating from a research paradigm that generally did not question a detached, objective approach to scientific research. Research was an unproblematic concept for the most part, whereby one might alter the specifics of how to do research but not the basic assumptions of research. The critical incident technique was just that—another technique—drawing from the Greek word for "of an art or skill." The name for this research approach has persisted, and one of the questions pursued later in this chapter is the degree to which this technique is a neutral tool, applicable to a variety of research perspectives. In keeping with the tradition associated with this research approach, I am holding on to the name critical incident technique. Readers will face the task of deciding whether it is appropriately seen as *teknikos* or *paradeiknunai*.

In his seminal work, Flanagan (1954) was interested both in the occupational performance (job tasks) and also in resulting psychological constructs.

Metaphorically, he was Elwood, leaning over the fences of a few thousand aviators, finding out what had worked for them in their bombing missions. The appeal of the critical incident technique of research lies largely in this systematic approach to inquiry—into what significance others place on given events.

In its earliest form, the critical incident technique was used primarily to investigate "activity requirements" (Flanagan, 1954, p. 354) of particular jobs, and this continues to be an important use of the technique (Anderson & Wilson, 1997). The research technique proved to be a powerful way to get at the requirements for being a pilot, a researcher, or an industrial manager. By examining common experiences shared by a broad range of an occupational community, critical incident researchers could claim to have uncovered important patterns— and these findings led to selection criteria, training programs, and evaluation tools.

As the technique gained wider acceptance, other researchers moved beyond activities, to look at characteristics, traits, and perspectives. However, the technique is rooted in careful observations (by the subject or an outside observer) of particular behaviors, thus lending it to an analysis of activities.

Components of a Critical Incident Study

Flanagan (1954) articulated the basic components of a critical incident study, though other researchers have adapted the process depending on their applications (Cohen & Smith, 1976; Freeman et al., 1991). Flanagan (1954) laid out five phases of a critical incident study: establishing general aims, establishing plans and specifications, collecting the data, analyzing the data, and interpreting and reporting (Figure 5.1). Each of these steps is elaborated below. As a cautionary note, it is important to remember that Flanagan himself saw this technique not as a rigid set of rules, but as a "flexible set of principles which must be modified and adapted to meet the specific situation at hand" (p. 335).

Flanagan's (1954) first stage involves the clarification of the general aim of the activity. He argues that one cannot inquire into what makes effective or ineffective behavior unless one knows the goal of this behavior. Clearly, if the focus is on activities, the governing issue is one of intent. In the case of Flanagan's early research, it made sense to clarify the aim of such activities as "combat leadership." For a participant to speak meaningfully about the effectiveness of a leader, that participant must understand the goal of such leadership. However, there are areas of interest where the concept of a general aim may be less relevant. For example, Woolsey (1986) used the technique to inquire into same-sex social bonds and women's self-actualization. Although she reports working to define the aim of the activity, one wonders how meaningful this is for such a concept as self-actualization. Does a person set out to self-actualize in the same way a soldier sets out to lead in combat? Or does self-actualization and social bonding occur in the

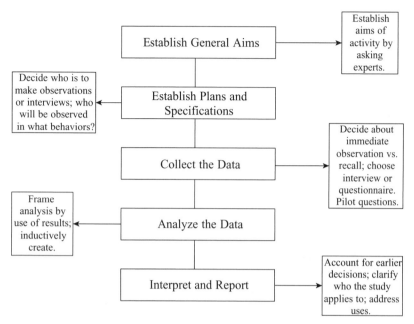

FIG. 5.1. Flanagan's five stages for the critical incident research technique, elaborated.

course of other aims? As the focus of interest shifts from the activity as significant to the significance of the activity, clarifying the aim of the activity becomes less important.

The second component outlined by Flanagan (1954) is the establishing of plans and specifications. This entails a laying out of who will make observations (e.g., a supervisor or a participant), which persons or group will be observed, and what sorts of behaviors will be observed. Flanagan maintained that the best observers for most jobs are the supervisors, who have a broader perspective and opportunities for numerous observations. If you wanted to know about critical events in the work of ticket takers interacting with inebriated fans at a football stadium, you could ask the supervisors to report on such incidents. Supervisors would have the opportunity and perspective to address multiple events. Supervisors could recount incidents where they observed ticket takers confronting intoxicated fans who attempt to enter the stadium. Thus, we have the key parts of the plan: who observes (supervisors) which group (ticket takers) in what behaviors (confronting intoxicated fans).

To draw on a more education-related example, suppose you wanted to know how teachers became adept at using an innovation such as cooperative learning. From the Flanagan (1954) recommendations, we could ask administrators (the teachers' supervisors) to report on events where teachers (the observed group) were particularly effective or ineffective at implementing cooperative learning (the behavior of interest). However, as anyone who has worked in schools knows, the supervisors would not observe most of the behaviors of interest. Teachers who are just implementing an innovation are unlikely to do so during the infrequent visits of their evaluators. Even if they were to do so, the nature of teaching is such that nearly all of the incidents of implementation would occur outside of the observational opportunities of the supervisor. Clearly, this case argues for designating the teachers themselves (and possibly their students) as the appropriate observers and reporters of incidents. However, principals and their assistants might have adequate opportunity to observe effective and ineffective classroom discipline practices, making these supervisors appropriate reporters of critical incidents.

When Fris (1992) wanted to explore how principals handled conflict, he went directly to the principals (as opposed to their supervisors) and asked them to describe challenging school-related conflicts. In a study of team planning for interdisciplinary teaching experiences, I went to the team members themselves (as opposed to their supervisors) to ask them to describe what they did to create successful collaborative interdisciplinary learning opportunities (Kain, 1997). The point is this: Before collecting a set of critical incidents, it is crucial that the researcher establish a defensible plan for who will provide what information about what persons or groups.

Flanagan's (1954) third component of a critical incident study is the collecting of the data. He discussed the relative advantages and disadvantages of collecting data through direct observations and through recalled incidents. Although direct observation is preferable, he argued, recollections are acceptable if such recollections provide "full and precise details" (p. 340). Flanagan laid out four means of collecting incidents from observers: through individual interviews, group interviews, questionnaires, and written records. Anderson and Wilson (1997) described an incident-writing workshop as yet another means of collecting incidents. This workshop approach seems to offer the potential of blending research and professional development, moving the critical incident technique into an action research mode. For example, one could conduct an incident-writing workshop where teachers reflected on key issues in their practice, offering them the growth possibilities about which Tripp (1993) wrote, while providing the basis for a researcher's inquiry into the same key issues. Whatever means one uses, Flanagan indicated the most important criteria for incidents are as follows: (1) Actual behavior is reported, (2) the relationship of the reporter to behavior is clear, (3) the relevant facts are provided, (4) the reporter makes a clear judgment about what makes the incident critical, and (5) the reasons for this judgment are clear.

Put simply, the critical incident interview invites the respondents to tell a story and explain why it is significant for a given context. For example, if our researcher is interested in teachers' implementation of cooperative learning, the researcher might seek information in the following manner:

> "Think of a time when you were especially effective at using cooperative learning in the classroom." (Pause). "Tell me what you did that that made this successful." "Why were your actions effective in making cooperative learning work?"

The researcher invites the respondent to describe several incidents where this sense of success was strong, and, of course, the respondent also would be asked to describe incidents where he or she was not effective. One interviewee might provide a dozen or more incidents.

It is obvious that a researcher must give careful thought to how a question is phrased. The tradition in research is to regard questions merely as a means to gather information. Schwartz (1999) demonstrated that questions also provide information, encouraging respondents to engage in meaningful communication. Flanagan (1954) cautioned against using leading questions, a notion that Schwartz (1999) expanded on by pointing out the effects on respondents of such things as the researcher's affiliation, adjacent questions, and the context of questions.

Data collection continues until enough critical incidents have been gathered so that in the analysis of these incidents no new critical behaviors (categories) appear. Flanagan's (1954) rule of thumb is that if adding 100 critical incidents only adds one or two critical behaviors, the data collection is adequate. However, various researchers have reinterpreted this rule of thumb, so that anywhere from 16 to 4,000 incidents have served as an "adequate" data set. Clearly, judging the adequacy of the set of incidents implies a concurrent analysis of data. That is, the researcher must be categorizing the reported incidents in order to establish that the incidents are merely adding to existing categories rather than suggesting new ones. If data analysis were left to a final and separate stage, a researcher might find either that far too much or far too little data had been collected to perform an acceptable analysis.

In your opinion, what is an "adequate" data set for a critical incident approach?

The fourth component of the critical incident technique is data analysis. Flanagan (1954) made a case for analysis that is useful—analysis that leads to practical purposes, such as training or evaluation tools. He explicated three features of data analysis. First, the researcher must select a frame of reference, by which Flanagan meant the general classification scheme. The subsequent coding of incidents will be inductive; that is, the categories will arise from the data. By attending to a frame of reference, the researcher directs the inductive activity of generating categories. As Woolsey (1986) indicated, selecting a frame of reference establishes limits on the exploratory use of the method. Flanagan (1954) indicated that the frame of reference is largely determined by the uses to which the research will be put. For example, if the target use will be training, the general frame of reference builds a classification system that translates easily into a training course. However, if the ultimate goal of the research project were to identify selection criteria (as in a job description), the frame of reference would differ from that of a study aiming to build a training course. Woolsey's (1986) study of same-sex bonds was intended to help counselors deal with their clients, so an appropriate counseling frame of reference was adopted, whereby clients could identify strength and closeness in bonds. An investigation of exemplary teaching in higher education, which drew on a critical incident questionnaire (Rahilly & Saroyan, 1997), used a classification scheme that enhanced the possibilities for improving teacher development: knowledge, processes, goals, and actions.

Having selected a frame of reference, the researcher then begins to create categories. This inductive category construction is a tentative, interactive process, where the researcher sorts incidents into groups derived from the frame of reference. A researcher might do an initial sort, starting with incidents that are nearly identical and moving to incidents that blur categories. As this inductive piling up of incidents occurs, categories are created. For example, my colleagues and I have used a modified critical incident inquiry to understand what our secondary teacher education students perceive as particularly influential in helping them make a transition from being students to being teachers (Kain, Tanner, & Raines, 1997). We ask students to recount (in writing) one or more critical incidents in making this shift during the semester before they begin student teaching. Such incidents fall readily into a number of categories: experiences with children in the schools, experiences or conversations with practicing teachers, crucial moments in completing assignments, and so on. (No one has, to this point, identified one of my lectures as the critical turning point.)

Reading through students' incidents generates the categories, and an important check on such categories is to have others review this work. This review does not consist of blindly generating the same categories, but given the category names and definitions, could another researcher place incidents into the same groupings with a high degree of agreement? In one study of teacher job satisfaction, researchers classified 694 critical incidents into 14 categories (Engelking, 1986). As a check on the inductive generating of categories, this study used two coders to categorize incidents, with less than 2% disagreement on the categories. Anderson and Wilson (1997) described an analysis where subject-matter experts rate the incidents on a 7-point scale. Thus, not only can the researcher check for agreement on categorical assignment among raters, but he or she also can compute means and standard deviations on the effectiveness of each incident.

The final decision in data analysis, according to Flanagan (1954), is a judgment call about the level of specificity to use in reporting data. Essentially, Flanagan makes a case for a logical organization that is useful to the consumer of the research. Whereas one could report out hundreds of specific behaviors in the context of activity requirements, a dozen more general behaviors might prove more useful. To return to the example of teachers' implementing cooperative learning, it would be more useful for consumers of research to encounter a manageable set of 10 to 15 effective actions than an intimidating, overly specialized set of 100. In my study of interdisciplinary team planning (Kain, 1997), I found it useful to look at three levels of categories. First, was an incident seen (by the provider) as positive or negative? At the next level, what was the basic type of interdisciplinary teaching situation (e.g., a "canned" unit vs. developing a theme or focusing on a skill)? Finally, I categorized team actions and organizational features that supported or inhibited such team planning.

Flanagan's (1954) fifth component of the critical incident technique is the interpreting and reporting on findings. He stated that the report must account for decisions made in the four previous stages, allowing the readers to make judgments about how the study should be generalized. Although Flanagan described a goal of generalization consistent with the positivist perspective ("The aim of the study is usually not a functional description of the activity as carried on by this sample but rather a statement relating to all groups of this type," p. 345), his admonition to describe fully and carefully is consistent with recommendations made by qualitative researchers who see generalization more as a case of reader-based transferability of the findings of a study (Lincoln & Guba, 1985; Stake, 1995).

Beyond this clarification of decisions made, Flanagan (1954) called for the researcher to emphasize the value of the findings. Is there something worth knowing in the results of this research? Flanagan argued that someone has to make that sort of judgment, and no one is better suited to do so than the researcher. The researcher shirks his or her responsibility by not indicating the degree of credibility in these findings.

Design a study using the critical incident approach. Account for each component described here.

ADVANTAGES AND DISADVANTAGES OF THE CRITICAL INCIDENT TECHNIQUE

One of the professed advantages of the critical incident technique is its connection to real-world examples and behaviors, minimizing the subjective input of the researcher (Stano, 1983). In this way, the critical incident technique is similar to the notion of grounded theory (Glaser & Strauss, 1967). As Glaser and Strauss put it, "In discovering theory, one generates conceptual categories or their prop-erties from evidence; then the evidence from which the category emerged is used to illustrate the concept" (p. 23). This is the means employed in critical incident research.

A second advantage of the critical incident technique is its usefulness in the early stages of understanding a phenomenon. As Woolsey (1986) wrote, "Critical incident studies are particularly useful in the early stages of research because they generate both exploratory information and theory or model-building" (p. 252). The critical incident technique can identify issues that may deserve further at-tention and research.

Another advantage of this technique is its systematic approach to gathering portraits of significance from a wide variety of participants. Unlike participant ob-servation activities, which require focused, long-term field experiences, the crit-ical incident technique allows researchers to access the perspectives of many re-search participants through one of the most accessible human discourse avenues, the narrative: "Tell me about … ".

This approach to research also has a number of potential disadvantages. Because the technique has not broken into the ranks of high-status research practices, it is unfamiliar to most readers, except in industrial and organizational psychology (Anderson & Wilson, 1997). This novelty can make it difficult to convince grant committees or editors that the approach is warranted.

Also, despite Flanagan's (1954) fairly thorough articulation of the research process, its flexibility leaves researchers to work out specifics of each study in a manner that may not be comfortable for many. Although this flexibility can also be viewed as an advantage, a researcher must consider whether or not such a working out of details fits the researcher's style and preferences. The critical inci-dent technique requires, as Flanagan argued, "insight, experience, and judgment" (p. 344), and it has many subjective decisions embedded in it. For researchers who prefer a more formulaic system, the critical incident technique is a poor choice.

To a certain extent, the critical incident technique suffers from an identity crisis. Not wholly in the qualitative camp, the technique is also not completely in or out of the quantitative alliance. Most critical incident studies make some attempt to count category membership. Engelking's (1986) study, for example, categorized 53% of all teacher satisfaction incidents as "recognition" incidents. In a study of Swedish grocery store managers, 1% of the incidents were categorized as "cooperates with colleagues and superiors" (Andersson & Nilsson, 1964, p. 398). Obviously, such reports of percentages make an appeal to a quantitative way of thinking. However, the persuasiveness of such research is not based on inferential statistical analyses; one is unlikely to encounter a p value, or any other statistical reporting, except reliability checks. Similar to ethnographic research, much of the persuasiveness of critical incident research arises from a careful explanation of the process followed and attention to rich descriptive detail, providing the reader with a basis to judge the applicability of the research.

Another potential disadvantage of the critical incident technique is that in relying on self-reports (as it often does), the technique is subject to criticism that such reports may be inaccurate. Schwartz (1999), speaking of behavioral reports in general, reviewed research that indicates such reports are "highly fallible and strongly affected by the specifics of the research instrument used" (p. 100). For example, Schwartz reported how the order of questions affects a respondent's recollections. Respondents who are asked to recall positive life events report more life satisfaction than those who recall negative life events. Schwartz also illuminated how context information alters self-reporting. When respondents were asked about their attitudes toward the Republican Party, their responses varied by whether the question identified the party as the group to which retired general Colin Powell had recently aligned himself or as the party that Colin Powell rejected when asked to run for president. One safeguard built into the critical incident technique in relation to faulty self-reporting is the use of multiple sources of information, and thus the need to generate many incidents. This, in turn, minimizes the effects of a particular faulty recall on the part of an individual participant. However, a competent researcher must bear in mind the possibility of informants being mistaken.

Similar to other qualitative research approaches, the researcher does not rely on a tested instrument to conduct the study. Instead, the researcher becomes the instrument. The researcher asks the questions of the respondents; the researcher probes responses, potentially guiding a respondent in this direction versus that direction. The researcher then categorizes the incidents in an inductive process and synthesizes the various categories in order to interpret results. In short, through its dependence on the researcher as instrument, the critical incident technique is subject to the critique of subjectivism that has been directed at qualitative research in general.

> What other advantages and disadvantages do you see in using this technique? What do you like and dislike about it? How does it compare to the techniques described by deMarrais in Chapter 4?

USES OF THE CRITICAL INCIDENT TECHNIQUE

Flanagan (1954) identified a number of appropriate uses for critical incident research, but the intervening years have expanded these uses substantially. Not only is the technique used for activity or job requirements, selection and evaluation criteria, training programs, and counseling, but it is also useful for a host of circumstances where the researcher is interested in shared patterns among a specific group. Some of these nonactivity requirement applications of the critical incident technique include the following: patterns of library use (McClure

& Bertot, 1998), higher education teaching behaviors (Rahilly & Saroyan, 1997), ethical misconduct among graduate students (Fly, van Bark, Weinman, Kitchener, & Lang, 1997), and group learning in a museum visitation (Gilbert & Priest, 1997).

It is interesting that the critical incident technique has been used as a means for reflection and enhanced understanding apart from its use as a research tool. For example, Tripp (1993) advocated the use of critical incidents as a means for teachers to come to a better understanding of their own practices and beliefs. Critical incidents become, in Tripp's model, a form of action research, where participants themselves frame the parameters and applications of the inquiry. In addition to guiding teachers in how to articulate a critical incident, Tripp provided a variety of analytic lenses to expand the conceptual perspectives of teachers. Cooper (1998) used the critical incident technique as a component of the written reflection on service learning among college students. In counseling, critical incident work has been seen both as a tool for inquiry and, more commonly, a tool for therapy (Cohen & Smith, 1976) or "critical incident stress debriefing" (Juhnke, 1997). Critical incident counseling is often used in debriefing trauma victims (Mitchell & Everly, 1995; Mitnick, 1996), and although this counseling has a similar emphasis on the actions associated with a traumatic event (the second phase is one of fact gathering, which focuses on what one did), the technique clearly departs from the research approach advocated by Flanagan (1954). Indeed, it is important to be aware that references to the critical incident technique in the context of counseling are quite different from the more general research technique and, in particular, to research in curriculum and instruction. Perhaps most significant, in counseling, the critical incidents are predefined by virtue of their traumatic nature, such as the 1996 bombing of a military dormitory in Saudi Arabia (Budd, 1997) as opposed to being created by participants' attaching meanings to events.

Even as the previous examples depart from what we normally think of as research, they highlight what research is really about: increased understanding. Whether that understanding is of oneself as a teacher or how one implements cooperative learning, how one reacts to a stressful event or even how one greens a lawn, it is understanding. I find myself agreeing with Stake's (1995) comment: "The function of research is not necessarily to map and conquer the world, but to sophisticate the beholding of it" (p. 43).

RESEARCH ASSUMPTIONS: ONTOLOGY, EPISTEMOLOGY, AND METHODOLOGY

What can be said about the paradigmatic assumptions of the critical incident technique? The question I raised earlier was this: Is this research merely technique, or does it imply a way of seeing the world?

The critical incident technique has strong positivistic roots. In its earliest forms, it would seem to assume a fixed reality, accessible to the careful, detached observer. Throughout his explication of the research approach, Flanagan (1954) strived to give scientific credibility to the critical incident technique. He wrote, for example, that "one of the primary aims of scientific techniques is to insure objectivity for the observations being made and reported" (p. 338). He apologized for the necessarily subjective classification of incidents, given the absence of an "adequate theory of human behavior" (p. 335), later saying it is unfortunate that the inductive creation of categories in data analysis is "more subjective than objective" given the current "stage of psychological knowledge" (p. 344). In short, it seems that Flanagan endorsed the method enthusiastically, with the only qualification being that it is not as objective as he would have liked.

But does this link to positivism necessarily pervade critical incident research? I don't think so. It is important to note that the entire premise of critical incident research is a handing over to research participants the power to deem whatever they choose as "critical." Tripp (1993) put it well: Critical incidents

> are not "things" which exist independently of an observer and are awaiting discovery like gold nuggets or desert islands, but like all data, critical incidents are created. Incidents happen, but critical incidents are produced by the way we look at a situation: a critical incident is an interpretation of the significance of an event. To take something as a critical incident is a value judgment we make, and the basis of that judgment is the significance we attach to the meaning of the incident. (p. 8)

Tripp pointed out that critical incidents are not observed, because viewing from the outside cannot reveal the criticalness of an incident. Critical incidents are created by the person to whom they are critical. Of course, the collection, analysis, and interpretation of the body of incidents is performed by a researcher or researchers. However, the focus is still on the meanings that research participants attach to events.

This view of knowledge does not match traditional positivism well at all. Instead of knowledge existing independently, awaiting "discovery" by a detached observer, the knowledge Tripp (1993) spoke of must be created by an individual. Again, it is important to remember that Tripp was using critical incidents as a means for teacher reflection, with limited attempts to go beyond the individual's perspective. (Clearly, by using theoretical analyses, Tripp did invite a form of generalization.) Still, even in a case where the intent to generalize is clear—how principals handle conflict, for example—it is only the observer–reporter, and not the researcher, who assigns significance to an event. The researcher is left to interpret that significance in the context of significances assigned by other participants.

At the same time, there are features of the model that cannot be twisted to fit an interpretivist view of the realities undergirding research (Guba, 1990). If the interpretivist researcher is concerned exclusively with the idiosyncratic world of the one, there is really no attempt to generalize. The premise of critical incident research, in contrast, is that in seeking the unique experiences and meanings of individuals, we can illuminate patterns that may apply to other persons and contexts. As Cohen and Smith (1976) put it, "The critical incident concept evolved with the observation that certain critical situations emerge and repeat themselves time and again in different groups and at various developmental stages" (p. 115). The nature of the technique—drawing on multiple incidents, created by multiple sources, and brought together by a researcher to derive patterns—argues for a shared reality as opposed to a completely unique reality. At the same time, this shared reality is tentatively constructed and offered to the research consumer to determine its applicability.

CRITICAL INCIDENT TECHNIQUE—A BRIEF EXAMPLE

To bring my discussion of the critical incident technique out of the abstract and into research in curriculum and instruction, I would like to present an example of the approach applied to education. I am drawing on my study (Kain, 1997) of the collaborative planning that teachers engage in when they are creating interdisciplinary experiences for their students.

Researchers rarely articulate their assumptions about the nature of knowledge or reality. I will explain what I believe were my assumptions in this study, recognizing that in looking back at the experience, I may not get it quite right. I was interested in what I consider to be an important issue that is faced by a variety of teachers in many different contexts: How do teachers work together to create interdisciplinary learning experiences, when most teachers are educated to be subject-matter specialists and socialized to work alone? We can tease out quite a bit from that question alone. First, it is apparent that I see a shared reality— a common set of problems and experiences that people face across contexts—as opposed to conceiving of the interesting reality as being idiographic, unique to each individual. Second, and this is far less apparent, I am interested in a variety of perspectives, indicating that I do not conceive of a fixed, single answer to my question.

Given these assumptions—that there is an interesting shared reality, but it is not single or fixed—I had to work out how I might come to know something about this reality. I reasoned that if I wanted to understand how groups of people successfully planned together, I would have to talk to them about their experiences. Thus, I am opting for an epistemology that conceives of research as an interactive venture: I, as researcher, would have to talk to people whose experience was relevant to my question. No test or survey would provide me access to what interested me; observation alone would be insufficient, because I wanted to understand how the teachers perceived their experience.

The critical incident technique was a methodology I could adapt to my purposes. It allowed me to target what I found important—the perceptions of teachers about what worked for them—in a systematic way. In addition, this research approach provided me with a means to bring together the unique experiences of many teacher groups so that I could offer some help to other teacher groups facing the same basic problem. I wanted to go beyond describing what a particular teacher team did (a case study) so that others might seek some general principles to help them in their work.

I followed the Flanagan (1954) approach quite closely. For example, I began my study (after all the necessary institutional negotiations) by contacting experts in the field of interdisciplinary learning to ask what the aim of collaborative planning was. I do not think the responses I received informed my study much, but I was thrilled to get letters from some of the people I admire most in my area of research.

Next, I developed a plan for who I would talk to about what. I wanted to speak to teacher teams (mostly at the middle school level, because that is generally where one finds such interdisciplinary teaching) who were successfully working together to create interdisciplinary experiences. Clearly, I was not interested in a sampling strategy that would permit me to make claims about teamed teachers in general. I simply wanted to talk to teachers who had done it. My approach was, thus, to get permission to talk to teachers in a district (no easy task) and then to ask where I might find such successful teams. Sometimes I would ask a district curriculum leader where to find good teams (and it surprised me how wrong these leaders might be); sometimes I would ask a principal (who could also be quite mistaken about what teams were doing). When I talked to a teacher or a team, I would ask if there were anyone else I should talk to. In short, I used whatever means I could to seek successful team members.

What did we talk about? I had developed a protocol and piloted it on several teachers. My interview essentially asked teachers to "think of a time when you and your team members were especially effective [and in a later question, ineffective] in working together to create an integrated or interdisciplinary unit or activity for your students," and then to tell me about this. There were probes and follow-ups associated with my basic questions, and I had a series of other questions designed to examine the role of teachers, the specific actions teachers took, and the support or nonsupport of the institution (both as it was organized and as it was administered). I found that teachers had difficulty talking about the collaborative planning they engaged in, so I added a question to my protocol where teachers were invited to offer a similar team advice based on their experience. This question proved to be extremely helpful. Although teachers had trouble articulating what they did from my basic question, they became far more loquacious when asked to give advice. (They were, after all, teachers.)

I conducted a variety of interviews, sometimes with one team member, sometimes with several. I spoke to some people on the telephone, though most interviews were conducted face to face. I tape-recorded when I could, but sometimes the circumstances (environmental or social) prohibited this.

Immediately after the interviews, I, or a research assistant, would type up the transcription or interview notes. I entered the incidents into a HyperQual2 stack (Padillo, 1993), and the data analysis began. First, each incident was classified as positive or negative. It was interesting that one team member might offer an event as a positive incident, whereas another member of the same team might see that event as negative. I preserved whatever valence a respondent attached to an event. Next, drawing on the literature about interdisciplinary teaching, I categorized each incident according to the nature of the focus of the incident. For example, some incidents involved a focus on a topic or a theme; some incidents arose from prepackaged, or "canned," units. Finally, I categorized the incidents according to explanatory features that might lead to better conditions for enhancing the success of collaborative planning of interdisciplinary experiences. For example, some incidents highlighted the positive contributions of physical facilities; some incidents might highlight the negative effects of the mandated curriculum.

Categorizing incidents was an ongoing activity. I continued to interview teachers and categorize incidents until I sensed a good deal of repetition in the categories. That is, as I talked to more teachers, their incidents fleshed out existing categories but did not add new ones. As often happens in such projects, a new category might emerge from the data that sent me back to earlier work so that I might reanalyze data. To facilitate this, I kept careful records of the category descriptions and the dates when each category had been created. When I felt confident that the categories represented my data well, I wrote the report, which is the stage at which the interpretations are created.

> Could you use this approach to data analysis in your research? Why or why not?

In reporting the results of my investigation, I maintained a tentative posture. That is, I was not claiming to have found universal principles. I did not feel as though all questions were answered. Instead, I presented the results as preliminary, inviting readers to seek a place for their own experience. For example, I reported that many teachers spoke of having some sort of framework to talk about interdisciplinary experiences when they were successful. A math teacher reported that one must plan objectives first, so her team used this as the organizing mechanism for planning an experience. I did not argue that teachers must or should have such a framework, but that this worked for some teams. In the same manner, I reported on the experiences of teams when they were not successful, leaving it for readers to situate their own contexts and experiences.

One characteristic of my reporting was to use the actual words of teachers often in my text. I described the categories I had created from the data, but I continually provided the "raw data" that led to the creation of such categories. The intention here was to permit readers to create an alternative reading, to see the data behind my interpretation.

In keeping with Flanagan's (1954) recommendation that a researcher identify the value of a study, I concluded by taking a broader perspective on the issue of collaborative planning and the use of the critical incident technique. For example, my discussions with more than 85 teachers who were identified as having created successful interdisciplinary work led me to question how seriously educators take the notion of "interdisciplinary." Further, I was able to comment on the effectiveness of this research approach in getting at a complex phenomenon, and I think the critical incident technique did provide a powerful means of helping teachers articulate how they work together—though there were limitations as well. I think the teachers' perspectives on what the institution of schooling does to impede their collaboration were particularly promising findings.

CONCLUSIONS

I began with a conversation between Elwood and Harvey to demonstrate the commonsense appeal of the critical incident technique. People assign meanings to their experiences, and when we group together collections of such meanings in order to make sense of the world, we engage in a kind of research, a seeking of understanding. The critical incident technique provides a systematic means for gathering the significances others attach to events, analyzing the emerging patterns, and laying out tentative conclusions for the reader's consideration. Although it has positivistic roots, the critical incident technique does shift the focus of interest to a decidedly nonpositivistic target—the meanings individuals make of events in their lives. Finally, I provided a brief example of how to conduct a critical incident study of joint teacher planning.

6

Focus Groups: More Than a Method of Qualitative Inquiry

Pamela B. Kleiber
University of Georgia

MEET THE AUTHOR

Pamela B. Kleiber is the associate director of the Honors Program and the coordinator of the Center for Undergraduate Research Opportunities at the University of Georgia. She received a bachelor of arts in English literature and a master's degree and doctorate in education from the University of Georgia. She joined the University of Georgia as a public service faculty member in 1994. Before joining the Honors Program, she served as department head for University System of Georgia Independent Study. As the department head, she led efforts to use the World Wide Web as a distance learning modality. She received the Leadership Award from the Association for Collegiate Independent Study in 1997.

Dr. Kleiber is adjunct faculty in the Department of Educational Psychology at the University of Georgia, a fellow in the Institute of Higher Education, and a member of the UGA Teaching Academy. She teaches and writes on qualitative research, with a specialty in focus group methodology. Dr. Kleiber has written numerous articles and has coauthored a book, *The Electronic Forum Handbook*, on the use of technology in support of learning. She maintains a collaborative relationship with the National Issues Forum network and the Kettering Foundation in Dayton, Ohio, and Washington, DC.

The focus group method of inquiry has become immensely popular and influential in contemporary culture. It has been used in a wide variety of ways, from developing advertising campaigns for toothpaste to managing images of public figures, including presidents of the United States. Cartoons about focus groups abound in major newspapers and high-profile magazines. One cartoon depicts people in a focus group as "out of focus," and another portrays Jesus with his disciples as "the first focus group." Although focus groups were not likely used in biblical times, they probably did find their way into early fieldwork of anthropologists and sociologists. But it wasn't until Paul Lazersfeld and Robert Merton implemented the "focused interviews" with groups in the 1940s to study the response of soldiers to "morale" films that the technique was legitimized and widely disseminated as a method of inquiry (Merton, Fiske, & Kendall, 1990). This work led Merton and Patricia Kendall to write an article about the method for the *American Journal of Sociology* in 1946, which was followed by *The Focused Interview* in 1956 (Merton, Fiske, & Kendall, 1956/1990.) Although these seminal contributions to the focus group literature continue to be recognized, the focus group method came of age not in the social sciences but in its applications in the arena of marketing (Morgan, 1988; Templeton, 1988). Apparently, whatever value it had for purely scientific purposes, it also became extremely useful in the business of determining consumer preferences and promoting products. Nevertheless, its place in the repertoire of alternatives for basic and applied qualitative research remains secure.

This chapter provides a general introduction to focus groups as a qualitative research method. I begin with the transition of focus groups from market research to social science research. I then consider how focus groups in the social sciences differ from those in marketing and the implications of these differences for how they are best conducted. Finally, I discuss common practices and issues for further consideration. As in most introductions, only the basics will be highlighted here. The intent is to give the reader the necessary background for a healthy respect for the method and to introduce other sources for closer study. Having conducted focus groups in a wide variety of settings for the past 20 years and teaching and training focus group researchers, I can say with confidence that, despite its deceptively simple appearance, the focus group process is profound in its potential for revealing socially constructed meaning and underlying attitudes.

With respect to research questions, the focus group can be used in addressing issues associated with nearly any theoretical or applied problem. Symbolic interactionists, critical theory feminists, action researchers, social constructivists, or market researchers all may find value in employing focus group methods. Whatever the perspective or problem, however, focus groups are most useful when employed with the assumption that knowledge is socially constructed and where the reality of interest is the result of social interaction. I operate from the perspective that research is a series of negotiated acts, dependent upon language, that results in shared knowledge (Stake, 2000).

Generative group interaction is the defining feature of the focus group (Morgan, 1988). During focus groups, the moderator is able to observe how people make private opinions public and how that process shapes the formation of their stated opinion (Krueger, 1988). Experts in the focus group method acknowledge that participants are informing one another (Krueger, 1988; Morgan, 1988; Templeton, 1987). Rather than providing short responses to structured questions, focus group participants engage in thoughtful discussion and may actually influence one another. Motivation for interacting can usually be assumed when participation is voluntary; people generally give of their time—at least with serious research subjects—when they have more personal investment in the subject. In market studies, however, prizes or monetary rewards may be necessary to generate a similar degree of investment. In either case, the motivation of participants required for effective focus groups calls for caution in the interpretation and extension of study findings.

THE EVOLUTION OF FOCUS GROUP APPLICATIONS IN MARKETING AND SOCIAL SCIENCE

Respect for the personal investment of participants in topics of inquiry is far more obvious to social science researchers than marketing researchers; "events and issues [are] manifestly more important to participants" than selling and buying

(Morgan, 1988, p. 27). Morgan's focus group research included studies of heart attack patients and widows. Personal investment alone is not a guarantee of self-understanding, however. In his examples, Morgan made a case for using focus groups to generate the thought processes that produce statements of opinion. He recognized that without interaction, individuals are often unaware of their own opinions and perspectives. The desire to explain one's perspective to someone with a potentially differing viewpoint is often the motivation for formulating and articulating an opinion (Morgan, 1988).

The development of focus group applications in marketing was a "mixed blessing" in Morgan's (1988) view. Its different motivational premises and eliciting techniques made comparisons with social science applications risky, but it still offered an abundance of new data on attitude and opinion formation. Morgan attributed the popularity of focus groups in marketing, and their neglect in the social sciences, to Merton's original emphasis on the introduction of a stimulus through radio and film clips. Social science research typically examines phenomena that do not have a tangible stimulus—a problem, an issue, or an experience, for example (Morgan, 1988). Nevertheless, many of the common practices in social science and marketing focus group applications are similar.

In the same year that Morgan's (1988) book was published, Krueger (1988) contributed the first practical guide for applied focus group research in the social sciences and, along with Morgan, is responsible in large measure for recovering the method for the social sciences in recent years. These books continue to offer fine introductions to focus groups as a method of qualitative inquiry in the social sciences. Since 1988, Morgan, Krueger, and others have written and edited other useful monographs and books examining issues and common practices in focus group research (see especially Barbour & Kitzinger, 1999; Morgan, 1993; Stewart & Shamdasani, 1990). Merton's and Kendall's classic treatise, *The Focused Interview,* was republished (Merton & Kendall, 1990) and continues to be valuable for anyone interested in focus groups. In the Forward, Gollin notes that "rarely can close scrutiny of a classic be recommended for both its historical value and its contemporary utility. *The Focused Interview* is one such case" (p. ix).

Focus groups can be utilized inappropriately, however, as is commonly the case in organizational settings, according to Greenbaum (1987). Executives often assume that focus groups are easier and cheaper to employ than they generally are, and when expedient shortcuts are taken to save time and money, they usually have problems of research design and fail to yield useful outcomes. My own experience as a focus group consultant in a variety of industrial settings is consistent with that observation; when managers understand what is required, they may decide the process is more costly and time consuming than expected, and sometimes more provocative as well. However, with adequate investment in time and resources, focus groups can yield extremely useful information for decision makers.

Focus group participants who find themselves in agreement on a topic may decide to take action as a result, though taking action was not the purpose of the study. In contrast, for action research and critical feminist work, change may well be a desired outcome. This blurs the usual lines between method and intervention. People using focus groups understand the influence the method may have on participants and their lives (Kleiber, 1993; Swenson, Griswold, & Kleiber, November 1992). The question of purpose and impact of focus groups in marketing and social science research may be primarily with the sensitivity of the topic and the investment of the participants in the outcome and use of findings.

Focus Group Design

As a method of inquiry, focus groups typically bring together 7 to 12 people for an average of an hour to an hour and a half to discuss the topic of inquiry. The participants are selected on the basis of common characteristics in order to obtain their perceptions, opinions, and attitudes on the research topic. The moderator may take a more or less structured approach to posing questions to the group. The more structured the approach, the less opportunity for discovery and the less "chaotic" the data. Less-structured questioning usually produces more discovery and proves more challenging to analyze. Usually five to six general questions are used with probes to obtain range, specificity, depth, and personal context (Merton et al., 1956/1990). At least three and as many as five sets of interviews on the same topic with different groups generally ensure that themes common across groups emerge and that data idiosyncratic to one group can be identified.

The focus group operates on the assumption that the whole is greater than the sum of its parts. In other words, the choice of focus groups is not justified simply by being an efficient alternative to conducting, say, seven interviews in sequence. Rather, the method depends on the interaction of the group to stimulate participants to think beyond their own private thoughts and to articulate their opinions. It is in having to formulate, represent, give evidence, receive feedback, and then respond that individuals move beyond the private. It is far easier to avoid addressing inconsistencies in our thinking if we keep our thoughts to ourselves rather than making them public (Doble, 1987). Trained focus group moderators encourage participants to express their points of view in an atmosphere of mutual respect and to facilitate interaction among the participants in order to understand underlying attitudes and beliefs. An atmosphere that is structured to be nonjudgmental and to promote candid expression allows for a range of opinions to surface. Consensus is never a goal of focus groups. This atmosphere can be developed through ground rules, given at the beginning of each focus group, that address confidentiality, the goals of the focus group, intended use of the information, moderator responsibilities, and expectations of participants.

Common Practices in Focus Group Research

Focus groups may be used alone or in combination with other methods of data collection. For example, focus groups may be very useful in designing a survey instrument, because participants can provide insight into how those who will be surveyed think and talk about a topic. Focus groups can also be very useful for understanding the responses on a survey, because people from the sample can assist in the interpretation of what respondents may have been thinking when they answered a question. Individual interviews and focus group interviews can be used in combination in order to gather information that participants may be reluctant to share publicly. In such cases, the focus group first may be used to stimulate thinking by having the members hear one another, and then one can follow up with individual interviews on aspects where participants were reluctant to self-disclose. As a matter of course, I begin focus groups by letting participants know that they are not expected to self-disclose beyond their comfort level, and I ask them to contact me if there is something they wish to discuss further. I also let them know that I may also contact them individually as I continue with the research.

The decision to use focus groups is the first in a series of research decisions that will all influence the data collected. The use of focus groups requires planning that takes into consideration questions such as: Who will moderate? Who will be sampled? How will the participants be recruited? Where will the focus groups be conducted? What will participants be told about the purpose of the research and how will the information gathered be used? What ground rules are necessary? How long will each focus group last? What questions will be asked? What probes will be used? Each of these decisions will have a profound influence on the quality of the data.

Participant characteristics are a particularly important consideration. Consider, for example, that you are planning to research barriers to women's participation in evening classes at the local college. If the focus groups are held in the evening at the college, some of the same barriers to participation in classes may be barriers to participation in the focus group. A focus group study of the perceptions that individuals with disabilities have toward public transportation may not be fruitful if the focus groups are held in a location that is not easily accessible. In some cases, it may be tempting to use a preexisting group in which people know one another, but personal and professional relationships may inhibit candid dialogue and self-disclosure. It would not be advisable, for example, for a teacher to use a focus group to conduct a midway evaluation of her own course. In contrast, asking students in the course to identify faculty members with whom they would feel comfortable critiquing the course in a focus group setting might yield very useful data. Once the planning is effectively completed, the techniques used in moderating the groups are the primary concern. The quality of the data collected will depend on establishing a rapport with participants, and this requires communicating appreciation for participants' time and their willingness to share opinions and perspectives on the research topic. Group facilitation skills are extremely useful in ensuring that all participants have a voice that is respected and heard. If the researcher moderates the group, she or he must guard against any reflection of bias in the questions, responses, and nonverbal language.

Once ground rules are established, it is important for the moderator to establish that no opinion or perspective is unacceptable and that a wide range of perspectives on a subject can usually be expected. If an assistant moderator is available, this second person can help orchestrate productive dialogue by encouraging those who are reticent, perhaps as a result of having a differing perspective, to contribute. A round table and name tents are also useful in facilitating participant interaction. In my own work with focus groups, I have found it useful to begin by having each person give an introduction that is easy and nonthreatening so that everyone has a turn speaking. Some amount of time to warm up can ease unfamiliarity among group members.

In addition to moderating, audiotaping and note taking are important functions in the data collection process. Videotaping is also useful when nonverbal behavior is of interest and when there are sufficient resources and expertise for the coding, analysis, and interpretation of nonverbal data. However, the potential this provides for enriching the data gathered must be weighed against the potentially intrusive impact of the camera that, in my experience, tends to be inhibiting to participants (Kleiber, 1993). The general rule of only using technology when it helps achieve the goals of the research should be applied in any case. If technology is appropriate and necessary, an assistant moderator can take responsibility for any technical equipment, which frees the moderator to concentrate on facilitating group interaction. An assistant moderator can also be useful in reviewing any taped material with the moderator, thus decreasing the likelihood of inaccurate interpretation.

Addressing such considerations will optimize the effectiveness of focus groups. But unless the dynamic social interaction of participants on the research topic is necessary, other methods may be preferred. In fact, the focus group is very similar to that of the qualitative individual interview, except that considerations of the dynamics of the interview are more complex due to the number of people who are interacting. The complexity of the group interaction is, in part, the reason that focus groups are not just an efficient way to handle a number of individual interviews.

When multiple focus groups are employed, I prefer to use a method of constant comparison in identifying emerging themes and issues after the first group and before each subsequent group. Although this can be labor intensive in the short periods of time between groups, it allows for the tailoring of interview questions for more effective introduction in addressing the research questions. Data in the form of transcriptions of audiotapes or videotapes and field notes from each focus group should be analyzed across groups for recurrent themes and issues. Writing up focus group research revolves around answering the research question for the audience. Recurrent themes and issues across groups can be illustrated using transcripts from the interviews.

Focus Group Scenarios

The following scenarios characterize two different contexts for using focus groups. In the first scenario, a nonpartisan public policy foundation is using focus groups to identify issues of concern to the American people regarding the role of the newspaper in American communities. In the second scenario, focus groups are used as an exploratory tool by a university research team with a grant for drug and alcohol education. The results of this focus group application were used to develop a survey for workplace education on substance use and abuse.

Focus Group A

Ten people sat in a circle in a hotel conference room in a suburb of Seattle, Washington, discussing the role of the newspaper in a community in the United States. The moderator was hired by a public issues foundation to ascertain current public opinion on this issue. The data gathered from the groups was used to develop a professional education program for a newspaper association. Some of the opinions expressed were critical of specific newspaper coverage; other perspectives were more supportive. But as points of view were expressed and deeper consideration of the issues given, participants shifted their opinion toward consensus around the importance of having three newspapers available to cover local news, even when a newspaper's stand on issues is at odds with an individual's. Though the moderator's goal was to gather a range of opinions, not necessarily to develop consensus, consensus did develop.

Focus Group B

Eleven people discussed drug and alcohol abuse for 2 hours in a conference room in a social sciences department of a major state university. The focus group moderator investigated attitudes and perceptions of adults on the topic. The participants were all on the staff of affiliated departments. The participants began by defining and listing drugs with which they were familiar. Halfway into the discussion, they were asked what they would do if someone they knew abused alcohol. One of the participants moved from the hypothetical situation to a self-disclosing personal experience. Another participant followed suit, disclosing a very personal story in order to "give the other side." The focus group discussion became polarized and emotionally charged at its conclusion.

Anyone who has ever moderated or participated in a focus group or read reports from data collected in focus groups realizes that it is a very powerful method. The richness and meaning of the data indicate that the effects of the focus group may extend beyond the mere sharing of information. Particularly when the topic is one in which the participants, as well as the researchers, are invested, the effect on the participants should be considered (Kleiber, 1993). In Focus Group A, participants were not highly invested in the topic. They were paid for their focus group participation, and they did not have well-developed opinions on the different newspapers in Seattle. The focus group was an appropriate method for data collection, because the participants informed one another about the various newspapers' options. The group came to the conclusion that having three newspapers was important, because they heard and valued the different reasons each had for selection of the newspaper to be read.

In Focus Group B, the group was also an appropriate method for development of a survey instrument. However, the fact that a preexisting group of fellow workers was used to form the group and that the moderator was also a fellow worker caused dynamics that were counterproductive to gathering data. The self-disclosures were threatening within the group and to the working relationship of the members after the focus group ended. The same focus group could have been conducted with considerably greater ease and productivity with people who had no shared history.

The moderators of Focus Groups A and B knew the opinions of group participants at the conclusion of the discussion, as well as some of the underlying beliefs and attitudes. Each moderator conducted at least three and as many as five focus groups from the same sample population on the topic of inquiry. This practice allowed for common themes to develop across groups and assisted in identifying themes that may be idiosyncratic to a group. In Focus Group A, the research was commissioned by a professional newspaper association to determine the viability of newspapers in various metropolitan areas across the United States. Men, women, minorities, and a range of ages of adults comprised each focus group. A report was delivered to the association based on the results of the group and was shared with its membership. In Focus Group B, the researcher was on the staff of a federally funded grant in a public university. The results were used to develop a survey in order to generalize to a larger population (Kleiber, 1993).

Focus Group A was very successful in meeting the objectives of the researcher in eliciting a dynamic discussion of why people read the newspapers they do. There are many factors that influenced the success of A: the design of the study and the skills of the focus group researcher. On the other hand, Focus Group B did not meet the objectives of the researcher. The design was faulty in using existing staff on the project. The moderator was also unable to establish a safe environment to discuss a sensitive topic like drugs and alcohol use. Focus Group B was a much greater challenge because of the topic, so the design and the moderation skills required greater expertise.

> Contrasting Focus Groups A and B, which group do you think produced the most useful results, and why?

Impact on Participants

Very little attention has been given in the focus group literature to the meaning of the experience from the participant's perspective. In the study using Focus Groups A and B (Kleiber, 1993), in addition to interviewing moderators, I also asked participants in individual interviews to describe their personal experiences as a participant in the focus group. In each case, the goal of the research in Focus Groups A and B was to inform the researcher on the topic, and each moderator had a metaphor explaining her or his role. The participants who discussed the role of the newspaper in their community were asked to discuss their feelings about being asked to share their opinion and hear others share theirs. Participants continued to think about the topic and were not particularly invested in the outcome, even after the focus group experience. A number of them felt that it was a stimulating conversation and remarked that they realized how seldom they discussed such topics outside the context of a focus group. The common reason for participating was that they felt it was an interesting topic for which they were paid to voice their opinion. A number also remarked that they were always aware of the video camera and felt that there was always somebody else watching, though they could not specify the extent to which it inhibited their conversation.

When I asked the participants in Focus Group B (the study of drug abuse) to discuss their experience, a different picture emerged. Because all of the participants were working on the research topic as part of their responsibilities, all were interested and invested in the topic. They participated in large measure because they felt it was part of their responsibility. They were paid to the extent that it was part of their job and the amount they were being paid for their job. However, they had varying degrees of comfort in discussion on the sensitive topic of drug use, which had affected some of the members personally. Most were uncomfortable with the group dynamics and the unexpected self-disclosure.

Swenson et al. (1992) also investigated these same questions in a follow-up study of the use of focus groups in a rural revitalization project in Georgia and found that participants learned as a result of their experience and, in some cases, took action. The impact of focus groups on the participants, when they are discussing issues of importance to them, suggests that it may be more than a method of inquiry; it may in fact have the effect of an intervention. If the topic is sensitive, as is often the case in issues surrounding race, gender, class, health, land use, and other factors that have compelling influences on participants' lives, the level of investment is often high and sometimes emotionally intense. The researcher should be aware that bringing people together to discuss low-income housing with public housing residents, for example, is likely to provoke an orientation to action. In the case of action research in a community where grass roots movement is the goal, this may be the desired outcome for the researcher. The ethics of the responsible conduct of focus group research requires full attention to the potential and actual influence of the experience on the participants and the possibility of creating intended or unintended consequences.

STRENGTHS AND LIMITATIONS OF THE FOCUS GROUP METHOD

The major strength of the focus group method is its ability to elicit opinions, attitudes, and beliefs held by members of the sample. Because the tendency of our society is to be too busy and isolated to find opportunities to discuss important issues, participants usually enjoy the novelty of the focus group process. The data generated are typically very rich as ideas build and people work to explain why they feel the way they do. The focus group moderator has the chance to "listen in" on people's conversations, gathering data not available through individual interviews or surveys.

Morgan (1988) and others who write about the focus group method value it for its power in both exploratory and descriptive social science research. Depending on the research question, focus groups can be usefully combined with other methods, such as face-to-face interviews and participant observation, with an effort to distinguish the methodological appropriateness of each. According to Morgan, the focus group method offers more control for the researcher than participant observation but less control than in traditional face-to-face interviewing. Focus groups can also be used in combination with surveys, both in developing the items for the survey and in interpreting the results of its administration.

Among the limitations of focus groups are that they are often time intensive and expensive, and possible underwriters of the cost may have a vested interest in an outcome that is apparent (and often objectionable) to the participants, and this can compromise the integrity of the process. Further, the group financing the research may not want to share the results with participants for a variety of reasons. The moderator/researcher may therefore negotiate for sharing information if it is in the interest of the participants. Sharing information may include how the information will be used, who is funding the research, and access to the results. Negotiations over the conduct and outcomes of the research can be quite complex. Morgan (1988) is quick to point out that social sciences have institutional restraints, suffer from limited funding and competing demands, and have multiple "clients," including journal editors and promotion committees (p. 13). Nevertheless, with the goal of increased understanding and the opportunity to ask better questions that generate productive discussion, focus groups may still be the method of choice. And as is common in qualitative research, the moderator/researcher in focus groups must be recognized as the instrument of influence. Designing, facilitating, and analyzing focus groups that provide authentic, useful information and understanding requires extensive training in qualitative research methods and, when possible, apprenticeships with successful focus group moderators.

Can you list any additional strengths and weaknesses? Is saving time in data collection a strength? Is unwillingness to share personal information in a group a weakness?

Because focus groups are often the preferred method for understanding how people think about topics, especially those with social significance, they are worth the investment. And, as long as modifications or limitations are understood, respected, and noted, they can be fruitful. In most instances, the data collected in individual interviews is qualitatively different from that collected in groups. The focus of the study should be the determinant in how data are collected.

ADDITIONAL PRACTICAL CONSIDERATION IN CONDUCTING FOCUS GROUP RESEARCH

In planning focus groups, determining the stakeholders—those who will use the information collected—should be done deliberately. Preliminary interviews with all the prospective stakeholders can reveal the level and nature of interest in the topic and suggest the best questions to be asked in the group setting. This should be done carefully, because the number of questions used should be limited. Generally speaking, five to six main questions will be ample, though probing questions and other techniques may also be incorporated where necessary. It is important to consider how long the focus group will run and how many participants will be involved. The formula I use is to limit the group process and the number of participants in each group to between 7 and 12; in a focus group lasting 90 minutes with 7 participants, each person would be able to speak about 12 minutes. Using too many questions can interfere with getting clarification and deeper meaning. When possible, a pilot focus group can be very helpful to ensure that the questions will elicit useful data. Adjustments can thus be made before conducting the actual research. Although this practice may add some additional cost, it is good insurance for usable information.

One focus group does not constitute a "study" under any circumstances, and two is usually not enough. In most cases, a set of three focus groups will be required to collect data on the research question. During data analysis, common themes emerge across groups. In this way, data idiosyncratic to a particular group are better understood, as are themes common across groups. Additional groups may be necessary in order to reach theoretical saturation.

Although it is possible to conduct focus groups within your own working environment, it can be problematic. In the example noted earlier, the teacher using a focus group to find out how her students feel about the course should probably not expect to generate honest discussion or useful information. In order to minimize bias and provide a neutral group environment where participants can be candid, it is desirable to have an objective moderator who is not personally invested in the delivery of program, instruction, or services.

Sampling for focus group research should be done purposefully. In many cases, purposeful sampling from the target population is the goal. Participants should have experience with the topic or research question and feel comfortable sharing what is on their minds. Situations with clear power inequities should be avoided. For example, an employee may not feel comfortable talking about working conditions if the employer is present. In contrast, a group of people who have a similar interest in a topic—teachers who are involved in using an innovative teaching initiative, for example—are likely to enjoy the discussion and participate eagerly.

Homogeneity and heterogeneity with respect to gender, race, class, or level of experience should be taken into consideration in planning focus groups. The most advantageous composition depends on the research question. Recruitment of participants requires a neutral location that is easily accessible to those from whom you wish to hear. An obvious example is that sampling low-income individuals would likely require access to public transportation or special transport provision, or the focus group should be conducted in local neighborhood schools or churches. It may also be necessary to pay participants directly in order to ensure participation and/or by covering the cost of child care. If the issue is one that is potentially very sensitive, such as race, it may also be important to ensure enough representation of the groups involved to ensure comfort and safety. By contrast, busy professionals, such as physicians or business executives, may only be willing to participate in a teleconferenced focus group; long-distance carriers can arrange conference calls for this purpose. Although this has the disadvantage of losing the value of face-to-face interaction with other group members and also requires some special moderating skills, I have been able to do it in a way that meets the needs of all stakeholders.

To create a relaxed and comfortable environment, it is beneficial to allow participants to mingle for a few minutes while everyone arrives and before they are seated in a circle. Providing beverages and snacks can sometimes contribute to warming up the atmosphere. The room should offer comfortable circular seating that will allow cross talk and enable the moderator to see everyone. It is almost impossible to conduct a focus group in a rectangular arrangement.

The moderator typically begins by welcoming people, thanking them for coming, and giving ground rules. Ground rules stated by the moderator at the beginning of the focus group experience can prevent possible problems such as domination by a few individuals, lack of attention to one another, or artificially and prematurely reaching consensus. Participants should understand that this is an opportunity for them to give their opinions and perspectives and to be heard. The object is not to reach a consensus but to cover a diversity of opinions. This is also the time for the moderator to explain that her or his role is to ask questions and keep the conversation on track, and that participants should feel comfortable talking to and asking questions of one another. The moderator also should inform the participants that he or she is responsible for enforcing ground rules. This understanding contributes to the establishment of trust. An explanation of the purpose of the research and addressing the management of confidentiality and the ultimate disposition of findings will help ensure a more open and constructive discussion.

Beginning with short introductions allows each person to become immediately active as a participant. A general question that all are asked to answer can also be used to lubricate the conversation by giving everyone a "voice." In this regard, the moderator may be most effective, by seeing him- herself as a conductor of an orchestra. This initial work of exercising voice is analogous to a conductor allowing the members to "tune their instruments." Although this metaphor is quite different from those offered earlier—water and boats—I believe the orchestra metaphor is most useful at this particular point, because it focuses on hearing the individual voices and tones before the discussion.

How are metaphors helpful in understanding roles and purposes in focus group research? Can a metaphor ever inhibit communication? If so, what are some examples?

More generally, metaphors such as concert orchestras and boats in water can be helpful in understanding the roles and purposes of a focus group during the moderator training. The metaphor may give the aspiring focus group moderator a simple image which can aid in transfer of the skills to the practical setting. Because the responsibility for a focus group can be quite intimidating for the novice, a metaphor can help put them at ease when they are actually moderating. Although, I suggest that the teacher/master of the method continually ask the students if the metaphor works for them and, if not, what metaphor better describes the moderation from their perspective. So, understanding the students's alternate metaphors, may help in providing constructive guidance.

After the initial turn taking, the moderator asks the first question intended to provoke discussion. "What do you consider to be the greatest challenge facing continuing legal educators?" is the type of broad question that can be used. The answer requires that participants think before answering, prioritize their possible responses, and listen to one another. The moderator ("conductor") is able to turn to those who have not been heard on the topic and ask if they agree or disagree with the comments that have been made to that point, and the focused discussion thus begins. From this point on, the moderator should inquire further, asking questions such as "What do you mean when you say ——?" or "Would you give us an example of what you are talking about so we can better understand?" One of the most important techniques at this point is to give the participants enough time, or silence, to consider what they think before giving an answer. Another important technique is to listen carefully and respectfully, modeling the ground rule of listening and respecting differences. Neutrality is critically important. If a moderator shows bias by nodding to some responses consistent with his or her own opinions and cutting off opinions that do not reflect his or her own views, he or she will fail to gather important data. Probing and asking for clarification ensures that the data will be helpful in interpretation and analysis.

It is usually necessary to tape-record focus groups and, to hear what is being said in a group, it is important to remind participants to speak one at a time. To encourage participants to converse with each other, the moderator may employ the technique of "withdrawing" while taking notes. It is useful for the moderator to take notes in case the tape recorder fails or more than one person speaks, but this activity also allows participants to talk with one another more directly and assume some leadership in the group while the moderator relinquishes eye contact and thus disengages a bit from the "conductor" role. Of course, the moderator is silently listening and ensuring that everyone has a voice. She or he reenters when it is necessary to hear from others, probe for clarification, and/or introduce new questions.

It is useful to end the focus group by asking participants if there is anything that has come to mind during the course of the conversation that they have not had an opportunity to add, or if they have a response to a question that has not been asked but should have been. This question often results in rich data and is a good technique for drawing what might be a very lively conversation to a close. After the conclusion of the focus group, the moderator should spend at least 30 minutes jotting down observations, questions, or comments that contribute additional data for analysis. The data are the transcripts of the focus groups and the postgroup notes that are analyzed collectively for themes that emerge across groups.

Focus groups should be recognized by all researchers as a legitimate and important option for some questions for the unique yield they can contribute to understanding the world. On the other hand, while the method requires the same rigor as any other methodological tool, there may be more potential for harm to the participants than other methods because of the social setting of the group. Only with a healthy understanding and respect for the method should designers of current research studies elect to venture into the realm of focus group methodology.

CONCLUSIONS

Since the first dissemination of information on focus groups as a method of qualitative research by Lazersfeld and Merton in the 1940s and Morgan and Krueger
in the late 1980s, focus groups have been widely used and often misused. Other
social scientists have joined Morgan and Krueger in beginning to refine and
diversify this powerful method (see especially Barbour & Kitzinger, 1999; Morgan,
1993; Stewart & Shamdasani, 1990). Issues related to the effects of sampling,
moderator skills, and group composition are being addressed. The possibilities
for application within alternative theoretical paradigms, and for action research
in a wide variety of settings, suggest that the use of focus groups will continue
to be a paradigm-challenging and creative process and one that is well worth
watching.

7

Exploring Life and Experience Through Narrative Inquiry

Mary Kay Kramp

MEET THE AUTHOR

After teaching for 30 years, **Mary Kay Kramp** is retired and living in the mountains of Georgia with her husband, W. Lee Humphreys. Teaching was the focal point of her disciplinary study, academic research, and professional practice. Her undergraduate degree in American history and education is from St. Mary's College, in Notre Dame, Indiana. She has a master's degree in human development from Saint Mary's College, in Winona, Minnesota, and a doctorate in cultural studies in education from the University of Tennessee, Knoxville. Her entrance into the doctoral program at the University of Tennessee did not mark the beginning of her professional career; rather, she saw it as opportunity to enrich and extend her prior years of teaching in high school and college. Through her doctoral program, she formalized past experience, having brought to her study a recognized research record and an active research agenda focused on students' and teachers' narratives of learning. The latter was supported by grants from Alverno College, in Milwaukee, Wisconsin, where she was a member of the faculty for 13 years; the National Center for Adult Learning; and the Fund for the Improvement of Postsecondary Education. Her dissertation, a phenomenological study of college teachers' experience of their students' stories of learning, built on prior classroom research. Narrative as a method of research was at the heart of this research. Throughout her career, the classroom energized and motivated her work with narrative. In 1998, she retired from Dalton State College, in Dalton Georgia, where she was the Regents' Distinguished Professor of Teaching and Learning.

It is the research question—what it is you, the researcher, wish to know—that influences your choice of research method. As a qualitative research method, narrative inquiry serves the researcher who wishes to understand a phenomenon or an experience rather than to formulate a logical or scientific explanation. The object of narrative inquiry is understanding—the outcome of interpretation—rather than explanation. Narrative inquiry changes the question the philosopher Richard Rorty identifies as the epistemological question that has historically preoccupied Anglo-American philosophy, from "How do we come to know the truth?" to "How do we come to endow experience with meaning?" (cited in Bruner, 1986, p. 12).

Narrative is a vital human activity that structures experience and gives it meaning. As a research approach, it provides an effective way to undertake the "systematic study of personal experiences and meaning: how events have been constructed by active subjects" (Riessman, 1993, p. 70). What distinguishes narrative as a mode of inquiry is that it is both a process, a narrator or participant telling or narrating, and a product, the story or narrative told. Thus, it is both the means by which you, as researcher, gather data, and the discourse or form of the data gathered. At times, it is even a form you might select to write up and report your research.

In response to the invitation, you, as researcher, extend to the participant to "Tell me about . . ."active subjects construct a narrative that is particular, personal, and contextualized in time and place. Having heard the narrative or having been told the story, you as researcher use any one of a variety of frameworks to analyze and interpret its meaning and understand the phenomenon you are researching. Through narrative inquiry, you gain access to the personal experiences of the storyteller who frames, articulates, and reveals life as experienced in a narrative structure we call story. In narrative inquiry, this story is the basic unit of analysis.

> At this early juncture, what does the term *story* mean to you in the context of narrative research? What are the challenges in convincing audiences of the value of research results called stories?

Historically, qualitative researchers have assigned value to context. They understand that behaviors, events, and actions are meaningful as embedded in context. Context enables the researcher to make meaning where previously there was no meaning. So they typically study subjects in their native surroundings, in their own settings. Qualitative researchers engaged in narrative inquiry share this respect for context, especially time and place. They understand that, in terms of narrative, time and place provide a setting for plot and character. The researcher using narrative inquiry anticipates the storyteller's use of context to connect and situate particular experiences so they cohere and structure life as experienced. In this process of reflecting, structuring, and narrating, disparate events are made meaningful. A narrative or story is constructed.

Unlike context, *narrative* is an ambiguous term for qualitative researchers. It has traditionally been understood in a general way, inclusive of various responses, from short-answer questions to write-ups of field notes and transcriptions of interviews, case studies, and autobiographies. Although such responses may be prose, that is, complete ideas written in sentences, and may even reflect "narrativelike" qualities, they are not necessarily always "narratives." In this chapter, we will come to understand and use the terms *narrative, narrative inquiry,* and *story* in a more particular way, within the context of a different paradigm of knowing. This paradigm is shaped and informed by the recent research and writing of scholars who, across disciplines, have been engaged in an ever broadening conversation on narrative (Baxter-Magolda, 1992; Bruner, 1986, 1989, 1990, 1991, 1996; Carr, 1985; Connelly & Clandinin, 1987, 1988, 1990, 1994; Goodson, 1988, 1995; Grumet, 1988, 1991; Kerby, 1991; Polkinghorne, 1988, 1989, 1995; Ricouer, 1988; Witherell & Noddings, 1991). We will use the term *story* interchangeably with *narrative.*

People tell stories. The word *story* is more appropriate when speaking in a familiar, personal, or conversational way. The word *narrative* calls to mind a particular genre with formal characteristics. A story is an example of a narrative—a kind of narrative. A story is always a narrative, but narrative structure is not limited to story. By using the two interchangeably, or as fits the context, you can capture the experiential quality of "telling a story." At the same time, a particular way of thinking or knowing and a framework for telling—that is narrative—is revealed. Usually experienced as more formal, the term *narrative* is a distant term, even if it is more inclusive. When I use the word *story*, it is to be understood as a narrative structure that organizes or emplots human events. It is a construction by the teller or narrator. Although this narrowing does not fully remove the ambiguity, it does inform our understanding and use of narrative inquiry as a research method.

To clarify the concept and experience of narrative inquiry, this chapter is organized into two main parts. Part 1, "Understanding Narrative Inquiry: What It Is and What It Does," addresses concepts basic to narrative theory and narrative itself. Part 2, "Engaging in Narrative Inquiry," suggests ways of practicing narrative inquiry as a kind of qualitative research. Throughout the text, I make frequent reference to scholars and researchers who are actively engaged in narrative inquiry, whether practicing it or thinking and writing about it. These references serve as resources for you to pursue to further your own study of this method. By personally examining the writings and the research of those presently contributing to this work, you will note the absence of any single, universal theory that shapes narrative research. Rather, you will encounter many thinkers in a variety of disciplines exploring narrative inquiry as a viable method in doing qualitative research. You will note not only the many issues that remain unresolved and even unexamined, but also that these are the very issues that energize an ongoing dialogue and encourage the exploration of ideas.

What is your speculation on the meaning or a working definition of the research method of "narrative inquiry"?

UNDERSTANDING NARRATIVE INQUIRY: WHAT IT IS AND WHAT IT DOES

Essential to utilizing narrative inquiry as a method of research is the understanding that narrative is a way of knowing. As such, it is natural to us and is part of our cognitive repertoire. Narrative knowing is expressed in a narrative form we call stories. We are not formally taught to tell stories, rather, "Narrative is a conventional form, transmitted culturally . . . " (Bruner, 1991, p. 4). Stories are valued by some as "culturally constructed expressions [which] are among the most universal means of organizing and articulating experience" (Turner & Bruner, 1986, p. 15). More recently, we have recognized that "the sounds of storytelling are everywhere today" (Greene, 1991, p. 1). Respect for stories and appreciation of their value have grown as we have come to understand more fully how they assist humans to make life experiences meaningful. Stories preserve our memories, prompt our reflections, connect us with our past and present, and assist us to envision our future.

> Narrative is the fundamental scheme for linking individual human actions and events into interrelated aspects of an understandable composite . . . a meaning structure that organizes events and human actions into a whole, thereby attributing significance to individual actions and events according to their effect on the whole. (Polkinghorne, 1988, pp. 13–14)

Implicit in Polkinghorne's description of narrative are assumptions that narrative is a cognitive scheme and that it has a particular form. Thus, any understanding of narrative as a mode of inquiry is shaped and informed by narrative as a way of knowing and narrative as a genre with formal characteristics.

As a way of knowing, narrative enables the storyteller to organize the story told by linking events, perceptions, and experiences. Didion (1961) suggested that narrative fills the space between "what happened" and "what it means." Donald Polkinghorne and Jerome Bruner are two of the scholarly and authoritative voices who have shaped the conversation on narrative knowing over the past two decades. In 1984, Bruner gave an invited address to the American Psychological Association meeting in Toronto in which he presented his thesis outlining two types of cognition: paradigmatic and narrative. In the next decade, he developed his thinking and further clarified the distinctions through his writings (Bruner, 1981, 1986, 1989, 1990, 1991, 1996). Polkinghorne (1988, 1989, 1995) extended and enlarged the conversation with his writings on narrative knowing.

Narrative inquiry is predicated on the narrative way of knowing. What follows is a brief summary of important distinctions between the paradigmatic and narrative modes of knowing gleaned from the writings of these scholars. For a more extensive and technical discussion of these two modes than is appropriate in this chapter, consult Bruner's work, *Actual Minds, Possible Worlds* (1986).

Paradigmatic, or logicoscientific, knowing answers Richard Rorty's question referenced above: How do we come to know the truth? This way of knowing is based on positivist assumptions and is driven by reasoned hypotheses. It results in a rigid principle or law, an abstraction or generalization that leads to a theory, information, or both that are used to predict or control human behavior or natural forces. Paradigmatic thinking pursues empirical truth and requires logical proof. The researcher–scientist works to eliminate ambiguity and uncertainty. Logical proof is singular and compelling for the scientific researcher, and explanation is preemptive (Bruner, 1996). There cannot be two equally credible accounts.

The observable—what is seen, heard, and so forth—is the significant evidence for the researcher who seeks to explain or explicate. Language used to express paradigmatic knowing is typically denotative—"I mean what I say"—emphasizing definition, abstraction, conceptual analysis, evidence, and truth.

Narrative knowing responds to Rorty's question, How do we come to endow experience with meaning? as we have come to extend it: What is the meaning of experience? This way of knowing is grounded in a worldview of contextualism and, as Ricouer suggests, is built on a concern for the human condition. Narrative knowing results in a story, which, though structured, is flexible and attends to the personal, the specific, and the particular. As the researcher engages in narrative inquiry, one interprets experience and events as told by the storyteller. This is no simple task. "To understand well what something 'means' requires some awareness of alternative meanings that can be attached to the matter under scrutiny, whether one agrees with them or not" (Bruner, 1996, p. 13). Alternate meanings derived from alternative, often even contradictory, accounts are accepted by the qualitative researcher utilizing narrative inquiry. The researcher understands that each story has a point of view that will differ, depending on who is telling the story, who is being told, as well as when and where the story is told. Consequently, verisimilitude—the appearance or likelihood that something is or could be true or real—is a more appropriate criterion for narrative knowing than verification or proof of truth. What the storyteller "tells" is what is significant for the researcher, who desires to understand the meaning of a particular phenomenon rather than to gather information about it. Connotative language best expresses narrative knowing—"I mean more than I say"—revealing effective causal thinking, which creates order, reveals intentionality, and structures human experience. It is what McEwan and Egan (1995) called "straight talk." Clear accounts of an experience, typically jargon-free, are structured in story form, constituting a meaningful story, sometimes not known to the storyteller until it is told.

> What are the contrasting characteristics of paradigmatic versus narrative knowing? Do they have any elements in common? Is one perspective superior to the other? Make a case either way.

Narrative inquiry is a by-product of narrative knowing. The researcher who engages in narrative inquiry is interested in determining the meaning of a particular experience or event for the one who had it, and tells about it in a story. Anthony Paul Kerby (1991) reinforced the usefulness and appropriateness of such a process when he wrote, "Narratives are a primary embodiment of our understanding of the world, of experience and ultimately of ourselves" (p. 3). It follows, then, that narrative inquiry readily accesses such understanding, whereas impersonal research instruments reveal neither understanding nor meaning to the researcher, nor typically even to the one who had the experience and is telling the story. "Narrative and life go together and so the principal attraction of narrative as method is its capacity to render life experiences, both personal and social, in relevant and meaningful ways" (Connelly & Clandinin, 1990).

It is with stories, told or read to us and told or read by us, that we typically acquire our first and most vivid experiences of narrative. We know narrative experientially as a kind of literature, a literary genre that has a recognizable structure and formal characteristics. As structured, stories organize, or "emplot," human events in time. Each story has a plot and one or more characters. Each story, as a narrative, reflects the perspective of the narrator, or a point of view. Each story has a setting in time and place. Each story has a beginning, middle, and ending, although not necessarily presented in that order as it is told. "At a minimum a 'story' (fictional or actual) involves an Agent who Acts [character] to achieve a Goal [plot] in a recognizable Setting [context] by use of certain means [plot]" (Bruner, 1996, p. 94).

The plot, one of the formal elements of a narrative, is a construction by the teller or narrator, whose perspective, or point of view, it reflects. The narrator constructs a plot by selecting and sequencing actions and events, thereby imposing a meaning on these actions and events that comprise the story. This process, often referred to as emplotment, reflects the intentionality of the narrator, who does the arranging or sequencing. The plot "grasps together" these multiple and scattered actions and events, binding them into a temporal unity, or "mental model," that reveals " . . . time that is bounded not simply by clocks but by humanly relevant actions that occur within its limits" (Bruner, 1996, p. 133). Time is integral to plot because it is integral to human experience. Narrative organizes lived or human experience. Because it is human time, we are not speaking of Western time only. Time as humanly experienced may be understood and expressed in various ways. For example, it is possible for cultural and religious practices to reflect cyclical patterns even in a culture that uses calendars and clocks to measure time as linear. According to Ricouer (1988), "Human time is nothing other than narrated time" (p. 102).

Point of view is another formal element of a narrative. A narrative that is emplotted reflects a point of view. We might think of point of view as someone's "standpoint" (Harding, 1987), or "angle of vision" (Rimmon-Kenan, 1983). The expression of experience and of "human," or lived, time requires a form that is perspectival, that reflects a point of view. A narrator constructs a plot, that is, orders, emplots, or configures actions, events, and experiences. This very ordering, or sequencing, is perspectival. To further particularize the narrative and to enhance perspective, the narrator not only "tells" the story from a point of view but also situates it in a particular social, cultural, or political context. The context or setting assists you as researcher to interpret the story and understand its meaning.

Narrative and narrative inquiry may appear to be deceptively simple. An understanding of what narrative is, as a way of thinking and as a literary genre, is critical to your use of narrative inquiry as a method of qualitative research. Narrative inquiry cannot be reduced to a formula or an itemized listing of component parts. It is a very rich and enriching process that is informed by disciplines such as education, psychology, literature, philosophy, history, anthropology, and others. The more you familiarize yourself with the works of writers and thinkers in different disciplines who are engaged in conversation on narrative inquiry, the more prepared you will be to produce research that can be held to rigorous standards, demonstrating an inherent respect for both storytellers and the stories they tell.

> What rigorous standards could be used, in your opinion, to make the results of narrative inquiry believable?

Having a conceptual understanding of what narrative *is*, it is imperative to reflect on what narrative *does* or *can do*, for it is both what narrative is and does that makes it a viable method of inquiry for you as researcher. Keeping in mind that it is both a process and a product, then "perhaps the most essential ingredient of a narrative accounting (or storytelling) is its capability to structure events in such a way that they demonstrate, first, a connectedness or coherence, and second, a sense of movement or direction through time" (Gergen & Gergen, 1986, p. 25).

A narrative connects events, actions, and experiences and moves them through time. The narrator or storyteller constructs a story by structuring and framing relationships. The resulting narrative presents itself to you as researcher to interpret, constructing meaning where perhaps there was none, or where it was unknown. The subject's story compels you as researcher to consider what typically complicates research—a particular voice "telling about" a particular experience. You come to recognize that neither the particularity of the voice, with its richness of color and detail, nor the storyteller's point of view become obstructions to be sacrificed for you as researcher to achieve understanding. The narrative told to you is not merely a listing of events and actions, nor simply a series of anecdotes. Rather, it is a perspectival construction that enables you to see differently, to move between the particular and the generic, aware of what each says to enrich the other.

By structuring or framing relationships, typically causal, the storyteller translates knowing into telling. Then the story told is an emplotted form through which storytellers give shape to their experiences in story form, enabling them to be shared with others. Grumet (1988) put it nicely when she wrote, "To tell a story is to impose form on experience" (p. 87). This is what narrative does. If you think of story as "life as told," then it is through story that you come to know "life as experienced." It is in the telling that meaning is given to experience. It is in telling that we come to understand. Important to note, however, is that there is no already existing story for the narrator to tell; rather, the story comes to be in the act of telling, where meaning is assigned to experience, and intentionality becomes apparent. Observation alone provides only part of the picture for you as researcher. Narrative inquiry yields what careful observation cannot—a way of coming to understand by being open to the stories individuals tell and how they themselves construct their stories and, therefore, themselves.

The historian Hayden White (1981) regards narrative as a possible "solution to the problem of how to translate knowing into telling, the problem of fashioning human experience onto a form assimilable to structures of meaning that are generally human" (p. 1). Although White was writing about what narrative does for the historian, it functions similarly for one using narrative inquiry as a research method. Believing that narrative is uniquely suited for expressing lived experiences as contextual and meaningful, narrative inquiry as a method does assist you as researcher in arriving at understanding. As researchers, we come to understand what Witherell and Noddings wrote in *Stories Lives Tell* (1991): "The stories we hear and the stories we tell shape the meaning and texture of our lives at every stage and juncture . . . they contribute both to our knowing and our being known" (p. 1).

Narrative privileges the storyteller. It is through the personal narrative, a life as told, rather than through our observations as researchers, that we come to know a life as experienced. The subject of our research is not the object of observation, but is the narrator, the storyteller. Consequently, narrative inquiry reconfigures the relationship between the interviewer and interviewee that is characteristic of traditional research. You as researcher give authority to the storyteller, whom you acknowledge as the one who knows and tells.

Narrative functions as a connective medium for knowing, whereas narratives become the embodiment of an intimate relation between knower and the known, between storyteller and listener, between researcher and subject. The lesson learned by Dr. Robert Coles, author of *The Call of Stories* (1989), from one of his mentors while he himself was an intern in psychiatry is no less important for the researcher who uses narrative inquiry. Coles was reminded by his mentor, Dr. Alfred Ludwig, that

> the people who come to see us bring us their stories. They hope to tell them well enough that we understand the truth of their lives. They hope we know how to interpret their stories correctly. We have to remember that what we hear is their story. (p. 7)

Marcia Baxter-Magolda heard her students' stories and described her experience of them when she was analyzing the research for her book on the gender-related patterns of intellectual development of college students, *Knowing and Reasoning in College* (1992). Dr. Ludwig's advice resonated in Baxter-Magolda's own experience of the power of personal stories. Although the context for each is quite different, both became immersed in the personal stories—he in his patients' stories and she in the stories of her college students. Moving beyond the initial categorization and statistical analysis of her data, Baxter-Magolda reviewed her analysis in light of her students' stories. She

> became immersed in the students' stories and lost track of the categorization system that had become so ingrained in my thinking as I listened to their experiences and what they thought about them. The experience transformed my thinking. . . . *The stories were richer than my statistical operations were able to communicate.* (my emphasis, pp. 10–11)

She elaborated: "*The varied themes of student stories that existed within the categories were hidden when this type of interpretation was employed alone*" (my emphasis, p. 11). In this instance, "Statistical analyses of gender similarities and differences were less helpful than the actual words and stories of the students" (p. 12). In "Studying Ways of Knowing," chapter 1 of her 1992 work, Baxter-Magolda clearly and sensitively described the impact of the stories and the consequences they had for her as researcher and for her research. Her forthright discussion provides insightful reading for anyone using narrative inquiry as a research method.

In traditional research, we look for answers to particular questions using various forms of data collection. How is the role of researcher different in narrative inquiry?

Would you ever choose narrative inquiry to conduct research? Discuss with your colleagues reasons for selecting narrative approaches to inquiry.

Having reflected on what narrative is and what it does, you are better able to appreciate the power and the potential of narrative inquiry as a research method. Initially, it would provide your research participants a natural and unselfconscious way to order their experiences. Because lived experience is the object of your research, narrative inquiry would serve you as an appropriate research method. As your method of choice, it would result in narrative constructions that we call stories. These stories would explicitly contextualize the particular lived experience you wish to understand more fully through your research. The stories you elicit tell this particular experience—an experience *of* something *had* by someone who tells about it. In this way, narrative reveals to us how the persons we are studying construct themselves as the central characters and narrators of their own stories. Your research participants are the actors in the story who, according to Bruner (1987, p. 17), develop as a person, becoming in turn a self and eventually an individual. Narrative inquiry has the power and the potential to reveal these individuals in all of their complexity and uniqueness to you, as researcher, in ways observation alone cannot.

ENGAGING IN NARRATIVE INQUIRY

Narrative inquiry is a process that calls forth your best and most exacting abilities as a researcher. Beginning with the careful articulation of what it is you wish to know, through your listening and relistening to your participants' stories, to your analysis and interpretation of them, and then your final formulation, construction, and presentation of your findings, narrative inquiry is laborious and time consuming. You must not only be aware of this before you commit yourself to it as your method of choice, but you also must anticipate how it might play out for you as a researcher in your discipline. This is so because narrative inquiry may appear to be seductively simple. As it is still a nontraditional form of research whose practice is evolving, there are few preformed protocols. The value of your research, for example, will not lie in the generalizability or replication of your findings, for generalizations will not capture what your participants' stories speak to you. This awareness must shape any assumptions that guide your research.

In a research project (Kramp, 1995) I undertook, I was eager to know and understand more fully the experience of college professors who had engaged their own students' stories of learning. The focus of my study became the lived experiences of these professors who heard the stories of learning told by their own students, contextualized in particular classrooms and disciplinary contexts. From prior studies, I noted that there had been a link between the stories these students told their professors and these veteran professors' own renewed reflections on themselves and on their practice (Kramp & Humphreys, 1993). What was still to be identified and remained to be researched was the particular experience of each of these teachers who engaged their students' stories of learning—the "what" that was experienced and the "how" or mode of experiencing. Phenomenologists call these the noema and the noesis.

Given that understanding was my research goal, the stories the teachers or professors told me in our interviews not only described their experiences but also revealed to us together how these experiences led them to rethink their past, present, and future selves. Their narratives brought us closer to confronting the complexities of teaching. Through narrative inquiry, I explored their particular experiences—thoughts, feelings, ideas, examples, and situations—as narrated by them. These teachers made themselves present to me in their interviews. In telling me their stories, they invited me into their lives. Clearly, I was not the objective bystander or observer. My connection to them was real, and I was most conscious of my role in the research process. I approached them as a colleague in higher education—an experienced college teacher and researcher who had engaged my own students' stories of learning. This experience reinforced my prior realization that when the situation, research method, and research question warrant it, I agree with Ann Oakley, who urges that

> the mythology of "hygienic" research with its accompanying mystification of the researcher and the researched as objective instruments of data production *be replaced by the recognition that personal involvement is more than a dangerous bias—it is the condition under which people come to know each other and to admit others into their lives.* (my italics, cited in Weiler, 1988, p. 62)

Narrative inquiry assumes "personal involvement" as the very condition that makes it possible for you, as researcher, to gather and interpret narratives of participants in your study. Narrative inquiry is not about the business of dispassionately chronicling experience and events. In the case of the study I just described, my research question—What does it mean to engage your students' stories of learning?—shaped the way I conceptualized my study and the format in which I chose to write it and to present it. My interview prompt—"Tell me about a time you were aware of your students' stories of learning"—was an invitation to each participant to construct a narrative detailing particularities of this experience and contextualizing them in a specific time and place. I initiated the interview by saying, "Think about some times you experienced your students' stories of learning. Tell me about a time." This open-ended prompt made it possible for the teachers to tell me what they wanted to say. Although the researcher may ask the question, it is the research participant—the teacher in this case—who owned the response and subsequent narrative.

How do the questions just presented allow the college teachers to own the response? Would they still own the narrative if they were asked, Can you explain to me how you teach so that you encourage students to tell their stories of learning?

What is essential to this type of interview is for you, as researcher, to hear what the participant has to tell. Hence the appropriateness of the phenomenological interview as a technique. This type of interview complements and enhances narrative inquiry. The informality of the discourse lends itself to telling stories. When invited, participants speak readily and easily. Each story is typically detailed and is constructed as it is being told. Following research protocols on confidentiality and permission for doing human subjects research, these interviews are taped and transcribed at a later date. As transcripts, they become the "texts" rich in "thick description," each typically 30 or more pages. Most participants take great effort to set contexts for their stories and several tell more than one story. It is the "tell me about a time . . ." that sets up the single focus and detailed narration of a particular story. The particular prompt you select provides a frame that allows the narrator great personal freedom and choice. This is critical to the process of narrative inquiry, because the more that the process is focused on the participant and the power of each to construct the narrative, the greater the understanding derived from the telling.

As researcher you have engaged the process—your research participants "telling" or "narrating" their stories to you. You gathered the products—the stories narrated or told by your research participants. These become the object of your study, analysis, and interpretation, the next stage of your inquiry.

Two resources that will facilitate your work with the interviews and the transcripts are a bracketing interview and a research group. The former should ideally take place before you begin your interviews. The second, a small group of colleagues with knowledge of qualitative research in general and narrative inquiry specifically, functions most effectively and efficiently when set up to be ongoing through the entire research experience.

In a "bracketing interview," you, as researcher, ask a colleague to interview you and ask you to respond to the same prompt you plan to give to each of your participants (Thompson, Locander, & Pollio, 1983). This interview is designed to make you, as researcher, aware of the presuppositions you bring to your research and the perspectives your own experience provides. This self-awareness on the part of the researcher is especially critical in narrative inquiry, a method sometimes thought or used to give "voice" to those who have none or "power" to those who are powerless. (See Munro, 1993, for a discussion of this point from a feminist perspective.)

A bracketing interview brings forward the researcher's prejudices. It is only with this awareness that we can truly be open to what are our own experiences. What came through in my bracketing interview, done at the outset of the study I have described, was a strong orientation to process and a bias that my pedagogy is and should be influenced by my students' knowledge of themselves as learners. My willingness to move away from traditional models and metaphors of teaching and learning could also translate into a kind of missionary zeal—a sense of urgency that might not always be shared by colleagues, let alone appreciated. Through this experience, I became aware of presuppositions and the assumptions that influence me as a teacher and a researcher. An excellent reference on the bracketing interview is Steinar Kvale's "The Qualitative Research Interview: A Phenomenological and Hermeneutical Mode of Understanding" (1983).

Although as a researcher you want to recognize the biases you bring to your research, you do not want to overlook the value of your own perspectives, which can lead to insights derived from a particular way of seeing. Gadamer (1976) reminded us that our "prejudices are the biases of my openness to the world." Biases need not be obstructive or intrusive for you, as researcher, if you interact with an awareness of them and are sensitive to their potential. Indeed, a knowledge of your biases can inform you as you work to achieve a clearly stated description of the experiences of those to whom you listen, and whose stories you engage in the process of narrative inquiry.

With the tapes of your interviews and the transcripts, or of texts, in hand, you are ready to begin your analysis and interpretation of the stories you have gathered. There are a variety of frameworks that can shape your analysis. A discipline might dictate a particular and appropriate framework for you to use. In this chapter, we use a generic framework that focuses on the text as a narrative structure. You begin with the text, the story, and end with it. Be aware of the language used by your participant, or narrator, because the language used by your narrator constructs what it narrates. Attend carefully to each story. Engage the whole story before you address singular excerpts that stand out for you. Repeatedly read and reread, listen and hear the stories you have gathered. It may help to read a story aloud, either alone or with your research group. Familiarize yourself with the narrator's language, inflection, and especially the story itself. This may be the most tedious part of your research. Your compensation, however, is that your study of the narrative texts will affirm your choice of method as you repeatedly experience narrative as

> the linguistic form uniquely suited for displaying human existence [and experience] as situated. . . . [and in particular that] storied narrative is the linguistic form that preserves the complexity of human action with its interrelationship of temporal sequence, human motivation, chance happenings, and changing interpersonal and environmental contexts. (Polkinghorne, 1995, pp. 5–6)

Your research group will be most helpful in this process, because they will offer you good support and clear insight. By reading and reviewing the texts aloud as a group, your research colleagues collaborate to assist you by suggesting and identifying possible themes. The meaning of the lived experience you are researching is to be found in these themes. In your reading and reviewing of the texts you open yourself up to the themes, which are the very structures that make up the lived experience you are researching (Van Maanen, 1990, p. 70). Work with the text until the particular themes in each narrative emerge and become clear. Even though themes express the essence of an experience in abstractions, they do fix the experience in a temporal and exemplary form, providing a "for instance." Your research participants construct themselves in their stories. They describe the content of the experience, enabling you, as researcher, "to touch the very essence" of that which you are hoping to describe (Van Maanen, 1990, p. 88). This is significant, because in narrative inquiry you are committed to describing the phenomenon you are researching rather than to explaining it.

In your mind, what are the important distinctions between describing and explaining? Does each make a contribution or hinder the trustworthiness of research results? If so, why?

The themes that will reveal themselves to you in each narrative are like threads that, when woven together, create a pattern with a plotlike structure. Your task is to grab on to these themes by lifting appropriate words and phrases of the narrator from the text. By using the storyteller's own words, typically more colorful and distinctive, you can best communicate the unique particularities of what the experience is really like for each of your participants.

For example, in the research project I describe above, "connection" was a theme common to the college teachers' experiences of their students' stories of learning. The presence of this theme came as no surprise. The surprise came in the idiosyncratic way the theme was revealed for each teacher. We hear Chuck, a psychology professor, tell us he was surprised by the way a student connects course content to her own life and its subsequent personal impact on her life. "Never in my wildest dreams" did he anticipate such a powerful and influential "connection" between his students and the course content. Another teacher, John, a professor of agronomy, experienced "disconnection" from his students when he was delivering a lecture: "I was just breezing along. I became aware this isn't connecting. I just didn't feel I was connecting with the students." John describes his experience, which was one of "disconnection" where he had anticipated "connection."

Margaret, a professor of early childhood education, made very clear that her experience was the absence of connection, rather than disconnection. As she experienced and described it, hers was the absence of connection between the self as the "teaching person I am" and the "college teaching professor" she thought she was expected to be. She speaks of "mesh/not mesh." Her language nicely captures the lack of connection between reality and expectation that she experienced. For Florence, a professor of mathematics who is hearing disabled, connection was a "linking together" of herself and her hearing disabled students. Her experience of their stories was "I get to know the students better." She connected with her students and realized she could facilitate that connection. She did that by rearranging her classroom so as not to be physically separated from her students: "I decided to move the desk so that the students would not feel any barriers in the classroom." "Connection," for Florence, was quite tangible and spatial.

For Yulan, a professor of romance languages, his experience of connection was a kind of "being with." He told of making eye contact, knowing students' names, and working with small groups. Clearly, his experience of "connection" was found in meaningful student–teacher relationships. In contrast, Tim, a professor of philosophy, experienced "connection" as being between the student and the course content, a connection that he, as teacher, could facilitate. So, unlike Chuck, who expressed great surprise at such a connection, Tim actively intervened to structure learning so as to enable the connection. He planned and anticipated such a connection—"so I am much more conscious of trying to find out, actively find out, where the students are and what is happening with the class in order to plan what I am going to do."

It is clear that while the theme of "connection" is common to the experience of all these teachers, there is a range of experience across the narratives that is delicately nuanced and personalized. This range, revealed in the teachers' stories, speaks to the uniqueness of each teacher's experience of their students' stories of learning.

The shared theme, or category, of connection suggests a general description of the teachers' experiences of their students' stories. However, a common theme does not do justice to the richness of the experiences of the teachers or the fullness of the narratives they tell. Margaret's "mesh/not mesh" speaks much more specifically and particularly than simply "connection." Because "theme formulation is at best a simplification" (Van Maanen, 1990, p. 87), it comes as no surprise that the common themes that emerge from the teachers' narratives appear disembodied, lacking affect, particularity, and temporality. To enrich your description and your understanding of the themes, carefully attend to the nuances of each example of your common theme. If I merely identify "connection" as one of the themes common to all the teachers' narratives, I lose sight of the distinctive character of the teachers' stories and what they reveal to me about their experiences. The teachers' experiences *are* embodied. Because they tell about their lived experiences, their experiences are also temporal. The common themes are nuanced in the teachers' particular experiences—embodied and in time—that they "tell" in their narratives. Consequently, as you analyze and interpret the texts, it is important that you capture these experiences in the words of your participants themselves. When you are satisfied that you have done this, you may move inductively to identify any common or shared themes that structure the stories of your participants. Preserving the language of your participants will reappear as an issue for you later in the process because of the implications affecting the way you present your findings and report your research.

The personal nature of each narrative you gather reveals a self who is sensitive and complex. The narrator often makes use of metaphors to clarify and communicate the complexities of this self. As a result, metaphors frequently serve as organizing images for descriptions of oneself and of one's experiences. A metaphor has a precision and a directness, allowing it to work effectively as a "central vehicle for revealing qualitative aspects of life" (Eisner, 1991a, p. 227). This centrality of metaphor in life and language comes as no surprise if we agree with Lakoff and Johnson (1980), that if "our conceptual system is largely metaphorical, then the way we think, what we experience, and what we do every day is very much a matter of metaphor."

In all the students' and teachers' narratives gathered by my colleagues and me over the years, it is rare to find one without metaphor (Kramp & Humphreys, 1993). Within the context of the story each tells, the teachers' most vivid descriptions are the metaphors they employ in telling their stories. Note the language of everyday experience used by these teachers in their narratives when they tell what the experience of their students' stories of learning is like:

"Never in my wildest dreams . . . "—a teacher of psychology
"The whole thing changes . . . "—a teacher of agronomy
"I was run over by a Mack truck . . . "—a teacher of early childhood education
"I was shocked . . . and very inspired . . . "—a teacher of mathematics
"I had no idea what I was getting into . . . "—a teacher of romance languages
"Listening for clues . . . "—a teacher of philosophy

These powerful metaphors introduce and bring into focus the particular descriptive orientation and holistic image that shapes each teacher's particular experience as told in each one's story. Themes that eventually emerge in each story are implicit in these metaphors.

> What are metaphors? How might their use in narrative inquiry help or hinder the clarity of the story? What is your opinion about this practice?

Having acquired a holistic understanding of each narrative, you are ready to illustrate first the themes particular to each story. Introduce each participant/narrator. Make every effort to capture the experience narrated, using the language of your participants to articulate themes revealed in each story. Inductively generate a set of common themes from individual sets of themes in each narrative. For example, in my study of the college teachers, the particular themes of "revelation–mystery," "able–unable," "connected knowing–disconnected knowing," "aware–unaware," "confirming–affirming" found in individual narratives suggested the common theme of "knowing–not knowing."

This identification of themes within each story and those common to all is what Polkinghorne (1995) called an "analysis of narrative," essentially a paradigmatic approach to narrative inquiry. The "analysis of narrative" characterized in this approach "moves from stories to common elements." The example I related above moves from the teachers' stories to shared themes or themes common to all. This is a clear example of Polkinghorne's "analysis of narrative." Data, such as shared themes, that you derive from the stories is then organized to make it accessible. Typically, the researcher uses an appropriate paradigmatic structure such as a matrix, a taxonomy, or categories. A matrix is an especially effective way to bring together the common themes and individual themes. All aspects of a matrix stand in relation to each other. The variations on a theme remain explicit and meaningful at the same time that the common themes are identified and illustrated. The integrity of each narrative is also maintained as you enable your audience to move readily between individual themes and common themes. Whatever the structure you use to illustrate your themes and their relation one to another, select or construct one that assists you in illustrating and communicating what you are describing.

This "analysis of narratives" is one of two types of narrative inquiry Polkinghorne (1995) identified. Modeled on Bruner's two kinds of reasoning or two kinds of knowing, he referred to the one based on paradigmatic reasoning as the "analysis of narratives"—the type described above—and the other based on narrative reasoning as narrative, or "narrative analysis." Although your preference for a particular type of narrative inquiry relates to the purpose of your research and your research question, understanding Polkinghorne's distinctions proves to be especially helpful in your analysis and in the reporting of your research. Stories are the basic unit of analysis in each. In the paradigmatic type or analysis of narratives, your purpose in using stories is generally to understand a concept or abstraction such as consumerism or an experience such as buying a new car. As researcher, the stories provide you with data. Your analysis of the narratives begins in each story. You separate the data, after which you proceed inductively to your identification of common or shared constituents such as themes, one way to organize your findings. Next, you present your findings in an appropriate paradigmatic structure that ideally allows you to move between the particular and the shared or common elements.

"Narrative analysis," the second type of narrative inquiry (Polkinghorne, 1995), moves from the particular data gathered to the construction of stories. A case study is an example of a "narrative analysis." In a narrative analysis you, as researcher, construct a narrative, or what I call a storied analysis, using the data gathered from each story. The story you write "must fit the data while at the same time bringing an order and meaningfulness that is not apparent in the data themselves" (Polkinghorne, 1995, p. 16). Attending to the characteristics of a narrative—plot, setting, characters—discussed earlier in this chapter, you construct a story in which you integrate the data rather than separate it as you would do in an analysis of narrative. Given the personal quality of your research and the potential of narrative discussed earlier, a storied analysis is a "method that returns a story to the teller that is both hers and not hers; that contains herself in good company" (Grumet, 1988, p. 70). By "restorying" the narratives you receive, you return the stories to your participants. When done well, you, as researcher, set the stage, frame the time, and relate or sequence the events, happenings, and experience, conveying a sense of meaning and significance. You reconfigure individual and shared themes, emplotting them into stories.

It is possible but not necessary in your research to do both an analysis of the narratives and a narrative analysis. These methods of narrative inquiry are not inherently contradictory. They can be complementary. Used together, they provide a rich analysis of the stories your research participants shared with you in their interviews. An analysis of the narratives that leads you to identify the individual and the shared outcomes would certainly inform and shape the plots you construct when you create your storied analyses.

Further, given the personal nature of the stories you analyze and those you would construct in a narrative analysis, you demonstrate respect and consideration for the participant, or narrator, when you ask each one to review the appropriate product of your research. In demonstrating such respect—returning to the storyteller—you affirm your findings. You begin and end with the storyteller.

> What might be gained or lost in sharing each participant's story with that participant?

CONCLUSIONS

As you bring your research using narrative inquiry to some closure, you become increasingly aware you cannot superimpose a traditional template of research on your study. Your written presentation cannot be in tension with your topic and method of research. Your participants told their stories to you. You have analyzed and interpreted their stories. Narrative processes are a way of knowing for you and for the storyteller. As researcher, you made use of narrative as a method of inquiry and an object of interpretation. Through your interpretation, the story is told and retold.

As a research approach, narrative inquiry is as an appropriate way to gather data about lived experience. Narrative itself is one way to order and give meaning to experience. The stories told to you illustrate the relationship between one's life and one's stories. "A life as led is inseparable from a life as told" (Bruner, 1987). Aware that the story you hear is constructed, as a researcher using narrative inquiry, you accept the story "as told." The story as told, as it is constructed, becomes your object of analysis in narrative inquiry. As a qualitative researcher, you understand that "there is no telling it like it is, for in the telling there is making. The [your] task is to do justice to the situation and yet to recognize that all stories, including those in the natural sciences, are fabrications—things made" (Eisner, 1991a, p. 191).

8

Enjoining Positionality and Power in Narrative Work: Balancing Contentious and Modulating Forces

Juanita Johnson-Bailey
University of Georgia

MEET THE AUTHOR

Juanita Johnson-Bailey is an associate professor at the University of Georgia in the Department of Adult Education and the Women's Studies Program. Her book, *Sistahs in College: Making a Way Out of No Way* (2001), received the Phillip E. Frandson Award for Literature in Continuing Higher Education. She is also the coeditor of *Flat-Footed Truths: Telling Black Women's Lives* (Holt, 1998), a collection of constructed narratives.

Dr. Johnson-Bailey specializes in researching race and gender in educational and workplace settings. She has written and lectured nationally and internationally on power and positionality in the research and teaching process. She is currently writing a series of essays about her experiences as a professor at a research university entitled, *Where's Our Authority in the Classroom: Women of Color in Women's Studies.*

Over the last decade, the use of narratives in qualitative research has steadily increased. This growth can be primarily attributed to the accessibility of narratives to both researchers and consumers. Because stories are the familiar and are easily understood as the discourse used to frame our everyday lives, the method has universal appeal. Researchers are attracted to the seemingly uncomplicated nature of narrative methodology as a means of collecting data. Readers are drawn to narratives for the unobtrusively intimate format and the ease of understanding. Tappan and Brown (1991) concluded that narratives are the preferred way of communicating when we must tell "the way it really happened" (p. 174). They further posited that disclosures related in narratives are told with moral authority and are representative of the cognitive, affective, and conative dimensions of the experiences.

Also, we find and construct meaning in our lives by telling our stories. In particular, the narrative as a style of telling and researching has been widely adopted by feminist scholars when working with the words of other women. The format has been relied on heavily by this group of researchers, especially those doing work on women of color, because the implicit collaborative and interactive nature of the design is recognized for attending to the power disparities involved in research. In addition, this format gives preeminence to displaying data in its original state, which is acknowledged as a trustworthy way of giving "voice" to the participants. However, such assumptions about the control of the story and cooperative structure are tenuous because the power still remains in the hands of the one who will ultimately leave the field, write the story, and benefit from publication.

This chapter examines how the narrative format is used to collect and present data. It also explores the broader and more familiar use of narratives as a means of presenting a story that is embedded in other qualitative products, such as ethnographies, phenomenological studies, or case studies. Further, the discussion explores how narratives are used by feminist researchers as a way of depicting women's lives and their societal circumstances, and includes an extensive exploration of the "Other" by using a comparative lens to discuss the power dynamics inherent in the outsider and insider positionalities.

NARRATIVES AS A WAY OF COMMUNICATING AND KNOWING

Overall, women have been invisible or have not benefited from positivistic representations of data in history, literature, science, and contemporary anthropological recordings of lives documented (music, newspapers, magazines, art, etc.). Primarily, the domain of personal and private depiction has been left to women as a way of recording their own lives. This solitary telling by women has historically taken the form of journals, diaries, and letters, many of which are lost, destroyed, or abandoned—and when recovered are often discounted as subjective knowledge collected or recorded using unsystematic and unscientific procedures. This place of nonacceptance for women's histories has a basis in the prejudice against the ordinary ways in which diaries, journals, and letters tell the lives of women. This bias is motivated by the importance that Western society places on definitive scripts or truths, told objectively and with distance, that do not vary from previous accounts. Therefore, any new information, which is collected using a different lens and presented in a different voice claiming multiple realities, is suspect.

In general, life story and oral narrative historians have set forth that women's tales are bound differently from men's in several important ways. Gluck and Patai (1991), in their foundational work, *Women's Words: The Feminist Practice of Oral History*, made the broad contention that women have an order to language, cultural cues, and reasoning encompassed in the telling that is driven by the consciousness derived from being female in a patriarchal world. They further conjectured through the text's collective essays that to avoid losing details in data collection, researchers should attend to the special nature of how women relate information through such nonverbal indicators as silences, code words, and communication patterns. In addition, many narrativists agree that in interpreting the accounts of women's lives, the researcher is obliged to consider the complex social spheres that order women's lives (Alvarez, 1996; Cotterill & Letherby, 1993; Etter-Lewis & Foster, 1996; Gluck & Patai, 1991; Witherell & Noddings, 1991). As keepers of the cultures in which they exist, women tend to speak with an awareness of the community and their surroundings, seldom advancing an individual or isolationist perspective in the ordering of their lives.

How might narratives provide a more authentic view of women's lives? Or, do they?

Although life stories provide people with a way of revealing their lives, narratives are also used in a much broader societal context. Basically, stories exist on several levels—the macro through the micro—which include the community, regional, national, cultural, and individual. Yet stories consistently portray the element of individual knowing and awareness, making them ideal as bridges across the personal barriers of the mind and the political alliances of the conscience. As a consequence, narratives have become the select method for exploring the lives of the "Other."

There are sound reasons to employ narratives to investigate the lives of people who reside on the margins of general knowledge that are beneficial to the participants and the researchers. The processes of data collection for narrative methodologies (and in qualitative work in general) are responsive to the implied communication differences that might exist between the researcher and the researched. Such variations frequently occur when there are societal experiences and circumstances attached to distinct lived positionalities such as class, race, gender, and sexual orientation. There are of course words, cultural codings, gestures, and silent or expressed political rhetoric bound into these unique cultural circles.

The flexible structure of narratives also allows for a study's design to be changed to more appropriately address power disparities. For example, I conducted a study on the feminist perspectives of African American women in which a diverse group of women were interviewed concerning their definitions and experiences with feminism (Johnson-Bailey, 2000). In the process of conducting the study, I realized that the women who were economically disadvantaged and who were lacking in educational credentials (especially high school diplomas) did not feel comfortable talking to an academician, even one of the same gender and racial background. Because I was using narrative analysis and a feminist theoretical framework that was sensitive to power differences, the interviews with the hesitant women were eventually accomplished by interviewing them as a group. Talking with them as a collective gave them power. Four important details emerged that affected our assembly:

1. The group of five women outnumbered me.

2. The women perceived that their numbers gave them the ability to control the interview.

3. The stories of their peers emboldened the members to take risks in relating information.

4. The stories told by the group (who knew each other previously) were instantly subjected to member checks (Denzin, 1994).

The richness of the resulting data evidenced the importance of a flexible method in doing fieldwork where manifestations of power, specifically one's ability to find support and resources based on group affiliation, varied within the sample and between participants and the researcher. Invariably, all parties were assisted by the adaptable narrative method. The participants were bolstered in finding the license to claim their stories, and the researcher profited when the previously resistant women relented and shared their narratives.

What do you think might be the advantages and disadvantages of using group rather than individual interviews? Compare the group interview approach outlined here with the focus group data collection described by Kleiber (Chap. 6, this volume).

The tendency among those of us who collect stories has been simply to compile and present them (Mercier & Murphy, 1991), casting them into the scholarly literature collective as if their presence should automatically compensate and do penance for the years of omission. However, we often fail to ask what is being done with the stories. How are they being used and whose interests were being served by this raw offering of difference? Scott (1999) pointed out that presentations of the unexamined stories of the "Other" confer on the stories a misplaced authority to represent the whole of the group. Although she concedes that there is a vital need to expand the historical record by including the accounts of the others, Scott cautioned that using these differently scripted narratives as "fact" limits their importance. If they are seen as final and "irreducible," this precludes the possibility of critical examination and debate, and thus violates the intent and spirit of poststructuralist thinking—which currently dominates the theorizing of social scientists by examining the political construction of definitions and categories of meaning. As such, neglecting to analyze the narratives of the "Other" also compromises their overall significance by subjecting them to the inevitable claims of being presented without rigorous examination, therefore making their content questionable.

How would you describe to a colleague what is meant by the term *Other*?

THE DYNAMICS AND DIMENSIONS OF THE "OTHER"

Before further exploring the concept of "Other," it is necessary to acknowledge that representing women as an enigmatic populace is a favorable step removed from the original celebratory abstraction of women as a monolithic group. This idea of sameness initially set forth in early feminist writings of the 1970s and 1980s, although innocently presented, simplified the complex existence of women, mistakenly omitting class, race, sexual orientation, and other distinctions. Although the common ground of living in an androcentric world unites all women under the banner of gender oppression, denying the structural inequalities that privilege some over others serves to reproduce and reflect the hegemonic dragon we, as feminists, are trying to slay.

In the last decade, feminist scholars have turned to a more inclusive paradigm that attempts to speak for and address the concerns of the disenfranchised, and in doing so have sought a method that encompasses the actual group voices. No other technique or formula has been more appropriate than narratives as a way of letting the "Other" speak. The concept of the "Other" in feminist research is principally based on deBeauvoir's (1968) concept as the female other to man's primary being. In extrapolation, the term has come to mean the "different" when compared with the "norm." The essentialized other is an ever increasing popular and present character in current qualitative studies. Other commonly dichotomized pairings occurring in the literature are Black/White, gay/straight, women of color/White women.

In feminist research, the different, or the "Other," is recurrently manifested as women of color. This prevalent appearance of differentiated participants has been explained in several ways. First, the inclusion of women of color adds a needed dimension to a research discussion that previously neglected such groups or made exotic their conditions, because of a proclivity toward enthocentrism. In general, feminist researchers now present the ethnographic others' words as a critical and insightful corrective force to the stereotypical ideas implanted by colonialism. This postcolonial framework for presenting "authentic data" was intended to open a much needed dialogic space that would sponsor new understandings and foster social justice.

Second, bringing in the "Other" represents underexplored research opportunities and provides new avenues for scholarly inquiry. Current work, especially in the social sciences and education, is highlighting significant gaps in the literature and stimulating further research. Finally, there are two types of exploitation occurring within this dilemma. First, Western theorists and scholars are using non-Whites and non-Western cultures as grist for their theoretical mills. When a researcher uses groups from which they are removed by culture and geography, this is an apparent means for establishing instant objectivity and distance. Second, using the different adds excitement by tendering the fresh and exotic. hooks (1999) declared that this perspective is used in academic writings and specifically in popular literature:

> The commodification of Otherness has been so successful because it is offered as a new delight, more intense, more satisfying than normal ways of doing and feeling. Within commodity culture, ethnicity becomes spice, seasoning that can liven up the dull dish that is mainstream white culture. (p. 179)

However, it is well to remember that the exotic, entertaining, and harmless "Other" can only exist in contrast to the uninteresting, observing, and authoritative norm. Therefore, the essentialized average or representative culture occupies a place that is replete with power. This advantageous location held by the norm is the dominant position that is consistently assigned power in the duality of the comparison and contrasting analogy.

NEGOTIATING POWER IN "OTHERING"

Indeed, power is an optical illusion in any narrative. It is clearly there but is hidden from view, especially if the narrative is skillfully constructed. Still, the unseen force directs the lens of the researcher, negotiating how cultures and the people who live in them are observed and analyzed. Power is ever present in the presentation of the lone participant's story or in the oral traditions of a group, because the communities that surround each are encased within social systems. And these systems control and significantly order the operations of our hierarchial Western society with laws, customs, educational systems and programs, and organized religions. So when narrativists work with stories they must be aware of how power, this hidden companion, shapes views and relations with the world.

Such concerns are compounded for feminists, because a major tenet said to drive feminist research is the obligation to deliver "a critique of traditional concepts and structures that have marginalized women materially and psychologically, in the world and even in their own souls" (Patai, 1991, p. 139). So for feminists working with women, particularly women of color, there is a weighty awareness that the lives of women of color are usually invisible in most academic arenas and that when their stories are present, they are often ensconced in sensationalism and stereotype. Invariably, the responsibility, often internally imposed, falls on feminists who work with narratives to accurately and sensitively represent women of color. This circumstance is problematized by the position of the researcher in relation to the position of the women of color being studied. Simply put, it matters whether the researcher stands as an outsider or as an insider to the group.

The location of the researcher to the "researched" has been characterized in the anthropological literature in myriad ways: the endogenous or exogenous, the native and the colonializer, the observer and observed, the participant observer and the participant. But the stance of the researcher is not easily defined despite obvious oppositional pairings of terminology. The experience of the researcher as an insider or outsider cannot be a fixed one, because we are all at some point an insider and an outsider, given the setting. In addition, the perspectives of the researcher can be multifaceted and can be susceptible to shifts influenced by interactions with others, the changing research context, time, and other unpredictable factors.

Banks (1998) offered a four-part typology that recognizes the complexity of the researcher's position: the indigenous–insider, the indigenous–outsider, the external–insider, and the external–outsider. The first part of his binary pairings refers to the circumstance of researchers as being indigenous or external members in relationship to those being studied. The second component references the political and cultural position of the researchers: Do they hold the values, beliefs, and views of the people they are studying? Banks' sociologically based definitions are extensions of Merton's insider–outsider (1972) and Collins' outsider–within (1990) concepts. However, Banks' hierarchy implies that the categories are fixed and seems to assume that researchers are cognizant of their positions and the ways in which personal perspectives influence their work. Such points seem misplaced when dynamic research conditions are considered. Most researchers can relate to going into the field sure of one's perspective and emerging from the field with shredded philosophies. Standpoints can shift, and power can intervene to problematize data collection and postfield analysis.

For the most part, despite the various possibilities, only the two extremes of the outsider and insider statuses are widely recognized and discussed throughout the literature. The deliberations have been primarily twofold: people of color discussing how they research within their own groups and Whites reflecting on their research on people of color. A fascinating quandary emerges in this two-part dialogue in which the conversation is seldom expanded to include people of color researching Whites or Whites researching other Whites. Failure to have such evolutionary continuations of the discourse are easily attributed to the way in which power operates to objectify the "Other," while allowing the "norm" to continue invisible to and unchecked by examination. It is important to note that this objectification of the "Other," is not necessarily precluded when the scholar is a member of the disenfranchised group being studied.

> What is your definition of the "objectification of the Other," and how might it influence researchers? How might being aware of this improve the authenticity of research?

RESEARCHING WITHIN CULTURAL BOUNDARIES

The current explorations on researching as an insider are optimistically positive. Black women scholars in particular have been most prolific on this subject. It is generally set forth that the common bonds of gender and race provide a groundwork on which to construct trust and dialogue and that an empathy will be extended across racial lines (Beoku-Betts, 1994; Foster, 1996; Johnson-Bailey, 1998; Nelson, 1996; Vaz, 1997). Foster (1996), a Black woman academician, recounted how her race and gender helped in her interviewing other Black women teachers: "There is no doubt that the teachers' view of me as an insider influenced their willingness to participate, and shaped both their expectations and responses" (p. 223).

Collins (1999) warned of assuming that insider rank gives one the steadfast ground of knowing correctness in one's work and detecting it in the work of others. She adds, however, an the important disclaimer in support of politically conscious platforms. Collins believes that scholars who themselves are members of disenfranchised groups will bring an insider's political stance to their work. Her idea operationalizes the notion that groups are bound by race, gender, class, or all of those factors so tightly that they share common concerns and that therefore only someone who has walked in the same cultural shoes can speak for the culture. She expresses this thought concisely regarding her perspective on Black feminist thought: "In contrast to views of culture stressing the unique, ahistorical values of a particular group, Black feminist approaches have placed greater emphasis on the role of historically-specific political economies in explaining the endurances of certain cultural themes" (p. 157).

This belief, which Merton (1994) called a new type of ethnocentrism, is also echoed in Alvarez's (1996) and Lal's (1999) respective essays on Puerto Rican and Indian women. Alvarez (1996) expressed that oral history is a method and a grounding that allows her a way to negotiate her subjectivity and intrasubjectivity status to her Puerto Rican community. According to Alvarez, the heterogeneity of her people based on class, gender, and race disallows most claims of insider status that rest on the concept that minority groups are monolithic. Likewise, Lal (1999) saw Indian women as distinctly divided along class lines, which establish educational, work, and basic life choices. And Lal also rejects the idea that she can not have valid and critical insights on her own cultural group. Describing herself as a political and historical being, Lal attempts to "disrupt this binary" (p. 125) of the outsider–insider perspective and escape the postmodernist theoretical quandary (concerning the problem of self-representation and the difficulty of characterizing "the" social reality). Lal admits that her efforts are difficult but significant, because they are situated in the politics of reality.

However, women scholars who research as insiders also report on the inconsistency of the insider's terrain, which often varies in accordance with perceived degrees of difference. Nelson (1996), another Black woman researcher, explained how her naive hypothesis about sisterhood was dispersed:

> The women in this study received me with varying degrees of intimacy, from tepid politeness to sisterly or motherly generosity. Beneath the obvious and sustaining bonds of gender, race, and class lay more subtle features, artifacts of the various microcommunities of our individual enculturation processes, features that either drew us together or set a distance, however slight, between us. (p. 184)

In a study that I conducted on the schooling narratives of Black women, race, gender, and class played major roles in determining the flow of data

(Johnson-Bailey, 1999). Race and gender were uniting forces. The women and I enjoyed a bond of comfort as we discussed our similar racialized and gendered stories of what it meant to grow up a "colored girl" in the segregated American South. There was no lack of trust exhibited when we talked about our similarities, and the dialogue flowed easily between us, because an understanding was assumed. Routinely, they would make statements like, "You know how it was" or "You know what I mean."

However, class issues were an unwelcome intruder to the fragile community that the participants and I had formed. As discussions progressed, with some of the participants referring to their current educational pursuits of community college degrees and teaching certificates, my terminal degree seemed an indicator of middle-class status, and I was faced with skeptical inquiries concerning my previously alleged impoverished background. The women made cynically couched statements like "Well, look at you now" or "Well, you wouldn't know it to look at you." Class was not easily discussed, and the class differences between us eroded our common ground. The fact that I was no longer the "sister" who instinctively understood was disconcerting, because I had been "seduced by that sense of mutuality" so often created when women interview women (Olson & Shopes, 1991, p. 196). Forfeiting the researcher's ground and moving toward the participants' perspective is dangerous, especially for the insider who most probably harbors a sympathetic grasp of the participants' belief systems. This position of being an insider who is in sync with the group provides a tempting platform from which to speak for the group and to know the right and moral way that is in the group's best interest.

> Why do the "shifting sands" of being an insider at one point and an outsider at another make doing narrative research more complicated?

Other concerns lodged against insider research are the mistaken notions that insider research is simpler (Johnson-Bailey, 1999), that insider work is merely an extension of the researcher's own concerns (Cassell, 1977), and that insider research is not real (Vaz, 1997). First, it is assumed that insider research is easier, because insiders have to mediate fewer boundaries and share a sense of identity with those they research. A prevalent belief found in the literature claims that cultural membership connotes the higher moral and correct ground (Beoku-Betts, 1994; Foster, 1996; Nelson, 1996; Vaz, 1997). This view, which is usually supported and debated within the same writing, posits insider status as beneficial, but certainly not a guarantee when researching within your own group. Yet the possible benefits of being closer to the participant in shared positions is embraced as the stronger of the concepts, as evidenced by its primary position as the foundation for critiquing and presenting insider standpoints.

Second, most research is in some way connected to the researcher—through special interests, individual connections, and psychological ties, and emotional ties, or both. But the idea that when people on the margins examine those who are similarly situated, the examination is based entirely on personal agendas, is mere self-examination and is sympathetic, and favorable propaganda seems steeped in positivistic elitism. Although it would certainly appear that overlapping concerns would be more common within the same groups, such a position disregards the differences that exist within groups and discounts the researcher's ability to maintain intellectual and ethical integrity.

Such a perspective also gives little consideration to how internalized oppression could negatively affect the way researchers from within the culture are perceived by the group members being studied and how researchers might perceive their own culture. Internalized oppression is defined simply as being prejudiced against one's self, one's group, or both (Collins, 1990). In this instance, it refers to a member of a disenfranchised group who is enculturated in the ways of the dominant group and rejects the mores and traditions of the home culture as inferior but accepts all things in the dominant culture as superior. For the academic insider as an anthropologist, cultural critic, or researcher, it translates into viewing one's own culture through harsh eyes: The home culture would be possibly judged as primitive, lacking, and unsophisticated. An example of this is seen in Gloria Naylor's (1988) novel *Mama Day*. In the opening chapter, she tells the story of a former boy from the island who has received a university education and has returned home as a man with tape recorder in hand to do ethnographic research among his people. From his stance of superiority, he assesses his community as having, "unique speech patterns," because they do not speak "proper" English, of "asserting their cultural identity" in mistaken but explainable forms, and of "inverting hostile social and political parameters," because they are resisting improvement to land developers who want to build resorts and disrupt their lives and community.

Finally, the third point, that research that is produced by an insider is not real research relies on two ideas: Subjectivity can be equated with bad research, and only an outsider who has distance can observe and analyze clearly. The idea of the outsider as a person who does not have an agenda or a clouded perspective is soundly rejected by qualitative researchers. The mantra of the constructivst qualitative paradigm is that everyone and every story is shaped by the situation, context, and culture. In addition, modern social scientists of the last two decades have decried the ethnocentric stances taken by their predecessors. Moreover, the qualitative research paradigm views subjectivity, especially when it is forthrightly stated, as a propitious stance that allows readers to know the lens through which the research is presented and to then make their own evaluations about the legitimacy and worth of the research.

Succinctly, the perspectives that inform the insider position are politically charged and bolstered by a history of injurious outsider research in which people at the margins are not only seen as different, but as deficient. Issues set forward as concerns, such as those expressed by Merton (1994), that insiders are practicing a kind of reverse ethnocentrism are too easily given credence. Is it not seemingly logical that insiders would have a larger knowledge base from which to interpret their own culture more so than outsiders? Consequently, little consideration is accorded the insider's previously denied right to self-define. The right to self-define has long been the basis of the dominant group's enthnocentric discourse. So, one might ask why this same vantage point is troublesome when used by disenfranchised groups.

There are no definitive answers to whether researching within the culture is less intrusive, less harmful, more politically correct, or more politically astute. The major areas of discussion are certainly that the groups on the boundaries of research are there because of existing societal power disparities. It is debatable whether self-examination is a way of equalizing the forces that structure the inequities. However, attempting to name the source of the problem, and then controlling the predicament, is presented by marginalized insiders as the first and most important step in equalizing the playing field where research on the "Other" takes place.

Who are examples of "marginalized insiders" who might be the subjects of narrative inquiry? Why study these individuals?

RESEARCHING ACROSS CULTURAL BOUNDARIES

Characteristically referred to as crossing boundaries, cross-cultural research, or representing the "Other" (research conducted by White scholars on people of color) is oversimplified by any brief descriptor. There are three levels ever present in this type of dynamic: the researcher, the researched, and the societal contexts where the power relations between the two are situated.

In examining the discussions on outsiders researching women of color, the territory is not easily negotiated. Certainly, there is enormous precedence in the social sciences, because historically researching humans meant researching those outside of your tribe. Yet, feminist scholars (Collins, 1990; Etter-Lewis, 1993; Gilligan, 1982; Gluck & Patai, 1991; Hesse-Biber, Gilmartin, & Lydenberg, 1999; hooks, 1989; Wilkinson & Kitzinger, 1996; Witherell & Noddings, 1991) declare that a primary reason for collecting and presenting the voices of all women, and especially disenfranchised women, is to disrupt the traditional canon and to challenge alleged objectivity. But the idea of women using other women as subjects to further a goal raises immediate ethical concerns: How will the women studied benefit from the work and what will we give back? We must also ask how the work of feminist oral historians and narrativists differs from the anthropologists who studied the newly encountered tribes of distant non-Western lands. Are we the neocolonist oppressors? Are we studying down? In her essay on ethics, Patai (1991) pointedly framed the problem:

> The dilemma of feminist researchers working on groups less privileged than themselves can be succinctly stated as follows: is it possible—not in theory, but in the actual conditions of the real world today—to write about the oppressed without becoming one of the oppressors? (p. 139)

Patai answered her own question within the same essay: "In an absolute sense, I think not . . . ". And then she went on to declare that feminists must wade into this ethical quagmire and do their best to disrupt the structures in their final products. She later warned that some feminist researchers try to assuage their conscience by putting all of their effort into the window dressing of data collection. They attempt to speak to the power disparities solely in the researcher–participant relationship by demonstrating their "feminist commitments" when they involve the participant as a coresearcher.

In her essay, "White Woman Researcher—Black Women Subjects," Edwards (1996), a White woman, wondered

> On the one hand, I want my arguments about black—and other—women's lives in specific situations to be heard and to be accepted as having a valid academic status. . . . I also wonder what power relations I perpetuate when I take part in the academic "survival of the fittest" process. (p. 87)

Edwards finally concluded that the end is justified in her work, which seemed to be inclusive and to present an authentic depiction of Black women. However, her statement about needing to publish so that she won't perish in academia is not as simple a concept as Edwards presented. She set forth that the academic publishing game is a fair one and that inevitably the better work will be published. However, she neglected to explore the political dimensions of publishing related to work on race. This concern was expressed by McIntosh (2000) in her now famous list, "White Privilege and Male Privilege: A Personal Account of Coming to See Correspondences Through Working in Women's Studies." McIntosh stated, "If I want to, I can be pretty sure of finding a publisher for this piece on white privilege" (p. 31). She explained that her opinion on race will be more easily accepted as valid and objective than the opinion of a person of color and that it will most probably find easier inroads toward publication. In essence, she was saying that work by Whites about people of color finds more ready acceptance. This exactly parallels the dilemma of Whites writing about the "Other" when compared with the "Others" writing about themselves or their group members.

The conclusions reached by Edwards are shared by Russell (1996), a White South African woman, who is questioning her right to write about the lives of

Black South African women. Russell stated that she refused to confine herself to examining her own group "to avoid accusations of colonialization" (p. 92) and further refused to include statements about her personal stance in her publications as a way of proving the worthiness of her work. Russell continued to muddy the academic waters by claiming that the Black South African women she interviewed did not object to her whiteness. Because she did her work during apartheid, there were certainly too many complex issues between the races for participation by Black participants with a White researcher to be construed as valid proof of her right to represent Black South African women. But her supposition that doing antiracist research provided her permission to do research on disempowered people is a recurrent theme among feminist researchers who do narrative work on less powerful groups.

What arguments do you have for and against Russell's case for not describing her personal stance? How might her decision influence the quality of data or study results in this case?

Although Russell claims that she is practicing resistance by refusing to explain her own politics in print or in media interviews, the claim rings hollow. According to her, the trend to explain ones's position in order to rationalize the research can have a potentially harmful impact on the careers of women researchers. Her profession of refusal juxtaposes possible career difficulty against the life-threatening risk that her participants are taking as Black South African women speaking out against apartheid and relying on a White expatriate South African to represent them and to protect their identity. If it is as Cotterill and Letherby (1993) claimed, and researchers weave threads of their lives into the stories of those they research, then to definitively extend the discussion to include who you are as a researcher seems only ethical.

Russell's predicament is a familiar one in the research relationship: The participants risk more than the feminist researcher. Repeatedly, however, the reason for asking the respondents to take chances is to fulfill the need of the researcher to do her part, answer her political convictions, and become an advocate fighting for the "Other."

Gluck (1991) expanded on this advocacy theme in explaining how her belief and advocacy on the part of Palestinian women shapes her work. However, unlike Russell (1996), Gluck was explicit about her politics:

> One of my goals in collecting Palestinians women's stories is to bring the issues of their national and social liberation to the attention of the American public. Because I am not simply a propagandist but also a scholar-advocate, I have had to construct, self-consciously, my public presentations and continually assess how to present my materials. (p. 213)

Patai (1991) elaborated on the importance of declaring one's politics and of recognizing the safety of the researcher's academic tower. She stated that research with the intent to transform is done from safe academic distances and that scholars who engage in such efforts are caught in the tenuous bind of pleasing two masters—not wanting to bite the hand that dispenses the research dollars and not wanting to "caress it too lovingly" (p. 139).

In summary, resoundingly the answer in the literature about whether or not people of color should or can be researched, understood, and represented by outsiders is yes—with added codicils: if you are working as an advocate, if you use a compassionate lens, and if you present the legitimate message. However, it must be conceded that research about such groups, particularly research that endeavors to tell the stories of the "Other," is treading the dangerous waters charted long ago by anthropologists and their predecessors, missionaries who were the emissaries of conquerors, who exoticized entire civilizations and used their writings to diminish cultures. Of late there are voices in the field calling for research away from essentializing those who are different.

What is your position on whether or not people of color should be researched and represented by outsiders?

Previously, the research focus was partially aimed at providing the "Other" with a look at themselves through a Western and more civilized mirror. This new shift is to turn the focus primarily on influencing the dominant in the direction of self-examination. Patai (1991) set forth that ethics must prevail and that researchers must reveal the part that they and their removed compatriots play in the subjugation of entire groups. Lengel (1998) built on the work of Patai (1991) and stated that ethnographers should attempt to use their work to change the attitudes and perceptions of the dominant culture toward the "Other," so that self-reflexivity and shifting our own paradigms would be the highest calling of telling the story of the "Other."

CONCLUSIONS

In final analysis, reconciling power and positional statuses seems impossible to accomplish with any degree of finality. The powerful forces that structure our world exist in the major systems that give essence to the hierarchy: the government, social organizations, communities, and family units. People are educated formally and informally in how to order the world based on their group fidelities or positions. Often, we learn how to think about and behave toward others through what we read, seldom coming face to face with the "Other." How do we change this fundamental way of exercising power through the lens of our own position-alities? How do you see and then represent the lives of those who are different from you? The literature poses these questions but fails to answer them, leaving open the assumption that merely contemplating transformation is sufficient and honorable. Indeed, merely discussing these problems is insufficient, but the pursuit of trying to examine and reexamine one's motives and perspectives is decent and ethical.

> How would you plan and carry out narrative research if your participants were not like you in significant ways (e.g., culture or gender)? Argue for why you should or should not be the one to conduct this research.

We are left struggling with fundamental questions: Who owns the story, the researcher or the participant? What happens when there is disagreement on interpretation or analysis? What are the ethical boundaries in telling the story—to edit or not to edit? Are we reproducing the status quo when members of the norm group write about those who are members of less powerful groups? Are the calls of the marginalized best responded to by a group member? These unrelenting questions are cyclical in that any response spawns new questions. But failing to ask them is unconscionable, given the ongoing dialogue that is occurring in the literature between position and power.

No research methodology can provide a perfect balance for telling and representing. Power can affect the relationships or the historical positions and patterns of relationships between the researcher and the researched. In a narrative where the storied script that reveals in integral and accessible ways while simultaneously functioning as the research structure, the design dilemmas are intense. Therefore, a research scholar using narratives must remain vigilantly aware of power issues—the balance of voices, competing political agendas, and the societal hierarchies enveloping the process. Each story and the accompanying data collection and analytic process is a balancing act. The forces to be reconciled change as positions shift: a White person studying a person of color, a man researching women and their place in society, a scholar of color doing work within her or his own culture. There is no righteous ground. There are people of color who can accomplish a synchronously sympathetic and critical examination of their kin, and there are those who bring a jaundiced gaze sponsored by internalized oppression to self-group examination. There are Whites who can negotiate the privilege of their whiteness and represent the "Other" in ways that are generally accepted as accurate by the group, and there are those who are trapped and blinded by their privilege. But then there are those fortuitous instances when all the margins are traversed, the inevitable biases contained, and the fortunate story, told well, reverberates universally.

9

Ethnomethodological and Conversation Analytic Studies

Kathryn J. Roulston
University of Georgia

MEET THE AUTHOR

Kathryn J. Roulston is an assistant professor in the College of Education at the University of Georgia and teaches in the Qualitative Inquiry Program. Before moving to the United States to make her home in Athens, Georgia, she completed her Ph.D. in education at the University of Queensland, Australia. Kathy's research interests include music education, qualitative research methods, and the application of ethnomethodological and conversation analytic methods to the study of talk-in-interaction. In the area of music education, she completed a master of music degree (with an emphasis on Zoltán Kodály) at the University of Calgary and has worked as a music specialist with children from preschool through eighth grade in Australian schools. She is currently engaged in research concerning young children's music preferences. Her articles are published in *Qualitative Inquiry, Qualitative Research, Music Education Research, Oxford Review of Education,* and *Text.*

Ethnomethodology as an approach to sociological analysis derives from the work of Garfinkel (1967). Garfinkel's theoretical endeavors have focused on problems central to sociology—those of "the theory of social action, the nature of intersubjectivity and the social construction of knowledge" (Heritage, 1987, p. 225). Put simply, this qualitative approach to research seeks to examine how members make meaning of one another's utterances and actions, and what that meaning might be in any specific encounter. Researchers using ethnomethodological approaches to research are keenly interested in how members' knowledge is constructed in and through talk and text. In this chapter, I briefly outline relevant terms and features of ethnomethodological studies before providing an overview of conversation analysis (CA), a field of study deriving from ethnomethodology (EM). I then provide examples of different types of ethnomethodological and conversation analytic studies, review suggested ways to begin such work, and conclude by proposing contributions of this type of work.

BACKGROUND

The approach taken by Garfinkel to the investigation of problems is highly original in that he avoided working toward a "large-scale systematic theory of social structure" (Heritage, 1984, p. 4) such as accomplished by Max Weber or Talcott Parsons. Instead, Garfinkel (1967) aimed to focus on the methods members use in activities of everyday practical reasoning. Rather than take as a "point of departure" scenes from everyday life—as is common in sociological work—Garfinkel was interested in rediscovering "how any such common sense world is possible" (p. 36). This concern with what members make of everyday, ordinary life contrasts with conventional sociology, which "conceives of ordinary social life as an arena where theoretically conceived structures and factors are played out and as nothing more than a reflection of these entities" (Hester & Francis, 2000a, p. 3). Rather than study retrospective accounts of members' actions (as is common to interview studies), researchers using approaches informed by ethnomethodology seek to study the ongoing achievement of social practices. Rawls (2002, p. 6) stated that the object of ethnomethodological work is to "discover the things that persons in particular situations do, the methods they use, to create the patterned orderliness of social life" (p. 6).

Garfinkel (1967) acknowledged his debt to the work of Alfred Schutz, and reported a series of " breaching"activities undertaken by his students through which he and his students sought to examine some of the commonplace scenes of the "world known in common and taken for granted" (pp. 36–37). Students were instructed to detect the invisibility of background expectancies by making "trouble" through a series of activities. For example, they were asked to imagine themselves as boarders in their own home and act as such, or engage with others on the assumption that their interactants were attempting to mislead them. In another set of exercises, students were instructed to insist that others (with whom they were engaged in ordinary conversation) clarify their remarks. Through these simple "experiments," it becomes apparent how members anticipate that others will understand "the occasionality of expressions, the specific vagueness of references, the retrospective-prospective sense of a present occurrence," and that these are "sanctioned properties of common discourse" (p. 41). One such case is reported as follows:

> The victim waved his hand cheerily.
> (S) How are you?
> (E) How am I in regard to what? My health, my finances, my school work, my peace of mind, my . . . ?
> (S) (Red in the face and suddenly out of control.) Look! I was just trying to be polite. Frankly, I don' t give a damn how you are. (p. 44)

In this simple example, we see the trouble caused when the common question "How are you?" is treated as other than a greeting (cf. Sacks, 1992, Vol.1, pp. 549–566).

Given this interchange, how does situational context determine meaning?

Garfinkel's ethnomethodological enterprise has been described elsewhere as simply a working out of the "implications of Schutz's arguments about the nature and foundations of sociological knowledge" (Cuff, Sharrock, & Francis, 1998, p. 150). Certainly, the encounters as described above deal explicitly with Schutz's

concern with the "world known in common" and the "conduct of everyday affairs." Holstein and Gubrium (1998, p. 140), however, argued that EM, although
indebted to Schutz's phenomenology, is no mere extension of Schutz's work. How
might the ethnomethodological enterprise be defined then? Garfinkel (1974)
described EM as

> an organizational study of a member's knowledge of his [or her] ordinary affairs, of
> his [or her] own organized enterprises, where that knowledge is treated by us as part
> of the same setting that it also makes orderable. (p. 18)

The focus of research problems for the ethnomethodologist is to investigate
and explicate

> the body of common-sense knowledge and the range of procedures and consid-
> erations by means of which the ordinary members of society make sense of, find
> their way about in, and act on the circumstances in which they find themselves.
> (Heritage, 1984, p. 4)

Sharrock and Anderson (1986, p. 38) outlined three "investigative maxims"
for researchers taking up Garfinkel's project. These are the following:

1. Treat activities as reflexively accountable.
2. Treat settings as self-organizing and commonsense as an occasioned corpus
   of knowledge.
3. Treat social actors as inquirers into those settings and accountings.

In these principles, we see the invocation of two essential properties that are
important to an understanding of ethnomethodological work. These are indexicality and reflexivity. The nature of indexical expressions (such as "here," "now,"
"this," "that," or "it") has been widely discussed within the field of linguistics
(Heritage, 1984, p. 142). The problem posed by indexical terms for the analyst
of social interaction is that the referents of terms and "truth values of the statements in which they occur" vary with the circumstances (p. 142). Put another
way, meanings of utterances and actions depend on the social situation. Rather
then treat indexical meanings as problematic, Garfinkel proposed to examine the
nature of indexicality as a phenomenon. How, for example, do language users
"routinely and unremarkably make sense of indexical expressions" (Sharrock &
Anderson, 1986, p. 43) in everyday settings? How do members utilize indexical
terms as a resource?

Reflexivity refers to the notion that activities are "simultaneously in and about
the settings to which we orient, and that they describe" (Holstein & Gubrium,
1998, p. 143). Garfinkel (1967) noted that reflexivity is taken for granted by members as an ever present feature of reality: "Members know, require, count on, and

make use of this reflexivity to produce, accomplish, recognize, or demonstrate rational-adequacy-for-all-practical-purposes of their procedures and findings" (p. 8).

Both indexicality and reflexivity are properties of everyday life, and as such are central topics to ethnomethodological studies. Garfinkel's concern with these topics departs from previous treatments. First, ethnomethodology's concern with "reflexive phenomena as applied to actions" is quite different from that of more traditional phenomenological treatments of reflexivity (Heritage, 1984, p. 109). Second, Garfinkel's focus on the indexicality of language sought to investigate the "nature of language use and the practical reasoning which informs it"—until then an overlooked topic within sociology (Heritage, 1984, p. 135). (For further discussion of these topics, see Heritage, 1984, Chapters 5 and 6.)

"STRAIGHT-AHEAD" AND "APPLIED" ETHNOMETHODOLOGICAL STUDIES

Heap (1990) explored a number of questions related to the value of pursuing ethnomethodological studies. Characterizing ethnomethodological work as "straight-ahead" or "applied," he argued that EM studies can deliver two types of findings, "critical news" and "positive news" (Heap, 1990, pp. 42–43). The "critical news approach"—prevalent in early EM work—offers an alternative way of viewing problems, that is, "others got it wrong as to how things are" (pp. 42–43), and often addresses new audiences outside the field of sociology. The studies Heap proposed here have investigated the nature of practical reasoning, the properties of indexicality and reflexivity, and the nature of the documentary method of interpretation. In contrast, Heap argued that the "positive news" approach aims to show how "X is organized in this way" (p. 43). Examples of this type of work are studies of conversation, and studies of workplace interaction.

Although the value of straight-ahead EM studies is primarily to inform professionals within the field of EM, the applied EM approach advocated by Heap (1990) was aimed at a lay audience. In summing up why researchers might take an applied EM approach as a guiding framework, Heap noted that

> such effort may deliver news about the structure of phenomena, and especially about the consequences of those structures for realizing ends and objectives regarded as important outside of ethnomethodology's analytic interests. The states of affairs may be other than they appear, other than they have been reported to be by others, or may be of interest independently of what others have said, rightly or wrongly. (p. 44)

In advocating for applied EM studies, Heap (1990, p. 69) argued that this type of work is multidisciplinary and must be undertaken by researchers conversant in disciplines other than EM[1] who are interested in investigating the "missing what" (Garfinkel, Lynch, & Livingston, 1981) of interaction within their field of study. Hester and Francis further explained the concept of the "just whatness"[2] of social practices:

> . . . virtually all studies in the social and administrative science literatures "miss" the interactional "what" of the occupations studied: studies of bureaucratic case workers "miss" how such officials constitute the specifications of a "case" over the course of a series of interactions with a stream of clients; studies in medical sociology "miss" how the diagnostic categories are constituted during clinical encounters; and studies of the military "miss" just how stable ranks and lines of communication are articulated in and as interactional work. (Lynch, cited in Hester & Francis, 2000a, p. 3)

Thus, researchers working in any discipline might take an ethnomethodological approach, and this has certainly been the case. What topics, then, have researchers using this approach investigated?

ETHNOMETHODOLOGY IN EDUCATION

Ethnomethodological studies have been conducted in diverse fields, including education, law, communication, medicine, human–computer interaction, mathematics, and science, contributing significantly to our understanding of social life in a wide variety of settings.[3] Studies have investigated social interaction in courtroom proceedings (Atkinson & Drew, 1979), educational settings (Baker, 1997a; Hester & Francis, 2000b), scientific settings (Lynch, 1993), human–computer interaction (Hutchby, 2001; Suchman, 1987), and the workplace (Heath, Knoblauch, & Luff, 2000). It is pertinent here to use the field of education to exemplify the diversity of topics that have been addressed through ethnomethodological approaches. Hester and Francis (2000a, pp. 8–11) identified six broad themes addressed by ethnomethodological studies within education:

1. The organization of educational decision making includes work that addresses allocating, assessing, testing, sorting, and grading students (see, e.g., Mehan, 1991).

---

[1] In Garfinkel's view, such research must be carried out by a researcher who is also a competent practitioner in the domain of activities under investigation. Fulfillment of this "unique adequacy requirement" will ensure that the "constituent details of occupationally competent activities will be depicted with as much precision and specificity as possible" (Heritage, 1987, p. 264).

[2] Garfinkel's term for this concept is "quiddity" (Heritage, 1987, p. 262).

[3] A bibliography of empirical and conceptual work in ethnomethodology may be found in Coulter (1990).

2. Studies concerning standardized educational assessment and standardized testing (e.g., Heap, 1980) show how assessment practices are based on unstated and unacknowledged background knowledge, beliefs, and assumptions.

3. The area of classroom order and management has addressed classroom control, the management of deviance, and the sequential organization of talk (e.g., Danby & Baker, 2000; Hester, 2000; Mehan, 1979).

4. The production of classroom activities and events (e.g., Payne, 1976) examines the interactional and collaborative production of particular types of activities (such as lessons, storytelling, classroom writing, or a lecture).

5. The practical organization and accomplishment of academic knowledge investigates how disciplinary knowledge is organized. For example, McHoul and Watson (1982) showed how geographic knowledge is organized and accomplished within a classroom lesson, whereas Armour (2000) examined how an artist teaches the concept of color to students. Other researchers examined the organization of knowledge in mathematics and science (Livingston, 1986; Lynch & Macbeth, 1998) and story reading (Rymes & Pash, 2001).

6. Studies investigating the child as a practical actor show how adult–child relations and the cultural world of childhood are organized (see, e.g., Baker & Freebody, 1987). This type of work has shown the educational implications of adults' neglect of and lack of appreciation for children's competence as social actors.

As may be seen from this brief overview, a wide variety of topics are identified within the auspices of ethnomethodological research in education, and this listing of themes is by no means exhaustive. It would seem, then, that EM as an approach to research is available to any qualitative researcher interested in investigating topics from an alternative frame. How, then, might one proceed? Baker (1997a) outlined eight features of ethnomethodological work that we might consider. These features provide pointers to beginning ethnomethodological studies:

1. Ethnomethodological analyses begin by studying actual instances of talk-in-interaction or other interactional activities rather than beginning with a theory or theoretical position.

2. Detailed transcripts are made from recordings and are aids to analysis. Analytic claims are referred continuously to the details of the recorded talk or activity.

3. Ethnomethodological analyses are concerned to reveal the methods people use to organize their talk and activity such that it is orderly and accountable. For example, analysts begin with "how" questions concerning how particular kinds of work gets done before proceeding (if at all) to "why" questions (Silverman & Gubrium, 1994).

4. Ethnomethodological analyses are not motivated by a belief in a particular theory, nor do they result in prescriptions.

5. Ethnomethodological analyses treat talk as social activity. The concern is in what people do with words and how and when this is achieved.

6. Talk is understood to be systematically organized by speakers and hearers in a setting. The "systematics" of talk are both context free and context dependent. For example, although speakers' methods for gaining a turn are similar in different settings, speakers nevertheless design talk for particular settings and are sensitive to hearers, tasks, and prior turns.

7. Speakers and hearers are treated as competent analysts of ongoing talk as social activity.

8. Talk is part of, and reflexively constitutive of, the setting itself. "Context" is understood to be produced by the talk as much as talk is designed for the context.

As noted above, ethnomethodological studies frequently use detailed transcriptions of audio- or video-recorded talk or interaction. Harvey Sacks (1992), whose work I shall discuss in a later section on CA, was explicit in his use of transcriptions of recordings. He noted, for example, "I'm trying to develop a sociology where the reader has as much information as the author, and can reproduce the analysis" (Vol. 1, p. 27). Thus, transcriptions make available to readers information in ways not normally available to readers of reports that utilize field notes as a source of data. As noted by Silverman (1998), detailed transcripts serve other purposes. First, they provide a public record of data, available to other analysts. Audio and video recordings can be replayed, transcripts improved, and other analyses pursued. Further, other researchers can inspect sequences of utterances without being limited to topics chosen by the first researcher.

Hester and Francis (2000a, pp. 4–5) noted the diversity of methods adopted within ethnomethodological studies and suggested that there cannot, nor should there, be a "standard method" for such research. Therefore, the use of transcripts of audio- or video-recorded talk is a strategy pertinent in relation to the phenomena under investigation and should not be thought of as a "universal method." For example, other types of data used in ethnomethodological studies include origami instructions (Livingston, 2000), an excerpt from a textbook (Sharrock & Ikeya, 2000), student responses to an exercise from a statistics course (Livingston, 1987), and a newspaper report (Jayyusi, 1991). I turn now to further explanation of CA.

In your own words, how would you characterize ethnomethodological studies at this point in the chapter?

CONVERSATION ANALYSIS

Garfinkel (1991, pp. 14–15) included conversation analytic studies as one branch of ethnomethodological study that seeks to examine "naturally organized ordinary activities" (pp. 14–15). The interrelationship between EM and CA has been explored further by Clayman and Maynard (1995). These authors outlined the continuities and interrelationships (in theory, method and substance) between the two enterprises, rejecting pejorative critiques of CA by ethnomethodologists (1995, p. 27). Clayman and Maynard argued for complementarity between the two enterprises, noting that

> conversation analysis without ethnomethodology risks proliferating findings that are detached from their roots in members' ongoing constitutive activities. Ethnomethodology without its conversation analytic branches risks becoming rootbound, probing ever more deeply into the autochthonous ordering of society, but lacking an analytic apparatus that reaches for the sky. (p. 28)

How, then, might CA be defined? Developed by the late Harvey Sacks in the 1960s, CA "studies the order/organization/orderliness of social action, particularly those social actions that are located in everyday interaction, in discursive practices, in the sayings/tellings/doings of members of society" (Psathas, 1995, p. 2).

Sacks (1992) was quite clear about the purpose of his enterprise and his own contribution, noting in a lecture in 1972 that "there's an area called Analysis of Conversation. It's done in various places around the world, and I invented it" (Vol. 2, p. 549).

Sacks (1992) endeavored to systematically investigate and analyze the "machinery" of interaction through an examination of two features of talk-in-interaction: sequential organization and membership categorization. Sacks' lectures—which have been posthumously transcribed and published by his colleague Gail Jefferson—are an invaluable source for analysts wishing to investigate these issues. Preferring the term " talk-in-interaction," Psathas (1995, pp. 2–3) outlined seven basic assumptions of CA:

1. Order is a produced orderliness.
2. Order is produced by the parties in situ; that is, it is situated and occasioned.
3. The parties orient to that order themselves; that is, this order is not an analyst's conception, not the result of the use of some preformed or preformulated theoretic conceptions concerning what action should or must be, or based on generalizing or summarizing statements about what action generally, frequently, or often is.
4. Order is repeatable and recurrent.

5. The discovery, description, and analysis of that produced orderliness is the task of the analyst.

6. Issues of how frequently, how widely, or how often particular phenomena occur are to be set aside in the interest of discovering, describing, and analyzing the structures, machinery, organized practices, and formal procedures—the ways in which order is produced.

7. Structures of social action, once so discerned, can be described and analyzed in formal, that is, structural, organizational, logical, atopically contentless, consistent, and abstract terms.

CA studies are committed to the elucidation of "the local logic and emic rationality of situated practices" (ten Have, 1999, p. 199). Broadly speaking, inquiry has been pursued by researchers in two traditions—similar to those already outlined within the broader field of EM—"pure" or "straight-ahead" CA and "applied" CA.

Now what do you think EM studies are, what their focus is, how they are carried out, and the purpose for conducting them?

"Pure" Conversation Analysis

"Pure" (ten Have, 1999) or "straight-ahead" CA (Heap, 1997) examines the institution of interaction (Heritage, 1997, p. 162). This type of work produces "fine grained sequential analyses with the goal of describing and documenting the operation and organization of sequences of talk-in-interaction" (Heap, 1997, p. 218). Sacks, Schegloff, and Jefferson (1974) investigated the mechanism of turn taking in minute detail. Subsequent work on sequential organization and turn taking illuminates some of the features—normally taken for granted—of conversation that Silverman summarized as follows (1998, p. 103):

1. People talk one at a time.
2. Speaker change recurs.
3. Sequences that are two utterances long and are adjacently placed may be "paired" activities.
4. Activities can be required to occur at "appropriate" places.
5. Certain activities are "chained."

Researchers seeking to investigate further these gross features of talk-in-interaction have investigated many facets of the sequential organization of talk-in-interaction. For example, analysts have investigated such local features as the preference for certain kinds of utterances such as agreements (Frankel, 1990);

openings and closings (Button, 1990; Schegloff & Sacks, 1973; Zimmerman, 1992); topic management and topic shift (Jefferson, 1993); repairs (McHoul, 1990); agreement and disagreement (Bilmes, 1991; Greatbatch, 1992; Pomerantz, 1984); introducing bad news (Maynard, 1991, 1996); and troubles telling (Goldsmith, 1999; Jefferson, 1984, 1988).[4] Reports of pure CA are commonly addressed to a professional audience of conversation analysts and students working in the field.

"Applied" Conversation Analysis

Researchers working in an applied CA tradition seek to examine the management of social institutions *in* interaction (Heritage, 1997, p. 162). Applied CA studies add an ethnographic dimension and are concerned with investigating the organization of talk involved in the accomplishment of some interactional encounter (Heap, 1997, p. 218). In speaking of research in the field of education, Heap listed the work of Mehan (1979), Baker (1997c), and Baker and Keogh (1995) as exemplifying an applied CA approach. In these studies, researchers investigated the structure and organization of talk in different educational settings—these being a classroom, a staff meeting, and teacher–parent interviews, respectively. With reference to the use of CA in education, Heap (1997) noted a "productive tension" between applied and straight-ahead studies (p. 223). He argued that although the former can tell us "what to look at," the latter "tells us how to look, and what we must do in order to show how the features of institutions . . . are produced *in situ*, in real time, interactionally." Although Heap was primarily addressing work in educational settings, researchers working within other disciplines might usefully adopt this concept.

In applied CA studies such as those cited above, the social order of institutional settings is investigated through the tools of CA and membership categorization analysis (MCA). MCA investigates the categories that members of society use in their descriptions (Silverman, 1998, p. 77), and Sacks' work in this area was intertwined with his investigation of the sequential organization of talk. Sacks formulated a number of rules and definitions to explain how members employ categories.[5] Jayyusi (1984) (see also Eglin & Hester, 1992) significantly extended Sacks' work in this area, whereas Baker (2000) and Lepper (2000) demonstrated how this work might be applied to the analysis of texts, and Emmison and Smith (2000) showed how MCA might be used to analyze visual data. Central to an understanding of MCA is the notion of the "membership categorization device"

---

[4]This list merely provides some examples concerning a small amount of topics. Extensive bibliographies may be found at http://www2.fmg.uva.nl/emca/

[5]For further explanation, see Sacks (1992) and Silverman (1998).

(MCD), which Sacks (1972) defined as

> any collection of membership categories, containing at least a category, which may
> be applied to some population containing at least a member, so as to provide, by the
> use of some rules of application, for the pairing of at least a population member and a
> categorization device member. A device is then a collection plus rules of application.
> (p. 332)

Watson (cited in Silverman, 1998) has outlined the central features of Sacks'
work in MCA as follows:

1. A concern with social activities: "Categorization was to be analyzed as a
   culturally methodic (procedural) activity rather than in terms of an inert
   cultural grid."
2. Categories came to have meaning in specific contexts: "He did not see categories as 'storehouses' of decontextualized meaning."
3. Category use did not reflect psychological processes (such as information
   processing) but depended on cultural resources that are public, shared, and
   transparent.
4. The issue was not the content of the categories but the procedures through
   which they are invoked and understood. (pp. 129–130)

These features provide a glimpse of the type of issues that MCA addresses and
show how this work focuses on the contextual, social, and practical procedures
that members rely on to make sense of social action and interaction in everyday
settings.

What does it mean that "order is a produced order"and that "the parties orient
to that order themselves, that is, this order is not an analyst's conception"?

I have cited some examples of applied CA studies from the field of education.
Applied CA work is not restricted to this field, however. Just as ethnomethodological studies have been fruitfully conducted in many disciplines and fields of
study, so have CA studies. In the next section, I examine further how a researcher
might examine research problems from a CA perspective.

THE PRACTICE OF CONVERSATION ANALYSIS

As noted earlier, work in CA relies on transcripts of talk-in-interaction from either audio- or video-recorded events. Sacks (1992) was highly critical of the use
of interview studies as used in ethnographic work of the time (such as the Chicago

school). For instance, he noted in 1964 that

> the trouble with [interview studies] is that they're using informants, that is, they're asking questions of their subjects. That means that they're studying the categories that Members use . . . they are not investigating their categories by attempting to find them in the activities in which they're employed. (Vol. 1, p. 27)

Therefore, Sacks' early studies in CA utilized transcriptions of naturally occurring data—such as telephone calls to a suicide prevention center and a series of group therapy sessions (ten Have, 1999, pp. 6–7). Indeed, Goodwin and Heritage (1990, p. 289) noted that only data drawn from "real life" situations should be analyzed and exclude the use of role plays, experiments, or invented materials. As has already been noted, CA studies have expanded far beyond an initial interest in mundane conversation and telephone calls. This has already been noted in the extensive work devoted to the study of talk at work (Drew & Heritage, 1992) and other institutional settings such as schools.

> Why is it so crucial that the study of talk come from "naturally occurring data"? What other ways is talk studied?

More recently, researchers have examined interview talk using the tools of CA (Baker, 1983, 1997b, 2002; Baker & Johnson, 1998; Johnson, 1999; Mazeland & ten Have, 1998; Rapley, 2001; Rapley & Antaki, 1998; Roulston, 2000b). In their discussions of CA, Hutchby and Wooffitt (1998) and ten Have (1999) devoted significant sections to how interview talk—ranging from standardized telephone surveys through to open-ended unstructured interviews—might be productively analyzed using CA. Although other qualitative researchers commonly investigate interview data for the content of what is said, the focus of EM and CA analyses of such data is on a different order of data (e.g., how accounts are produced or the social orders invoked by speakers).

Whatever the choice of data, how might the analyst begin? First, as Myers (2000, p. 194) pointed out, detailed transcripts of talk-in-interaction must be undertaken. Transcription conventions developed by Gail Jefferson were outlined in numerous sources (Atkinson & Heritage, 1999; Hutchby & Wooffitt, 1998; Psathas & Anderson, 1990; ten Have, 1999). As Ochs (1979) and Baker (1997d) noted, transcription practices are not neutral, and the level of detail included in any transcription requires the analyst to make theoretical choices that are consequential not only for how research participants are represented, but how data might be analyzed. For the type of work under consideration here, prior to transcribing any talk, the analyst needs to ask what details are relevant to the type of analysis being undertaken. Who will be the audience? Will the report be addressed to an audience of conversation analysts or lay members in the analyst's own disciplinary area of study? Answers to these questions will determine the detail required in the transcription. For example, if turn taking is to be examined in depth, then details of any overlaps, interruptions, and pauses in recorded talk are essential to the analysis. A detailed guide to transcription practice may be found in ten Have (1999). To undertake CA, the analyst needs to familiarize him- or herself with literature within the field to gain an awareness of features of talk that could be of interest. Further, the analyst commonly undertakes transcriptions, because these are an acquired skill requiring practice.

Different analysts recommend a variety of procedures to beginning conversation analytic work. Schegloff, who was a fellow student with Harvey Sacks "at the University of California at Berkeley," proposed an initial procedure for "roughing the surface" of a transcript (cited by ten Have, 1999, p. 104):

Analytic Procedure 1

1. Check the episode carefully in terms of turn-taking: the construction of turns, pauses, overlaps, and so forth; make notes of any remarkable phenomena, especially on any "disturbances" in the fluent working of the turn-taking system.
2. Then look for sequences in the episode under review, especially adjacency pairs and their sequels.
3. Finally, note any phenomena of repair, such as repair initiators, actual repairs, and others.

As may be seen from this sequence of steps, Schegloff's interest in CA is within the arena of pure CA; therefore, sequential organization of talk is stressed in this guide.

Another approach to examining transcripts has been demonstrated by Pomerantz and Fehr (1997). These authors presented and demonstrated a five-step process:

Analytic Procedure 2

1. Select a sequence.
2. Characterize the actions in the sequence.
3. Consider how the speakers' packaging of actions, including their selection of reference terms, provides for certain understandings of the actions performed and the matters talked about. Consider the options for the recipient that are set up by that packaging.
4. Consider how the timing and taking of turns provide for certain understandings of the actions and the matters talked about.

5. Consider how the ways the actions were accomplished implicate certain identities, roles, relationships, or all of these factors for the interactants.

This guide differs from the one offered by Schegloff in significant ways. First, although turn taking (see Step 4) is considered, identification of the "actions" being accomplished by speakers and how those actions are "packaged" are included in the sequence.[6] Second, the identities, roles, and relationships invoked by speakers in the sequence of talk are considered. This sequence of steps would be a useful starting point to those analysts interested in pursuing applied CA work. At this point, it is worth mentioning a dividing point between practitioners of pure and applied CA. Information that is external to what can be seen and heard in recordings is excluded from analyses within the pure CA tradition. In contrast, those doing applied CA may well be interested in external phenomena (such as roles, identities, and relations of individuals) that are not explicitly invoked in the interaction (Heap, 1997, p. 223).

> Revisit "pure" and "applied" CA. In your estimation, what are the important differences? Is one a more effective research methodology than the other?

For those interested in investigating institutional talk by way of an applied CA approach, the work of Drew and Heritage (1992) may be of relevance. Heritage (1997, pp. 163–164) directed the analyst to search for three features in institutional talk:

1. Institutional interaction normally involves the participants in specific goal orientations that are tied to institution-relevant identities: doctor and patient, teacher and pupil, and so on.
2. Institutional interaction involves special constraints on what will be treated as allowable contributions to the business at hand.
3. Institutional talk is associated with inferential frameworks and procedures that are particular to specific institutional contexts (see also McHoul, 1978).

By locating these features of institutional talk, Heritage (1997) argued that a unique "fingerprint" of institutional interaction may be identified that includes "specific tasks, identities, constraints on conduct and relevant inferential procedures that the participants deploy and are oriented to in their interactions" (p. 164). Heritage suggested six basic places to probe for the

---

[6]This is not to suggest that Schegloff would not be interested in these features of talk. To the contrary, the steps outlined in Analytic Procedure 1 merely set forth an initial sequence of steps to inspect a data set.

"institutionality" of interaction as outlined above and demonstrates what to look for in data.

Analytic Procedure 3

1. Turn-taking
2. Overall structural organization of the interaction
3. Sequence organization
4. Turn design
5. Lexical choice
6. Epistemological and other forms of asymmetry

Taken together, the features of institutional talk as outlined by Heritage and the places to look for these in data present a clear demonstration of how one might examine data in any institutional setting. The analyst may find, however, that any particular sequence of talk may feature sections that are more "institutional" than others.

I conclude this section by presenting a fourth series of analytic steps proposed by ten Have (1999, pp. 107–108):

Analytic Procedure 4

1. Work through the transcript in terms of a restricted set of analytically distinguished but interlocking "organizations":
   • Turn-taking organization
   • Sequence organization
   • Repair organization
   • Organization of turn construction, or design
2. Working turn-by-turn, consider the data in terms of practices relevant to these essential organizations.
3. Present "remarks" as "analytic descriptions" on the transcript, or as "codes and observations" in a separate column.
4. Try to formulate some general observations, statements, or rules that tentatively summarize what has been seen.

This sequence of steps includes a number of procedures seen in steps previously considered. What ten Have's (1999) sequence contributed is some practical features of analysis that may be helpful to the novice. For example, consider each utterance turn by turn and formulate a description of each. Although this is certainly an implicit feature of the sequences of analysis shown earlier (see, for example, Step 2 of Pomerantz's and Fehr's guide), here it is stated explicitly. To summarize, each of the analysts cited here focuses on different aspects of the talk at hand, and each analytic procedure provides a different point of entry into the method known as CA.

Some Examples

In this section, I include short excerpts from transcripts that demonstrate an analysis of talk-in-interaction from different types of settings. These excerpts are drawn from a 3-year study of music teachers' work (Roulston, 2000a).

Excerpt 1: Pedagogic Interaction

In the following excerpt, we see an example of the initiation–response–evaluation sequence (see arrowed lines below) identified by Mehan (1979). This talk is found commonly in classroom talk, and here we see it in evidence in a music lesson with fourth- and fifth-grade students. At lines 2 and 5, the teacher provides an initiation in the form of an invitation to bid (for a response).

1.　　　T　　OK ((pointing to the musical notation of the note G on chalkboard))
2. (I)　→　so that's a?
3. (R) Ss→ G
4. (E) T → G good
5. (I)　→　What's this one then ((on the chalkboard, draws the note E on staff))
6. (R) Ss→ E
7.　　　T　　hands up hands up hands up
8. (E)　→　good show me a G on your recorder please
9.　　　　　the (map) of the fingering is down the bottom of the page
10.　　　　　(3.0)

In this interaction, the students respond as a chorus to their teacher's questions (lines 3 and 6) with short, factual responses (in this case, letter names). At line 7, after they have delivered a correct response, the teacher gives further instructions as to how students should respond (by raising their hands). This utterance provides a clue as to how turn taking should take place within this particular classroom—that is, the teacher should normally nominate the next speaker. This appears not to have occurred at line 6 (and possibly line 3).[7] Here is an example of reflexivity in action. The teacher's utterance at line 7 is directed specifically to the students' utterances at lines 3 and 6, yet also contributes to the constitution of the setting itself (i.e., "doing" classroom talk in a music lesson). This interaction

---

[7]This transcription is taken from an audiotape, complemented by descriptions from field notes. However, this type of interaction shows how video recordings of events can provide material for more precise analysis by showing us, for example, whether or not the teacher gestured to a student or students to provide a response.

was produced within a regular classroom setting when the music teacher visited for the weekly 30-minute lesson. Here, the production of "music" knowledge is accomplished through the use of the symbolic language of musical notation (to which the teacher refers on the chalkboard), and physical actions involving the production of musical sound (in this case, utilization of recorders by the teacher and her students). At line 8 the students are directed to "show" the teacher the finger pattern for the musical pitch G on the recorder (an instruction to act), but at line 9, she gives an instruction to "look." Although symbolic representations of the pitch G may be found in staff notation on the chalkboard (lines 1–3), and "down the bottom of the page" (line 8) in a diagrammatic representation of the finger pattern found in the music books on students' desks, at this point the students must produce the correct bodily expression of a G. Through her use of the direction "Show me," the teacher is asking her students to prepare their body for the production of a sound by placing their fingers in the appropriate position on their instruments. Thus, at line 10, we have a 3-second silence rather than the production of an actual musical tone.

Although the students in Excerpt 1 have little problem identifying *what* their teacher is looking for with her questions (lines 2 and 5) and producing correct verbal responses, at other times, speakers must "sort out" and jointly elaborate on the business at hand. This may be seen in the next example. In Excerpt 2 below, we see how speakers elaborate at length on the meaning of an interview question. This occurs when the respondent, Maria (M) is faced with a question for which she can provide no immediate "satisfactory" response. To the researcher's question, "What kind of things would happen on a good day?" this first-year teacher provides an immediate response that she immediately discounts as inappropriate and facetious (line 3). At line 5, she notes that this is a "hard question," and after a pause of 3 seconds, asks for an example from the researcher. Over several utterances, the researcher and her respondent negotiate the kinds of responses that would be appropriate in this "research setting" (lines 8–15), and it is not until line 16 (not shown here) that Maria begins to formulate a response to the researcher's initial questions at lines 1 and 2.

Excerpt 2: An Interview Question

1. R   yeah .hhh u::m (.) next one is just *what* u:m is a good day for you
       w- what
2.   kind of things would happen (1.0) on a good day
3. M   u::m get a lunch time? no [heh heh heh um
4. R   [heh heh heh ·hhh
5. M   o::h (.) it's a hard question
6.   (3.0)

      7. M   can you give me an example?
      8. R   well u:m what kinds of *things* (.) u:m (.) I guess work together for
              you to
      9.   enjoy a *day* cos you said that you enjoyed going to [base school] so=
      10. M   = yeah so w- why would I enjoy=
      11. R   =yeah
      12. M   (the day)
      13. R   what kinds of things *happen* yeah mm
      14. M   [u : : m
      15. R   [or don't happen maybe as the case may be mm
      16. (2.0)

In this excerpt, we see the researcher responding to her participant's request for clarification (line 7) by reformulating her initial question no less than three times. The initial question, "What kinds of things would happen on a good day?" (lines 1 and 2) is reformulated successively as "what kinds of *things* (.) u:m (.) I guess work together for you to enjoy a day" (line 8); "what kinds of things *happen*" (line 13); and finally, "or don't happen maybe as the case may be" (line 15). Although Maria has asked for an example of what might constitute a "good day," in her reformulated questions the researcher has resisted providing explicit examples.

Through close analysis of interview talk such as this sequence, it is possible to illuminate how the researcher and respondent on this occasion worked closely to formulate the topic of talk. We also see the kinds of interactional difficulties faced by interviewees responding to questions that do not match their personal experience. In Excerpt 2, we see Maria working hard to engage in the "work" of the research interview—that is, to produce appropriate responses for the researcher.

Excerpt 3: Meeting Talk

      1. MT   u::m (.) and I was actually thinking this year of starting up the um (.)
      2.   tour around (.) um the nursing homes and things like that again
      3.   (1.0)
      4. MT   cos I [think that's one of the
      5. P   [that wouldn't be part of your fund-raising=
      6. MT   =no that's [wouldn't be part of fund-raising that's just an extra thing I
      7. M   [no
      8. MT   was thinking about that I was thinking (cos I used to be)
      9. P   so so you haven't the idea of the going to the local *shopping* center and
      10.   en*hancing* the school is on *one* day is not on?

In Excerpt 3, taken from an inaugural music support committee meeting held at an elementary school, we see a second-year music teacher (MT) suggesting an item for a list of performance activities for the music program. This is that of a "tour around the nursing homes." At line 4, she continues by beginning an account for her proposal, but is interrupted by the principal (P), who reorients the talk to the business of the meeting—that of "fund-raising." This reorientation retrospectively acknowledges that the music teacher's proposal does not serve this purpose. With agreement for the principal's exclusion of this "item" to the formation of the list at hand by a mother (line 7) and the music teacher (line 6), the music teacher's account (begun at line 4) is discontinued at line 8.

Having discounted the music teacher's item for the list of "fund-raising" events, the principal makes a new proposal at lines 9 and 10, this time referring and re-presenting a suggestion that he has made in earlier talk. This short excerpt of interaction from a meeting shows how one speaker may discount a proposal by another and deftly accomplish a topic switch back to the "business" at hand. The talk examined here shows how participants in a meeting routinely orient to an "agenda," and certain speakers (e.g., the chair, or, in this case, the principal) can routinely change topics without being held accountable. In this case, this is accomplished by the utterance "that wouldn't be part of your fund-raising" seen at line 5.

In each of these examples presented here, I have located some of the different activities within talk that might be attended to through CA. For instance, in the preceding example, I have examined the talk for the "management of proposals."

At this point, what purposes do you conclude are served using CA research? Has your position changed regarding the importance of this research method? If so, how, and if not, why not?

CONCLUSIONS

As one might expect, advocates for ethnomethodological and conversation analytic approaches are laudatory in their claim for this approach to research. For example, Mehan and Wood (1975) envisioned EM as a "form of life" and a "collection of practices" comparable to those used by artists and craftspeople (p. 238). These authors argue that in "committing itself above all to reporting, social sciences has shown itself to be a form of life that denigrates the integrity of non-Western, nonmale, nonliberal, nontechnological realities" (p. 238).

Mehan and Wood (1975, p. 238) suggested that by investigating topics that have been previously overlooked and taken for granted, ethnomethodological studies can undermine this practice. Atkinson (1988) regarded EM's contribution to sociology as significant, noting that the "foundations laid by Garfinkel and Sacks have resulted in a radical reappraisal of sociology's subject-matter and procedures" (p. 462).

However, the fields of ethnomethodological and conversation analytic studies have been marked by both internal divisions and unrelenting external criticism (see Silverman, 1998, for one discussion). Rather than summarize these arguments here,[8] I take Silverman's (1998, p. 184) point that rather than taking sides in a debate, we are better served to examine what these approaches offer the field of qualitative research.

Silverman (1998) argued that Sacks' chief legacy was that of an "aesthetic for social research" that encompasses smallness, slowness, clarity, and nonromanticism." How might this work in practice? First, EM and CA offer the researcher in naturalistic settings many possibilities for changing the questions that might be asked (Baker, 1997a, p. 46). Taking the field of education as but one example, EM and CA studies have contributed in significant ways to show how educational problems—related to, but not exclusive to, topics such as classroom talk, classroom knowledge production, or classroom literacy—might be formulated differently, where they might be located, and how we might look at them (Baker, 1997a, p. 49).

Whether the ethnomethodologically motivated researcher investigates social interaction in interview data, or the socially situated and locally produced events that make up our everyday world in personal, workplace, or institutional settings, this approach to qualitative research provides a distinctive approach. For researchers in pursuit of theory-driven prescriptions for solutions to social problems, this approach to research will likely prove incomprehensible. For others, however, the self-reflective practice promoted by the detailed and in-depth analysis of real-world and everyday issues fundamental to this approach to research will be inviting. For example, in the study from which the earlier analytic examples were taken, the tools of EM and CA provided a means through which social interaction from three different settings—interviews, classroom interaction, and a naturally occurring meeting—might be investigated. This approach to the analysis of data enabled me as a researcher to not only examine familiar surroundings from a very different perspective, but also to challenge previous assumptions about the social world and qualitative research. I invite you to utilize the approach outlined in this chapter and to view anew "the world-known-in-common" as an "amazing practical accomplishment" (Silverman, 1997, p. 250).

---

[8]Sharrock and Anderson (1986) addressed charges against EM such as that it is (1) naive and simplistic, and (2) subjectivist and relativist. See Sharrock and Anderson (1986) for an overview of early critiques. Silverman (1998) addressed five criticisms of Sacks' work in CA—trivial topics, trivial data, use of nonrandom and incomplete data, and neglect of social structure.

NOTES

Transcription conventions:

T	Teacher
S	Student
R	Researcher
( )	words spoken, not audible
(( ))	transcriber's description
[	two speakers' talk overlaps at this point
[	
=	no interval between turns
?	interrogative intonation
(2.0)	pause timed in seconds
(.)	small untimed pause
ye::::ah	prolonged sound on word "yeah"
why	emphasis
YEAH	louder sound to surrounding talk
heh heh	laughter
-hhh	in-breath
hhh-	out-breath
°yes°	softer than surrounding talk

10

Fieldwork Traditions: Ethnography and Participant Observation

Judith Preissle and Linda Grant
University of Georgia

MEET THE AUTHORS

Judith Preissle and **Linda Grant** have been colleagues and collaborators at the University of Georgia since the mid-1980s, where they both are affiliated faculty in the Women's Studies Program. They have written together on gender study, qualitative research methods, the ethnography of education, and together with Xue Lan Rong on immigration and education. For 4 years in the 1990s, they led summer workshops in fieldwork methods for students from across the social and professional sciences from other universities. They have also eaten a lot of meals together, counseled each other on their gardens, and seen their ways through various academic crises.

Judith works in the social foundations of education program and in the College of Education's qualitative and ethnographic research program. Her degrees are a bachelor's degree in history from Grinnell College in 1964, a master of arts (from the University of Minnesota) in 1971, and a doctorate in education (from Indiana University) in 1975, concentrating in anthropology and education. Her major scholarly interests and publications are in sociocultural theory, gender studies, classroom social life, immigration and education, and the ethics, philosophy, and practice of qualitative research. She also enjoys reading, music, gardening, birding, miniature schnauzers, and ballroom dancing.

Linda works in the sociology department in the Franklin College of Arts and Sciences, and she is an adjunct faculty member in the Department of Social Foundations of Education. Her degrees are a bachelor's degree in journalism from the University of Kentucky in 1966, a master of arts in sociology from Wayne State University in 1973, and a doctorate in sociology from the University of Michigan–Ann Arbor in 1981. Currently, she is studying gender and scientific careers, social processes in desegregated classrooms, and the writings of early women sociologists in the United States. Her interests include wildflowers, hiking, herb and vegetable gardening, travel, her granddogs, and collecting old cookbooks, children's books, glassware, and far too many other things.

Fieldwork, the study of something in the natural environment where it occurs or that it inhabits, may be one of the oldest forms of human inquiry. Ancient scholars like Thucydides in Greece and Sima Qian in China studied events as close to firsthand as possible, reflected on them, and interpreted them. These are the basic elements of all fieldwork. Fieldwork traditions form the foundations of disciplines such as biology, botany, astronomy, geology, anthropology, and sociology. In this chapter, we discuss ethnography and participant observation, the two field traditions that developed from anthropology and sociology and that have been elaborated and refined by scholars in other human and professional sciences.

Newcomers to these approaches can be overwhelmed, as we once were, by how fieldwork inquiries are formulated, described, and assessed. Everything has multiple, overlapping labels, and research methods instructors respond to every query for clarification with "It depends." Ethnography and other forms of fieldwork can be particularly frustrating to study, because of the complexity of their origins and their development. Here are some of the questions most frequently posed by novices to ethnography and fieldwork:

1. What is it? What are its boundaries? How is it similar and dissimilar to other forms of inquiry?

2. How is it done? What techniques of data collection, analysis, and writing are used? How do I choose the appropriate ones? What are the determinants and consequences of those choices?

3. Is it good? How do I know if my work is worthwhile? How do I defend it to others such as committee members, editors, and readers? What are its implications and applications? What are its limits?

WHAT IS FIELDWORK?

What is fieldwork, then? Fieldwork in the human and professional sciences almost always is research on some aspect of human behavior in its everyday context. The researcher enters the social world of study, the field, to observe human interaction in that context. Participant observation is a label for research requiring some extent of social participation to document or record the course of ongoing events. The researcher observes through participating in events.

The nature and extent of participation vary, and kinds of participation have been classified in different ways. Raymond Gold (1958) proposed four participant observation roles: the complete participant, the participant as observer, the observer as participant, and the complete observer. Harry Wolcott (1967) was a participant as observer in his position as the village schoolteacher when he studied a Kwakiutl village and school in Canada. He had a role within the community, but he was also known by participants to be studying them. In contrast, researchers who take a complete participant role do not reveal their research intentions to those they study (Humphreys, 1975); these research positions have become increasingly rare, with the growing emphasis on informed consent of those being studied and on the closer monitoring of methods that require deception. Gold's (1958) third position, observer as participant, characterizes shorter forays into the field to gather interviews with individuals in their own environments, such as Thomas Gorman's (1998) interviews with parents in their own homes in his study of parental attitudes toward education. Finally, Gold (1958) formulates the complete observer role as one that requires no participation in social events. The researcher eavesdrops on participants from some position where he or she is un-noticed by them. Participant observation studies conducted in public venues, like David Karp's (1980) study of customers in adult bookstores, involve observations of participants during which they are unaware of the researcher's presence. Like the complete participant role, the complete observer role depends on some level of deception and raises special ethical concerns. Most field workers find themselves working back and forth throughout their data collection along a continuum of roles, primarily between the middle two, but occasionally slipping into one of the complete role positions.

> What experiences have you had with participant observation (or similar ob-servational activities)? What role or roles did you take in your work? How did your role influence your fieldwork?

Ethnography is the study of the culture of a group, usually as that culture is revealed, again, through the course of ongoing events. What makes ethnography separate from other participant observation studies is the emphasis on culture. Such cultures may be contested and unevenly shared among group members, as they are in Daniel Yon's (2000) study of an ethnically diverse Canadian high school, but are still assumed to be identifiable through investigation. Researchers sometimes say they are using participant observation to conduct an ethnography, and the vast majority of ethnographies are produced from observations in the field. However, as Wolcott (1988) noted, "An anthropologist might possibly em-ploy none of the customary field research techniques and still produce an ethno-graphic account (or at least a satisfactory ethnographic reconstruction)" (p. 200). Examples of non-field-based ethnographies are those produced from life histories of survivors of no longer existing communities (Groce, 1985) or from documents or other artifacts that may reveal cultural patterns (Comaroff & Comaroff, 1992).

> What do you think the authors mean by culture? How would you define cul-ture? How does the definition possibly shape field studies?

In this chapter, we examine ethnography and related forms of fieldwork orig-inating in 19th-century social sciences. As Annette Lareau and Jeffrey Schultz (1996, p. 3) emphasized, contemporary human science scholars do not always agree on what constitutes ethnography. The classical model of ethnography was developed primarily by anthropologists to document ways of life around the world presumed to be changing rapidly under the pressures of colonization and Westernization (Boas, 1940; Malinowski, 1922). Researchers took a visible role in a community or culture for an extended period of time and wrote a contex-tualized account attempting to portray the culture from the perspectives of its participants. What scholars mean by the term *ethnography* is further complicated by their practice of using the term to refer both to the process by which research is conducted and its product, the presented account (Agar, 1996).

A looser, broader idea of ethnography developed from the work of sociologists centered in the United States at the University of Chicago (Prus, 1996) and was elaborated by scholars in many other disciplines. This approach initially documented the lives and challenges faced by increasing numbers of urban poor in North America and Europe, whose plight the sociologists sought to ameliorate. We refer to the approach as fieldwork rather than ethnography because it used ethnographic methods of participant observation and intensive interviewing, but did not always demand such deep involvement with a culture or an account written from the perspective of participants. Instead, field workers used a range of roles, from peripheral to distant (Adler & Adler, 1987), and fieldwork roles were expected to shift over time. Accounts might be written from the perspective of an insider or an outsider, and a lively debate ensued about the advantages of differing perspectives (Becker, 1967; Merton, 1972). In its earliest days, Chicago-style fieldwork was coupled with the theoretical perspective of symbolic interactionism and a moral commitment to social activism (Deegan, 1988), but these commitments weakened over time (Fine, 1995) and as fieldwork expanded elsewhere.

Substantial overlaps, rather than clear boundaries, have developed between ethnography and other forms of fieldwork. We regard ethnography as a specialized form of fieldwork, in which culture is a central concept, where deep engagement over time with a culture is expected, and where a central goal is the presentation of an insider's view of that culture. However, because ethnography and other forms of fieldwork were developed by scholars from many different disciplines whose works often mutually influenced one another, formulations of these designs continue to vary from scholar to scholar and discipline to discipline (Gubrium & Holstein, 1997). We envision fieldwork techniques and presentation styles as variable in the degree to which they foreground experiences and perspectives of those studied, versus those doing the study. Ethnography in its classical form foregrounds the culture of the participants, their perspectives of the world, and backgrounds those of the researcher. Other forms of fieldwork might take this same stance, but many do not privilege the perspectives of participants over those of researcher. The theoretical concerns or practical interests of the researcher guide the research more explicitly, and this orientation is reflected in the written account. In our formulation, ethnography as conceptualized and practiced by early anthropologists is a form of fieldwork, but not all forms of fieldwork are ethnography.

Although often discussed as recent developments, insider ethnography and fieldwork within one's own community are longstanding practices in scholarship. W. E. B. DuBois (1899) studied the African American community of Philadelphia. He was invited to undertake the study by a group of philanthropists, because he was himself an African American scholar. The early symbolic interactionist and social theorist George Herbert Mead (1934) studied his own children from the vantage point of his armchair. Ella Cara Deloria wrote about the Sioux community from which she was descended in two genres: anthropological field reports (1933), in which she revealed little of her personal ties to the culture, and a novel, *Waterlily* (1988), in which her personal tribal identity was far more central.[1] Her contemporary Zora Neale Hurston likewise created both fictional (1937) and anthropological accounts (1935) of her fieldwork, in this case among African American communities. Later in the century, Margaret Mead regularly incorporated her daily observations of U.S. culture into astute cross-cultural analyses of human life (1949).

Some methodologists view ethnography as the category of participant observation that focuses on culture. Others view participant observation as an ethnographic technique. We are discussing them as more-or-less parallel, even overlapping, research approaches to underline their disciplinary histories and their conceptual frameworks. Both developed as means of studying and documenting the lives of those presumed to be different from those either funding or conducting the study. The first guide to what may be considered ethnography was written by the French philosopher Joseph-Marie Degérando (1800/1969) to instruct the crew of a French ship on the observations of indigines they expected to encounter on their exploration of the south coast of Australia. Degérando cautioned the French explorers to consider the perspective of indigenous folk themselves to understand responses to the Europeans of "fear, defiance, and reserve":

> The main object, therefore, that should today occupy the attention and zeal of a truly philosophical traveler would be the careful gathering of all means that might assist him to penetrate the thought of the peoples among whom he would be situated, and to account for the order of their actions and relationships . . . to become after a fashion like one of them. (p. 70)

By the end of the century, field workers like Beatrice Webb were attempting to systematize their own practices (published formally in 1926) as they studied the urban poor in Western societies. Throughout this period, researchers struggled to conceptualize their relationships to those they studied. Despite warnings to avoid "going native," field workers sometimes were natives of their settings, as we have shown in the preceding examples. Gold (1958) himself cautioned that risks of overidentification must be balanced against risks of ethnocentrism, which are rejecting "the informant's views without ever getting to the point of understanding them" (p. 220).

---

[1] A first draft of the novel was written at about the same time as her anthropological monograph, but her two anthropological advisers—Ruth Benedict and Franz Boas—disagreed about its importance and the desirability of its publication. Benedict advocated publication as rapidly as possible and attempted to assist in this endeavor. Boas was less favorable. The work was not published until after Deloria's death. She dedicated *Waterlily* to Ruth Benedict, because she always "believed in *Waterlily*."

> How do you see the relationship between ethnography and participant ob-
> servation? What disciplinary concerns, theoretical concerns, or both might
> guide your work in thinking about the type of research Preissle and Grant are
> describing here?

All these inquirers took to their fields, however familiar or strange, notions about human life and how to explain it. All were affected, albeit differently, by the scientific revolution that offered empirical evidence—information gathered by direct, sensory observation—and rational argument as the means to provide explanation and understanding of human life. Fieldwork itself is the eminently empirical method—study by firsthand, direct experience of life.

What to make of these observations and experiences has been the ongoing challenge. Early anthropologists emphasized theories of human differentiation and human similarity. They argued the relative influences on human behavior of biology and society—the nature–nurture controversy. These Westerners puzzled over why human societies differed and postulated the theory of ontogenesis, an invariant development of human society with their own version of civilization as the end result. Likewise, early sociologists addressed questions of human agency versus social structure as determinants of individual behavior and social order—a question unresolved and still central in that discipline.

HOW DO I DO IT?

How do I do it is a deceptively straightforward question, but its answers are complex. Students may approach fieldwork expecting a simple recipe for getting it right, and unfortunately it is sometimes taught that way. Embedded in this question are complex decisions grounded in assumptions about the nature of reality, the creation of knowledge and meanings, and the relationship of objectivity and subjectivity. We discuss the conduct of fieldwork as it is embedded in these philosophical assumptions (see Figure 10.1).

What Is Reality?

Field workers approach research with divergent beliefs about the nature of reality. We draw here on the work of Michael Crotty (1999), who outlined a continuum ranging from realism to idealism. Classical and contemporary fieldwork and ethnography can be located at various points along this continuum. Scholars at the realism end of the continuum work from an assumption that social life has a concrete reality, one that is uniform and that exists beyond the minds of researchers. This reality can be studied using empirical, or sensory, evidence.

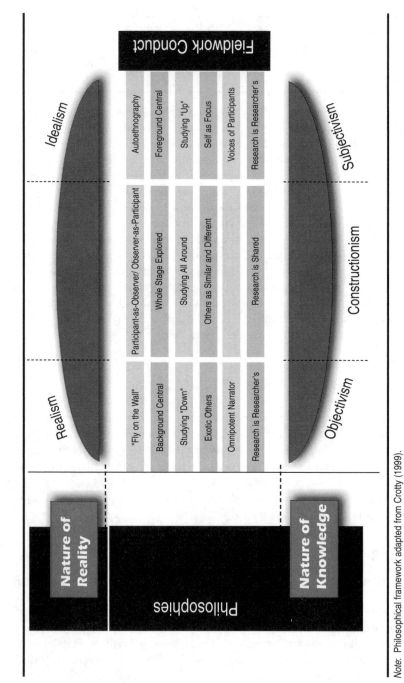

Note: Philosophical framework adapted from Crotty (1999).

FIG. 10.1. Philosophies and fieldwork conduct.

Systematic collection of empirical, not necessarily quantifiable, evidence is expected to provide a coherent portrait of a social setting, replicable within the same historical period.[2] Formal training in fieldwork technique and systematic data collection are thought to be important in producing valid, evidence-based reports that minimize the impact of researcher subjectivity.

Positivistic, quantitative research is based on realism, but so are many fieldwork studies and ethnographies (see Van Maanen, 1988; Wolf, 1992). Most of the early sociological fieldwork, conducted by faculty at the University of Chicago Department of Sociology in cooperation with the Hull House Collective, headed by Jane Addams,[3] was firmly located in the realist tradition. Researchers were interested in addressing problems facing South Side Chicago neighborhoods with large immigrant communities. Their research began with painstaking data collection from fieldwork in these neighborhoods on topics such as quality of dwelling units; work activities of women, men, and children; and family organization. These early researchers sought to document a world they believed to be real but little understood by scholars or policy makers. Their work, with its social reform orientation, embodied assumptions of a single reality to be studied systematically in carefully designed and executed fieldwork research (Deegan & Hill, 1987; Platt, 1995).

At the other end of the continuum in current debates about reality, Crotty (1999) posed idealism, the position that reality is a creation of the human mind and consequently is unstable, configured internally, and variable according to the mind apprehending it. Any social setting or set of events can engender multiple interpretations, inevitably linked to the vantage point of the researcher. The world beyond us may or may not exist only in our minds, but we can perceive and conceive it only with our minds. No commonality may thus be possible in how we understand it. Idealist researchers do not assume that there is a common reality "out there" to be studied, but rather that all accounts are inventions of a human mind (see Krieger, 1985). Unlike many quantitative approaches to social research, fieldwork does not necessarily assume a stable external reality. Rather, fieldworkers often assume that social conditions and meanings are fluid and changeable, and many advocate a fieldwork approach to allow researchers to become a part of this meaning-making activity and to gain perspective on how events develop and change (Blumer, 1969).

The idealist tradition most recently has been elaborated by women and minority scholars, among others, as a challenge to dominant understandings of

---

[2] We here define *empirical* in its classical sense, as evidence gathered through the senses, although we recognize that in recent eras the term empirical is sometimes misused to denote data that are or can be quantified (Polkinghorne, 1983).

[3] Although Addams is often remembered as a social worker, she was a full-time member of the University of Chicago sociology department, one of its most prolific publishers, and an affiliated editor of *The American Journal of Sociology*, the first sociology journal in the United States, published from that department.

reality that subordinate the experiences and perspectives of less powerful people. Many scholars have asserted that what is defined as "reality" is a world seen solely through the eyes of dominant groups. For example, sociologist Dorothy Smith (1987) argued that most sociological accounts are written from the perspective of those who control "the relations of the ruling." She urged scholars to look to the critical rifts—the points at which their experiences and subjective understandings differ from the received wisdom within their disciplines—to find other standpoints from which knowledge can be created. Relatedly, African American sociologist Patricia Hill Collins (1990, 1998) challenged researchers to consider what the world looks like from the vantage points of subordinated groups, such as African American women, who have not typically been part of academic knowledge production (see also Mullings, 1994). To scholars writing from the idealist tradition, it is essential to know researchers' standpoints to apprehend their accounts.

> Locate yourself within the realism–idealism continuum that these authors describe. Explain your reasoning for selecting that particular location in regard to the nature of reality.

Sometimes a researcher's orientation is established before starting fieldwork or ethnography. Beginners' choices often are constrained by the assumptions acceptable within their disciplines, or at least among their advisers and committee members. However, a perspective may emerge or become clarified in the process of fieldwork itself (see Glassner & Hertz, 1999; Hertz, 1997). Often, the movement is away from realism and toward idealism.

Although idealist approaches have been gaining popularity in many human science disciplines recently, this has occurred more rapidly in disciplines where women and scholars of color also have made the greatest inroads: education, anthropology, and speech communication, for example, more so than in sociology, psychology, and political science (see Stacey & Thorne, 1985). Finally, on the realism–idealism continuum, Crotty (1999) himself took the position that the material world exists apart from human consciousness of it, but he attributed all meanings for that material world to the formulations of the human mind. He argued that this view of reality supports the constructionist view of knowledge production, which he endorsed.

How Do We Know Reality?

Stances on reality are linked logically to how we build knowledge about that reality, using such inquiry approaches as fieldwork. Determining how we approach the knowing of reality involves making assumptions about the making of meaning. How objective or subjective are meanings, and what is the role of the self in meaning making? How much should self (versus other) be foregrounded in the research process and especially in the final account?

Building still from the work of Crotty (1999), we design our figure as a continuum of stances researchers take, ranging from objectivist through what he terms "constructionist" to subjectivist. As we elaborate, researchers' stances on meaning making are also linked to their assumptions about the nature of reality. The approaches to fieldwork conduct in the figure can likewise be considered as continua. Researchers may move back and forth along continua or take a single position in a particular study. They also vary in how self-consciously they connect their philosophical assumptions to their fieldwork practice.

Objectivism. The assumption of a single, stable reality lends itself well to an objectivist stance in fieldwork. Objectivism is the position that meaning is independent of any consciousness, that things have intrinsic meanings to be discovered or revealed by inquiry. Because a one-to-one match between observed reality and actual reality is assumed, the researcher uses techniques that allow a one-to-one correspondence between the researcher's observations and relevant aspects of that external reality. If reality exists out there in bounded time, space, and physical surroundings, then well-trained observers should "see" more or less similar things if they use similar systematic means of collecting empirical evidence.

The clearest manifestation of the objectivist stance is the "fly on the wall" technique, which journalists have been urged to cultivate (Hirsch, 1999). They are trained to avoid, or at least conceal, personal biases and stances and to cover "all sides of the story" regardless of personal viewpoints. The assumption is that well-trained journalists can hide or overcome personal biases through professional training so that they do not influence the story at all. A good journalist covers both sides of a political race, for example, develops equally strong ties with each candidate, and writes "fair" and balanced reports, sometimes consciously striving to give equal space or air time to the discussion of particular individuals or sides of an issue. Despite the recent movement toward more personal journalism and the blurring of journalism and entertainment in televised news shows, the classic model of the journalist covering breaking news is still one of detachment and objectivity.

Much early fieldwork and ethnography was influenced by a similar model. Although researchers were urged to use introspection and self-reflection in gathering data, much as journalists were encouraged to follow their hunches and use their "nose for news" in pursuing a breaking story, that process was not to be visible to readers of the final account. From an objectivist stance, the introduction of such material would make the account biased and hence less credible, in part because it would be less replicable by others. Evidence that multiple perspectives on the same event were consistent increased the credibility of the account. For example, in the Watergate incidents reported by Carl Bernstein and Bob Woodward

(1974), *Washington Post* editor Benjamin Bradlee (1995) insisted that each bit of information be confirmed by two, preferably independent, sources before it was printed. The research equivalents of this are techniques such as triangulation, using multiple research techniques to confirm some aspect of the research; member checking, sharing data or tentative interpretations with participants and revising them accordingly; or qualitative variations of reliability coding, verifying whether others classify evidence as the researcher does. The prototype of this approach was described by Leonard Schatzman and Anselm Strauss (1973). They outlined a "naturalist" approach to research in which field workers minimize the effects of their presence in studying a social reality perceived as largely external to them. Although they nevertheless described fieldwork as an emergent and flexible strategy, these authors outlined a series of techniques designed to minimize the intrusion of the researcher into data collection, data analysis, and presentation and writing of the final report.

At the objectivist end of the continuum, researchers report little about themselves or their relationships to those in the setting. The research participants are foregrounded, and self as researcher is backgrounded. Social relationships formed in the field are blurred or even obliterated. To the extent that researchers discuss themselves, it is usually to report mistakes, setbacks, or failures—problems in establishing a fieldwork role with grace, in keeping their emotions from intruding on the research process, or in gaining or maintaining the cooperation of key informants. These discussions often occur in methodological appendices, apart from the body of the text, or even in separate publications (compare Wolcott's 1967 account of schooling in a Kwakiutl village in Canada with his 1974 reflections on his relationships with the students).

Although approaches depending on the "researcher as instrument" (Pelto, 1970), where data are the recorded perceptions of the field worker, might appear inconsistent with objectivism, classical fieldwork has been written from a number of stances, including objectivist positions. From the perspective of readers trying to make sense of accounts or of novices hoping to emulate research practices (Cohen, 2000), values of objectivity and norms of silence on certain actions of researchers have removed from written accounts such important knowledge as sexual liaisons between researcher and participant (Wolcott, 1990a), covert espionage work by supposed social researchers (Horowitz, 1967), or ordinary human friendships (Hansen, 1976).

First, claims for the objectivist "fly on the wall" stance have been critiqued as naive, unattainable, and insensitive to the perspectives and autonomy of participants in the course of research (Fine, 1993). Powerful illustrations of this critique were offered by sociologist Barrie Thorne (1978) and educational researcher Alan Peshkin (1988). Each discussed an attempt to establish a neutral stance in a cultural milieu where such a position was impossible. For example, Thorne's (1978) attempts at neutrality and balance in her study of two draft-resistance groups with similar political stances but different tactical preferences were thwarted by the practices of one group. Its activities were episodic and dramatic rather than routinized. To do participant observation with this group, she had to become involved in the crisis-laden acts dominant among their activities—causing the other group to see her as a partisan of "them" rather than "us." Similarly, educational researcher Peshkin (1988) discussed the futility of trying to maintain a neutral stance in his study of a fundamental religious community and school whose members would not acknowledge a position of neutrality and whose doctrine allowed only two possible categories for him: a convert or a potential target for conversion.

Researchers discover that they are not wholly in control of roles and options in fieldwork, no matter how carefully they have designed their studies or mastered their techniques. Second, critics argue that the supposedly neutral, objectivist stance is a position of power, privilege, and control. This critique, elaborated more fully in chapters by Johnson-Bailey (Chap. 8), Lather (Chap. 12), and Noblit (Chap. 11) in this volume, argues that typical objective researchers exercise dominance and power by learning more about their participants' lives than they reveal about their own, overwriting others' stories with interpretations of their own and nearly always garnering more benefits and suffering fewer risks from the research process and product than do the research participants. As we have noted previously, Smith (1987) emphasized that priorities and methodologies established in academia are by no means divorced from power arrangements in society. They help to create and legitimate forms of knowledge and discourses in which researchers are more powerful than participants. Researchers, not participants, decide who will and will not be studied, which incidents will be reported and which will be shielded from scrutiny, and whose interpretation will be represented in the final account. These are not neutral decisions but expressions of power. Not surprisingly, those who traditionally have been marginalized in the production of formal knowledge in the academy are more critical of how so-called neutral scholarship represents a distinctive perspective, despite disclaimers to the contrary. Feminist scholars, minority scholars, and anthropologists who have studied developing societies and oppressed groups have been on the forefront of these critiques (Hymes, 1972; Lather, 1991; Mongia, 1996).

Constructionism. Crotty (1999) claimed that most current fieldwork is done from the middle positions of constructionism. The many varieties of constructionism (Velody & Williams, 1998) and their relation constructivism (Fosnot, 1996) assume that knowledge is created by an interaction between the knower and the known: "Subject and object emerge as partners in the generation of meaning" (Crotty, 1999, p. 9). This stance often emerges after field workers attempt, and fail at, an objectivist stance. Constructionism has been elaborated by anthropologists, who reflexively analyzed relationships between self and other in a variety of developing societies around the globe (Clifford & Marcus, 1986; Geertz, 1973) and by other social scientists espousing uses of empathy and introspection in field-work analysis (Blumer, 1969; Reinharz, 1979).

These and other researchers, reflexively mulling the actualities of fieldwork experience, questioned both the possibility and the desirability of a nonin-trusive position toward human and social settings (see Behar, 1996). In some instances, researchers' abilities to empathize with others, to relate participant triumphs, challenges, and pain to their own, is a strength and a hallmark of field-work (Reinharz, 1986). Indeed, fieldwork can be a process of self-discovery, where researchers learn as much about themselves—sometime more—than about those who are the participants in their study (Daniels, 1983; Ellis, 1991). Immersion in uncomfortable and unfamiliar circumstances—for example, in the shoes of a novice in the Moonie religious movement (Bromley & Shupe, 1995) or a pan-handler on an urban street (Lankeneau, 1999)—can create a valuable source of experiential knowledge unattainable from the "fly on the wall," minimally in-trusive, stance. The knowledge can enrich the validity of the interpretation. In anthropology, the field workers' grappling with the contrast between their own and their participants' cultures becomes a crucial source of social analysis (Wax, 1971).

In this section of the continuum, reality is seen as a construction via ongoing interaction between the self and the other (society, culture) in a physical and ma-terial world, and knowledge is based on meanings developed in social contexts. Herbert Blumer's (1969) notion of the "obdurate nature of reality" is relevant here because physical and material aspects of the world, as well as social and cultural history, place limitations on what researchers observe. From this stance, some as-pects of the world a researcher studies may be more "real," or knowable in an empirical sense, than others (Azevedo, 1997). In Jeanne Weiler's (2000) study of the experiences in an alternative high school of a diverse group of working-class women students, she treated their grade point averages and courses completed as stable, concrete, "real" indicators of their school achievement. In contrast, her conceptualization of their identity formation and the place of educational attain-ment in it was based on the sense individuals made of their experiences, and she made a case for how these differ by their individual histories and their racial and ethnic standpoints.

In the constructionist section of the scale, researchers become acutely aware that their studies are collaborations between themselves and their participants, who may cooperate or not, reveal or conceal information, and even allow or refuse to grant the researcher any access at all. A field worker's role as an insider or an outsider to the setting might be critical and might also be transformed in the course of the research. Insiders studying their own communities may become increasingly alienated from them as they produce accounts unpalatable to their comrades. Or, conversely, a researcher who begins as an outsider may become fully engulfed in the setting and the concerns of its constituent members, in the extreme case going native and subordinating research goals to the full participant member goals or foregoing the research altogether (Adler & Adler, 1987). More frequently, researchers discover that they are neither wholly insider nor outsider to a community or that their stances differ with different community members (Beoku-Betts, 1994; Reissman, 1987; Zavella, 1996; Zinn, 1979). Research is thus not necessarily replicable from one researcher to another, because each establishes a unique relationship with those in a setting (May & Patillo-McCoy, 2000). Multiple perspectives and multiple accounts illuminate variable aspects of reality.

For constructionists, producing a credible account also requires greater revelation of self. We have previously discussed the researcher as an instrument of data collection, and constructionists emphasize likewise the researcher's role in interpretation. Through reflexivity, field workers provide readers or other audiences insight into how their perspectives develop. Reflexivity is the field workers' self-conscious and critical study of their own standpoints and assumptions and of how these change or remain stable throughout the fieldwork and analysis and in relationship to participants, funding sources, and other interested parties (Alvesson & Skoldberg, 2000; Ball, 1990). Because the analysis depends on the web of social relationships formed in the field, audiences need an in-depth understanding of these relationships to be able to comprehend the final product. Although constructionism calls for greater revelation of self and a greater appreciation of how subjectivity can enrich research, most researchers working from this stance still foreground participant and setting more so than self and draw on multiple sources of evidence, including observations from the field, but also on their own reflections on their evidence in the production of the account.

Crotty (1999) regarded the label "constructionism" as a broad umbrella for many forms of fieldwork and ethnography, including symbolic interactionism, ethnomethodology, grounded theory approaches, and the like (see Garrick, 1999, for a critique of the philosophical assumptions in these traditions). The degree to which subjectivity is drawn on and valued varies across these approaches. Nevertheless, they share the notion that the process and the product of research are an interaction between the researcher and the outside world.

Subjectivism. Subjectivism is the position that the knower imposes meaning on the known. The known plays no role here; the knower uses past experience, dreams, or other sources to attribute meaning to the known. Researchers working from an idealist stance view all forms of research as inherently subjective. The very frames of meaning by which we comprehend the world (e.g., words, conceptual categories derived from our academic disciplines) are linked to social history and subjective experience. The evidence gathered during research is never separable from researchers' selves and is inextricably linked to the perspectives of the researchers, who are the only instruments of data collection. Rather than seeking a single meaning or interpretation, researchers explore the multiple, contradictory, and multilayered meanings inherent in a setting or an event. The meaning of any report derives not from the account itself, but from the interpretations placed on it by audiences and readers. Accounts may thus be read differently by different persons and in varying historical periods and cultural milieus.

Researchers working in this tradition try to give a more authentic, or at least a more introspective, account of self in the conduct of fieldwork. Because they believe that all knowledge is grounded in subjective experience, they try to convey as much as possible about themselves as the implementor and reporter of research. The prototypical form of subjectivist research is autoethnography, in which researchers themselves become the focal point of study (Ellis, 1991; Ronai, 1992). In this form of research, the field and other players within it sometimes fade to the background, the milieu in which the self-ethnography is developed. Issues of power and domination, in the course of data collection, analysis, presentation of the report, or efforts to affect the usage of knowledge that human scientists produce, are problematized (Davies, 1992; Lather, 1991; May, 2001). Alternative interpretations, rather than being suppressed or marginalized, are incorporated into the account, and audiences can become involved in the analysis of primary data. Scholars usefully draw on subjectivity by studying groups of which they are a part (Zavella, 1996), involving as collaborators those with genuine commitments in a field (Lather & Smithies, 1997), developing presentations with research participants (Lee & Jackson, 1992), or becoming involved in the real-world application of knowledge generated by research (Eder & Corsaro, 1999).

Scholars working in the subjectivist tradition do not regard presentation forms as neutral, either. Traditional modes of scholarly communication blunt subjectivity; they privilege the concerns of academic discourse (e.g., building theory) over those of research participants (e.g., direct action to counter social problems). Therefore, scholars embracing a subjectivist stance have experimented with alternative means of presenting research so that form better represents content rather than distorting it. Such forms have included poetry (L. Richardson, 1993), illustrated fiction (M. Richardson, 1990), performance science (McCall & Becker, 1990), multivocal reading (Ellis & Bochner, 1992), and film (Myerhoff, 1983). These representations are designed to portray the complexity of the study and the perspectives of those whose voices have been distorted in conventional presentations; they reveal an emotional depth for such experiences as death and grief or sexual exploitation, often flattened and diminished in traditional academic discourse.

Because subjectivist scholars regard self as central to knowledge generation, they share a great deal about themselves, their emotions, and their relations with others in the field in their accounts. Often, they study themselves and their experiences through critical life events, such as Norman Denzin's (1987a, 1987b) accounts of alcoholism and recovery from the perspective of a scholar with a family history of alcoholism or Carolyn Ellis' (1995) account of the death of and her grieving for her longtime partner. These reports involve revelations of private aspects of self, such as pain, humiliation, embarrassment, failure, and the like, and they may take on a confessional character. Scholars who undertake these studies may seek to reverse the power dynamics of greater shielding of self, which otherwise characterize conventional fieldwork reports.

These subjectivist approaches are controversial in most human science disciplines, although they are currently more acceptable in some fields than in others. They have been criticized by scholars whose work falls more toward the objectivist end of the continuum and reflects assumptions of a common reality. Critics charge that these newer forms of presentation are self-indulgent and narcissistic dialogues more appropriate for private writings, conversations, or therapy sessions than for scholarly venues. An even greater concern is that the field or social setting in which the account is based may be obliterated, relegated to a backdrop for an in-depth autobiography of the researcher.

> Where do you stand on the objectivist–subjectivist continuum? Explain your reasoning to a colleague. How might this continuum affect the credibility of research results?

In practice, many ethnographic and fieldwork studies are blends of objectivist, constructionist, and subjectivist approaches, and few researchers lie at the extremes of Crotty's (1999) continuum. Further, perspective is rarely static. Researchers move back and forth along the continuum in each direction, although in recent years more fields have nourished the subjectivist end. This movement may occur during a single study or over a career as a researcher. Beginning field workers should anticipate such evolution of their own perspectives and most importantly record such movements in their research journals (Janesick, 1999). The materials in such journals assist field workers in showing how good their work is and in displaying its strengths and weaknesses.

Making It Good

Standards for evaluation of research, like those for the conduct of research, are grounded in assumptions about the nature of reality and how knowledge and meaning are created. Standards also vary with the audience for the fieldwork; different readers bring different sets of assumptions to their assessment of fieldwork (LeCompte & Preissle, 1993, Chap. 9). In the rest of this chapter, we discuss the standards for truth associated with different traditions.

Assumptions of realism and objectivism are associated with the correspondence standard for truth: Claims are true if they match a detailed description of whatever has occurred. For some of what a fieldworker observes, matching claims with descriptions may be fully adequate. This is why rich descriptions are so prized; readers can decide for themselves whether the descriptions justify the claims. Lillian Rubin (1976) referred to this as the "aha" standard of validity. However, people disagree both about what may have happened and what it means. This makes correspondence claims difficult at times. Among some constructionist scholars, this match between claims and descriptions has been replaced by seeking agreement between the researcher's claims and participants' responses to those claims. Previously, we discussed such techniques as participant corroboration, informant debriefing, and member checking (Seale, 1999). Studies based on more subjective, idealist premises often depend on such checking. When the claims concern participants' views of what has happened, this may work well. However, even people who agree on the views toward events may disagree about the origin of or motivation for those views. Member checks can become member vetoes of sensitive or controversial views. Nevertheless, correspondence is one determining standard for assessing whether a study is good.

Another standard for evaluating fieldwork is methodological or procedural. Scholars frustrated with trying to match their claims to what really happened or even to what participants believe to be the case have sought to support their analysis by demonstrating how well they designed and conducted their studies. Documentation must be meticulous, and field workers must record evidence carefully and note rationales for decisions in the field, such as when to observe a setting or when to terminate interviews. The premise here is that following prescribed procedures and avoiding proscribed practices results in a more legitimate portrayal of events or groups. If the methods followed are sound, then the product is more likely to be legitimate. The procedural or methodological standard, however, is based on the assumption that communities of scholars agree on a set of valid procedures for some method.

Some traditions do have areas of common agreement. Among ethnographers, for example, remaining in the field for at least one complete cycle of events is regarded as crucial for establishing the range and variation of activities in any group. For most field workers, another common standard is the triangulation discussed previously. The more different ways that claims can be supported, supposedly, the more sound they are. Likewise, making arguments that use data to eliminate alternative claims is a procedural principle advocated by some. In these cases, the preferred claim is strengthened if the field worker can show that other claims are unlikely. However, sound procedures do not guarantee insightful interpretations, and some of the most illuminating research breaks procedural rules. Consequently, the procedural standard might be more useful in requiring that researchers provide an accounting of how they conducted a particular piece of work rather than specifying rigid recipes for how work is to be done. Introspective and reflective accounts of the researcher's conduct and experience offer audiences justification for procedural choices without assuming methodological orthodoxy.

Among critical, feminist, and other interventionist scholars, the pragmatic standard is often used in evaluating fieldwork. The pragmatic principle requires that the truthfulness of claims be judged by the outcomes or consequences of the research. If research results in some desirable goal such as uncovering injustice or empowering community members, then it is judged as good research. As we have noted, fieldwork traditions have a history of concern for social issues, justice, and equity, and some of the most acclaimed studies are valued because they reveal or substantiate patterns of human suffering (e.g., Anderson, 1978; Ladner, 1971). However, this standard too depends on agreement among communities of scholars, in this case on what constitutes desirable outcomes. Also, this overtly partisan work has been criticized by scholars who believe in neutrality (Merton, 1972). To them, it is unscientific and hence undesirable.

Finally, the challenges and controversies posed by postmodernist thinking in the arts and the humanities have likewise raised questions about standards and principles in the social and professional sciences. Postmodernists question whether stable correspondences, procedural criteria, and pragmatic standards are possible (Kvale, 1995; Schwandt, 1996). They emphasize how correspondence standards are at best approximations and at worst inventions, how procedural standards are contradictory and can limit creative approaches to human dilemmas, and how pragmatic standards deny plurality and human differences. In the aforementioned study of the diverse students and teachers at a Toronto high school, Yon (2000) used the postmodern notion of discursive space to reveal the fluidity, contradictions, and ambivalences in the experiences of his participants. He claimed that he could not have produced such a nuanced account using more conventional standards for fieldwork.

Postmodernists require field workers to examine their assumptions about getting it right and getting it all, to make these assumptions available to audiences, and to consider the applicability of such assumptions to the research questions and research participants at hand. The responsibility for assessing the quality of fieldwork becomes first and foremost that of the field worker, and such assessments must be contextual, local, and particular. Crucial to this assessment is an examination of the relationship between the studier and the studied and the acknowledgment of the researcher's representation of others as a construction primarily of the writer's (Lincoln, 1995).

Postmodernism makes researchers their own most critical audiences, it makes fieldworkers responsible for assessing the goodness of their work for those inside and outside the field, and it demands a rigorous honesty and integrity to accomplish these difficult tasks. It highlights the reflective, conceptual, and ethical aspects of fieldwork and emphasizes the centrality of fieldwork relationships to the scholarship. Researchers make these processes visible in their reports, which contribute to the ongoing dialogue with the literature and commentaries of others.

In thinking about the quality of this type of research or "what makes it good," what does each of the positions described (constructionist, critical/feminist, and postmodern) enable and constrain in the work?

However, all field workers, novices and the more experienced, still worry about whether they got it all and got it right. No one gets it all, of course. But researchers ask themselves whether they have captured the range and the variation of patterns relevant to their topics. Likewise, many, if not most, field workers would deny a single true or right interpretation of the data. But they do ask themselves whether their interpretations are authentic, credible, and coherent. The first and initial critic of any fieldwork research is the field worker him- or herself. Field workers must first develop confidence in the integrity of their material, convincing themselves of its quality through working and reworking the data analysis and the presentation in whatever format it takes. Commitment to adequate time is crucial for pursuing a process of iterative writing or other formatting, revising, checking sources, getting feedback, and reflecting.

Next, field workers must convince an audience of the worth of their presentations. The audiences for which work is intended also have standards for assessing the truth of claims. Researchers are always writing or creating for particular audiences. Certain kinds and forms of data are more or less acceptable to some audiences than to others. Many field workers draw their standards from the prevailing disciplinary norms, but these change and for most fields have been in a state of flux since the final quarter of the last century. When field workers elect to challenge prevailing norms, they should expect to make strong cases for so doing.

In your thinking now, how would you convince an audience of the worth and quality of your fieldwork? What strategies might you employ to accomplish this challenge?

Crotty's (1999) philosophical views of how research is done, we believe, indicate that how fieldwork is assessed depends on the anticipated audience, as well as on the standpoint of the researcher toward what is researched and who is being researched (cf. Hammersley, 1992, for a similar analysis). These standpoints are often associated with different fieldwork traditions and different philosophies of research. What we have attempted to present in this chapter is the range and variation of fieldwork traditions, their associated practices of ethnography and participant observation, and a philosophical framework to aid novice researchers in reflecting on the choices available to them.

11

Reinscribing Critique in Educational Ethnography: Critical and Postcritical Ethnography

George W. Noblit
University of North Carolina at Chapel Hill

MEET THE AUTHOR

George W. Noblit is a professor and chair of the Graduate Studies Division in the School of Education at the University of North Carolina at Chapel Hill. He specializes in critical race studies, the sociology of knowledge, anthropology of education, and qualitative research methods. His 1996 book, *The Social Construction of Virtue: The Moral Life of Schools*, was selected for a Critic's Choice Award of the American Educational Studies Association, and he recently published a set of studies covering his career, *Particularities: Collected Essays on Ethnography and Education* (1999). He won the Dina Fietelson Outstanding Research Award from the International Reading Association in 2000. Dr. Noblit is the editor of *The High School Journal* and coeditor of *The Urban Review* and a book series with Hampton Press, *Understanding Education and Policy*. He is past president (1999–2000) of the American Educational Studies Association.

Critical ethnography is currently at a crossroads. What was originally seen as a productive synthesis of ideas is now unraveling, because the two perspectives that were united had different assumptions. The two perspectives were brought together because each offered a solution to a perceived weakness in the other. Critical theory was largely philosophical and lacked a methodology to allow it to expand into the social sciences. Interpretive ethnography, in contrast, was beleaguered by charges of relativism and relegated to the status of a "micro" theory. It was seen by many as useful at the level of social interaction but lacking a theoretical base to also be a "macro" institutional and sociocultural approach. Both perspectives shared a leftist orientation and a need for what the other could offer. The synthesis was first seen as creating a "new" sociology of education, which gave way to "critical ethnography" as educational anthropology joined the synthesis. In this chapter, I will explore the history and current status of critique in educational ethnography. It is a story of mutual benefit and of heady and provocative accomplishments, all built on a difference that although repeatedly spoken, could not be directly addressed without dissolving the union. The difference is critical theory's claims to "objective reality and its determinate representation" (Hollinger, 1994, p. 81; i.e., there is a truth that can be definitively known and that specifies fixed relationships between things) and interpretive ethnography's claim that all knowledge, including critical theory, is socially constructed. The former accepted the latter's view that ideas emerge from specific contexts, or "situated knowledge" as referred to by Miron (1996). The latter accepted the former's view to the extent that it accepted the centrality of power and ideology in the social constructions of schools and classrooms.

There is a larger point to this chapter, however, that anyone interested in research methodology, whether quantitative or qualitative, should consider.

Research methods and theory are often taught separately and portrayed as being different kinds of ideas. Theory is taught as attempts to understand the world that have a history and thus are tentative, historically specific, and ultimately subject to the results of continued research. Research methods are often characterized as the arbiters of theory. As such, students are often left with the understanding that methods are different from theory. When research is taught as a series of techniques, students learn that there are right and wrong ways to do whatever methodology being taught. The implicit and often explicit lesson is that research methods are not like ideas. As arbiters of theory, methods have a higher status than theory and have explicit rules that separate good from bad ways to know. Students are smart. They learn this message. Unfortunately, qualitative researchers are often as guilty as quantitative researchers in this, but the point of this chapter is that methods are ideas and theories in themselves. They have histories, are best understood as tentative, and are not separate from the theories they are used to test or explore. Indeed, this is a key point of this chapter—the linking critique and ethnography came about in a particular historical and ideational context and was done by particular people. When ideas are joined in paradigmatically new ways, they produce an exciting program of "normal science" (Kuhn, 1970, p. 10) that over time reveals the problematic assumptions of the paradigm. This is the case with critical ethnography. Yet I do not want readers to interpret this point fatalistically. We are at a crossroads, and this gives us new possibilities. I do not think we should approach the crossroads thinking we are forced to choose one of the existing roads. We should not choose between critical theory and ethnography. Instead, I think we see that researchers are making new roads. They are cutting new paths to reinscribing critique in ethnography.

> How do you think methods of research and theories are tied together as suggested here?

My argument that theory and method are linked by people means that readers should know my relationship to critical ethnography. In important ways, I came of age with critical ethnography. I was in graduate school in the early 1970s and was taken by Marxist analyses. I studied what was then called the new sociology of education in graduate school and began my first ethnography by rereading Young's (1971) *Knowledge and Control*, Berger's and Luckmann's (1967) *Social Construction of Reality*, and a set of Habermas' (1971) readings that had only been recently translated into English (*Knowledge and Human Interests*). I have also written a number of pieces (Collins, Noblit, & Ciscel, 1978, 1980) that are, in substance and form, critical ethnographies. I have also written about critical ethnography as a genre (Engel & Noblit, 1989; Noblit & Eaker, 1989). Yet, critical ethnography is one of many genres that I use to represent my knowledge. I am politically aligned with the agenda of critical ethnography but also insist that critical ethnography is also a constructed form of knowledge, and as such can make no special claims to "truth" outside of its genre. This position, of course, means that I am on the margins of critical ethnography. Yet as I will show, my position enables me to turn the tools of ideology critique on critical ethnography itself and to suggest a new future for critical ethnography. I will call this future, and its present, manifestations postcritical ethnography.

WHAT IS CRITICAL ETHNOGRAPHY?

Critical ethnography has a history of some 30 years. It emerged following what was seen as a crisis in social science (Gouldner, 1970), when the boundaries between the social sciences and the humanities were fraying (Geertz, 1973) and when many Western democracies were being challenged by emancipatory social movements, including youth movements, antiwar movements, and the civil rights movement. Marxism was instrumental in challenging dominant social theories but was in transition itself to a neo-Marxism (and now post-Marxism), which did not assume that capitalism would be replaced by communism and be less associated with the Soviet Union. Hall (1986) characterized the current state as "Marxism without guarantees." As it has developed, critical ethnography has spanned disciplines and nations, and as such has multiple histories.

One of the central ideas guiding critical ethnography is that social life is constructed in contexts of power. Thus, the histories I discuss below must be understood as my social construction. Moreover, being included in this volume gives considerable prestige and power to my view. I encourage readers to seek other views, other inscriptions.

There are many different definitions of critical ethnography (Carspecken, 1996). In part, this is because critical ethnography is embedded in the expansion of qualitative research methods and because its origins were multiple. Indeed, Quantz (1992) argued that providing a definition of critical ethnography is not all that helpful: ". . . no answer is likely to satisfy critical ethnographers themselves, because to define the term is to assume an epistemological stance in which the social world can be precisely defined—a position that is not very critical" (p. 448). Nonetheless, many authors have struggled through this multiplicity of definitions with the goal of conceptual clarity. Thomas (1993) offered a distinction between conventional ethnography and critical ethnography: "Conventional ethnography describes what is; critical ethnography asks what could be" (p. 4). That is, "critical ethnography is conventional ethnography with a political purpose" (p. 4). As he explained, critical ethnographers are "raising their voice to speak *to* an audience *on behalf* of their subjects as a means of empowering them by giving more authority to the subjects' voice" (p. 4).

Carspecken (1996) elaborated the definition by specifying that critical ethnographer researchers have both a value orientation and a critical epistemology (theory of knowledge) that characterizes their work. To paraphrase (and quote), the value orientation of critical ethnography includes the following:

1. Research is to be used in cultural and social criticism.
2. Researchers are opposed to inequality in all its forms.
3. Research should be used to reveal oppression and to challenge and change it.
4. "All forms of oppression should be studied."
5. Mainstream research contributes to oppression, and thus critical epistemology should presuppose equal power relations. (pp. 6–7)

Carspecken then elaborates central points of critical epistemology. He argued that it is important to be explicit in a critical ethnography about

1. How claims to valid findings are acts of power in themselves and thus whose interests are being served by the research
2. How values influence what is seen as facts
3. How we choose to represent reality is also an act of power and alters the interpretations of reality

Taken together, then, Carspecken (1996) highlighted the centrality of working against power and oppression as key elements of critical ethnography. For him this acts on two levels. First, the critical ethnographer works against oppression by revealing and critiquing it. Equally important, though, is that critical ethnographers understand that knowledge itself is a social practice that employs power. To that end, critical ethnographers must explicitly consider how their own acts of studying and representing people and situations are acts of domination even as critical ethnographers reveal the same in what they study. In this, Carspecken asked that critical ethnography turn its value orientation and epistemological understandings back on itself.

These attempts to define critical ethnography help us understand what may be involved in doing critical ethnography, but this must come with a caution. As Quantz (1992) argued, critical ethnography is not so much a thing in itself as a project within a wider dialogue:

Critical ethnography is one form of an empirical project associated with critical discourse, a form in which a researcher utilizing field methods that place the researcher on-site attempts to re-present the "culture," the "consciousness," or the "lived experiences" of people living in asymmetrical power relations. As a "project," critical ethnography is recognized as having conscious political intentions that are oriented toward emancipatory and democratic goals. What is key to this approach is that for ethnography to be considered "critical" it should participate in a larger "critical" dialogue rather than follow any particular set of methods or research techniques. (pp. 443–449)

> How would you define *critical ethnography* from what you have read? What role does "asymmetrical power relations" play in your definition?

Quantz (1992) recognized that this type of definition favors the critical side over the ethnographic side but saw this as appropriate because critical ethnographers refuse to separate theory from method. As I will return to later, this privileges only one of the theories that were part of the origins of critical ethnography. Yet Quantz was quite correct in arguing that to understand critical ethnography, we must place it in both a wider dialogue and in the history of that dialogue. There are at least three accounts of this dialogue that are important.

Three Accounts

Anderson (1989) gave one account of the origins of critical ethnography in education:

> Critical ethnography in the field of education is the result of the following dialectic: On one hand, critical ethnography has grown out of the dissatisfaction with social accounts of "structures" like class, patriarchy, and racism in which real actors never appear. On the other hand, it has grown out of dissatisfaction with cultural accounts of human actors in which broad structural constraints like class, patriarchy, and racism never appear. Critical theorists in education have tended to view ethnographers as too atheoretical and neutral in their approach to research. Ethnographers have tended to view critical theorists as too theory driven and biased in their research. (p. 249)

In the 1960s and 1970s, there was a growing challenge to the dominant quantitative, positivistic paradigm for educational and social research. On the one hand, the functionalist theory (with its focus on the social functions and systems of social arrangements that contribute to equilibrium) that undergirds positivism was being challenged by Marxist theory, which emphasized class struggle and conflict as the basis of social life. On the other hand, positivistic science was increasingly seen as inappropriately applied to social and cultural life. Although positivism posited a social and cultural life that was objective, quantitative, or empirical, and governed by "laws," it was increasingly argued that social life was in many ways subjective and socially constituted. This required a research methodology that could capture the actual nature of social life and cultural beliefs. In some ways, the challenges by critical theorists and ethnographers were retribution for how positivists had denigrated other research approaches. Neo-Marxism and ethnography had both been attacked by positivists. As Marxism changed into critical theory, positivists charged that they were overly theoretical and had no methodology for empirical research. Positivists charged that ethnographers who rejected functionalist theory had no theory and were relativistic. Faced with the dominant positivist critiques and with a shared interest in the less powerful people, critical theory and ethnography were joined together.

There are at least three perspectives on Anderson's portrayal. To understand the progress and predicaments of critical ethnography, it is helpful to consider the history of critical ethnography from the perspectives of (1) critical theorists, (2) ethnographers, and (3) the combined critical ethnographers who came after the union. First, I will review Quantz's (1992) history of critical ethnography from the critical theory perspective. Second, I want to review critical ethnography from the perspective of ethnographers. Finally, Wexler (1987) will provide a history of critical ethnography once the union of critical theory and ethnography was in place. These histories, in turn, will lead to a reconsideration of the postmodern challenge to critical ethnography and ultimately to the possibilities of a postcritical ethnography.

A Perspective From Critical Theory

Quantz (1992) saw the discourse of critical ethnography as being based both in Great Britain and in the United States. In the United States, deviance studies, most notably the qualitative, symbolic interactionist studies of Becker (1963, 1964), in sociology were a call to take the side of the underdog and to do so by using the perspectives of the underdogs to challenge conventional worldviews. Becker's study (Becker, Geer, Hughes, & Strauss, 1961) made it clear that students could be understood similarly to be victims of schools and that educational research should be directed away from improving educational efficiency and toward legitimating student perspectives.

Similarly, social anthropology was developing through a series of case studies of British schools (cf. Hargreaves, 1967). Studies of this type were critiqued as portraying the deviant as an exotic and as a victim rather than revealing how ideology and power created deviance. As the British symbolic interactionist studies continued, they became more influenced by continental critical thought, which "attempted to get beneath the social consciousness to the material basis for that consciousness" (Quantz, 1992, p. 455). At the Centre for Contemporary Cultural Studies at the University of Birmingham, ethnographic methods were adopted as the methodology of choice for critical studies. There, culture was conceived as structured by economic and political forces, but was also highly complex and not reducible only to such forces. Quantz discussed the many ethnographies that resulted, including the now classic

Learning to Labour (Willis, 1977) and "Working Class Girls and the Culture of Femininity" (McRobbie, 1978). These ethnographies used resistance theory, arguing that students resisting domination of the school also reproduce (or create) that same dominance (Giroux, 1983).

In the United States, ethnography and field research in education had a long history but was a minor tradition. In the 1960s, interactionist, phenomenological, and sociolinguistic studies were increasingly common, whereas educational anthropology was traditional and used functionalist theory. By the 1970s, ethnography in education was becoming a worthy challenger to the positivist traditions. With the importation of the British critical studies and the theoretical work of Michael Apple and Henry Giroux, an American critical ethnography was emerging. Everhart's Reading, Writing and Resistance (1983) and the works of Simon and Dippo (1986) and McLaren (1986) from Canada signaled the end of traditional ethnography and the emergence of a fully developed critical ethnography. The result according to Quantz (1992) was that "the discursive traditions of critical theory have been strengthened by a method to incorporate experience, and the experiential methods of educational ethnography have been deepened by critical discourse" (p. 461).

> Have you read any ethnographic studies? What do you suppose are the purposes for conducting such investigations?

A Perspective From Ethnography

As Quantz (1992) acknowledged, there is another account of critical ethnography that focuses on the ethnography side of critical ethnography in education. Ethnography in education was reacting against positivism, and in doing so engaged in three "moves": importation of method, legitimization of method, and crises of representation and objectification.

Importation of Method

Ethnography is historically based in anthropology and the study of culture. Although there were qualitative traditions in sociology and other disciplines, anthropological ethnography was claimed to be the most thorough and rigorous qualitative approach. Other approaches, such as case studies and intensive interview studies, were seen as valid but only an approximation of ethnography. Ethnography was being brought into education as a challenge to the dominance of positivism, and the battles were heated and continue to be even today (Cizek, 1995). The "imported" ethnography in education was being fashioned as a weapon that was reshaped in reaction to outcomes of the battles. Early articles and books in education (Bogdan & Biklen, 1982; LeCompte & Goetz, 1982) directly accosted positivist claims about knowledge. Early studies often took the form of taking a generalization derived from quantitative research and demonstrating how it did not account for what was revealed in an ethnographic study. Ethnography in education soon looked different from the ethnographies of education done by anthropologists, and there were complaints from the anthropologists about the changes (Jacob, 1987; Spindler, 1982).

Legitimization of Method

In part, the complaints may have been about anthropology losing control over ethnography, but there was more to it. Anthropologists worked with ethnography in a context that largely defined ethnography as the accepted method, whereas educational ethnographers were fighting for the acceptance of their methodology. In the latter context, ethnography's form was altered to meet the strategic needs of seeking legitimacy as a form of educational research. In this struggle, it was assumed that ethnography was a superior method but ignored ethnography's origins in colonialism. Rosaldo (1989) characterized the ethnography that was to be imported into education: The "Lone Ethnographer" (p. 30) left his advanced civilization and traveled in search of a primitive native (school, clothing, etc.) guided by beliefs in objectivism, monumentalism (accounts that render culture as a museumlike display), timelessness (primitives did not change), and a complicity with imperialism (Geertz, 1988). In short, ethnography itself was overcoming the dominance of positivism.

The legitimacy struggle took place on many fronts. Overcoming the dominance of positivism involved broadening the methodology into a more generalized qualitative research, in which ethnography was but one variant. Although the legitimacy struggle took place widely across the fields within education (curriculum studies, social foundations, educational administration, etc., and is still engaged in areas such as special education), there were two major fronts in which the struggle took different forms: educational evaluation and educational research.

One of the key sites of the legitimacy struggle was in evaluation, where the press of producing useful knowledge was revealing the limits of quantitative methods. Positivism was unable to respond to the "political inherency" of program evaluation and was increasingly seen as arrogant (e.g., in demanding students be randomly assigned to treatment and control study groups), and irrelevant because the results did not address the real world of decision making (Greene, 1994). As the alternatives to positivism were being argued in the late 1960s and early 1970s, Scriven (1967) argued that evaluation was best understood as a process of valuing, and argued for a goal-free approach to evaluation (Scriven, 1973) that undercut the claims of scientific evaluators that programs should be goal based. House (1977) made his classic distinction between merit and worth in evaluation, arguing against positivism as he argued for evaluation being based on assessments of worth of the program to various stakeholders. Guba and Lincoln (1981) and Cronbach et al. (1980) also contributed to the movement, and by the 1980s, the struggle for legitimacy between quantitative and qualitative evaluation had eased into détente.

Lincoln and Guba (1985) did not, however, limit themselves only to evaluation and thus were key participants in the legitimacy struggle on other fronts as well. They and others (Bogdan & Biklen, 1982; LeCompte & Goetz, 1982) began to articulate qualitative methods as legitimate in educational research in general. Educational research had been not only positivistic, but largely psychological also. Qualitative researchers in education countered with appeals to their disciplinary bases in sociology and anthropology. Although qualitative researchers in education were also ultimately successful in achieving a form of détente in educational research, they did so by reinforcing positivistic assumptions that methods were to be justified by claims to disciplines outside of education. This also meant that the grounds for legitimation within education were to be essentially methodological.

Qualitative researchers had argued that positivism has a fetish with details of methodology, but the legitimation of qualitative research on methodological grounds ends up pushing qualitative researchers to focus on the details of method as well. Scholars worked on analogies for quantitative validity and reliability (LeCompte & Goetz, 1982), criteria for trustworthiness (Guba, 1981), improved techniques (Krueger, 1988; Miles & Huberman, 1994; Mishler, 1986), synthesizing multiple studies (Noblit & Hare, 1988), and paradigm and epistemological justifications (Guba, 1990). This qualitative methodological fetish has resulted in a burgeoning industry of texts and handbooks, including this one. Much of this work is interesting and provocative to read, but the point is that much of it was driven externally by concerns for legitimacy.

Legitimating qualitative research did not proceed by itself, either. Qualitative research was seen as better serving the interests of oppressed peoples by giving voice to the oppressed (Fine, 1994). Yet as Fine notes, voice all too easily gave way into ventriloquy, especially as the methodology struggled for legitimacy. The colonialist origins of ethnography, even with all the changes in qualitative methods, were and are hard to escape.

At this point, how would you distinguish between quantitative and qualitative research? What does voice and colonialism have to do with using qualitative approaches to research?

As ethnography and qualitative research were seeking legitimacy in educational research, in part by appealing to discipline heritage, it was being argued that the interpretivist perspective was spreading across the humanities and social sciences, obviating discipline claims and boundaries. The "blurred genres" posited that ethnographic accounts were interpretations of interpretations (Geertz, 1973). In many ways, Geertz did not anticipate that this move would both promote qualitative researchers exploring the "linguistic turn" (Toews, 1987, p. 879), semiotics, and poststructuralism, and ultimately contribute to a crisis of representation (Marcus & Fischer, 1986) within ethnography.

Crises of Representation and Objectification

The crisis of representation meant that qualitative researchers could no longer make a strong claim that what they reported was the truth about those studied. Instead, ethnographies are products of the ethnographers' culture more than accounts of another culture. McCadden, Dempsey, and Adkins (1999) argued that the crises of representation are actually a derivative of a more substantial crisis of rendering cultural beliefs as objects rather than subjective meanings or, as they term it, "objectification." If objective accounts are not reasonable, ethnography is not realistic. It can only be claimed to be partial attempts to understand what others believe and do.

The crisis, however conceived, has led to considerable experimentation in educational ethnography. Narrative (Vaz, 1997), literary (Noblit, 1999; Richardson & Lockridge, 1998), poetic (Glesne, 1997), impressionistic (Van Mannen, 1988), autoethnographic (Ellis & Bochner, 1996), and other approaches are all being elaborated. Similarly, many authors have experimented with how to display their positionality and reflexivity (Fine, 1994; Noblit, 1993; Weis & Fine, 1993). In this experimentation, the realist ethnography that was married to critical theory is left behind, and critical ethnography loses one of the legs on which its stands.

Conflicting Assumptions

The two perspectives reviewed above show the importance of history and context in research methods. Although they shared an interest in working in the interests of the less powerful people, critical theory and ethnography were primarily united in opposition to positivism and functionalism. That is to say, it was a common enemy more than a shared perspective that brought them together. The two perspectives also reveal that even when joined in a critical ethnography, each side worked to advance its own perspective. Critical theory advanced critique as a foundation of social analysis. Ethnography advanced a methodology. Together, they have re-created a new form of "historically reified knowledge" (Wexler, 1987, p. 4) in which critique is the legitimate form of social analysis and ethnography is the legitimate methodology.

Critical ethnography in the United States lost the sociology of knowledge base that it had in its origins in the United Kingdom and replaced it with a critique of ideology that reified structure, materialism, realism, and rationalism. Although the sociology of knowledge project was put aside within critical ethnography, it did not disappear from education. Rather, the antifoundational perspective it presented was elaborated in the struggle to develop and legitimate ethnographic and qualitative methods, accepting the methodological fetish of educational research. The sociology of knowledge also continued as a minor act in social theory, and as I am doing here, is being reinscribed in postmodernism and poststructuralism (Dant, 1991; Ladwig, 1996; McCarthy, 1996; Popkewitz, 1998). Antifoundationalism was also at the base of the criticisms of critical theory and ethnography. Bennett and LeCompte (1990) explained:

> In the middle and late 1980's, critical theory came under its own attack by social theorists such as post-structuralists, feminists (Delamont, 1989; Lather, 1986; Ellsworth, 1989); and anti-rationalists (Ellsworth, 1989). While these approaches differ in their emphases and are as varied as the researchers who espouse them, they all draw on the analytic constructs of earlier functionalist and conflict approaches, as well as the post-positivists' attack on "hard science." They also utilize the perspective of interpretivist theorists, accepting the premise that reality is constructed of the sum of the realities of individuals interacting in any given setting. These approaches place great importance on the presentation of "multiple voices" (Geertz, 1973, 1988) of all participants—especially less powerful participants such as women, members of minority groups, and students—in social interaction. (p. 29)

These critics argued that critical ethnography was in itself a form of hegemony— patriarchal, Eurocentric, individualistic, and White. Critical ethnographers responded to the challenges cited above with attempts to legitimate critical ethnography itself. The general strategy was to subsume the criticism. Thus, when the dominance of class-based analyses were challenged, the result was to declare a "parallelist" (Morrow & Torres, 1998) position in which critical theory was argued to be applicable to the study of gender domination, much in the same way it was to have worked with class. The challenge of race led to a further elaboration into a "nonsynchronous parallelist" position (McCarthy & Apple, 1988). In each of these moves, however, critical ethnographers and theorists refused to engage the fundamental challenge of relational knowledge and antifoundationalism. The result was "a theory which could never be wrong" (Ladwig, 1996, p. 40), revealing critical theory's ideological base. As Wexler (1987) explained, "A critical analysis which hides uncertainty and disjuncture in a coherent story is also ideological" (p. 104). In short, critical ethnography has ironically come to be a form of ideological practice. Critical ethnographers have tried to minimize the saliency of postmodernism and poststructuralism, claiming some insights as justified by critical theory but rejecting the salience of ideas that do not fit (Giroux, Lankshear, McLaren, & Peters, 1996; Kincheloe & McLaren, 1994; Torres & Mitchell, 1998). In doing so, critical ethnographers set the stage for postcritical ethnography. Yet, as I will argue, this is not something all that new.

> What do you think Wexler means when he argues that critical ethnography is "a critical analysis, which hides uncertainty and disjunctions in a coherent story"?

The Postmodern Challenge?

Critical theory in some ways is the ultimate product of modernity, and ethnography is the ultimate product of colonialism. That is, both play out dominant ideas of the epochs of their historical origins. Postmodernism and poststructuralism signal the end of these epochs. Some postmodernists and poststructuralists argue that it is better to think of postmodernity as a historically specific condition rather than as a theory. Lemert (1991) explained:

> Postmodernism, if it means anything at all, means to say that since the midcentury the world has broken into its political and cultural parts. The very idea of the world revolving on a true axis has proven finite. The axial principles of the twentieth-century world—European culture, British administration, American capitalism, Soviet politics—have come apart as a matter of *fact*, not of theory. The multiple identities and local politics . . . are not just another way; they are what is left. (p. 167)

Murillo (1999) went further, arguing that postmodernity has a racial face. People of color have had to live postmodernity for some time, but only recently has it come to privileged Whites and intellectuals. Postmodernity and poststructuralism are not different theories that coexist and complement one another. Defining these terms is decidedly difficult, because both question objectification of ideas. Therefore, I will simply use what many see as the central concept of each.

Postmodernity is marked by the end of grand narratives (Lyotard, 1984) that determine the play of human history. In this sense, then, critical theory and ethnography are both essentially modernist projects deploying notions of objectivity and definitive representation. Poststructuralism is linked to postmodernity but has its roots in linguistic structuralism of de Saussure. For de Saussure (1959), there was a "final signified" behind language. That is, there was the possibility of an objective reality. Poststructuralists reject the notion of a final signified, arguing that reality is constructed in contexts of power relations and that claims to final signifieds or truths in theory or research are instead claims to power. What both share is the claim that there are no fixed foundations to understanding social life.

Critical theorists and critical ethnographers are not the only ones concerned about the implications of postmodernism. There are many opposed to the ideas that people are calling postmodernism. Pearl and Knight (1999) pursued a "general theory" (p. 43) of democratic education and are decidedly not critical theorists. In fact, they argued that critical theorists have avoided specifying their ideas in practice and do not emphasize the importance of the balanced treatment of ideas. Pearl and Knight argued critical theorists "do not meet our definition of democratic education" (p. 54). In any case, they are even more concerned with the inadequacies of postmodernism: "We argue that postmodernism is the logical consequence of hostility toward not only all grand narratives but to democracy, specifically" (p. 27).

Critical theorists, for their part, share some of Pearl's and Knight's basic concerns. Torres and Mitchell (1998) also saw postmodernism as a threat to democracy, as well as to the possibility of race, class, and gender equality. They acknowledged critical theory's origins in modernism by arguing that what postmodernism is missing is an emphasis on "critical modernism" (p. 7). Ebert (1991) argued that "the postmodern is increasingly seen as the end of transformative politics" and calls "into question emancipation itself as a political agenda" (p. 291). She then proceeded "to write the political back into the postmodern" (p. 291) via a "resistance postmoderism" (p. 293), which she distinguished from the "ludic postmodernism" of Derrida (1978), Lyotard (1984), and Baudrillard (1988), which deny that ideas in themselves can lead to societal transformation. She clearly saw the challenge of "ludic" (or ludicrous) postmodernism to the critical agenda. For her, Lyotard's (1984) cultural policy of playful, experimental, and transgressive subversions of the "rules" of grand narratives denies the possibility of the critical project. Kincheloe and McLaren (1994) used Ebert's "ludic" characterization to rethink the linkage between critical theory and qualitative research. In their effort, they argued that ludic postmodernism "is decidedly limited in its ability to transform social and political regimes of power" (p. 143) and "tends to reinscribe the status quo" (p. 144). They saw resistance postmodernism or critical postmodernism as an extension and appropriation of ludic postmodernism that " brings to ludic postmodernism a form of materialist intervention" (p. 144). Put otherwise, postmodernism must be anchored in the economic and political determinism of neo-Marxism. In their formulation, postmodernism is a condition to be explained away by critical analysis.

Why must postmodernism and poststructuralism be contained by critical ethnography? First, as new approaches, they threaten the hegemony of the critical ethnography of education. For critical ethnography to remain dominant, these ideas must be repudiated and contained. Second, they must be contained because they are not new. As both postmodernism and poststructuralism are antifoundational, they represent a familiar challenge to critical ethnography. They revisit the struggle between interpretivism and critical theory at the origins of critical ethnography (Dant, 1991; Popkewitz, 1998). Popkewitz (1995) reframed the critical ethnography repudiation of postmodernism and poststructuralism as being relativistic: "... the concern of relativism is an attempt of critics to privilege their perspectives whose absence is defined as relativist and thereby worthless and not competent" (p. xvi). That is, a critique of relativism is a strategic move to remain dominant. Mannheim (1952) was aware of this phenomenon when he was writing in German in the 1920s and 1930s and argued that the appropriate characterization was not relativism but relationalism:

> Relationalism signifies merely that all the elements of meaning in a given situation have reference to one another and derive their significance from this reciprocal interrelationship in a given frame of thought. Such a system of meanings is possible and valid only in a given type of historical existence, to which, for a time, it furnishes appropriate expression. (p. 76)

Mannheim was concerned with ideology and power as well, but these are ever more evident in understandings of postmodernism and poststructuralism. Foucault (1980), of course, as a poststructuralist had an explicit focus on power/knowledge. As Popkewitz (1998) explained, "Foucault provides methodological strategies for interpreting how the constitution of the 'self' and 'individuality' are the effects of power. He joins that issue to a consideration of the social sciences as practices that deploy power" (p. 48).

The postmodern challenge to critical ethnography does not reject critique. Instead, it rejects a claim to objective knowledge, and this is precisely what critical theory was to bring to its marriage with ethnography. The postmodern challenges to critical ethnography have spawned multiple approaches to postcritical ethnography (in the sense that they ask critique to critique itself): Feminist critical (Fine, 1994; Marshall, 1997; Weis, 1995), critical race (Scheurich & Young, 1997), *mojado* (Murillo, 1999), queer (Hennessey, 1995; Seidman, 1995), postmodern (Scheurich, 1997), poststructural (Lather, 1991), postcolonial (Murillo, 1999), critical sociology of knowledge (Wexler, 1987), native (Benard & Pedruza, 1989; Jennings, 1999), and so on. Postcritical ethnographies directly challenge the epistemology of critical ethnography (Adkins & Gunzenhauser, 1999) and can be argued to constitute an alternative:

> Claims are not justified in the same sense that claims are justified in post-positivist research. Knowledge ceases to exist in the conventional sense of knowledge as justified true belief. Knowledge instead is understood as the product of a moment of mutual construction that at once converges divergent perspectives and preserves the divergence. Because knowledge and the process of knowledge justification are redefined, this is the beginning of what may be considered an alternative epistemology. In this way, we may begin to imagine an alternative epistemology with which to inform a postcritical ethnography. (p. 71)

Although there are clear differences in poststructuralism and postmodernism, it is clear that they are not about the elimination of the political as characterized by critical ethnographers. As Noddings (1995) summarized

> Postmodernists believe that the search for an all encompassing description of knowledge is hopeless. Instead they emphasize . . . how knowledge and power are connected, how domains of expertise evolve, who profits from and who is hurt by various claims to knowledge, and what sort of language develops in communities of knowers. (p. 72)

Rather than negating politics, particular ethnographies require the interrogation of the power and politics of the critic him- or herself, as well as in the social scene studied.

As a review, begin to develop your definitions for modernism, postmodernism, postculturalism, relativism, and critical ethnography. At this point, what do you judge each of their purposes to be?

Although critical ethnographers are disturbed by the implications of postmodernism for their practice, it is important to understand this in a broader context. If we look only at the conflicts between postmodernism and critical theory, we may think this is a special case in the history of critical ethnography. But it is not the case. As above, Bennett and LeCompte (1990) showed that critical ethnography has had a history of controversy about its exclusiveness, patriarchy, Eurocentrality, and its oversimplified view of asymmetric power relations. As Popkewitz (1995, p. xix) explained, it is better to view critical ethnography as a social field in which scholars struggle to define which views of critical research are to be authoritative. In this field, there is a recognizable form to the struggle. The "old left" issues the critique that postcritical challengers are threatening relativism, nihilism, or both, in addition to possibly authoritarianism (Popkewitz, 1995). They then proceeded to analyze the challenger's position for points of similarity and argue for a synthesis that privileges the old left position. The postmodern challenge is being played out similarly. As Popkewitz put it, critical ethnographer calls to reject postmodernism are strong rhetorically but ultimately contradictory. The structural categories central to critical ethnography "are historically constructed within power relations" (p. xix), and critical ethnography's refusal to problematize their intellectual and conceptual categories produces a form of authoritarianism.

The supposed challenge of postmodernism to critical ethnography then is not new. It revisits in new terms the origins of critical ethnography and signals the end of critical ethnography as it was initially constituted. LeCompte (1995) summarized postmodernism as a rejection of authors "who give *voice* to the authoritative canon" (p. 101). Moreover, "postmodernism as a conceptual (or nonconceptual) frame has incorporated the methods of social construction-ism and symbolic interactionism" (p. 101). In short, postmodernism returns to the interpretative ethnography that was joined to critical theory. Yet, postmodernism and poststructuralism move beyond the antifoundationalism of the sociology of knowledge and interpretivism. According to Scheurich (1997), antifoundation-alism functioned as half of a foundationalism–relativism binary in which each reproduced the other in their opposition. Postcritical ethnography works as part of a "postfoundationalism" that moves beyond the binary (Scheurich, 1997), with the more explicit focus on power than is present in interpretivism and the soci-ology of knowledge. This offers the possibility of reinscribing critique as well. As Ellsworth (1989); Lather (1986); Wexler (1987); Ladwig (1996); Murillo (1999); McCadden, Dempsey, and Adkins (1999); Adkins and Gunzenhauser (1999); and others exemplify, this critique undermines the objectivity and definitive represen-tation claims (Hollinger, 1994) of critical ethnography. Instead of grand narra-tives giving meaning to our research, postmodernism leaves us with the decidedly difficult understanding that we are responsible for creating the world we have and are responsible for what is coming. Further, postmodernism understands that social life is never simply rational, and thus acting responsibly is filled with unan-ticipated consequences (Giddens, 1979), irony, discontinuity, and contradiction. Under these conditions, postmodernists see reflexivity and playfulness as reason-able ways to approach acting responsibly. The focus here is on the possibilities offered through postcritical ethnographies.

Possibilities for Critical and Postcritical Ethnography

There are a number of possibilities for critical and postcritical ethnography at this juncture in history. Clearly, classic critical ethnography will continue to play an important role in educational ethnography, but other postcritical ethnographies are now possible.

Classic Critical Ethnography

I have discussed this model throughout this chapter, but it needs to be sum-marized here. Classic critical ethnography involves using ethnographic methods as part of a critique of ideology and domination. Although there are many varia-tions, doing classic critical ethnography involves a critic studying how a group is oppressed by ideas, social relations, and power. The critic represents the story for the oppressed as part of a larger theoretical project of social and political emanci-pation. The studies will focus on structure, material conditions, reproduction, re-sistance, contradictions, power and transformations evident in the lives of people, communities, schools, and classrooms. Classic critical ethnographies often em-ploy realist portraits of the oppressed and their oppression. Realism is important to the critical ethnographers' claim to have revealed actual oppression and having a theory that offers a definitive explanation of that oppression and the possibilities for eliminating oppression.

> How do you think knowledge and power are connected, if at all? How might these two ideas have a role in conducting research?

Postcritical Ethnographies

Postcritical approaches are many and diverse, as I have indicated. Each is and will continue to be significant for the foreseeable future. Although postcritical ethnographies are not one thing, it is possible to consider some issues that the many approaches address. The issues that need to be considered in conducting postcritical ethnographies include positionality, reflexivity, objectivity, and representation. These issues blend into one another and should not to be understood as criteria for a good postcritical ethnography. Rather, they are ways people have tried to think about what they are doing.

Positionality involves being explicit about the groups and interests that the postcritical ethnographer wishes to serve, as well as his or her biography. One's race, gender, class, ideas, and commitments are subject to exploration as part of the ethnography. Indeed, position may be so important that it can be seen as an epistemological claim, as in Collins' (1991) standpoint epistemology. Her point is that position and identity may be the basis of a theory of knowledge that then is explicated via research. Positionality also involves "studying up" in the sense that the focus of the ethnography may well be institutional arrangements and social movements (Wexler, 1987), or the more powerful, as with Whiteness studies (Kincheloe et al., 1998; Warren, 1999).

Reflexivity is about "redesigning the observed" (Marcus, 1995, p. 111) and about "redesigning the observer" (p. 114). The former involves recognizing that identities of those studied are dispersed and changing. In different contexts, identities and the ways in which identities change are different. Moreover, time and history are lived and constituted via social interaction rather than exist as a context to identity. Redesigning the observed also involves consideration of voice, polyphony, and montage. Redesigning the observer involves working toward dialogic and bifocal (emic and etic) accounts that elaborate the alternative possibilities, identities, juxtapositions, and outcomes in any scene studied ethnographically.

Objectivity is usually eschewed in postcritical ethnographies but is never fully escaped whenever ethnographic interpretations are offered. The act of writing inscribes a critical interpretation that exists beyond the intentions of the author to deobjectify, dereify, or demystify that studied. McCadden et al. (1999)

argued that reconsidering objectivity goes beyond writing: "Theorizing postcritical ethnography of education should be represented in the same tone as its writing—balancing tentativeness and surety and evoking a sense of temporality" (p. 33). Postcritical ethnographies worry the issue of objectivity. Cultures are not objects in a simple sense. They are ephemeral and multiple, whereas our interpretations are always partial and positional. Postcritical ethnographies try to work through this dilemma of objectivity.

Representation is about the issues involved in inscribing a postcritical ethnography. Representation may involve the genre (Glesne, 1997; Van Mannen, 1988), tropes (Geertz, 1988), metaphors, literary devices (Noblit, 1999), imagery involved an ethnographic text, or all of these. Yet, postcritical ethnographies may also be represented as performances, videos, montages, and other ways. Representation involves acknowledging the "uncertainty about adequate means of describing social reality" (Marcus & Fischer, 1986, p. 8) and working through the myriad decisions critically. Willinsky (1998) reminded us that the guiding ideas of ethnographic thought included the will to know in ways that demonstrated difference, the will to display an exotic other, and the right to educate according to the ethnographer's culture. The first pushes us to problematize why we wish to study and represent; the second to problematize the desire to, and ways of, creating a portrayal; the third to worry about the idea that our accounts or representations are to edify others.

It is the working through issues of positionality, reflexivity, objectivity, and representation that redefines critique as postfoundational. Yet, there still exists the issue of critique itself. Postcritical ethnographies still regard critique to be about power and ideology. However, postcritical ethnographies see the standard form of critical ethnography as a possible choice given specific historical and political contexts. As Cherryholmes (1988) explained

> Our choices and actions, in their totality, are pragmatic responses to the situations in which we and others find ourselves. They are based upon *visions* of what is beautiful, good, and true instead of fixed, structured, moral, or objective certainties. (emphasis in original, p. 151)

This means that it is inappropriate to think about precise research techniques and to imply that postcritical ethnographies should have similar forms or strategies. Rather, it is better to consider the question, How might we think through postfoundational critiques? Stone (1995) offered us one way to think about reinscribing critique as postcritical. She tried to think through an "agreement to work together . . . in spite of theoretical disagreement" (p. 155) within a feminist critical praxis. Although I would expect that different postcritical ethnographers would want to consider this differently, Stone's effort was sufficiently comprehensive to stimulate the thinking of anyone working to reinscribe critique in nonfoundational ways.

Stone (1995) offered eight elements of critical sufficiency when giving up modernist certainty. First, *epochal tension* involves acknowledging that today's conditions are different from those in the past and that there is the "tension of changing senses of the world" (p. 155). The play of critical and postcritical ethnographies, modernity, and postmodernity; structuralism and poststructuralism; race, gender, sexual orientation, and class; and so on are implicitly and explicitly part of sufficient critiques. *Historical non-necessity* replaces history with historicity or even posthistoricity. History is understood as lived, constructed, particular, and contingent, rather than as an external context to that studied. Giving up notions of "totality, singularity, sameness, or oneness"and "objectivity and foundationalism" (p. 155) is part of *antiessentialism*. At a minimum, identities, structures, cultural beliefs, and social practices are changing and multiple. *Contextualism* involves considering language as socially constructed and materialism as "theoretically non-essential" (p. 156). The meaning of context itself will vary from strong to weak and from creating possibilities to limiting possibilities, depending on specific social, cultural, and political conditions. *Theory ladenness* recognizes that "language is thought; thought is never neutral" (p. 156). In one sense, perception is culturally constructed and theory laden. In another sense, theories themselves are laden with other ideas and theories that emerge in specific social, cultural, and political contexts. Experience is partial, time specific, and located in conditions and contexts, meaning that *identities* are seen as partial and multiple for both the postcritical ethnographer and those studied. The privileging of the critic and rationality is replaced with understanding the positionalities of the critic and others. In the absence of a foundational truth, researchers and the researched move to *ethicality*. Postcritical ethnographies require moral commitments, because researchers and those studied are responsible for the social construction of everyday life. Finally, Stone argued that critical sufficiency requires *reconceptualizations of power* as "antipower":

> First as temporality—that is, as momentariness, ambiguity, dispersion, fluidity; second as plurality—that is as multiplicity, multivocality, multiculturalism; third as recreation—that is as reconstruction, recursion, reconstitution; and fourth as otherness—that is as difference, playfulness, irony, and contradiction itself. (p. 156)

Power escapes the containment of critical ethnography and establishes itself everywhere and everywhere critically analyzed.

Postcritical ethnographies obviously lack the certain form and substance of critical ethnographies. They instead require considerable theoretical and methodological thought. They involve working through positionality, reflexivity, objectification, representation, and critical sufficiency. Postcritical ethnographies, in an important sense, are not designed but enacted or produced as moral activity. Postcritical ethnographers then must assume they exist within a critical discourse that in part makes them responsible for the world they are producing when they interpret and critique.

How would you contrast postcritical ethnography with critical ethnography? Which is more appealing to you and why?

CONCLUSIONS

Although I see critical and postcritical ethnographies existing in dialogue with each other, it is important to recognize that the centrality of foundationalism to critical ethnography may well imply the end to critical ethnography. Indeed, Ladwig (1996) proposes just this with his "science with an attitude" (p. 161). Ladwig argued that critical theory's rejection of positivism was a mistake and argues for "strategic methodological stances" (p. 164) that includes "poaching mainstream issues" and "poaching mainstream tools" (pp. 165–166). His argument is that if the goal of critical analyses is to defeat mainstream educational research, then critical researchers should take over the theories and methods of positivism. It is important that he is strongly influenced by the feminist, postmodern, and poststructural arguments presented above as he argues for a strategic approach to win the paradigm wars. Where he falls short is in critiquing the war metaphor. I think that the point of much of the above is that if we accept the terms of battle we may reproduce war, if in a different form. The reason for a postcritical ethnography is arguably to replace war, not with peace, but with ending the ability of the concept, the metaphor, and the practice to be a reified thing. Nevertheless, Ladwig does remind us that the work of critical and postcritical ethnography was constructed in a warlike context. Revisiting and critiquing this history is clearly a project for postcritical ethnographies. My effort here obviously is but one attempt.

12

Critical Inquiry in Qualitative Research: Feminist and Poststructural Perspectives: Science "After Truth"

Patti Lather
Ohio State University

MEET THE AUTHOR

Patti Lather is a professor in the cultural studies in Education Program, School of Educational Policy and Leadership at Ohio State University, where she teaches qualitative research in education and gender, and education. Her work includes *Getting Smart: Feminist Research and Pedagogy With/the Postmodern* (1991) and, with Chris Smithies, *Troubling the Angels: Women Living With HIV/AIDS* (1997), which received a CHOICE Award as one of the best academic books of the year. Recent articles have appeared in *Harvard Education Review, Qualitative Studies in Education*, and *Educational Theory*. She has chapters in *The Handbook of Research on Teaching, Working the Ruins: Feminist Theory and Methods in Education*, and *The Handbook of Ethnography*. She is presently working on a manuscript, *Getting Lost: Feminist Efforts Toward a Double(d) Science*. Her favorite academic achievements thus far are a 1995 sabbatical appointment to the Humanities Research Institute, a University of California–Irvine seminar on feminist research methodology, and a 1997 visiting appointment at Goteborg University in Sweden. Her hobby aspiration is to learn to play the accordion.

Across the social sciences, unsettlement and contestation permeate discussion of what it means to do inquiry. For much of the 20th century, field-based "paradigms"[1] have been articulated and developed. Rooted in the research traditions of interpretive sociology and anthropology, such alternative practices of social research focus on the overriding importance of meaning making and context in human experiencing (Mishler, 1979). Over the last two decades, advocacy approaches to research that are openly value based have added their voices to this methodological ferment. For example, "critical ethnography" of education is constructed out of interpretivist anthropology and sociology as well as neo-Marxist and feminist theory (Anderson, 1989). Making an epistemological break with the positivist insistence on objectivity, "openly ideological" research argues that nothing is outside ideology, most certainly the production of social knowledge (Lather, 1986a, 1986b). As the concept of "disinterested knowledge" implodes and collapses inward, social inquiry becomes, in my present favorite definition of science, a much-contested cultural space, a site of the surfacing of what it has historically repressed (Hutcheon, 1988, p. 74).

In terms of my focus in this essay, a "critical social science" is intended to work toward *changing* as well as *understanding* the world (Fay, 1987). What Van Maanen (1988) called "critical tales" ask questions of power, economy, history, and exploitation. In the words of Poster (1989), "critical theory springs

---

[1]I put "paradigm" in scare quotes because of the deconstructive argument that we are in a "post-paradigmatic" era (Caputo, 1987).

from an assumption that we live amid a world of pain, that much can be done to alleviate that pain, and that theory has a crucial role to play in that process" (p. 3). Doing critical inquiry means taking into account how our lives are mediated by systems of inequity such as classism, racism, sexism, and heterosexism. Of late, such work has been profoundly challenged by postmodernism/poststructuralism/deconstruction.[2] Hence what follows will attempt to note these challenges, as well as to delineate the parameters of critical inquiry.

> What is your view of the relationship between "understanding" and "changing" in the context of social science research? Do you agree with Lather's stance here? Why or why not?

CRITICAL INQUIRY: PARADIGMATIC ASSUMPTIONS

Science is in crisis in both the natural and the social sciences. Quantum physics and chaos science have created a physics very different from the one the social sciences have aspired to in their quest for legitimate scientific status. This

---

[2] Although I am suspicious of the desire for definitions that analytically "fix" complex, contradictory, and relational constructs. I generally use the term *postmodern* to mean the shift in material conditions of late 20th-century monopoly capitalism brought on by the micro-electronic revolution in information technology, the fissures of a global, multinational hypercapitalism, and the global uprising of the marginalized. This conjunction includes movements in art, architecture, and the practices of everyday life (e.g., MTV). The code name for the crisis of confidence in Western conceptual systems, postmodernism is born out of our sense of the limits of Enlightenment rationality. All of this creates a conjunction that shifts our sense of who we are and what is possible in the name of science (Lather, 1991, 1993; Rosenau, 1992).

I generally use *poststructural* to mean the working out of academic theory within the culture of postmodernism, but I also sometimes use the terms interchangeably. Structuralism is premised on efforts to scientize language, to posit it as systematizable. Poststructuralism's focus is on the remainder, all that is left over after the systematic categorizations have been made (Lecercle, 1990). For such French poststructuralists as Barthes, Derrida, Foucault, and Lacan, structuralism's basic thesis of the universal and unconscious laws of human society and of the human mind was part of the bureaucratic and technocratic systems that they opposed. Their interest was in the "gaps, discontinuities and suspensions of dictated meanings in which difference, plurality, multiplicity and the coexistence of opposites are allowed free play" (Bannet, 1989, p. 5).

The goal of *deconstruction* is to keep things in process, to disrupt, to keep the system in play, to set up procedures to continuously demystify "the real," to fight the tendency for categories to congeal. Deconstruction foregrounds the lack of innocence in any discourse by looking at the textual staging of knowledge, the constitutive effects of the use of language. Though impossible to freeze conceptually, deconstruction can be broken down into three steps: (1) identify the binaries, the oppositions that structure an argument; (2) reverse/displace the dependent term from its negative position to a place that locates it as the very condition of the positive term; and (3) create a more fluid and less coercive conceptual organization of terms that transcends a binary logic by simultaneously being both and neither of the binary terms (Grosz, 1989). This somewhat linear definition is deliberately placed in the endnotes in order to displace the desire to domesticate deconstruction as it moves across the many sites of its occurrence, such as the academy, architecture, and the arts.

questioning of what science is and what role it plays or might play in our lives is within a larger context of what Habermas (1975) termed a "legitimation crisis" in cultural authority.

Hence it is both a dizzying and an exciting time in which to do social inquiry. It is a time of openness and questioning of established paradigms in intellectual thought. At some level, we're moving out of the cultural values spawned by the Age of Reason, the scientific revolution of the 16th and 17th centuries, and the Enlightenment and its material base, the Industrial Revolution. We're well into an age of late capitalism in which knowledge is increasingly configured in electronic language in a way that deeply affects our relation to the world (Poster, 1990). Furthermore, the profound effect that electronic mediation exerts on the way we perceive ourselves and reality is occurring in a world marked by gross maldistribution of power and resources.

Within such a context, the orthodox consensus about what it means to do science has been displaced. A proliferation of contending paradigms is causing some diffusion of legitimacy and authority. This situation is often characterized by the term *postpositivism*. This term refers not to the loss of positivism but rather to the end of its claim to being the only way of doing science. Within postpositivism, paradigms of disclosure are vying for attention with paradigms of prediction/prescription, and advocacy paradigms are competing with "neutral" paradigms. In Table 12.1, I added deconstruction to Habermas' (1971b) thesis of the three categories of human interest that underscore knowledge claims: prediction, understanding, and emancipation.[3] This table is but one way to present the proliferation of paradigms that so characterizes contemporary social science. Like any conceptual map, it has many problems. For example, feminist work goes on across the paradigms. Despite such problems, Table 12.1 helps to distinguish how each paradigm offers a different but not necessarily exclusive approach to generating and legitimating knowledge. I, for example, place my work in the emancipation column with great fascination for the implications of deconstruction.

How does the conceptual map Lather presents in Table 12.1 (based on Habermas' work) fit with your own conceptual mapping of research methodologies? What would you add to this mapping?

---

[3] Habermas would not approve of my addition of the column of "deconstruct," given his worries about postmodernity. In essence, Habermas identified postmodernism with neoconservativism and argued that the Enlightenment project is not failed, only unfinished. His polemical defense of universalism and rationality is positioned explicitly against what he saw as the "nihilism" of Foucault and Derrida and, implicitly, against Lyotard's challenge to the "great ideological fairy tales" that fuel Habermas' praxis of universal values and rational consensus (Calinescu, 1987, p. 274). For his own statements, see Habermas (1987).

TABLE 12.1
Postpositivist Paradigms of Inquiry

Prediction	Understanding	Emancipation	Deconstruction
Positivist	Interpretive	Critical	Poststructural
	Naturalistic	Neo-Marxist	Postmodern
	Constructivist	Feminist	Postparadigmatic
	Phenomenological	Race specific	Diaspora
	Hermeneutic	Praxis oriented	
	Symbolic interactionist	Freirean	
	Microethnographic	Participatory	

Note: Diaspora, as used by Jewish and African American historians, refers to the forced relocation of people from out of their homelands. Caputo's (1987) "post-paradigmatic diaspora," then, refers to the proliferation of frameworks for understanding contemporary social inquiry as well as to the incommensurability of these frameworks. The contesting discourses about inquiry force a researcher both to relocate away from secure, "one best way" approaches and to negotiate the resources of different inquiry problematics.

Positivism is not dead, as anyone knows who tries to get published in most journals, obtain grants from most funding agencies, or have research projects accepted by thesis and dissertation committees. What is dead, however, is its theoretic dominance and its "one best way" claims over empirical work in the human sciences. Philosophy and history of science, sociology of knowledge, the various voices of marginalized people, and developments in physics have combined to make positivism's dominance increasingly shaky. *Postpositivism*, then, refers to the great ferment over what is seen as appropriate within the boundaries of the human sciences. Postpositivist philosophies of science turn more and more to interpretive social theory, where the focus is on *constructed* versus *found* worlds in a way that increasingly focuses on the role of language in the construction of knowledge (Rorty, 1967).

In sum, there are many ways to do science. Positivism, with its claims of methodological objectivity and mathematized procedures, is one way. Critical inquiry, with its belief that there is no transhistorical, culture-free, disinterested way of knowing, is another way. Foregrounding the politics of knowing and being known, examples of critical inquiry are especially visible in the fields of anthropology, qualitative sociology, semiotics, and poststructural linguistic theory as well as the transdisciplinary fields of feminist and cultural/communication studies (e.g., Clifford & Marcus, 1986; Fine, 1992; Grossberg, Nelson, & Treichler, 1992). In the rest of this chapter, I position critical inquiry methodologically within the "uneasy social sciences" in what is generally referred to as "the postpositivist intellectual climate of our times" (Fiske & Shweder, 1986, p. 16). My particular focus is the challenge poststructuralism offers to the development of critical approaches to empirical research in the social sciences.

CRITICAL INQUIRY: METHODOLOGICAL ASSUMPTIONS

Critical inquiry views both method—techniques for gathering empirical evidence—and methodology—the theory of knowledge and the interpretive framework that guide a particular research project—as inescapably tied to issues of power. Methods are assumed to be politically charged "as they define, control, evaluate, manipulate and report" (Gouldner, 1970, p. 50). The point of the above is that "the role of ideology does not diminish as rigor increases and error is dissipated" (LeCourt, 1975, p. 200). Such a recognition of the pervasiveness of ideology provides the grounds for an openly value-based approach to critical inquiry. The central issue is how to bring scholarship and advocacy together in order to generate ways of knowing that interrupt power imbalances.

Oriented toward the interests of marginalized social groups, an emancipatory, critical social science develops out of the social relations of the research process itself, out of the enactment of research praxis that uses intellectual effort to work toward a more just society. Given poststructuralism's warnings that nothing is innocent, including intellectuals with change aspirations, Foucauldian (Foucault, 1980) questions come to the fore: How do practices to discover the "truth" about ourselves influence our lives? How can we learn to track the play of power across intendedly "liberatory" approaches to inquiry? What would it mean "to grow up in our attitudes toward science" (Fine, 1986, p. 2) in an era characterized by the loss of certainties and absolute frames of reference?

To explore such questions, I first sketch the characteristics of critical research designs and then call on a handful of exemplars[4] to flesh out those characteristics. I deliberately use feminist work in order to situate it as a fertile site for the generation of new research methods that take into account the growing lack of confidence on the part of social scientists regarding ways of portraying a world marked by the elusiveness with which it greets our efforts to know it.[5] This lack of confidence in the taken-for-granted patterns of Western science is often coded with the term *the crisis of representation*, and it has profound implications for rethinking the practices of the social sciences (e.g., Rosenau, 1992; Van Maanen, 1988).

---

[4]I use the term *exemplar* to mean not a cookbook recipe to follow or an instance of "the best of," but as a concrete illustration of a number of abstract qualities. Exemplars are not used in the Kuhnian sense of paradigmatic cases that dominate a research community's sense of both normal and revolutionary science. To the contrary, my exemplars are a quite idiosyncratic selection from the not-yet-published work of friends and dissertation students with which I happen to be familiar. Like Mishler (1990), I offer them as resources, "springboards" (p. 422).

[5]Kroker and Cook (1986) stated: *"Feminism is the quantum physics of postmodernism"* (p. 22, original emphasis). Quantum physics opened up a world other than Newtonian linearity, subject–object duality, and universal covering laws. Hence I read Kroker and Cook as situating late-20th-century feminism as the paradigmatic political discourse of postmodernism. For more on this, see Lather (1991, Chap. 2).

> What is meant by the crisis of representation? What are the implications of this crisis for research practice?

CHARACTERISTICS OF CRITICAL RESEARCH DESIGNS: FEMINIST POSTSTRUCTURAL EXEMPLARS

Critical research designs are characterized by the following: (1) they explore more interactive, dialogic, and reciprocal research methods that work toward transformative action and egalitarian participation; (2) they connect meaning to broader structures of social power, control, and history; (3) they work toward open, flexible theory building grounded in both confrontation with and respect for the experiences of people in their daily lives and profound skepticism regarding appearances and "common sense." Finally, given poststructuralism's cautions regarding the researcher as "The Great Liberator" (Foucault, 1980), (4) they foreground the tensions involved in speaking *with* rather than *to/for* marginalized groups. Rather than speaking *to* or *for* those struggling for social justice, the goal is to proceed in a mutually educative way that works against the central danger to praxis-oriented empirical work: "emancipating" people in a way that imposes a researcher's agenda. The following exemplars both embody and problematize this listing as they explore the implications of the critical paradigm. I begin with an example from medical anthropology and then turn to feminist poststructural inquiry.

Nancy Scheper-Hughes (1992), in *Death Without Weeping: The Violence of Everyday Life in Brazil*, presented an ethnographic portrayal of mothers, children, and child mortality among the poor in a Brazilian shantytown. Drawing on extensive fieldwork into people's daily lives, Scheper-Hughes worked within the framework of critical medical anthropology to challenge standard biomedical and social definitions, particularly the Western notion of maternal love. As infant mortality among the poor is related to larger political and economic forces, distinctions between official diagnostic definitions of disease and illness and patients' experience of them are positioned as cultural constructions and probed for whose interests they serve. Returning to give the shantytown residents copies of her book, she spoke of becoming involved in the lives of those she has studied: "They become closer to us [anthropological fieldworkers], more intimate to us sometimes, than sisters and brothers" (Scheper-Hughes, cited in Coughlin, 1992, p. A9). Exploring how the political and medical establishments have transformed the social problem of hunger into medical problems in ways that serve class interests, this example of critical medical anthropology demonstrates how critical ethnography connects meaning to broader structures of social power. As critical ethnography, it works to build theory in a way that is grounded in respect for the everyday lives of people who are disenfranchised.

A first example of feminist critical work that takes the crisis of representation into account is Richardson's (1992) essay about her interview with "Louisa May" as part of her study of unmarried mothers. "Consciously self-revelatory" in probing the lived experience of the researcher (p. 125), Richardson cheekily hopes that she has not "ventured beyond improper" as she "breache[s] sociological writing expectations by writing sociology as poetry" (p. 126). First presenting "a transcript masquerading as a poem/a poem masquerading as a transcript" (p. 127), her primary goal was "to create a position for experiencing the self as a sociological knower/constructor—not just talking about it, but doing it" (p. 136). Speaking autobiographically in order to provide "an opportunity to rethink sociological representation" (p. 133), Richardson evoked her need to break out of the "dreary" writing of "straight" sociological prose" (p. 131) as the part of her that has written poetry for 8 years is called on to provide new writing strategies.

Richardson concluded with five consequences to herself of the experience of producing and disseminating the story of "Louisa May." We hear about changed relations with children; spirituality; Richardson's integration of "the suppressed 'poet' and the overactive 'sociologist'" (p. 135), including her return of the advance from the book contract because she is no longer able to write conventional sociology; her increased attunement to differences in others and herself, including more caution "about what 'doing research' means" (p. 135); and, finally, some disillusionment at "the hold of positivism on even those I consider my allies" as she presented this work (p. 135). "I experience isolation, alienation, and freedom, exhilaration. I want to record what they are saying; I want to do fieldwork on them. Science them" (p. 136). Her "feminist mission . . . intensified," she positions herself as "a sociological revolutionist in community with others who are questioning how and for whom we write sociology" (p. 136).

I deliberately use this most scandalous exemplar first. Presenting the interview data from one single mother as a poem, Richardson blurred the lines between the genres of poetry and social science reporting. Theorizing out of autobiography, her practice collapsed the private/public distinction. Richardson is mother, wife, scholar, and poet in her desire to move toward some way of doing science more in keeping with her feminist poststructuralism. Bringing ethics and epistemology together, Richardson's authority came from engagement and reflexivity rather than some canonical "objectivity." Her practices of textual representation, by hegemonic standards, "go too far" with the politics of uncertainty, self-conscious partiality, and embodied knowing.

A second example of feminist poststructural work is a dissertation on African American women and leadership positions in higher education (Woodbrooks, 1991). Woodbrooks's study was "designed to generate more interactive and contextual ways of knowing" (p. 93), with a particular focus on openness to counter interpretations: "The overarching goal of the methodology is to present a series of fruitful interruptions that demonstrate the multiplicity of meaning-making and interpretation" (p. 94).

In analyzing interview data, Woodbrooks (1991) made extensive use of two familiar qualitative practices of validity: member checks and peer debriefing (Lincoln & Guba, 1985). Using both to purposefully locate herself in the contradictory borderland between feminist emancipatory and poststructural positions, she attempted to interrupt her role as the Great Interpreter, "to shake, disrupt, and shift" her feminist critical investments (Woodbrooks, 1991, p. 103). Peer debriefing and member checks were used to critique her initial analysis of the data, her "perceptions of some broadly defined themes that emerged as I coded the transcripts" (p. 132). After reanalyzing the data and her original analysis, Woodbrooks sent a second draft out to participants and phoned for responses. This resulted in a textual strategy that juxtaposed the voices of the White female researcher with those of the African American female participants.

In her textual strategy, Woodbrooks first tells "a realist tale" (Van Maanen, 1988) that backgrounds the researcher's shaping influence and foregrounds participant voices. Here the voices of the women she interviewed are presented, organized around the emergent themes of assertiveness, cultural diversity, identity construction, and the double jeopardy for women of color. Each "realist tale" is interrupted with "a critical tale" that reads the data according to Woodbrooks' theoretical investments. Here Woodbrooks used feminist and critical theory to "say what things mean" as she theorized out of the words of the African American women research participants presented in the realist tale. Finally, in a third-person voice, she tells "a deconstructive tale" that draws on participant reactions to the critical tale. Here, she probed her own desire, "suspicious of . . . the hegemony [of] feminism" (p. 140) in her analysis. Her feminist analysis marginalized both African American identity as a source of pride and strength (ascribing it totally to gender) and participant concerns with male/female relations. "This strategy [of feminist consciousness-raising] perpetuates feminism as a white middle class project and trivializes the deep emotional ties that black women share with black men" (p. 200). In sum, holding up to scrutiny her own complicity, Woodbrooks created a research design that moves her toward unlearning her own privilege and decentering the researcher as the master of truth and justice via her expanded use of the familiar techniques of member checks and peer debriefing.

> How might you use Woodbrooks' strategies of presenting a realist, critical, and deconstructive tale in your own work?

A third example of feminist poststructural work is that of an Australian dissertation student, Erica Lenore McWilliam. In a study of how students talk about their needs in preservice teacher education, McWilliam (1992a, 1992b) developed a research design that elaborated three research moments. First, researcher preconceptions were put under scrutiny by analyzing survey data from 314 preservice teachers that examined their attitudes toward New Right discourse and conducting a discourse analysis of avant-garde literature in teacher education. This initial reflexive phase was designed to allow contradictory evidence to inform the researcher's growing complexity of thought about the issues at hand, particularly to challenge her own preconceptions about the researcher's role as "transformative intellectual" come to "save" the oppressed that is too typical of critical, emancipatory research (Lather, 1991).

Second, a qualitative phase was designed that proceeded "from a new set of social relations in which the dominance of the researcher's 'versions' of student needs is already challenged" (McWilliam, 1992a, p. 11). This phase studied preservice teacher understandings of theory and practice over time by using interactive, dialogic interviews that situated preservice talk about needs "as fluid social phenomena . . . open to change over the duration of the pre-service course" (p. 12). A third and final reciprocal phase was designed as reflection in action. Moving toward practices of cotheorizing that created conditions for both researcher and researched to rethink their attitudes and practices, McWilliam performed multiple readings of the Phase 2 data in order to fragment researcher authority over data analysis. Of note is McWilliam's learning that research practices that interrupt researcher privilege must construct "an interrogative researcher text . . . a questioning text" that overtly "signals tentativeness and partiality" (1992b, p. 271).

Each stage paid particular attention to discrepant data, the facts unfit to fit tidy categorical schemes. Ranging across rather standard attitudinal surveys, dialogic, reciprocally self-disclosive interviews, and sustained interaction, McWilliam worked to decenter both her own expertise and the participants' common sense about teaching practices. Her "double-edged analysis" (1992b, p. 30) used feminist, critical, and poststructural theories to problematize one another. Remarking on the "untidiness" of "this straddling of agendas" (p. 91), she delineated the "state of tension" (p. 257) that exists between feminism and unproblematic siding with or against Enlightenment projects of social transformation via consciousness raising. As such, her work enacts what it means to let contradictions remain in tension, to unsettle from within and to position "facts" as a "discourse of the real." Dissolving interpretations by marking them as temporary, partial, and invested, she continues her paradoxical continuing investment in transformative praxis.

Like Woodbrooks, McWilliam is particularly noteworthy for attending to the creation of interactive social relations in which both researcher and researched can rethink their attitudes and practices, rather than focusing exclusively on textual strategies. In exclusively, textual strategies, questions such as "Who is speaking to/for/with whom, for what reasons and with what resources?" are displaced by "What is the object of my analysis? How have I constructed it? What are the conventions of disciplinary practice that I seek to put under erasure?" As Whitford (1991) noted in her book on Irigaray. "Playing with a text . . . is a rather solipsistic activity: it is not a dialogue with the other which includes process and the possibility of change" (p. 48). It is one thing to ask whether new voices are being heard and quite another to ask whether voices are hearing themselves and one another fruitfully.

My final exemplar of feminist critical work that gestures toward the problematics of representation is my beginning study of women living with HIV/AIDS (Lather, 1992). A Lyotardian (Lyotard, 1984) "small narrative," the following questions based on the early phases of my inquiry offer a specific pragmatic context for fashioning a field of possibilities for practices toward a *reflexive* science.

Following Foucault, I ask myself: Am I telling stories that are not mine? Do research participants become narrators of their own stories? In contrast, if I as the researcher tell the stories, do I work to not see so easily in telling the stories that belong to others? Do I try hard to understand less, to be nudged out of positions customarily occupied when viewing "the Other" (Brown, 1992)?

In terms of researcher/researched relations, who are my "others"? What dualisms structure my arguments? What hierarchies are at play? How can I use Irigaray's concept of the "We–you/I" to disrupt such oppositions, to create a constantly moving speaking position that fixes neither subject nor object, that disrupts the set boundaries between subjects (Game, 1991, p. 88)?

What does all of this have to do with we/they positionings? For example, what does my getting tested for HIV mean within this context? I am considering when to do this: now? at the end? midway through writing? There is a methodological interest here. Is this instrumental? exploitative? What does it mean to position these women and this project as a Gramscian (Gramsci, 1971) historical laboratory in which to explore a science marked by practices of productive ambiguity that cultivate a taste for complexity?

In terms of the role of the researcher, how do I struggle with the task of an I becoming an *eye* without the anxiety of voyeurism that entangles the researcher in an ever more detailed self-analysis (Quinby, 1991)? What are my practices of self-reflexivity? Do I as researcher address the inadequacies of language, or do I position myself as telling a "real" story with a "final" say? Do I use disruptive devices in the text to unsettle conventional notions of the real?

What is my goal as a researcher: empathy? emancipation? advocacy? learning from/working with? What is the romance of the desire for research as political intervention? What would it mean to "come clean" about my methodology? How is this work tied into what Van Maanen (1988) refers to as the by no means trivial "demands of contemporary academic careers" and disciplinary logics (p. 53)? What is this fierce interest in proving the relevance of intellectual work? To what extent is my work tied to "the pretensions of sociology toward politics" (Riley, 1988, p. 54)?

Situated so as to give testimony and witness to what is happening to these women with HIV/AIDS, I have the methodological desire to probe the instructive complications of this study. As I learn how these women make sense of their experiences, my hope is to generate a theory of situated methodology that will lead me to a place where I do *not* conclude that "I will never do research this way again."[6]

Offered as more problem than solution, the exemplars I have recruited as provocateurs of critical inquiry after poststructuralism are performances that work from spaces already in the making. Situated in the crisis of authority that has occurred across knowledge systems, I face the challenge of making productive use of the dilemma of being left to work from traditions of research that appear no longer adequate to the task. Between the no-longer and the not-yet lies the possibility of what was impossible under traditional regimes of truth in the social sciences: the "micro-becomings" of a science defined by a dispersal, circulation, and proliferation of becomings (Deleuze & Guattari, 1983, p. 70). My intent has been not to make a general recipe but to forge from a scattered testimony a methodology that is not so much prescription as "curves of visibility and enunciation" (Deleuze, 1992, p. 160). An experiment "that baffle[s] expectations, trace[s] active lines of flight, seek[s] out lines that are bunching, accelerating or decreasing in speed" (Deleuze & Guattari, 1983, p. 111), it evokes the "horizons toward which experiments work" (Ormiston, 1990, p. 239) as we try to understand what is at play in our practices of constructing a science "after truth."

Lather raises the question of the researcher's goal (empathy, emancipation, advocacy, and learning from/working with). How would you describe your goal as a researcher in your own work? How have your goals changed over time?

CONCLUSIONS

Post-modernism involves the development of new rhetorics of science, new stories of knowledge "after truth."... The postmodern world is without guarantees, without "method." ... All we can do is invent. We must construct and exemplify the rhetorics of the future ... through ... endless stories. Like this one. (Tomlinson, 1990, pp. 44, 57)

---

[6]This sentiment comes directly out of my experience of presenting a talk on my research project to a small gathering of women at the research conference of our dreams in Wisconsin, August 7–8, 1992. It is also spurred by P. Marienthal's (1992) dissertation experience with "participatory research," from which he concluded that "I will never do research this way again" when his use of "member checks" blew up in his face, causing great consternation on the part of everyone involved in the inquiry.

In this chapter I have probed the challenges of "the postmodern moment" to explore how critical and feminist research is reinscribing qualitative inquiry. The role of feminist critical work in reinventing the social sciences is both cause and effect of the larger crisis of authority in late-20th-century thought. Awareness of the complexity, contingency, and fragility of the practices we invent to discover the truth about ourselves can be paralyzing. Taking into account Martin Luther King's caution regarding paralysis of analysis, reflexively getting on with doing such work may be the most fruitful action we can take.

13

Case Study Research

Patricia A. Hays
Northern Arizona University

MEET THE AUTHOR

Patricia A. Hays earned a master's degree at the University of Illinois, a doctorate at Northern Arizona University (NAU), and is an associate professor in the Center for Excellence in Education at NAU. She was director of student services and is currently a team instructor in the Integrated Secondary Teacher Education Program (I-STEP) in the teacher preparation program.

Dr. Hays' selected publications include a book chapter *"Education in the Year 2000"* (1989, with A. Cropper, P. Baron, and P. VerVelde), and two articles, *"Evaluating Your Gifted Program"* (1994) and *"I-STEP and the Preparation of Middle School Teachers"* (2000, with D. Kain and K. Wunderlich). Her papers include *"An Application of Holland's Theory to Gifted Minority and Underserved Eighth Graders"* (1986, with K. Karol and J. Flores), *"Preparing Gifted Special Populations for Careers"* (1988), *"Early Career Planning for Gifted Youth"* (1993), and *"Problem-Based Learning and the Gifted"* (2000).

Dr. Hays received the Arizona Minority Education Access and Achievement Medallion Award (1991) and a Phi Delta Kappa special award (1997) for "outstanding service and contributions to education students."

Case study research can involve the close examination of people, topics, issues, or programs. These studies might explore student experiences in a law school, cheating at a community college, effects of school reform in a middle school, a special program for Gulf War veterans, or countless other entities. These entities are known as particular cases unique in their content and character. Case studies are unlike ethnographies in that they seek to answer focused questions by producing in-depth descriptions and interpretations over a relatively short period of time, perhaps a few weeks to a year. Ethnographies tend to ask much broader questions, observe and explain practices and beliefs, and make cultural interpretations in studies that may last for as long as a year or more. In addition, unlike biographies and other historical research approaches, case studies investigate contemporary cases for purposes of illumination and understanding. In some instances, case studies are used to provide information for decision making or to discover causal links in settings where cause-and-effect relationships are complicated and not readily known, such as school reform or a particular government policy (Yin, 1994).

In traditional research such as experiments, generalizability is a clear and main objective where findings are expected to apply to other similar settings and populations. Generalization is not a goal in case studies, for the most part, because discovering the uniqueness of each case is the main purpose. Case study researchers examine each case expecting to uncover new and unusual interactions, events, explanations, interpretations, and cause-and-effect connections. Generalizability, however, is quite possible when based on several studies of the same phenomenon. In addition, readers of these case studies often use their own experiences to give meaning to the case reports, using judgment to enhance their understanding of the case and comparing that to similar cases they have encountered. Unlike evaluation studies (see Chapter 14 in this volume), case study research ordinarily leaves the determination of meaning and worth to the consumer or audience who may construct their own naturalistic generalizations by drawing on the information in the case study (Stake, 1995, p. 85).

At this point, why do you think someone might conduct case study research?

A CASE STUDY EXAMPLE

Case studies can be best understood by reading them. Excerpts of a case study will be used to provide the reader with a practical example. This case study was written by Granada and Lapan (n.d.),[1] an unpublished report based on earlier case studies conducted by Granada and hereafter cited as Granada (1997). The case is that of an implementation of a program for gifted minority students in the southwest United States. My involvement with this case work began when I became the codirector of a teacher training project funded by a Jacob Javits grant (1990–1993).[2] The goal of the project was to prepare teams of classroom teachers over a 10-week summer period to develop and implement programs of gifted education for underrepresented populations in their schools. In addition, each school that was involved served large numbers of ethnic minority students. Each school involved agreed to send at least two teachers who would serve as the returning change agent team. Each teacher team, working closely with the school principal, was required to develop a site plan for the development and implementation of a program to serve gifted minority students. Sixty-three teachers received this training over a 3-year period. Follow-up case studies of these attempts at implementation were conducted at several sites.

What follows is material excerpted from one of these case studies (Granada, 1997). The reader should note that, as with most case studies, considerably more qualitative rather than quantitative data are collected and reported. Case study research can include both kinds of information.

---

[1] A thoroughly revised version of this unpublished case study appears as Granada and Lapan (2001).

[2] The project reported in this case study was supported under the Javits Act Program (Grant No. R206A90087) as administered by the Office of Educational Research and Improvement, U.S. Department of Education.

The Situation

In the summer of 1991, 15 potential change agent teachers arrived on the campus of Northern Arizona University (NAU) to become participants in a training project funded by a Jacob Javits grant. The goal of the training project was to prepare teams of classroom teachers, over a period of 10 weeks, to develop and implement programs of gifted education for underrepresented populations in their school. These teacher teams faced 10 weeks of intensive training, including practice in teaching methods, lesson and unit development, and analysis of their own teaching. They would be expected to learn how to identify underserved minority gifted youth and to develop a faculty collaboration and program plan to implement on their return to school in the fall. One particularly successful site was an elementary school in the southwest area of Arizona, an oasis in the middle of the desert regions near the border of Mexico. This is their story.

The Community

Agriculture, through irrigation of the desert area, was a part of the lifeblood of the economy. Drawn to the city, either because of the proximity of its location or the job opportunities that beckoned, were a significant number of Mexican families, representing more than 33% of the community's population (all Hispanics represented nearly 36%). The impact of the Mexican culture was prevalent throughout the area, most notably in the schools.

The School

The student population was relatively large, serving grades K–6, and portable classrooms were being used to accommodate growing numbers. Staff, including the principal, was primarily female, with several teachers at each grade level. An absence of diversity on the staff was quite obvious in relation to the student population. Only one of 40 staff members was Hispanic, although the school had a 52% Hispanic enrollment. Socioeconomic diversity was very apparent as one drove around the neighborhood.

The school offered a gifted education program that was similar to many across the state. Intelligence and achievement tests were used as criteria for placement (state mandated), and the program focused on acceleration and enrichment. Very few minority students had been identified for this program.

The Players

The key players in the NAU project training were Melinda, a fifth-grade teacher; Bart, a sixth-grade teacher; and Kelly, the school principal. Melinda had not been teaching long, but her classroom was very organized and structured. Routines were well established and the room environment was quiet and orderly. Bart had taught at the school for a few years and was known for his success with challenging students. It was no surprise to walk into his classroom and find a large number of boys (and a few girls) who had the potential to be very disruptive. Bart's classroom was very different from Melinda's; noise was quite common and the approach used was somewhat structured. Kelly had been the building administrator for a few years and steered her faculty and staff smoothly and efficiently. You knew where you stood with Kelly, and she ran the business of school with fair yet demanding expectations.

Bart cared about his students, but gave the appearance that he wouldn't be extremely nurturing in the classroom. One must remember that nurturing takes many forms. Bart was actively involved in sports, both as a participant and spectator, and had "coach" ingrained in his personality.

Melinda was the organizer. Her quiet leadership was able to reign in Bart's spontaneity when decisions had to be made. Melinda was efficient and linear in many aspects of her life. She held high expectations for herself, for her students, and for those with whom she worked. A natural at nurturing, Melinda was also very perceptive about her students' special needs and would do whatever was necessary to provide for her students or secure whatever they needed that she could not provide.

Kelly was a natural at being an administrator. She was a no-nonsense kind of decision maker when situations called for a "the buck stops here" kind of solution. Kelly also was an innovative instructional leader and recognized many needs not being met in her school, exploring creative ways to meet those needs under the funding constraints of the district.

> What kind of portrait has the case study painted for you? Can you picture the community, school, and the players involved? How can case study research add to our understanding?

The Case: Part 1—The Training

Early in the training, teams from each of the project sites were prepared for the curriculum and program planning that would take place as the training progressed. Units were to be designed by each team member that would cumulatively reflect an understanding of methods of teaching potentially gifted students, including materials that were culturally relevant to ethnic minorities found at each represented school. A site plan also was to be developed, in collaboration with the building administrator, that would outline a design of a gifted education delivery model that would identify and provide programming for underrepresented populations at each school. These site plans were highly specific to the needs of the school community and culture.

Melinda and Bart were very effective in the development of their site plan. Having full support and continuous communication with Kelly, their principal, they designed a plan that would focus on identifying students with potential in the areas of leadership and creativity. They both saw this as a need at their building and of the students they worked with. They determined that the most effective initial implementation of their design would be in two stages. Initially, they would go into classrooms at their assigned teaching levels (Melinda at fifth grade, Bart at sixth grade) and teach whole-class lessons that were designed to tap the creative and leadership talents of students. Together with the regular classroom teacher, they would begin collecting data to help them determine which students might benefit from a gifted program focusing on leadership and creativity.

Phase two of their program implementation would be to jointly select students who had demonstrated potential in either the leadership or creativity area and meet with the identified students on a regular basis by pulling them out of classes at scheduled times (called a pull-out model in gifted education). Bart would work with sixth graders and Melinda with fifth. With the help of teaching colleagues, they would identify students from all of the classrooms (including their own) who were not currently a part of the traditional gifted program, with a particular sensitivity toward finding untapped talent among minority students, girls, and underachievers.

The Case: Part 2—Fall Semester, 1991

In August, the first order of business was an optional in-service and orientation with teachers whose students might be selected for participation in the program. An information session was held early one morning during "prep week," with Melinda and Bart presenting an overview of the year ahead. The turnout for this optional session was reflective of site support. Much emphasis was placed in the presentation on the importance of the role of the classroom teacher. Bart and Melinda left the presentation enthused about the interest demonstrated by their peers.

The demonstration lessons would have a variety of targeted outcomes. Bart and Melinda would provide teachers with lesson models with the intention of motivating them to incorporate similar types of lessons into their daily teaching. Melinda shares what they had in mind as they began entering the classrooms to teach demonstration lessons:

> We had two goals when we went in. One was to let the teachers see their children doing things in a different way, maybe creative way by teaching in a new way that maybe they haven't seen. Hopefully they would start to identify [for gifted] and maybe see students responding to us that they didn't see responding to them in class when they were using lecture or questions. And hopefully we would be able to, by going in and working with their classes, help identify by giving us a chance to observe their kids.

Although the intent of the demonstration lessons had been broader, Bart and Melinda chose to focus on the use of the lessons as a means of identification. The classroom teachers for the most part shared this perception, but with more depth than perhaps Melinda and Bart were aware of.

A fifth-grade teacher, having experienced the lessons, recognized an expertise that Melinda and Bart now had in the identification of creative talent in kids. She recognized her own limitations and was very pleased that the two were able to share this expertise with her.

The Case: Part 3—Spring Semester, 1992

Second semester brought a quick start to the planned pull-out program. This would be a real test of collaboration, support, and teamwork for Melinda and Bart. They planned on meeting with newly identified students on a regular, weekly basis. As the semester progressed, a few more students were identified, and students were involved in a number of projects in the pull-out that tapped both their creative potential and critical thinking. Students were sharing their enthusiasm for being in the program with classmates and classroom teachers. Two especially perceptive students in the program shared some interesting insights. The first, in response to being asked why the program was being implemented, responded

> Because they [Bart and Melinda] felt that there was a need to get something because there were a bunch of kids being neglected. Nothing was being done with them, and they were not even ever thought of that way [as being gifted].

The second student recognized the extended benefits of being involved:

> You do activities to make you feel not that you're more special than another person, but to bring out your ideas. That way you get a better understanding, and then when you go to your regular class you can participate more and express your ideas in a way someone wouldn't.

Why may it be important to obtain student views in a case study? Would you give these the same weight when reporting findings? Why or why not?

Not only was the impact of the new program being felt at the building level, but Bart's and Melinda's undertakings were being recognized throughout the district. In-services were an additional opportunity for the novice change agents to spread the good word of their successful program. Melinda commented about a specific in-service opportunity she and Bart had the pleasure of being involved with:

> The whole district had an afternoon in-service on the Hispanic culture. We got to do a presentation on our program there. Our focus was on minority gifted, targeting minority students for gifted programs. Quite a few teachers came to that one.

An air of confidence was very much present as the two shared their experiences among the network of project staff and participants. They became quite eager to share the story of their success and, specifically, the success stories of the students they were serving.

Bart and Melinda, beyond the immediate changes they saw in students and their teaching, saw changes in their roles at the building level. Relative to students, the pair saw their program as the first steps toward at least a preliminary impact on the gang problems that were facing their community. There might be long-range effects from identifying kids who could "get lost in the cracks and maybe not even finish high school" and recognizing and valuing their talents. They also saw an impact on the teachers and a rethinking as to what "giftedness" meant. Both also saw themselves being recognized as leaders in the building and in the district. The opportunities to serve as in-service presenters were new to each of them, but they quickly grew comfortable with the new roles. Melinda commented on her new role as "novice expert":

> Well this past year I wasn't content in just teaching a lesson. I wanted to plan more. I think it's frustrating when you don't have that time and, you know, it takes a lot of time to plan. I didn't throw things together as quickly. I really put a lot of thought into it. I spent a lot of time looking at other materials out there . . . talking to other teachers . . . showing them what I had . . . giving them ideas, borrowing ideas from them. Before I went [to the training] I felt more like *I* just did it. [This year] I felt I pulled more from my staff to help out. We have a really cool staff and we've always shared and helped each other out. For some reason I felt that I was more available for the teachers. You know, provided more information, more input into things. Like when we would meet with the fifth-grade teachers, I really felt I had a lot more input. They took a lot of my advice and I shared a lot with them. Before when we met, we just talked about what we were doing. . . . Also I found teachers coming up to me and giving me things. "You'll like this," "Try this, I used this this morning and it's good." I was also getting a lot of materials from the teachers that I felt wasn't there before. I don't think that we didn't mean not to do that, we just never made a point of doing it.

Bart and Melinda, with the assistance of the teachers, began generating "waiting lists" of kids who were now being looked at in a very different way. In one instance, a classroom teacher was anticipating a future placement of a student who had just been moved into her classroom from an English as a second language classroom. This was quite a new way for the building staff to look at a non-English-speaking child, and credit for the heightened sensitivity stems back to Bart and Melinda.

Finally, the district itself was beginning to evaluate gifted education. Melinda offered this perception:

> I think we've probably stirred them [the district] up a little. I think we've gone in and we've asked questions that they couldn't answer. So I think they're looking at

trying to answer those questions on change. It may be slow in coming, but they're aware that they've got to do something, and I'd like to think that we've helped them become aware.

Melinda, Bart, and Kelly had a lot to be proud of as the year ended. A majority of their plan had been successfully implemented, they had been able to overcome the challenges of scheduling, and they had provided a special year for two groups of students. But they were all aware that, even as a threesome, they could not have done it alone. Melinda summed up what all agreed was the key to success:

> I think you need support from your staff and administration to help with your plan. I think you need to start small and then build up toward big. I think if you take on too much too soon, you'll fail. I think having a team was great because you've been there to help each other out the whole way. You can ask each other questions like "What are you doing?" and "How did this work?" "Have you tried this?" or you remind each other of things. Being in constant communication with others lets you know you're not alone.

What does this case study tell you about what contributes to implementing new programs in schools? What would you do with what you have learned from this case study?

In this case study, Granada (1997) provided a picture of two teachers involved in a school change project and in particular what happened with these two teachers following their Jacob Javits training. How does someone like Granada go about conducting a case study? The rest of this chapter is intended to answer that question.

CONDUCTING A CASE STUDY

Case studies are often viewed as an easy way to do research. All the researcher needs to do is make some observations and conduct some interviews and then write the story of what happened. As with most research approaches, case study work is actually quite demanding, requiring reflective and very focused research efforts. Reflecting on the case study presented above, let us have a look at how these studies are constructed.

Selecting a Site

The researcher's purpose in case study research is not to study everything going on in the site, but to focus on specific issues, problems, or programs. In every instance, there must be boundaries set before the study begins. One way of bounding the study is through the use of research questions. These questions will continue to focus the researcher throughout the study. Yin (1994) talked about defining the "case"; therefore, the first step in bounding the case study is to decide on the case. The case can be about an individual, a group of people, a school, a school district, decisions about programs, a program implementation process, an organizational change, or other issues. And, of course, they could be about issues and programs outside of education. Once the case is defined, the unit of analysis needs to be determined. The unit of analysis is defined as where the researcher obtains the data for the case study. If the case study is about an individual, the individual is the unit of analysis. If the study is about a school district, the unit of analysis is the school district and its policies. These decisions are made at the same time the research questions are being formulated. In the Granada case study, the decision was made to study two teachers at one school. Another decision to be made in the bounding process is the length of time for the case study investigation. Topics for case studies are dynamic topics that can be studied for years. In conjunction with determining the research questions, the definite times of the beginning and end of the study need to be set. If these times are not established in advance, there is a danger that the researcher may think that one more visit can produce additional interesting data. This can go on forever and result in no useful conclusion to the study. The time length in the bounding of the Granada (1997) case study was one year. Of course, the story continued and still continues today.

Research Questions

Once the researcher becomes involved in the case study at the site, the researcher will be tempted to focus on other issues rather then those planned. At a school site location, for example, the principal may tempt the researcher with other problems the school faces or stonewall if the topic could result in a negative view of the principal or the school. The teachers in a school always have a current problem they are focused on that has nothing to do with the researcher's interests, so the researcher has to work to refocus the teachers' attention on the topic of study. Observation in a classroom provides many temptations to draw the researcher's attention from the focus of the study. Each issue can appear to have a life of its own, drawing increasing attention as it becomes more complex and intriguing. Stake (1995) believed that the temptation to be drawn away from the topic of study is one of the most serious problems in case study research (p. 24).

The researcher needs to be entirely focused before beginning to collect data at the case study site, but at the same time flexible enough to see answers to research questions when they were not expected. The research questions provide this focus. The research questions can only be developed with extensive reading. As

Yin (1994) pointed out, "Budding investigators think the purpose of a literature review is to determine the *answers* about what is known on a topic; in contrast, experienced investigators review previous research to develop sharper and more insightful *questions* about the topic" (p. 9).

In Granada's (1997) case study, he needed to be well versed in the topics of change, change agents, use of teacher training to initiate change, giftedness, culture and education interaction, and giftedness and culture interaction. These are some examples of research questions Granada used to guide his study:

- Did the participants selected for the study change over the course of the school year during which a gifted program was to be initiated?
- If the changes in participants selected for the study took place, to what extent did those changes affect others?
- How effective were participants selected for the study as change agents?
- If the intended changes did not take place, what may have contributed to the lack of change?

Most case study researchers start with a general issue and, as background research evolves, the researchers try to generate a list of 15 to 20 questions focused on the issue. These questions then need to be pared down to a few questions to bound the study. As the researcher begins to work with the site, other questions may arise. The research questions must set the focus of the study, but the researcher needs to keep in mind that case study research is an evolving process. The researcher must be willing to allow questions to change and new ones to evolve as long as they relate to the focus of the study. An example given by Stake (1995) illustrated this. An original question was: What do the parents want from the music program? An evolved question was: What is the extent of disagreement across this music faculty regarding the teaching of music courses required of all students? The evolved question arose during teacher interviews. When case studies are conducted for examining innovative programs, the researcher needs to be able accommodate the program development.

When the program is implemented, it frequently develops in a manner that was not anticipated by the practitioners. The practitioners often adjust the program when various aspects of it do not work as planned. With this dynamic approach, the researcher is able to adjust the research questions and still maintain the focus of the study (Patton & Westby, 1992).

Why might the development of well-researched and refined questions be important in case study research? What do you think could go wrong if the study questions were not carefully defined?

Data Sources

Once the research questions have been determined, sources of data for each question should be determined. The case study researcher as a qualitative researcher needs to provide for triangulation (e.g., multiple sources of data and multiple methods for each question). Yin (1994) stated that a major strength of case studies is the opportunity to use many different sources of data. In Granada's (1997) study, he used an interview with the principal, separate interviews with the two teachers, classroom observations, interviews with students, and the school plan document created by the two teachers during the summer training. This is an excellent example of seeking multiple sources and multiple methods. Not all of these sources of data were used to answer each research question, but each research question did have multiple sources of information, as well as different methods to obtain the data. When initially planning a case study, some researchers create a chart listing each research question and the planned data collection methods and sources. For example, using a research question from Granada's (1997) study, Table 13.1 could be developed.

The use of multiple methods and multiple sources as forms of triangulation makes case study findings not only more comprehensive but also more complicated, because so many perspectives are represented. Finally, all categories of data need to be reviewed by the researcher as possible data sources (Yin, 1994). A review of some categories of data follows.

How does triangulation work, and what contribution does it make to case study validity?

Documents and Records

Examples of documents that might be used are letters, memoranda, meeting minutes, proposals, progress reports, grant applications, action plans, curriculum plans, lesson plans, and articles appearing in the media (in print or on tape). Examples of archival records that might be used are organizational charts; budgets; census-type data collected about the site, such as students in a free or

TABLE 13.1

Research Question	Possible Methods and Sources of Data
Were the participants effective as change agents?	Interviews with participants Interview with school principal Interviews with other teachers in the school Examination of the school plan document

reduced-cost lunch program, or the ethnic population distribution of a school; and personal records such as calendars, telephone notes, and e-mails.

All of these documents and records were written for a different audience, so accuracy of the information needs to be verified, even with the census-type data. These sources of data can be used to collaborate or elaborate data from other sources. They are also valuable in suggesting directions for interviews and observations. In his study, Granada (1997) reviewed the summer training the two teachers had participated in, the site action plan the teachers developed, and original agreements made among the grant directors, the school principal, and the two teachers. These provided directions for his on-site interviews and observations.

Interviews

Interviews are one of the richest sources of data in a case study and usually the most important type of data to be collected. Interviews provide the researcher with information from a variety of perspectives. Yin (1994) stated that

> Overall, interviews are an essential source of case study evidence because most case studies are about human affairs. These human affairs should be reported and interpreted through the eyes of specific interviewees, and well-informed respondents can provide important insights into a situation. They can provide shortcuts to the prior history of the situation, helping you to identify other relevant sources of evidence. However, the interviews should always be considered *verbal reports* only. As such, they are subject to the common problems of bias, poor recall, and poor or inaccurate articulation. Again, a reasonable approach is to corroborate interview data with information from other sources. (p. 85)

Early decisions need to be made if the interviews will be open-ended, focused, and with individuals or small groups of people. These are important decisions, and final decisions will be based on the interviewer's style preference, length of time for the study, and the research questions. For example, group interviews offer more data from more individuals in less time than a single interview. Confidentially, however, is sacrificed. As you read in his case study, Granada (1997) relied heavily on interviews to provide information. His important source interviews were conducted repeatedly with the same principal and teachers throughout the school year. He also interviewed students and other teachers.

Direct Observation

Observations are another important source of information in case studies. This is especially true in case studies involving classrooms or schools, because the interaction of individuals cannot be understood without observation. Early decisions need to be made about observations, including the number to be made and whether the observer and observed feel the researcher has received an accurate picture of the situation. Another decision involves whether to use observational protocols or more informal data collection. Observational protocols point the observer in specific directions and usually require tallies of different types of observed behavior. These tallies are a source of quantitative data. Deciding this often depends on purpose and study questions. Granada (1997) conducted several classroom observations of each teacher. He used both qualitative data of a general descriptive nature and quantitative data of a specific nature related to gifted education.

All of these sources of data are usable in a case study. In developing the plan for the study, the researcher will need to determine which sources of data are feasible. Many times, this feasibility is determined by the amount of money to support the length of time the study will be conducted. Case studies can be conducted over time, with the researcher visiting the site to collect data for a few days at a time over a school year, or the researcher can spend 1 to 3 weeks at a site collecting data each day to complete the study. It is most important that the researcher remember that triangulation requires multiple sources of data and multiple methods in answering each question. Findings in case studies are more likely to be trusted as true because of the use of triangulation of methods and sources. This triangulation also addresses any problems with construct validity (Yin, 1994). In case study research, construct validity refers to the extent answers to study questions are considered to be accurate representatives of the case.

Gathering Data

Gathering data begins when the background reading, research, and planning begin. Everything read and discussed has influence on the researcher. Even before formally collecting data, the researcher must visit the site to establish understandings between the researcher and those being studied on how the research will be conducted. Some of these understandings are:

- What is the purpose of the study
- How will the study be conducted
- How will confidentiality be established
- Who or what will be observed
- Who will be interviewed
- What documents need to be available for review
- Who will review preliminary findings to verify the information
- Who will receive the case study final document

Adding to all of this, the researcher tries to establish trust and rapport with those at the site. The initial personal contact should begin to allow the researcher to establish empathy with the individuals in the study. Establishing empathy is necessary for the researcher to be able to understand the feelings and experiences of individuals being observed and interviewed. Patton and Westby (1992) believed that "the capacity for empathy . . . is one of the major assets available for human inquiry into human affairs" (p. 11). If, over time, the researcher can establish a growing level of empathy between the researcher and those being studied, this relationship will provide the researcher with growing access to information. Those being studied will allow more open, true-to-life experiences in observations and provide more open, honest dialogue in interviews. Depending on the sites selected, these trust-building meetings may need to be held with people in a variety of positions. In the case of a school, the central administrative level must agree, the principal must agree, and the teachers must agree. Agreements also may need to be obtained from the teachers' union and school site council or Parent–Teacher Association. During all of these negotiations, the researcher is developing some beginning understandings about the site and is informally collecting data. Even though Granada knew the two teachers well from the summer training, in his study (1997), he had to establish his role as data collector and establish an open relationship with the principal.

> What is your definition of the term *empathy*? What makes its development so vital in case study work? What are the implications of being too empathetic in case study work?

Understanding the various power arrangements is essential in comprehending how a school operates. Because case studies are often viewed as a form of evaluation, the researcher must always keep in mind the natural tension that is created by the fact that someone is being studied. Also, if the researcher is observing in classrooms, it is important to remember that most teachers only experience is when they are being evaluated. Depending on each teacher's experience, observation of the classroom may be viewed positively or negatively, but in any case, it is usually viewed with apprehension.

Each day after the data is collected, the researcher needs to review what information has been collected and how various pieces of information need to be verified. Most researchers keep a diary of the day's events or begin writing the case study. Most important at this point is reflection. Stake (1995) argued that expertise in case study work comes largely through reflective practice used in doing case studies. Granada (1997) spent numerous days over one school year at the site collecting data. Each evening he would review his interviews and observations from that day, deciding which questions needed to be asked during the next day's interviews to verify or clarify his understandings. For example, in an interview with the principal, she talked about an upcoming in-service the two teachers were planning. Earlier in the day, Granada had interviewed one of the teachers who had not mentioned the upcoming in-service. As he reviewed his notes at the end of the day (knowing he would interview the other teacher the next day), he made plans to ask the teacher about the in-service, to learn about the teacher's thoughts during that experience.

Analyzing and Interpreting the Data

At this point, the case study researcher is faced with reams of data. Sorting out the data and making meaning can be likened to solving a mystery. The researcher acting as detective must search through the clues (data) to follow threads of evidence (patterns of consistency in the data) to a final decision. Reflection becomes as important for the researcher as it would be for the detective. Patterns that emerge when all the data are reviewed are important, but occasionally a single occurrence provides meaning and makes sense of all the patterns. Therefore, good case study researchers do not rely on repeated instances as the only means to reveal meaning.

The research questions must be kept foremost in the researcher's mind. They are the threads to be followed. There will be many pieces of interesting and exciting data that do not relate to the research questions in any way. This data needs to be set aside while the researcher focuses on the research questions. The intention of a case study is to answer questions, not to provide a complete picture of the site. Using the research questions as a guide, all of the data needs to be taken apart while the researcher is looking for relationships and then reassembled to tell the story of the case. This process requires data reduction as the data is analyzed with the purpose being to sort, focus, and reorganize data that allows for drawing final conclusions. Most researchers develop a system for sorting and categorization that results in a coding system. The sorting, resorting, organizing and reorganizing, and labeling and relabeling of data should lead to a set of categories that answer the research questions in a meaningful, thick description that provides a summarization.

Sometimes a pattern of important information that adds to the complete description of the case is revealed while collecting or analyzing the data. The research questions developed prior to the collection of data did not anticipate this information. These unexpected or unintended results need to be addressed in the analysis of data. For example, in Granada's (1997) study, there was very strong support by the other teachers in the building and the school principal. This was unanticipated. Certainly, the two teachers expected support, but not to the degree revealed by Granada.

This is very inductive work. It can be thought of as a series of puzzles to be worked through, with the researcher going back and forth through the data with an idea searching for substantiations of the idea.

> How would you organize and sort through data from a case study? Are you familiar with any computer programs than can assist in this task?

Writing the Final Report

Experienced case researchers suggest that much of the writing should be done during the data collection stage (e.g., Stake, 1995; Wolcott, 1990; Yin, 1994). This is more difficult for novices, but some parts can easily be done early, such as the site description and the explanation of how the study was done. The researcher needs to clearly understand who the audiences are for this research. For example, in a school setting, writing for administrators and writing for teachers or even parents can each require a different writing and presentation style. There are a variety of styles the final reports can follow, but all must include certain parts.

Near the beginning of every case study, there needs to be a rich description of the site. If case study research recognizes the individuality and uniqueness of each case, there must be a clear understanding on the part of the reader regarding what this place is like. This might be called a unique sense, a visual image, and a personality of place. Granada (1997) had such a description near the beginning of the case study. Because the two individual teachers are an important part of his study, he spends more time trying to acquaint the reader with these main players than describing the physical setting of the site.

Because much of the collected data is analyzed through the researcher's lens, the researcher needs to provide information concerning the researcher's perspective and relationship to the case. Was the researcher hired to conduct a case study? Is this a subject the researcher has studied during a lifelong career, or is this a study where the researcher is only familiar with the participants through documents that have been provided? The audiences need to understand the researcher's role and perspective if they are to accept the findings.

When the final report is in draft form, an important procedure needs to be employed. The researcher should provide the case study participants with a copy of the draft and ask them to corroborate or question any of the information or assumptions that have been drawn. Not only is this a professional courtesy, but it is part of the validity process referred to by some researchers as member checking. Often, case researchers will type out interview results and member check those with corresponding interviewees soon after the interview is done. Sometimes, the researcher will find that there is a misunderstanding in the description that can be eliminated by using more explicit language. Other times, there is definite disagreement between the researcher and the participants on the researcher's assumptions or interpretations. Some researchers decide to eliminate the assumption, whereas others keep the report as it is but publish the participants' opinions as part of the final report. If there is a disagreement about information in the case study, the researcher needs to rework through the issue. This may mean searching for data to corroborate the information in question. In this search, participants may remember information that was not shared with the researcher originally.

This process of member checking not only increases validity but also adds to the overall comprehensiveness of the case study.

Case study research can be all consuming for the researcher. Because it is an in-depth study, it is highly personal. As stated at the beginning, case study research results in a wonderful story to read, but it is not quick and easy research to conduct. Indeed, many case study researchers talk and think about the difficulties and stress of conducting case study research (Granada, 1997; Stake, 1995; Yin, 1994).

14

Evaluation Studies

Stephen D. Lapan
Northern Arizona University

MEET THE AUTHOR

Stephen D. Lapan earned a master of arts at the University of Illinois, a doctorate in educational psychology at the University of Connecticut, and is currently a professor in the Center for Excellence in Education at Northern Arizona University (NAU). He is director of the doctoral program in curriculum and instruction and teaches courses in approaches to research and evaluation. He is consulting editor for *The Journal of Research in Childhood Education*, past editor of the *Excellence in Teaching journal* and past editor of the *Center for Excellence* monograph series.

Dr. Lapan's selected publications include a book, *Survival in the Classroom* (1978, with E. House); book chapters, "The Evaluation of Teaching" (1989) and "Policy, Productivity, and Teacher Evaluation" (1997, with E. House); and journal articles, "Guidelines for Developing and Evaluating Gifted Programs" (1989), "Evaluation of Programs for Disadvantaged Gifted Students" (1994, with E. House), "Criteria for Gifted Programs" (1996), and "Students as Independent Learners" (1998, with P. Hays).

Dr. Lapan's awards include NAU charter faculty fellow (1988), first NAU Teaching Scholar (1989), and the Arizona Association for Gifted and Talented Life Achievement Award "for service to gifted education." His selected studies include evaluation of the Illinois Gifted Program for the Illinois legislature (1968–1970), assessment of the Florida Accountability Program for the National Education Association (1978), evaluation of the Cooke Magnet School for Gifted Children (1981), and evaluation of the NAU Jacob Javits Getting Gifted Grant (1993).

BACKGROUND[1]

The field of professional evaluation has developed over the past three decades as an interdisciplinary field with researchers from many areas of social science contributing to its concepts and practice. There are professional evaluation associations in more than 20 countries and half a dozen journals that specialize in evaluation. Evaluation studies are typically sponsored and funded by branches of government, including federal, state, and local agencies. Studies are carried out by professors, independent consultants, or companies that specialize in such work.

The accepted definition of evaluation is the determination of the merit or worth of some entity. The basic difference between evaluation and other forms of social research is that evaluators arrive at conclusions such as "X is a good program

---

[1] Ernest R. House served as contributing editor for this chapter.

or has merit," whereas other researchers arrive at conclusions such as "X causes Y." Some overlap can be found between evaluation and other forms of research, however, where evaluators sometimes look for causes as well as quality, and other researchers might produce conclusions about program quality along with making cause-and-effect connections. The logic of evaluation consists of four steps:

1. Establishing criteria of merit
2. Constructing standards
3. Measuring performance and comparing it with standards
4. Synthesizing and integrating the performance data into conclusions of merit and worth

This reasoning is similar to that found in publications like *Consumer Reports.* In evaluating cars, evaluators decide which specific cars to evaluate. Then they establish criteria of merit, such as acceleration, handling, durability, and cost. They measure the performance of the cars and compare it with the standards they have adopted. Sometimes the standards are comparisons with the other cars, such as "This car is best at handling." Other standards may be derived from expectations people have about cars: "This car turns over in emergency maneuvers."

These performance results are merged into conclusions about which cars are best among those studied or which cars are acceptable. Of course, it is the case that the cars differ in performance on different criteria. The car that handles best may not be the cheapest. Evaluators must somehow synthesize these performance results into summary conclusions, leaving consumers to make final decisions.

> What is evaluation and what does it accomplish? In what contexts are its applications meaningful and needed?

Evaluating educational programs is different in some ways. Programs serve constituencies, and what is best for one constituency on one evaluation criterion may not be best for others. Evaluators must weigh and balance these different considerations. Again, the evaluation criteria are derived from the nature of the entity being evaluated and what people expect from it. For example, what do people expect from reading programs: that the students improve their reading speed or analytical skills, or improve their reading for content or enjoyment? Evaluation audiences are likely to identify many different criteria for success in reading depending on what they value. Deriving criteria and standards of performance are critical components of evaluations. Once the criteria are derived, which may take some effort, evaluators use the data collection methods of social research to measure performance.

The focus of evaluation can be *programs, personnel, products, materials,* and *policies,* though the focus for this chapter is on programs. *Personnel evaluation* entails observing an individual's performance and what the person produces. For example, professors are evaluated on the basis of their teaching and their scholarly publications. Classroom teachers are judged on their ability to teach effectively and on student achievement. Evaluating *products* and *material* entails determining whether they meet the purposes set out for them. For instance, instructional materials in mathematics might be evaluated according to the standards of the National Council of Teachers of Mathematics and whether teachers and students can effectively apply these materials in classroom work.

Policy evaluation focuses on the effects of policies established by government agencies. A policy evaluation might ascertain the effects of retaining students by determining whether the failed students achieve more, drop out of school later, or suffer emotional problems from failing a grade.

Finally, *program evaluation* emphasizes how educational and social programs are implemented, how they operate, and what effects they have. In a school setting, a sixth-grade science program might be evaluated by studying how the program began, what happens in class, and what effect the program has on students, teachers, and parents. Evaluators might examine written program descriptions and talk with planners about the history of the program. Evaluators also might observe classes, interview students, teachers, administrators, and parents.

Fundamentally, there are about half a dozen different approaches to program evaluation. One of the most common approaches is to determine if the program is achieving the goals set out for it. If the program is designed to reduce the number of school dropouts, does it accomplish this? If the goal of the program is to increase female participation in math and science classes, does it do this?

There are other ways that programs are evaluated too, including the use of testing, indicators, and experiments. The use of standardized tests dates back many decades. Although standardized tests were originally developed to ascertain the educational needs of individual students (Binet & Simon, 1905), they currently are a dominant method for assessing educational programs. Tests are efficient to administer, require no outside expertise to analyze, and meet the reporting demands made by local school boards and state and federal agencies.

One task of program evaluation should be to establish a clear connection between the program and its effects on students. Tests do not always allow these connections to be made clearly, because test scores are influenced by many factors, including student ability, language background, and socioeconomic status. Thus, changes in test scores might be caused by factors that have little to do with the quality of the program being evaluated. Although tests can make a contribution to an evaluation, their limitations make them unsuitable as the sole means of measuring program effectiveness.

Measurement of indicators is another method used to determine program success. Some indicators can be tied to program goals and can be sensitive to the particular program. Indicators might include parent requests for student inclusion, student dropout rates, teaching effectiveness, student classroom performance, and student ratings of the program. Using several indicators rather than one provides a more comprehensive picture of the program's influence. A potential shortcoming of this indicator approach is the failure to discover unknown effects. If only program goals are used to generate indicators, unanticipated program effects might be overlooked.

Many experts have called for the inclusion of experimental methods to increase the rigor of an evaluation. Comparison and control groups permit more precise estimates of program effects in some cases. Well-conducted experiments rule out rival explanations for effects, such as student ability or socioeconomic status, and provide strong evidence. Indeed, experiments can work well in situations where the rules of rigorous investigation can be followed. However, in settings like schools, experiments are difficult to use, because experimental manipulation and random assignment of students, teachers, and treatments (usually instructional programs) are not ordinarily possible. Parents do not like their children to be randomly placed in classes. When experiments are conducted, considerable expertise is also required in carrying out and interpreting results correctly.

What are the pitfalls of using any single approach to evaluation, such as only goals or only test scores?

QUALITATIVE VERSUS QUANTITATIVE EVALUATION

In past years, there was a debate over whether evaluations should be based on qualitative or quantitative data. Qualitative proponents argued that thick descriptions and particular knowledge gained from program participants outweighed quantitative indicators like test scores. Quantitative proponents argued that test scores and other numerical findings provided more objective evidence of the effects of programs. This debate has been resolved by both sides recognizing the place of both quantitative and qualitative data and that the best studies would incorporate both kinds. However, selecting data collection methods should not be the first concern in planning evaluations. Evaluations should be based on the content, purpose, and outcomes of the program, rather than being driven by data collection methodologies.

Doing Program Evaluation

For convenience, school settings have been used in this chapter to illustrate program evaluation. However, just as evaluators can evaluate school districts, schools, and classrooms, they also can carry out evaluations of counseling activities, social service agencies, and federal and state educational delivery efforts.

First Steps

Program evaluations typically begin when program developers or school leaders contact a professionally trained evaluator (often located at a university), requesting an evaluation of a program. The evaluator meets with those who want to sponsor the study to discuss why the evaluation is being done and for whom. The "why" answer might range from local concern over improving a program to reporting requirements of funding agencies. The "for whom" answer relates to who has a stake in the program and who wants to know how well the program is working. It is important for evaluators to find out the limitations placed on the study and who the audiences are.

At this point, the evaluator develops a description of the program based on information obtained from early meetings and from documents such as program proposals. The evaluator might talk with teachers and other participants who have not been in the meetings to be certain that all appropriate perspectives are represented in the plan. This program description might be shared with sponsors and program participants to gain clarity about how everyone sees the program at this stage. This exchange encourages different views of the program to be expressed and promotes a broader understanding. During these meetings, the evaluator might request that sponsors and participants indicate evaluation questions they want answered. Other questions may come from outsiders, such as school board members, those who fund the program, or program evaluators themselves.

It is the evaluator's job to develop a plan based on program descriptions, needs of the stakeholders and audiences, and the specific questions generated, as well as raise issues and questions not covered by those interviewed. The plan could include the program description along with evaluation questions and a time line for collecting data and reporting findings. Some plans are detailed in specifying exactly how questions will be answered. Other plans are less specific, perhaps listing a few evaluation questions and deadlines for the work.

Evaluators address several questions in each evaluation. Ordinarily, they also use multiple sources of data and multiple methods of collecting data to answer the questions. In addition, the sponsors of the evaluation and the evaluator should develop an evaluation agreement between them to clarify these issues. This agreement includes the distribution of responsibilities for the evaluation and who will see the results of the completed study. The agreement answers questions as to who will conduct the evaluation, who will write and present the findings, when the evaluation will be completed, in what form the results will be reported and to whom, whether preliminary findings will be reported early for purposes of feedback, whether there will be a minority report if there are disagreements with findings, and the costs of the study. For example, sponsors may not want parents to know that the program is not working if it is not. If parents are stipulated as audiences in the agreement, chances are reduced that they will be left out. Putting such issues in the agreement reduces conflict later.

> How is it important that evaluation, like most research, should be designed around content and questions rather than techniques for collecting data?

Data Collection

Instrument selection and development are key components in planning. The quality of the data is only as good as the instruments used to collect it. Ordinarily, evaluators develop new items or protocols, because the purposes of programs vary and often there are no standardized instruments to fit the particular characteristics of a given program. Whether adaptations of existing instruments are made or new ones are developed, testing the instruments in the field is essential to their readiness for use. This field testing also provides practice for the novice evaluator in administering questionnaires, conducting interviews, and observing classrooms.

In evaluation studies, especially those using qualitative data, the evaluator is an integral part of the data collection. This is particularly so in observation and interview work, where the evaluator's judgment and influence on those being observed can influence the data collected. For example, in an interview, the evaluator might ask questions that encourage frank responses, thus making the evaluation results trustworthy. Or, the evaluator may convey that certain answers are desirable, resulting in information influenced as much by what the evaluator believes as what the interviewee was thinking.

The major data collection techniques used in program evaluation are interviews, observations, tests, questionnaires, and inspection of documents.

Interviews. The face-to-face interview is one of the best sources of information. Perspectives gained through this give-and-take process represent more than points of view; they offer insights into special knowledge that only participants possess. For example, teachers can recount how classes work or what is emphasized in lessons. Students can disclose personal views of what class is like for them. Interviews sacrifice coverage to gain depth, but depth is important, although it is also time consuming.

Developing and conducting interviews are not easy tasks. Interview protocols developed by professionals can be used, but most must be adapted for particular programs. In developing interview questions, one must avoid those that suggest certain answers (e.g., The parents really like the program, don't they? Would you say the materials are the real strength of the program?). Novice evaluators need to practice using protocols and listening to their taped interviews to sharpen their questioning ability.

Observations.   Observations are used to gain insights about program operations. Although there are many observation schemes available, the evaluator may have to adapt or develop one that suits the program. Again, practice and study is necessary to learn effective observation techniques. For instance, it may be helpful if two observers watch the same taped lesson independently and compare how each described what was happening. A few practice attempts improve the accuracy of the observations.

Tests.   The use of standardized tests is a popular method for data collection in program evaluation, but such scores do not adequately reflect the content and purposes of any given program under review. A better choice would be to construct tests that parallel the students' program learning experiences, although test reliability and validity evidence should be produced for these measures. As noted earlier in the chapter, tests of any kind should not be the exclusive means for evaluating a program.

Questionnaires and document inspection.   These approaches are useful in providing background information. Questionnaires might be sent to parents to verify their child's involvement in a program and obtain their views on observed effects at home. Documents may reveal aspects of program history and goals that can be corroborated with sponsor and participant views. These approaches do not explore the depth of meaning that interviews do, but can complete the picture the evaluator is developing.

Sampling

Purposeful sampling, the deliberate selection of information-rich sources, drives most program evaluation efforts. This sampling procedure is part of the evaluation plan, where the best data sources are defined by the study questions. Program teachers know most about day-to-day lesson planning, whereas administrators know most about program funding. Additional sampling occurs during the evaluation, when evaluators learn of information sources they could not have known about when the evaluation was planned. This is known as "emerging design," adjusting evaluation plans as the study unfolds.

Evaluators sometimes use random sampling to obtain statistically representative samples so that generalization to larger populations is accurate. This sampling approach is used in cases where large groups are being surveyed. For example, analyzing test scores of large groups of students in school districts requires knowing precisely which students the data came from or what groups were represented in the data collected.

Trusting Evaluation Results

The term *validity* is commonly used in research to describe whether a study's results can be believed. Trusting results in program evaluation is a serious issue, especially when qualitative data are employed. Sometimes audiences are unfamiliar with this kind of information and may want numbers and percentages so they can feel more secure about the objectivity of the findings. Two approaches used in validating qualitative studies are *member checking* and *triangulation*.

Member checking.   Program evaluation often involves many program participants over extended periods of time. Data are collected at several intervals, and the evaluator may choose to provide preliminary summaries to participants. Unlike traditional research, where data are gathered and analyzed before reporting, in program evaluation it is appropriate to share findings during the study, especially when participants have finished providing observations about the program. By sharing preliminary findings, the evaluator is able to gauge how early results fit with the understanding of participants and sponsors. This participant or member checking allows teachers and others to question the findings or request clarification, thus challenging the evaluator to reveal evidence, change interpretations, or collect additional data. Sharing increases evaluator credibility.

Triangulation.   Triangulation, another technique, refers to the collection of data from two or more sources (e.g., students and teachers) using two or more methods (e.g., interviews and observations). For example, if an evaluator wants to learn how the program operates at the classroom level, use of classroom observations (a method), student interviews (a source and a method), and teacher interviews (different source, same method) produce the triangulation. The evaluator generates overlapping evidence rather than obtaining just one perspective. Each method and source has strengths and weaknesses, and using several methods and sources builds on strengths.

Another form of triangulation has been found useful when the evaluator is also a program participant and is possibly biased by being too close to the program. Researcher triangulation is where an outside evaluator analyzes the data collected by the in-house evaluator and draws conclusions without knowing the insider's interpretation. These conclusions are compared.

How can evaluation studies be considered valid? When would evaluation results not be trusted?

Analyzing and Reporting Study Results

Evaluation studies transform interview, observation, test, questionnaire, and document data into descriptions and explanations. Often, these data are voluminous and must be interpreted by reading over the material several times. The evaluator might begin by highlighting thoughts or phrases that emerge as patterns, then writing summaries that capture these emerging patterns. In most cases, these summaries are formed by linking the findings with the evaluation questions formulated at the outset. This approach allows the evaluator to discover effects not anticipated in the original evaluation plan while adhering to the original evaluation questions.

These findings can be presented in writing, as well as through videos, multimedia presentations, and discussion formats. The goal is to formulate the findings so that audiences understand and respond. For example, educators and parents need different words and images to comprehend meaning. It is also helpful that findings are linked to recommendations that give stakeholders guidelines to follow for improvement, though making recommendations is not a necessary part of the evaluation. This depends on what was agreed to at the beginning of the study.

Final evaluation reports contain complete findings and data summaries where possible. Minority reports and testimony from those who disagree with the findings can make the reports more balanced and credible. Also, frequency counts and percentages improve clarity, but they should not replace description and rich detail. Final reports usually begin with an executive summary containing concise statements of the evaluation questions, findings, and recommendations (if requested). A rule of thumb is that a summary longer than three pages exceeds the attention span of audiences. The length of the total report depends on the breadth and depth of the evaluation.

An Example

A practical example will provide a more concrete way of thinking about how evaluations work. What follows is the description of an educational program and how it might be evaluated.

Program description.   An independent study program has been developed for seventh graders in two social studies classes for those students who complete required assignments early or demonstrate a grasp of material before it is introduced. In most cases, the two classroom teachers use pretests, checklists, or both to determine which students might pursue independent projects, but students also may volunteer for project work if the teachers agree.

The two primary goals for the independent study (IS) program were to offer students opportunities to gain greater depth in school curriculum areas and to learn how to become more self-directed learners. Consequently, selected IS students were encouraged to study areas that are linked to classroom content and challenged to take more responsibility for their own learning decisions.

Typically, selected IS students develop a contract with their teacher that specifies project content, deadlines, proposed products, and plans for evaluating the end results. Students would devise project schedules that could include all or a portion of their social studies class on a daily, weekly, or monthly basis. Teachers would hold planning, progress, and culminating conferences with each student throughout the IS schedule. Planning would include topic selection, setting deadlines, determining work locations and needed resources, and devising plans for judging project results. Because IS students receive grades for their required classroom work in social studies, no grades are given in IS. This is intended to encourage more student responsibility over decisions about learning rather than waiting for teacher direction. Progress conferences are used to monitor student work, whereas culminating meetings address project results, effectiveness of student self-direction, and any future project plans.

The IS program has been in operation for a little more than two school years, and approximately 15 students from the two classes have been involved in the IS project work each year. These students have produced videotapes, articles, small books, slide and PowerPoint presentations, and three-act plays on topics such as the World War II Japanese American concentration camps, power and corruption, causes of war, and gender politics in the 20th century.

The teachers have concluded that an evaluation would help them decide if the program should be retained or at least improved. They believe it is working well, but know that their judgments may be clouded by closeness to and personal investment in the program. A professor from the local university has agreed to conduct the evaluation. She is an experienced evaluator who has studied similar IS programs in other schools.

Evaluating the IS program. Following the framework outlined in the chapter, the evaluator would seek written and verbal descriptions of the program to obtain a preliminary idea about its purposes and functions. Soon after this, she would want to determine the evaluation's focus and specific questions by talking with the program teachers, some program students, and any administrator who may know about the IS program.

In this instance, the program evaluator used input from these individuals along with her own expertise to develop a list of areas the program teachers supported. These areas usually explicitly or implicitly offer the criteria and standards crucial to conducting any evaluation, but often are not labeled as such. These areas would then be used as guides for the evaluator in developing questions to be answered in the study. In this evaluation study example, the areas developed were

- Appropriateness of student selection
- Teachers' role in encouraging or discouraging independence

- Students' role in encouraging or discouraging independence
- Resources and environments that encourage or discourage independence
- Student progress toward more self-directed learning
- Student depth of understanding in the curriculum
- Quality of student independent study products
- Continuity of monitoring student independence from one project to the next

In addition to this list, the teachers wanted to know about the program's overall strengths and weaknesses and what they might do to improve things where needed. Subsequent to this planning, the evaluator would develop evaluation questions reflecting the areas of concern and ways to answer these. Note that the areas, as well as the evaluation questions that follow, go well beyond just determining if the two program goals are met (content depth and self-direction).

First, the evaluator may want to determine how students are selected to participate in the IS program. Do students have an equal opportunity if they meet the stated criteria? Are teachers making selections based on reasons other than those indicated? Why do some students who volunteer become IS students but other student volunteers do not? Here, the evaluator would piece together the selection process by interviewing teachers and students and by examining the match between classroom content and the pretest items, the checklist items, or both. Sifting through these data will allow the evaluator to construct how the selection process works along with ways it might be improved.

Following this, the evaluator will want to study how the program operates once students are identified. Of particular interest here and elsewhere will be the extent to which students are encouraged to be self-directed (one of the two primary program goals). Questions to be answered at this stage might include

1. What occurs during the student–teacher planning conferences?
2. How are topics and projects selected and by whom?
3. How are study schedules, plans, work locations, and resources decided and by whom?
4. To what extent are student independence and decision making encouraged or discouraged by the teachers?
5. Overall, what roles in decisions are taken by teachers and by students?

Again, following the guidelines presented in the chapter, multiple methods and sources would be used to increase the validity of the findings. The evaluator would probably observe planning conferences, tape-record them, or use both methods, as well as interview students and teachers about what usually occurs during these meetings. The evaluator would use this information to develop answers to the questions posed, possibly uncover other important findings not anticipated, and provide an explanation of how the planning conferences operate.

It also would be useful to study how the program works for students once they are engaged in independent study, once again by observing conferences and interviewing teachers and students. In addition, observing students while they work on their projects may provide useful insights. Are students working alone? Do they have access to necessary resources? Does their workplace support their project efforts? Are projects linked to the regular curriculum (the other primary program goal)? The answers to such questions will provide the evaluator with case scenarios that typify different project work patterns and might reveal needed changes in how students are guided or supported in these efforts. Also of interest would be the determination of how students are handling the new learning environment. It is often at this stage, for example, that students feel lonely or lost, because they are not able to gauge their progress compared with their peers. However, perhaps the teachers have prepared the students so that these concerns do not arise.

Another step in the evaluation process might be to observe culminating conferences, as well as inspect the projects developed by the students. In addition, it would be useful to find out how the IS students view the experience and whether or not they are gaining confidence in making more independent decisions. Questions in this portion of the evaluation could include the following:

1. In which areas are students making study decisions and in which areas are teachers taking the lead?
2. What are students learning beyond what they have obtained from regular class material?
3. What is the quality of the final IS projects?
4. How are the projects evaluated and by whom?
5. Is curriculum content or becoming more independent emphasized most in the culminating conferences?
6. To what extent are future projects and ideas about becoming more self-directed emphasized during these culminating conferences?
7. Why are some IS experiences effective but others are not?

It may appear that there is no end to the areas and questions that might focus an evaluation. Important guiding factors, however, limit the evaluator's scope. The needs of the primary audiences and stakeholders are paramount in designing the evaluation, as well as the expert judgment of the evaluator. Limits are in place as well. The amount of time and resources often constrain what the evaluator can accomplish.

In this plan, administrators and outside agencies were not the primary audiences, whereas the teachers and students were. Also, time and limited resources may not allow the evaluation to include parent perspectives, for example, although such data are often useful. Thus, although there is no one way to design and conduct an evaluation, selection of methods and data sources are formulated with the stakeholders and limitations in mind.

> What is the significance of audiences and stakeholders in evaluation studies?

ACKNOWLEDGMENTS

The author wishes to thank those who provided insightful comments on earlier drafts of this chapter. They are Deanne Falls, Gila Garaway, Patricia Hays, Bob Holloway, Dan Kain, Ellen Menaker, Frances Riemer, Enid Rossi, and Frank Vogel.

EVALUATION RESOURCES

Books

House, E. R., & Howe, K. R. (1999). *Values in evaluation and social research*. Thousand Oaks, CA: Sage.

   An advanced analysis of the value issues in evaluation and how they might be resolved.

Madaus, G., Kellaghan, T., & Stufflebeam, D. L. (Eds.). (2000). *Evaluation models*. Boston: Kluwer.

   An analysis of the different approaches to evaluation in the language of the originators.

Patton, M. Q. (2002). *Qualitative research and evaluation methods* (3rd ed.). Thousand Oaks, CA: Sage.

   A very comprehensive and easily accessible introduction to evaluation methodology and issues.

Shadish, W., Cook, T., & Leviton, L. (1995). *Foundations of program evaluation*. Thousand Oaks, CA: Sage.

   A more advanced analysis of the views of the founders of the field.

Worthen, B., Sanders, J. R., & Fitzpatrick, J. L. (1997). *Program evaluation* (2nd ed.). Reading, MA: Addison-Wesley.

   A textbook on various approaches to evaluations with detailed examples.

Associations

American Educational Research Association (AERA), www.aera.net

American Evaluation Association (AEA), www.eval.org

Journals

American Journal of Evaluation (formerly *Evaluation Practice*), published by the AEA

Educational Evaluation and Policy Analysis, published by AERA

Evaluation, published by Sage in London and Thousand Oaks, California, in association with the Tavistock Institute (London)

New Directions for Evaluation, published by AEA

15

Participatory Evaluation

Gila Garaway

Reprinted from *Studies in Educational Evaluation*, Vol. 21, 1995, pp. 85–102, Garaway: "Participating Evaluation." Reprinted with permission of Elsevier Science.

MEET THE AUTHOR

Gila Garaway is an evaluation consultant who has lived and worked in the international arena for the past 18 years, with work spanning beyond the educational area to the fuller context of international development. She has worked in both relief and development settings, in the Middle East, in India and Nepal, and in Rwanda, Burundi, Congo, Uganda, Kenya, and Nigeria, and has spent a good part of the past 6 years in countries experiencing active conflict. In addition to teaching a course in participatory evaluation at Tel Aviv University, she has evaluated a wide variety of programs, from formal educational programs to those aimed at emergency care of accompanied children, refugee camp social services, emergency shelters, community rehabilitation, child-headed households, child development, resource action mapping, agricultural rehabilitation, hygiene promotion, and water supply. Her primary professional interest is participatory process and the development of evaluation models that catalyze interactive process learning. In addition to a number of journal publications, she has recently written a chapter on evaluating education programs and projects in third world countries for the *International Handbook of Educational Evaluation* (Kluwer).

House (1993) defined evaluation as "the determination of the value or worth of something . . . judged according to appropriate criteria, with those criteria explicated and justified" (p. 1). Since the 1960s, the field of evaluation has expanded into a myriad of approaches, models, and persuasions (Cook, 1991; Cronbach, 1980, 1982; Eisner, 1976; Guba & Lincoln, 1989; House, 1980, 1993; Patton, 1990; Phillips, 1990; Popham, 1988; Provus, 1971; Rossi & Freeman, 1993; Scriven, 1969, 1974; Stake, 1983; Stufflebeam, 1966; Tyler, 1949). An array of analyses (Guba, 1990; House, 1983; Nevo, 1983; Patton, 1980; Scriven, 1983; Stake, 1983; Stufflebeam & Webster, 1980) have dissected, compared, and contrasted the numerous emergent and emerging models on a number of different points, including theoretical assumptions, ideologies, and political/social orientations.

Illuminating in their places of overlap, as well as in their divergence of views, the analyses as a whole suggest several avenues, which have been incompletely addressed. While their approaches are different, Stake's (1983) responsive evaluation and Guba and Lincoln's (1989) responsive constructivist evaluation come closest to giving full consideration to stakeholder concerns. Both leave evaluation, however, as an externally controlled process. The question arises, is evaluation always an external process, or is it/can it be part of an internalized process, an inward *and* a group process dialogue, a causal analysis that promotes people's creativity in reaching solutions? These and other questions like them have led to the development of what can be loosely called "participatory evaluation."

This article intends to look at current conceptualizations of participatory evaluation: some definitions, various rationales for its use, and finally, a general discussion with implications for future applications.

DEFINITION

What do we mean when we say "participatory evaluation"? Clearly, participatory activity in evaluation has a wide range of meanings. Looking first at participatory activity in research helps to lay a foundation for looking at participatory evaluation.

Participatory Research

In research, participation can be as limited as simply answering a questionnaire or being part of an interview, or as extensive as full, active involvement in all phases of the research process. In the field of education, the notion of teachers as participants in curricular research was first given currency in the work of Stenhouse (1971). Teacher as researcher has appeared more recently in the literature under the rubric of "action research" and has found expression across all disciplines (Daiker & Morenberg, 1990; Elliott, 1991; Ellis, 1990; Goswami & Stillman, 1987; Nias & Groundwater-Smith, 1988; Oja & Smulyan, 1989; Ross, Cornett, & McCutcheon, 1992; Schubert & Ayers, 1992).

In the educational field, much has been said in support of the action research process. A particularly revealing teacher comment appears in Rowland (1988): "it was as much about my own learning experience as that of the children so exposing my preoccupations and inadequacies" (p. 64). Atkin (1991), in his presentation to the American Educational Research Association, comments that it is in that gap between what a teacher actually does, and what his or her ideals are—that place of dissonance—that fertile ground for the seeking of new knowledge lies. In these comments, classroom-based research is seen as a process of exploration and discovery, where teachers themselves are involved in a growing learning process.

Whyte (1991) defined participatory action research (PAR) as a form of applied research, where the researcher becomes a facilitator in helping those being studied to also become actively engaged in the quest for information and ideas to guide future efforts. Widely used in the developing world, the PAR concept was originally conceived as a means of helping small farmers assess and solve problems, as well as a means for westerners to learn more about locally adaptive agricultural practices. It is in the extension of PAR to evaluation—to the evaluation of development projects in the developing world—that participatory expression.

What do you see as the difference between action research and participatory action research?

Participatory Evaluation

Cousins and Earl (1992) defined participatory evaluation as, "applied social research that involves a partnership between trained evaluation personnel and practice-based decision makers, organization members with program responsibility or people with a vital interest in the program" (p. 399). They differentiate participatory evaluation from PAR and other forms of action research by maintaining that PAR is limited to a normative and ideological research orientation rather than an evaluative one.

Brunner and Guzman (1989) defined participatory evaluation as "an educational process through which social groups produce action-oriented knowledge about their reality, clarify and articulate their norms and values, and reach a consensus about further action" (p. 11). They elaborated by detailing an approach where evaluators are chosen from a group of project participants to work alongside a professional evaluator, and where the indigenous evaluators are responsible for organizing and implementing the evaluation and disseminating the results to all other members.

Cookingham (1992) perhaps expressed the ultimate commitment to the participatory approach—a result of numerous experiences evaluating development programs—in his transformed definition of evaluation: "the facilitation of informed judgments about the merit and worth of something, based on verifiable evidence" (p. 21).

Greene (1990) maintained that the participatory approach grew out of a refined definition of evaluation's purpose—utilization—with responsiveness being a key to local utility. How then does participatory evaluation differ from the "responsive" stakeholder approach to evaluation?

Stake (1976), in an elaboration of responsive evaluation, suggested participation as the ongoing dialogue with primary stakeholders, the "primary stakeholders" being the actual program participants. The intention of such dialogue is to inform the evaluation, so that it might be "responsive" to stakeholder concerns. Here we see a deeper level of participation than in a one-time questionnaire, yet the participant still remains on one side of the evaluation. The bulk of the control and decision making remains in the hands of the professional evaluator, with the primary stakeholders generally involved only on a feedback, consultant basis. It is the professional evaluator who remains the primary investigator.

In evaluation carried out by the participants, the external evaluator goes beyond being the primary investigator and participant observer to becoming a facilitator. As facilitator, his or her aim is to help transform a fairly natural process (evaluation being something we all undertake, personally, continually) into a more broadly utilizable process. As a facilitator, he or she becomes a learner, arbitrator, and teacher, developing local skills and promoting an interactive learning environment. Evaluation becomes a team effort, with the team not constructed of professionals first, but drawn from the variety of strengths within the participant pool. It is more in the process then, than in the products, that participatory evaluation finds itself differentiated from other approaches to evaluation.

In participatory evaluation, the pool of participants tends to be a smaller group. Although there is still pluralism, with the concomitant problem of conflicting interests, there is the added aspect of interaction, which somewhat spreads the role of adjudication among the participants. In responsive evaluation, however, the evaluator seeks to engage a broad audience, to obtain as many perspectives as possible in the interest of delivering up an evaluation that is representative, just, and fair. The evaluator's purpose in that case is not necessarily to get people to interact with each other.

Who then are the participants in participatory evaluation? Following Mark and Shotland (1985), Greene (1986) maintained that the criteria used to define and select participants varies according to the rationale for using a participatory approach. Rationale thus provides a vehicle for examining different interpretations of a participatory approach.

RATIONALES

Greene (1986), in an early discussion of participatory evaluation and lessons learned from the field, suggested a number of rationales for choosing to use a participatory approach to evaluation. Among those discussed are increased utilization of evaluation results, empowerment of low status stakeholders, and greater congruence with decision-making processes. Cousins and Leithwood (1986) also articulated the notion of the creation of linkage mechanisms or an interactive-process learning environment. And Rugh (1986) combined all of these rationales into a larger purpose, what he called "partners in evaluation." Each of these rationales represents a different perspective on choice and role of participants. In addition, research support for effectiveness varies according to rationale.

Utilization

Within the utilization rationale for participatory evaluation, Greene (1986) suggested that the notion of use be considered broadly to include instrumental, conceptual, and symbolic uses. Here she means instrumental as action oriented, conceptual as learning or education oriented, and symbolic as persuasive or political. In choosing participants then, Greene claimed that criteria center around not only potential for making use of findings, but also having the power to do so, given a particular intended use. In Greene's utilization-oriented studies, insiders with some authority (program staff, administrators) were used in making participant selections rather than only evaluation coordinator/facilitators. Although this was in keeping with the criteria mentioned above, a power base selection force may have been a limiting factor in gaining a full view of participatory evaluation. Some of the lessons learned regarding choice of appropriate participants in her utilization-oriented studies indicate that participants should include "legitimate program stakeholders" who have sufficient program knowledge to be considered potential users or contributors to the evaluation process. "Legitimate program stakeholders" were considered to be those directly involved with the evaluand, and both those adversely and beneficially affected by the evaluand. Program knowledge, in turn, was found to be a function both of a participant's perceptions of his or her knowledge base concerning the program and of his or her sense of "having something to offer." Stakeholders who perceived that they had something to offer were the ones most likely to define themselves as participants.

In terms of credibility of findings (utilization to some degree being dependent on credibility), there are, within the issue of participant choice, issues of representativeness and diversity of perspective. Although this becomes a far more political and value-oriented issue in evaluation with an empowerment rationale, within a utilization orientation it still demands careful attention and would suggest the need for more than power/authority perspectives in selection.

In terms of participant roles within the evaluation, a utilization focus would tend to suggest that roles and responsibilities should be divided in such a way as to promote greatest utilization. Greene (1986) suggested a shared decision-making model where the structural guidance process and all technical responsibilities remain with the facilitator. Identification of substance/content (the evaluation questions) would be the arena of the stakeholders. This is perhaps a somewhat limited perspective, reflective of perceived operational constraints. Although this type of division does not necessarily preclude participation by each member across all levels, it does limit the extent to which participants will become "invested" in the evaluation, as well as recipients of levels of learning to be had via responsibility. Both of these effects could be said to be potential promoters of utilization.

The utilization rationale has received considerable support in the literature in terms of effectiveness (Cookingham, 1993; Cousins & Earl, 1992; Greene, 1986, 1988; Rugh, 1986). In addition to direct reports of increased utilization of findings by all participants, part of the support comes from underlying related factors. Increasingly, the cognitive processing perspective on evaluation use has found attention in the literature (Greene, 1988). In addition, as participatory approaches involve an extended period of time (for training and follow-up), possible cognitive limits are expanded by repeated processing, resulting in greater intake of findings and greater potential for use. Cousins and Leithwood (1986) and others maintained that the mere psychological processing of results constitutes use, providing powerful support for a participatory approach.

EMPOWERMENT

Given the inherently political nature of evaluation, there is always some particular interest being served by an evaluation. The question is whose interest, and can an approach to evaluation actually have an effect on whose interest is being served? Have those involved become empowered?

With an empowerment rationale, participant selection focuses on including low status/low power stakeholders. How these stakeholders are identified is not clear, but it would seem that identification and selection of participants would need to be conducted by the group representing the lowest power/lowest status to ensure that their interests are represented. Mark and Shotland (1985) maintained that seeking to attain empowerment goals of justice and democratization begs the question of balance of voice in participation, and of what balance will lead to goal attainment.

Assignment of roles requires at least equal access to decision-making roles (content and design decisions), as well as a rotational approach to roles, with evaluation "team" members periodically exchanging roles (Brunner & Guzman, 1991).

Empowerment has been and remains a central rationale for participatory evaluation in the developing world (Brunner & Guzman, 1991; Cookingham, 1993; Feuerstein, 1986) and has been reported to be effective in attaining that goal, at least on a local level. Greene (1988b) suggested that participation and "voice" by those with lower power provides the context for local stakeholders to work through diverse views—a major point in a pluralistic environment. Greene (1986) questioned, however, whether this approach is an appropriate strategy (or the proper use of evaluation) for the political goal of empowerment.

Mark and Shotland (1985) suggested two types of participation that result in what they call "pseudoempowerment": participation that is controlled by the professional evaluator in such a way as to preclude real stakeholder input, and bona fida participation that results in improvements and other benefits, but fails to result in the accumulation of power necessary to control issues. Brunner and Guzman (1991, p. 16) have proposed that true empowerment is a function of strong organization of the dominated groups, which in turn is a function of shared values and a common vision.

An interesting comment on effectiveness comes from an agricultural development program in India. McNee and Wood (1993) found that even though participatory efforts had led to some real improvements in local conditions (support for an improvement rationale), the people involved were no better prepared to face the power issues involved with dealing with government officials. When they took their own independent steps to become involved in other projects, their efforts met with no government response, although they made repeated attempts. It was not until the development agency (power) took steps on their behalf that the government responded.

Decision Making

In a decision-making rationale, the idea is participation that accurately represents the decision-making process and thus promotes representative decisions (Mark & Shotland, 1985). This rationale reflects a recognition that there are multiple groups in any evaluation, and that these multiple groups reflect decision makers with potentially different questions. Participant selection thus involves representative identification of those with status and power as decision makers, as well as sufficient status and power to see a decision implemented (Greene, 1986). Mark and Shotland (1985) suggested in addition that stakeholder groups be weighted evenly, according to their expected ability to influence the process, implying that participant roles be evenly distributed.

In looking at this rationale in terms of educational evaluation, there are some basic realities affecting effectiveness: Most educational evaluation is designed to be decision oriented (Cousins & Earl, 1990) systematic evaluation of educational programs is rarely a part of the curricular process (Slavin, 1989), and the fundamentally most powerful decisions are made at the local curricular level. Although Weiss (1983) and others contend that this rationale for a stakeholder (or participatory) approach is no longer viable, the problem may not be the rationale but how it has been conceptualized.

Interactive Environment

Cousins and Leithwood (1986) proposed development of linkage mechanisms or an interactive process environment as a rationale for participatory evaluation, the aim being the promotion of organizational learning. The focus of evaluation is not only reconciliation of differences, but also development of a joint interactive learning atmosphere. Senge (1990), a major proponent of systems thinking and organizational development, argued that individual and group learning requires a foundational exploration and understanding of some of the assumptions underlying practice.

Cousins and Earl (1992) maintained that participatory evaluation provides a bridge between this prerequisite reflection and action. They further maintained that organizational learning provides a theoretical framework for the whole concept of participatory evaluation. In support of this proposition, they cited a number of educational studies that link organizational learning with utilization of research/evaluation results. As one case, they presented Huberman's (1987, 1990) findings related to a multisite "tracer" study designed to follow a number of research result dissemination efforts. Findings included an ongoing, in-process feedback network was essential; interorganizational sharing was best created when interactions took place over a period of time; and interaction required both sides to more thoroughly consider the meaning of findings.

> Describe how participatory evaluation could serve as a bridge between reflection and action.

Partners in Evaluation

Numbers of programs in developing countries have for some time been utilizing participatory evaluation as a means of generating a sense of project ownership (Cookingham, 1993; Feuerstein, 1986; Rugh, 1986; Srinivasan, 1992; Voorhies, 1993). Their experiences suggest that for a program or project to be sustainable, it has to be "owned" by the community. This sense of ownership has resulted from community participation and shared control in all phases of the process. No longer external participants in a decision-making process, as might be the case in Stake's stakeholder model, they are included in the actual reasoning process of making the decisions. Project ownership comes about through community-led research, design, implementation, and evaluation.

Rugh (1986) aptly named this, "Partners in Evaluation," or self-evaluation as partners. The participatory rationale is based not only in decision making, with local planning promoting establishment of more realistic objectives, but also in improved performance (a result of utilization), in a systems approach to and understanding of resource need and allocation, and in community involvement in the determination of policy (empowerment). It is an overall development and change rationale.

Potential participants include a wide range of people, chosen for a variety of purposes. Included, in addition to the facilitator as partner, are:

1. Community members who are directly involved in the project—the purpose for their involvement is related to all of the rationales just stated.
2. Community members not yet involved, but who could benefit from an increased understanding of the project—the purpose is not only to promote future involvement with the project, but also to obtain bystander perspectives.
3. Project staff—again, the purposes for their involvement are directly related to the rationales given above.
4. National headquarters (or the equivalent)/the major decision maker—their inclusion is based in an understanding of the importance of reckoning with

power sources and the fact that power decision makers are more likely to heed evaluation findings if they feel they had a part in the evaluation.

5. Donors (if different than national headquarters)—involvement geared to fielding questions of accountability.
6. Development agencies—involvement geared at promoting dissemination of information and learning across various development agencies working in a particular area.

The various roles played by this myriad of participants would be dependent on the situation, but it is Rugh's (1986) contention that the underlying theme is "partners," and thus a democratic approach to role assignment, with those most closely involved in the daily workings having the greatest representation. Clearly, the professional evaluator's role is that of adjudicator, as well as facilitator of the dissemination of the adjudicator role, in situations where there is conflict of interest. In addition, Rugh suggested that the professional evaluator's role is to assist partners to identify and become familiar with the use of methods most suitable for their needs.

Initially, facilitation consists of outlining levels of evaluation and monitoring as a means of providing an example and a framework from which the evaluation group can expand. As the process continues, expansion and creativity are encouraged. It is the partners who set the times and seasons when evaluation is to occur.

Underlying Rugh's (1986) conceptualization there is the notion of the need for self-examination. It is Rugh's contention that before evaluation can place the magnifying glass on a project or context, it must begin with a magnifying glass turned to itself. It is only in this way that participants can obtain a full picture of context and the biases that are brought to the evaluation effort. It is the professional evaluator as facilitator who provides the example and guidance in this, as he or she openly explores and discusses his or her own presuppositions, and continues to personally examine presuppositions that may be hindering the evaluation's progress.

In the context of a development and change rationale, the participatory process is based on three principles (World Vision, 1993): (1) People, no matter what their condition, have great creative capacities; (2) change is most likely to occur when people are engaged in an experience with all the senses, emotions, and personal experiences that they bring with them; and (3) change is most likely to occur when people are creatively using the resources they have to learn more about their situation.

Support for this conjoining of rationales comes from a number of development sources. The experiences of Cookingham (1992), Feuerstein (1986), Hutchinson (1986), and Shani and Perkins (1991) all suggest that facilitated participant evaluation, in the broad conceptualization presented here, is more likely to have a positive impact on development in all its aspects than an external evaluator's pronouncements or judgments.

Summary

Although each of the rationales has been presented as a distinct entity, in real life boundary lines are rarely clear, with most participatory evaluation efforts seeking to serve several purposes within a single evaluation. What is clear is that there is both room for expanded definition and a need for further evaluation of effectiveness within each of the rationales.

Having utilized a rationale approach to examine different conceptualizations of participatory evaluation, there still remain a number of overarching issues, which need to be discussed.

DISCUSSION

There are a number of issues that were not discussed within the framework of rationales that warrant examination. These include characteristics required of the professional evaluator/facilitator, methods; related issues of bias, validity, and credibility; costs; and finally, implications for future use. Although each of these issues is quite clearly affected by the particular underlying rationale for use, a more global overview provides sufficient perspective for conveying the concept of participatory evaluation.

Professional Evaluator Characteristics

World Vision (1992), in an editing of four earlier articles dealing with participatory evaluation, summed up the role of the evaluator by stating:

> The role and attitude of the [evaluator] development worker are crucial. She must be a facilitator and not an authority figure. He must be willing to become vulnerable as a learner, as a person taught by community members. [He or she] must recognize that people are "experts" in their own environments, they have the wisdom to better their lives. The worker needs to create an environment in which people can express themselves about their own reality. (p. 1)

Adapted from Cousins and Earl (1992), World Vision (1992), Hutchinson (1986), and others, the following list of professional evaluator requirements is meant to serve as a portrait shedding additional light onto the concept of participatory evaluation:

1. Commitment and ability to work with others—a personal desire to participate and be a participant in an interactive process
2. Sufficient commitment to a participatory approach to support the necessary additional time commitment

3. Technical expertise and training in a wide variety of research disciplines and methodologies
4. Teaching skills and a comprehensive enough knowledge of evaluation to be able to synthesize as well as adapt it to a variety of teaching contexts
5. Tolerance for imperfection, balanced with the ability to diplomatically preserve sufficient technical quality to ensure evaluation viability

In support of, and as an extension to these, it is notable that in a development project in the Philippines, the staff listed the following as characteristics of a good participatory evaluation facilitator: spends time with people, encourages people, expects people to be creative, supports people, brings out the ideas of others, listens first, asks questions second, and only then gives information (World Vision, 1992).

> What other characteristics would you expect to see in a professional evaluator? Would you expect different characteristics for differing contexts? Why or why not?

Methods

In terms of choices and use of methods, participatory evaluation is not very different from the multimethod approaches that have gained currency in the field of evaluation. The guidelines for choosing a particular method are basically the same—appropriateness to underlying assumptions and to questions being asked—with the addition of the need to consider technical difficulty and adaptability to a particular level of expertise, and practicality given a particular location or situation. The following listing includes, in addition to some of the more standard methods, some techniques that are particularly suited to a participatory approach:

Surveys	Tests
Interviews	Participant observation
Audio and video recordings	Diaries
Analysis of records and reports	Case studies
Unobtrusive measurements	Group meetings
Individual and community drawn pictures	
Mapping	
Problem stories using fictional characters	
Problem stories using real events, evaluated as a group	
Creative expression—drama, role plays, songs, dances	
Locally generated counting charts/measuring devices	

This is by no means an exhaustive list; it is included to convey the notion of the creative potential for methodological extension.

Bias, Validity, and Credibility

Participatory evaluation understandably raises questions of credibility and bias. Some of these questions are addressed via the process of conceptual analysis and explication of world views discussed in Rugh's conceptualization. It can be argued here that the standard accepted practice of external evaluation brings its own bias, and that the separatist ideology and its demand for separation of subject and object is altogether unrealistic and inappropriate for studies involving social interactions (Scriven, 1983, p. 231). The nature of education, development, and learning *is* subjective. It can be further argued that the process of discovery for the evaluator entails understanding that subjectivity in order to understand a bit more about teaching, learning, and the educational and development process as a whole. Perhaps the key question here is: Is participatory evaluation a means to an end product, a set of findings, or is it, and can it be more than that—a vibrant, sustainable component of a program?

Extending the discussion of credibility to include the notion of validity further highlights the importance of all involved evaluators making their own personal world views, values, and beliefs, explicit. "All involved evaluators" means all of the participants involved in the evaluation process. This is particularly true when one considers increased validity a function of an increased awareness of all potential subjective elements, with explicit analysis statements allowing for reference back later, when data itself is being analyzed: "To what degree does data gathered reflect my biases?"

Usually, evaluation is a proces carried out by an external judge, an "objective" observer/data gatherer, where objectivity is intended to guard against bias and preserve the validity of the findings. In evaluation, however, objectivity can be said to be more an aspiration than a quality, as no evaluation is ever totally objective. Somewhere, there has been subjective decision making, whether it be in the problem statement, in the interpretations, or in the motivation for conducting the evaluation.

Traditional notions of validity assume that programs, policies, etc., are static. In fact any educational endeavor is by its nature highly dynamic—taking on its own shape as it goes along, a function of the interaction between a conceptualized program (the program design), the actual program implementation, and the participants. It is because of the very dynamic nature of human programs that measures of validity must be based in deeper foundations via full participant involvement in the evaluation process.

Finally, and perhaps most importantly, participants are potentially good judges because they alone experience the full impact of a program. It is through the "experiencing" that they have a knowing, a knowing that observation and testing can't attain. "Now each man judges well the things he knows, and of these he is a good judge" (Ethics I:3). Ideally, we'd like an educational or any other kind of a program to have a positive effect on a community. Participation means that those most closely involved become part of the process of determining how best to reach that goal.

Costs

Understandably, in addition to the many benefits that have been articulated in this discussion, there are a number of costs inherent in participatory evaluation. It is important to fully consider these costs before embarking on a participatory endeavor. Failure to do so could easily result in ill-preparedness, frustration, and failure with a resultant and unfortunate disillusionment with participatory approaches.

Greene (1988) suggested that there are or can be serious operational challenges with shared decision making. This can be especially crucial if the technical demands of the evaluation (a certain level of technical expertise is required to meet policy-making expectations) are combined with severe limitations in understanding the technical elements of evaluation, and insufficient evaluator/evaluation time to provide training.

All of the authors cited have noted that the participatory approach involves an increased investment of time, implying that this type of approach is most suited to longitudinal, long-term evaluation efforts. It further implies the possible need for a reconceptualization of evaluation and its role, with the need to consider that evaluation as an internal part of a program might better serve some of evaluation's purposes. In this case, time would not be a cost factor.

And finally, Stake (1983) noted that the inherent pluralism of participatory or stakeholder approaches brings about a concomitant problem of conflicting perspectives. And in commenting on early stakeholder use he noted, "the attempt to be useful to many may well have prevented it from being useful to any" (p. 25). Thus a very real cost of participant involvement is the emotional and psychological cost of adjudicating conflict. This involves deep value and justice questions. Mark and Shotland (1985, p. 607) maintained that value issues arise in stakeholder-based evaluations to a greater degree than they do in evaluations that ignore stakeholders.

How might this notion of the "psychological and emotional cost of adjudicating conflict" be useful in thinking about other research contexts? What other authors in this book have raised similar issues with regard to researcher–participant relationships? What do you think is important about researcher–participant relationships?

IMPLICATIONS

There are a number of implications in terms of participatory evaluation's potential for both development and formal education. Although addressed here separately, both of these can and do overlap considerably.

Development

Often, in the development model, participatory research or PAR has been limited to a one-time, or short-term, identification of needs or productivity in order to direct future policy. Extending beyond the development model, participatory evaluation has attempted to be more than an initiating "research" effort, where the focus is an initial participatory process of determining a community's needs. Instead it seeks to be an ongoing problem-solving activity that looks at how well a project is progressing based on a set of standards. As such, it can further benefit participants via the acquisition of improved problem-solving/critical thinking skills, and the discovery of values in interactions, experiences, and situations.

In the real world of development projects, and government and sponsor agency agendas, the ideal goals and purposes of participatory evaluation—use, improvement, empowerment, learning—are often subverted. There are exceptions however, with some of these having been mentioned above. It is Hutchinson's (1986) discussion of findings that provides one of the more powerful reasons for bearing with participatory evaluation, in any of its uses. In her work in Kenya, she found that not only did participatory evaluation result in an increased sense of ownership in the local development project and a shift in decision making from the powerful elite down toward the people, but more importantly it sparked in the people a sense of efficacy and newfound hope.

These are just some of the reasons for continuing to explore this largely uncharted path in evaluation. The potential for expanded definition and use is limitless, as varieties of peoples undertake to participate in numerous new ways in the structuring of their own futures.

Formal Education

In the formal educational arena, participatory evaluation has not been widely explored or implemented. As early as 1979, Koppelman (1983) proposed what he called an "explication model" of evaluation. Basically, his use of the term *explication* is an attempt to avoid some of the negative connotations of evaluation, and to emphasize the exploratory and explanatory aspects involved in the improvement-based goal of looking for strengths and weaknesses. The basic technique employed is "systematic" observation, beginning with an exploration of the teacher's understanding and perceptions of program functioning. The observation process, in turn, is carried out by the teachers and the students. It is fully participatory in terms of data collection. Further, the professional evaluator is conceived as a coordinator who helps organize and bring all the pieces together, so that meaning can be constructed as a group. Koppelman maintained that the key to this approach is the active involvement of all.

Interestingly, there are few reports of the implementation of this model in the literature. More recently, there has been some increase in the use of more participatory procedures, with all of the studies reviewed reporting positive benefits related to participatory activity (Cousins & Earl, 1992; Dawson & D'Amico, 1985; Green & Kvidahl, 1990; McColsky, Altshuld, & Lawton, 1985). In addition, most of them indicated that involvement in an evaluation process, with the training in research that that entails, resulted in a greater tendency to pay attention to and use not only their own findings but also other research and evaluating findings.

The question that arises is, What are some of the possible ways of applying a participatory approach in a formal educational setting? In addition to some of the ways covered in the studies just mentioned—rotation of evaluation roles among students and staff, training in research, teacher-developed surveys—there are probably numerous as yet untried applications.

Only one of these is Participatory Informed Evaluation (PIE; Garaway, 1993). As a facilitated process, PIE was designed to help teachers to explore beliefs, to analyze concepts, to assess a situation or an event, and to make informed propositional statements that can serve as viable evaluations on any decision-making level. In terms of broader purposes, PIE was developed in order to promote greater teacher involvement in a full curricular process. This is accomplished by promoting in the teacher an awareness of each curricular component and his role in it. It is intended that in the process of analysis and evaluation, the teacher will not only become better informed about the problems at hand, but will become better informed about how to address those problems.

Participatory evaluation encompasses a discovery approach to teaching and learning, explicitly stated and reported. It brings the notion of lifetime learning back into the schoolroom as teachers also become involved in an ongoing process of exploration. It also encompasses the adventure aspect of being creative, the excitement of discovery, and the sense of community that results when teachers are able to skillfully solve problems together.

From the developing world, numbers of recent reports suggest the need for more participatory approaches to evaluating educational programs. Ryan (1992) noted, "There is a clear need to complement trickle-down with bubble-up approaches. Local-level program administrators and practitioners have to be induced to diagnose their problems and actively seek out support in solving them" (p. 41). And Lawrence (1992) suggested,

> Ideally, innovative concepts of literacy will result in enhanced teacher training that encourages teachers to go beyond simple 'black-boxing' of students, where one expects a given set of inputs to produce a given set of outputs with little attention paid to the students' information processing. (p. 52)

There is a tremendous untapped wealth of knowledge contained within teachers. Has the educational community shortchanged teachers by not fully equipping them to become competent and creative evaluators?

CONCLUSIONS

This study has attempted to present an overview of current conceptualizations of participatory evaluation. Using rationale as a framework for examining conceptualizations of participatory evaluation, the study explored utilization, decision-making process, empowerment, creation of an interactive organizational learning environment, and finally establishment of partners, as rationales for a participatory approach to evaluation. Within this framework, various selection criteria and participant roles were discussed.

Moving to a more general discussion, the study then looked at characteristics required of an evaluation facilitator, methodology, validity, and costs. Characteristics required of an evaluation facilitator included faith in others' innate abilities, a desire to work together with people, and tolerance for imperfection. Methods and adaptations of methods were discussed, with the implication being that participatory approaches stimulate creativity in technique choice and construction. A discussion of validity, credibility, and bias concluded that it is the participant, the one directly involved with an endeavor, who is the best judge of its effectiveness. Although his or her judgment may be "subjective," it is quite possibly the most valid. And finally, in terms of costs, participatory evaluation requires a greater personal investment not only on the part of the professional evaluator as facilitator, but also on the part of the participants themselves.

The implications for the future use of participatory evaluation are powerful. Participatory evaluation creates a learning environment in which evaluation findings are processed and accumulated by end-users in the very process of their being gathered. Growth, development, and in many cases renewed hope are an immediate by-product of the process. In addition, by enhancing and supporting organizational learning and interactive support processes, participatory evaluation has the potential for strengthening educational systems.

In conclusion, Whyte's (1991) comment stated the challenge well: "Science is not achieved by distancing oneself from the world; as generations of scientists know, the greatest conceptual and methodological challenge comes from engagement with the world" (p. 21).

ACKNOWLEDGMENT

The author wishes to acknowledge the invaluable input received from Steve Lapan.

16

Multimethods Research

Paul A. Schutz, Courtney B. Chambless, and Jessica T. DeCuir
University of Georgia

MEET THE AUTHORS

Paul A. Schutz, is an associate professor in the Department of Educational Psychology at the University of Georgia. He earned his doctorate from the University of Texas at Austin in the Department of Educational Psychology. He currently teaches courses on classroom motivation and research methods. His research interests include the nature of goals in self-directed knowing, learning, and emoting; emotions and emotional regulation; and goals and goal development. He has publications in *The Educational Psychologist, The Journal of Educational Psychology*, and *Contemporary Educational Psychology*, as well as several book chapters.

Courtney B. Chambless received her master of arts in educational psychology at the University of Georgia in 2001. Originally from Georgia, Chambless earned a bachelor of arts in psychology also from the University of Georgia. Her research interests include issues in qualitative methodology and intervention strategies for emotionally disturbed adolescents. Although presently working in public mental heath, she intends to attain a doctorate in counseling psychology.

Jessica T. DeCuir is a doctoral candidate in educational psychology at the University of Georgia. DeCuir, a native of Baton Rouge, Louisiana, attended Louisiana State University as an undergraduate, where she earned her bachelor of science degree with a double major in psychology and Spanish in 1998. She later earned her master of arts degree in educational psychology at the University of Georgia in 2000. Her research interests include (adolescent), racial and ethnic identity development, motivation, assessment, and research methods. In her dissertation, DeCuir examined how sociohistorical issues, including race and skin tone, are affecting African American adolescents' construction of their identities as students.

During the past several decades, those who engage in research in the social and behavioral sciences have witnessed the paradigm "debates," or "wars," between the constructivist and naturalist positions on the nature of inquiry in one camp and positivist/rationalist positions in the other. These paradigms, or worldview discussions, have engaged questions related to the nature of reality, the nature of the knower and knowledge, and the nature of inquiry. In the long term, time and those who engage in the history and philosophy of science will judge whether these worldview discussions represented a minor border dispute or a significant shift in our thinking about science and inquiry. In the short term, however, one thing that has clearly increased, in part as a result of these worldview debates, has been discussions about the nature of multimethods research.

Our purpose in this chapter is not to rehash the worldview debates. For those interested in that discussion, there are a variety of places to engage the issue (e.g., Datta, 1994; Gage, 1989; Guba & Lincoln, 1989, 1994; Hammersley, 1992; House, 1994; Rossi, 1994; Smith, 1983; Smith & Heshusius, 1986; Tashakkori & Teddlie, 1998). We take the position that it was a useful discussion that resulted in a closer examination of the assumptions that are critical to any inquiry effort and, in addition, the discussion has provided some impetus for an increased interest in multimethods research.

We have four purposes for this discussion of multimethods inquiry. First, we present our current thoughts regarding two key questions related to the use of multimethods research. Those questions are: Can research methods be separated from the philosophical worldview from which they may have originated? and What are the assumptions about the nature of reality, nature of the knower and knowledge, and nature of inquiry that guide multimethods research? Then we will discuss some general guidelines for conducting multimethods inquiry. This will be followed by some of the potential benefits and potential problems with using multimethods research. Finally, we will make some concluding remarks about the role of multimethods research in the social and behavioral sciences.

METHODS: THEIR ORIGINS AND ASSUMPTIONS

There are at least three potential general categories of multimethods research that revolve around the basic distinction that has been constructed between qualitative and quantitative approaches to inquiry. In other words, once you create a distinction or binary between qualitative and quantitative approaches, you have the potential for multimethods research that involves: (1) two or more quantitative approaches, (2) two or more qualitative approaches, or (3) inquiry that involves a combination of at least one qualitative and one quantitative method.[1] The main focus of the current chapter is related to the third category of multimethods research that includes both qualitative and quantitative methods.

An additional distinction that will be useful when discussing the nature of multimethods inquiry is to consider the potential use of multiple methods in three different situations: (1) multiple methods used within a single study (e.g., a study on motivation in the classroom), (2) multiple methods used within a program of research in a sequential manner (e.g., a series of studies on motivation in the classroom), and (3) multiple methods used within an area of research (e.g., all researchers doing inquiry on motivation in the classroom). The main focus of the

---

[1] In the literature, several other labels, such as mixed models or mixed methods, have been used to describe studies that involve a combination of at least one qualitative and one quantitative method. We use the term *multi* here because we feel the term *mixed* in this context tends to legitimize the methods binary that developed during the debates between constructivist and positivist positions on inquiry. In this chapter, we will attempt to develop a position on inquiry and how the use of multiple methods can be justified from that position.

current chapter is the first category, which involves the use of multiple methods in a single study; however, we will also discuss some issues related to multimethods sequential inquiry.

Multimethods research that includes a combination of qualitative and quantitative methods in a single study has tended to be problematized by both camps involved in the previously mentioned paradigm disputes. This problematization is, in part, related to (1) what has been termed the incompatibility position that was and, in some cases, still is held by some in both camps and (2) the belief that methods are somehow inexorably linked to the paradigm from which they originated. However, we will argue that methods should be seen as tools (House, 1994). From this pragmatic position, the usefulness of a method for a particular study or program of research is not judged by its origin but whether it will help in solving a particular research problem or answering a particular research question. To help make this point, we think it is useful to make a distinction between the use of a method and what can be implied from the data that was gathered using that method. This distinction is similar to the one made by Smith and Heshusius (1986) in discussing the difference between methods such as "how-to-do-it," "logic of justification," and Bryman (1984), who distinguished between methods (ways of gathering data) and methodologies (epistemological positions).

> When thinking about research, what does the term *method* mean to you? How would you explain the difference between method and methodology?

Our discussion of methods as tools is at the level of the how-to-do-it. The use of a particular method can be thought of in much the same way that a skilled carpenter might approach his or her craft—with a variety of tools. Thus, different methods have different purposes. Some methods work well for certain research questions, whereas others may only work for other questions. It is the researcher's job to choose the best tool for the particular research problem and question at hand. To limit one's "tool box" by dismissing all the tools that were developed by researchers who endorse either the qualitative or quantitative label puts one into the position of only being able to investigate certain problems or questions. As any skilled carpenter knows, if the only tool you have is a hammer, you treat everything as a nail.

The second aspect of this discussion represents what we think is a more critical issue: What can be said about the data gathered with a particular method? This is a discussion at the level of the "logic of justification" (Smith & Heshusius, 1986) or methodologies (Bryman, 1984). Therefore, this is also where the researcher's assumptions about the nature of reality, the nature of the knower and knowledge, and the nature of inquiry come into play. These are the issues that were at the heart of the paradigm debates. These are also the issues that proponents of multimethods research have been charged with explicating (Datta, 1994). This explication is critical because these assumptions provide the context from which research problems and questions emerge, methods are selected, and how the data is collected, analyzed, and interpreted.

Before we start that discussion, it is necessary to state that we are aware that other multimethods researchers may not agree with our positions on some or all of these assumptions. It is also clear there are probably other useful assumptions that we do not address within this short chapter. However, we are confident that as we engage these issues within our own research, we will probably change our ways of thinking related to these issues. We see this continual examination as fundamental to a healthy emerging program of inquiry and for the larger inquiry community.

Nature of Reality

First, we feel there is an external reality, or a world of physical objects. We interact within that reality from our own, sociohistorical, subjective view of that world. In other words, we construct meanings within our world of physical objects, and we interact, as part of that reality, based on that social construction. In addition to this physical reality and our subjective experiences and thoughts about that reality, Popper (1972) also made a useful distinction that he referred to as "world 3," or the objective contents of thoughts. *Objective*, as it is used here, is not meant to indicate "the rational," but that the content of our subjective constructions have the potential to become objects separate from the person doing the thinking. Thus, the content of books and articles, the theoretical systems, and the problems and problem situations they contain can become objects similar to those in the physical world. This objectification does not concern the "truthfulness" or "usefulness" of the contents of thoughts; it only implies there is the potential for these thoughts to have a "life" outside of the thinker. For the social and behavioral sciences researchers, this means that in most cases our interest is not in physical external reality but in the sociohistorically constructed contents of the objective realities of our thoughts.

In addition, external realities, as well as the objective realities of our thoughts, are complex and layered. Thus, there is always the potential for discovering or constructing more complex layers that may help to explain other layers (House, 1994). One way to think about this is to consider that students and teachers transact within classrooms, these classrooms transact within schools, and schools transact within communities. Therefore, to understand, describe, and potentially help to solve the problems of a particular student's classroom behavior, it may be important to have some understanding not only of the student but also the student's classroom, school, family, and community. This suggests that inquiry at a single level may be misleading. For example, if a particular student or groups of students are not doing well in the classroom, research at a single level might suggest that these students lack ability. In contrast, if the classroom, school, and community are included in the analysis, we may find a systematic bias within the system that creates problems for a particular group of students.

Finally, external reality and the objective realities of our thoughts are open systems. By this, we mean that there is the potential for continual change and emerging properties that have not been seen before. Thus, what may currently seem like a pattern may not look that way in the future. For example, the schools that students go to today are not the same as the schools of 25 years ago. Yes, the school building, the time when school starts, and many of the activities that occur in the classrooms may look and may actually be the same. Yet, 25 years ago, you could go to a lot of classrooms before finding one with even a single computer, and few, if any, people in those classrooms would have been talking about HIV, the Internet, or global warming.

> What are open and closed systems, and what might these have to do with planning research studies?

Nature of the Knower and Knowledge

Knowers are enmeshed within their complex and layered sociohistorical context. This creates situations where there are potentially multiple layers or boundaries between the knower and what the knower might consider external reality. Thus, as indicated, students transact within classrooms and schools. The families these students come from transact within the community in which the school is located. At any particular point in time, students may identify with themselves, their family, their ethnic group, or even their school. Thus, when someone is identifying at the level of the family, the external reality becomes the nonfamily. In addition, human action is intentional, including a capacity for monitoring and second order monitoring (House, 1994). This reflective potential is what provides the opportunity to construct sociohistorical subjective views of reality and the examination of those sociohistorical subjective views. Further, humans have open-system properties such that although much of human action is repetitive, there is always the potential of new activities and new ways of looking at external reality and our socially constructed views (Csikszentmihalyi, 1985).

Finally, knowledge is fallible and changeable (Reichardt & Rallis, 1994); thus, what we think we know is subject to change based on changes in the external world or in the way we construct our understanding of the external world. This has critical implications for what we can say about what we find in our research. In essence, "truth," in some absolute form is probably an illusion. Thus, research whose goal is to establish truthfulness in some absolute form, in the long run, is probably not possible.

Nature of Inquiry

Given the aforementioned assumptions about the nature of reality and our abilities as researchers to know the world around us, the knowledge of our worldview will influence our perceptions of the research problems we choose, the methods we use, and the interpretations we make. This idea has been referred to as the "theory-ladenness of facts and inquiry" (Guba & Lincoln, 1994; Reichardt & Rallis, 1994). This view suggests that because we see reality is socially constructed and, as knowers, we are enmeshed within a complex and layered sociohistorical context, what we choose to investigate and how we choose to investigate it will be a function of that constructed worldview. In addition, because our conception of reality is socially constructed, there may also be many useful versions of "reality," or ways of looking at the world. For the researcher, this means that any and all data have the potential to be explained by many different theories. This idea has been referred to as the "underdetermination of theory by fact" (Guba & Lincoln, 1994; Reichardt & Rallis, 1994). This view suggests that because there are a variety of sociohistorical contexts from which to view the data, there may be many possible ways in which the data can be collected, interpreted, and used.

Yet, in the end, we feel that inquiry should attempt to develop an explanation of how factors of different kinds influence events within particular sociohistorical contexts (House, 1994). However, it should be kept in mind that a theory of causation, which is based on assumptions of invariant regularities, is probably untenable (House, 1994). In other words, as suggested by the earlier assumptions about the nature of reality and the nature of the knower and knowledge, we are fundamentally involved in an ever changing system. Therefore, change and the potential for change may be the only constant.

> What does it mean to believe that reality is socially constructed? What is an alternative belief about reality, and how would holding either view influence your research? How have other authors in this text treated this idea?

Worldview Summary

We make distinctions among our subjective experiences, the objects of the physical world, and the objective realities of our thoughts. It is in the realm of the objective realities of our thoughts that most behavioral and social science inquiries occur. In addition, we suggest there are two key characteristics for each of these three areas: (1) They are complex and layered, thus providing the opportunity for many different vantage points, and (2) they are open systems where there is the potential for continual change.

In addition, we see human action as intentional, or goal directed. This includes the capacity for monitoring and second order monitoring. In addition, knowers are enmeshed within a complex and layered sociohistorical context. The capacity for intentionality and monitoring provides the potential to reflect on the sociohistorical context and the objective realities of our thoughts that we use to explain and transact within that context. The understanding developed through reflection represents our understanding about the nature of our subjective experiences, the objects of the physical world, and the objective realities of our thoughts. This understanding is fallible and changeable.

So where does this leave us? It is clear from the nature of these assumptions that inquiry as a search for some ultimate "truth" is probably untenable. We would not know the ultimate "truth" if we saw it, and what might be "truth" today may not be so in the future. It is also clear that the limits of our generalizibiltiy become the boundaries of our sociohistorical contexts in which we are investigating. As such, we suggest that the usefulness, or problem-solving potential, may be the most useful goal for inquiry. In other words, from the perspective presented here, inquiry should be considered a problem-solving activity, or as ways of investigating and working to solve problems within a sociohistorical context rather than attempting to predict or discover universal principles.

These problems range from conceptual and theoretical to "real world" problems. They may be problems related to gaps in our current level of knowing, problematic phenomena, or current ideas that are challenged by new hypotheses (Brewer & Hunter, 1989). These problems emerge from transactions within a sociohistorical context and need to be addressed with that sociohistorical context in mind. When we conceptualize research as a problem-solving activity, we also suggest that any method, within moral and ethical constraints (see Tisdale, Chap. 2, this volume; Howe & Eisenhart, 1990), can and should be used. Thus, the questions of whether or not one should combine different types of qualitative and quantitative methods becomes secondary to questions of how one can combine them and what the benefits and constraints are when combining various methods during inquiry.

GUIDELINES FOR CONDUCTING INQUIRY

First, with any form of inquiry, it is important to be well grounded in the literature related to the problem under investigation (Howe & Eisenhart, 1990). As indicated earlier, research is most useful when it is focused on and used with problem solving in mind. As a problem-solving activity, the inquiry process begins with the development of useful and interesting research questions that address two general aspects of the potential problem: (1) a useful definition of the problem and (2) the development of approaches aimed at solving the problem.

An important part of developing a useful definition of a problem is an understanding of the inquiry that has previously engaged this issue. This does not necessarily mean a blind adherence to the literature. In fact, in many cases, it may be more useful to take a fresh or questioning look at the literature. Oftentimes, it may be that a fresh or questioning look helps to develop a more useful definition of the problem. However, in the final analysis, in order for inquiry to make an impact, it must be judged in relationship to the existing literature. For example, if the findings of a study contradict the existing literature, there is a need for a rationale as to why this was the case. It is through comparison and resolution that different ways of defining and solving problems have the potential to emerge.

There also needs to be a fit between the research questions, how the data is collected, and the analysis techniques used (Howe & Eisenhart, 1990). This seems to be a simple and straightforward statement, yet anyone who has taught a research methods course or who has been asked to be on a dissertation committee has heard a statement from a student or a colleague such as, "I want to do a qualitative study." When the researcher begins with the method, it limits the potential questions that can be asked. Therefore, the researcher may or may not end up with useful questions for the problem to be addressed. As indicated by Howe and Eisenhart (1990)

> it is incumbent upon educational researchers to give careful attention to the value their research questions have for informing educational practice, whether it be at the level of pedagogy, policy, or social theory, and then to ground their methodology in the nature of these questions. (p. 7)

Why might it be important to avoid using methods to guide the formulation of a research study? In your estimation, what should guide the development of a study design?

It is also important to apply the technique's specific standards that are relevant for any particular method (Howe & Eisenhart, 1990). For example, there are some more-or-less agreed on guidelines for interviewing, developing a survey instrument, or being a participant observer. For useful information to emerge from the inquiry process, the data collection and analysis processes need to proceed in a manner that facilitates adherence to the guidelines of the particular method. It does little good to collect and analyze data in ways that violate the standards and assumptions of the methods. For the multimethods researcher, this becomes a more complex issue, because the use of multiple measures brings with it more technique-specific standards to keep in mind during the research process. This also means, for example, that simply adding a few open-ended questions to a larger quantitative study will probably not meet the guidelines for conducting useful inquiry. An additional guideline that is also particular to multimethods research was suggested by Fielding and Fielding (1986), who indicated that "what is important is to choose at least one method which is specifically suited to exploring the structural aspects of the problem and at least one which can capture the essential elements of its meaning to those involved" (p. 34).

As indicated, the nature of reality is complex and layered, which makes it important to attempt to deal with that characteristic by using one form of data collection to help describe the context in which the transactions occur and an additional measure to describe the transactions themselves. This suggests that the usefulness of multimethods research emerges in the potential to investigate different aspects of the phenomena under study.

Howe and Eisenhart (1990) discussed the importance for judging the usefulness of inquiry as basically being able to answer the "So what?" question. Thus, the external value of inquiry is related to its actual problem-solving usefulness. In addition to problem-solving usefulness, Howe and Eisenhart (1990) suggested that findings from educational research should also be accessible to the educational community. For example, inquiry has limited potential to help in solving educational problems if it is not in a form that is understandable to teachers, administrators, and parents.

Finally, the internal value of inquiry relates to the research ethics. Howe and Eisenhart (1990) referred to this as "internal value," because it is related to how the inquiry is conducted. For this guideline, it is important to keep in mind what is generally referred to as the risk–benefit ratio. In other words, the risk to the participants needs to be weighed in relationship to the potential benefits to the problem-solving task at hand (Crowder, this volume). Howe and Eisenhart (1990) suggested that ". . . researchers must weigh the quality of the data they can gather (and whether they can gather any data at all) against principles such as confidentiality, privacy and truth-telling" (p. 8).

PURPOSES AND POTENTIAL BENEFITS AND PROBLEMS WITH MULTIMETHODS RESEARCH

Most discussions of multimethod inquiry in the social sciences trace their origin to the Campbell and Fiske (1959) article on the multitrait–multimethod matrix. In that article, it is argued that the use of more than one method in the study of a phenomenon is helpful in the development of construct validity. Related to that discussion, Knafl and Breitmayer (1989) indicated that the triangulation construct was used as "a metaphor to characterize the use of multiple methods to measure a single construct" (p. 210). From the Campbell and Fiske (1959) perspective, triangulation involved the use of multiple methods in the study of the same phenomenon with the basic purpose being the goal of seeking construct validity through the establishment of both convergent and divergent evidence for the task or test under consideration that confirms expectation. As suggested by Denzin (1978), "No single method ever adequately solves the problem of rival casual factors" (p. 28). Thus, the use of multimethods in a single investigation allows for the potential consideration of rival casual factors.

How might methodological triangulation contribute to the trustworthiness of research findings? Are you aware of other forms of triangulation in research?

In addition to the purpose of potentially providing confirmative evidence for the task or test under consideration, Jick (1983) and Fielding and Fielding (1986) suggested that combining methods also provides the opportunity to develop completeness, depth and breadth, or elaboration (Rossman & Wilson, 1985) to the understanding of a phenomenon. Thus, multimethod inquiry is not an end in itself; rather, it is a research approach that may serve at least two rather distinct ends: confirmation or completeness (Knafl & Breitmayer, 1989).

With those two basic purposes in mind, the combining of qualitative and quantitative methods during inquiry has the potential for many benefits, as well as problems. For the remainder of this section, we will elaborate on some of the potential benefits of multimethods research, as well as acknowledge some of the potential problems that may emerge when planning inquiry with a multimethods approach.

Potential Benefits

One benefit of using multiple methods is that it provides the opportunity to look for corroboration in the results from different methods (Brewer & Hunter, 1989; Denzin, 1978; Greene, Caracelli, & Graham, 1989; Rossman & Wilson, 1985, 1994). In corroboration, the attempt is to use at least two methods to investigate the same social phenomenon. For example, this may involve the use of an existing survey measure to investigate students' self-efficacy related to math, as well as interviewing the participants about their self-efficacy related to math. The use of these different methods allows for the opportunity to look for compatible findings between the methods. The idea is that if one comes to the same or similar conclusion using different methods, it lends credibility to the theory being developed and used to investigate the problem.

However, it should be kept in mind that the goal here should not simply be corroboration. Corroboration as a goal allows for the possibility that those interesting and useful differences in the findings could be ignored for the sake of seeking convergence. Therefore, the goal should be to investigate to see if and where evidence for corroboration exists. If it does, this may lend support to the usefulness of the theory. However, if the results of the study do not lend convergent support, then the potential for other, sometimes more interesting, issues emerges. In other words, a lack of corroboration is also a benefit of using multiple methods in that it provides for the opportunity to develop different and potentially more useful ways of thinking about, and attempts to deal with, potential problems.

A related benefit of using multiple methods is the potential to find complementarity (Greene et al., 1989; Rossman & Wilson, 1985, 1994). This is similar to corroboration in that it seeks similar patterns of findings; however, the difference is that in complementarity, the focus is on studying different aspects of a phenomenon rather than the same aspects. For example, a combination may include the aforementioned existing measure of math self-efficacy, along with interview data related to the participants' strategy use while learning math. The goal for complementarity is to elaborate and enhance the results of one method with the results of another method. There are a variety of combinations and advantages to combining methods in this way. A quantitative study may also employ a qualitative dimension to guide the sample selection or to help explain unusual results. A qualitative study may implement a quantitative dimension to guide sampling or help determine what to pursue in depth or to help generalize results to different samples and test emerging theories.

In addition to the previous potential benefits, researchers may engage in multimethods research as a means of advancing a study or program of research. In this situation, the researcher could use the result from one method to help guide the development of the next phase of research in areas such as sampling, measurement, or both (Greene et al., 1989). Thus, the potential for development within a program of study is the attempt to use the results from one method to help develop or inform another method. In this situation, development is broadly constructed to include sampling, measurement decisions, or the implementation of the research plan.

Another potential benefit for using a multimethod approach is the opportunity to use the results for expansion (Greene et al., 1989; Rossman & Wilson, 1985, 1994). By involving both qualitative and quantitative measures, one can expand the breadth and depth of a study to examine different aspects. This is particularly helpful, because certain components of research questions are better addressed through particular methods. For example, it might be more useful to assess math competency through math achievement tests resulting in standardized scores, whereas class participation may be better understood through repeated participant observations. By combining them, one may gain insight not only into differences in math achievement but also the possible relationships between participation and achievement.

Finally, the use of multiple methods also provides the opportunity to investigate potential paradoxes and contradictions that emerge from the data. It allows for the recasting of questions or results from one method with questions or results from another method (Greene et al., 1989; Rossman & Wilson, 1985, 1994). Denzin (1978) indicated that

> each method implies a different line of action toward reality—and hence each will reveal different aspects of it, much as a kaleidoscope, depending on the angle at which it is held, will reveal different colors and configurations of objects to the viewer. Methods are like a kaleidoscope: depending on how they are approached, held, and acted toward, different observations will be revealed.

These different observations allow for the recasting of questions or results, which becomes an excellent opportunity for potentially taking a fresh look at the problem.

> What are the many advantages to using multimethods in research? Are there disadvantages that come to mind?

Potential Problems

In addition to the potential benefits of multimethod research, there are also potential problems involved in developing inquiry that uses multiple methods. We have categorized these potential problems into two areas: philosophical and practical. In the philosophical area, although the heated rhetoric that marked the paradigm discussions has subsided to some extent, there is still what Rossman and Wilson (1985) called purists on either side of the debate. These purists tend to consider those who are involved in inquiry on the "other side" or those who attempt to use methods that emerged from both camps to be misguided. Thus, purists from both groups have the potential to cause problems for those attempting to use multimethod approaches. This resistance may emerge at any level of the inquiry process. For example, it may take the form of an advisor who discourages a student from developing a dissertation involving multimethods. These philosophical disagreements could also occur when multimethod grant proposals, conference proposals, journal manuscripts, or books are reviewed less favorably simply because of their approach to inquiry. Thus, the problem is similar to the potential problems that many qualitative researchers have encountered when trying to conduct and publish qualitative research in quantitative journals, the difference being that multimethod research has the potential to be dismissed out of hand by purists from both camps.

At a more practical level, developing a multimethods approach to inquiry involves acquiring knowledge and skill in two areas of inquiry. For example, in most doctoral programs, these methods of inquiry are currently being taught as two distinct bodies of literature. This, in effect, would basically double the course load for a doctoral student wanting to develop skills in both areas. In addition, there has also been a proliferation of methods courses in both areas. For example, in the quantitative area, during the past few years, there has been the addition of courses like structural equation modeling and Rasch modeling. In the qualitative area, it is now becoming more common to see specific courses on interviewing and case study inquiry. Further, there are very few places that offer multimethods courses that deal with the practical issues involved in combining different methods. Thus, the best piece of advice for graduate students interested in becoming researchers is to take both qualitative and quantitative research courses and apply what they learn to the constructs and contexts they plan to investigate.

Finally, by its very nature, the cost involved in multimethods research tends to increase over a single-method study. This increased cost can be seen in the amount of time it takes to collect, make sense of, and write about the findings, as well as the monitory cost of the materials involved. When writing up the results, again, because of the nature of the process, you also end up with the potential of having more to write about.

This could also be coupled with the potential to write about results that may not converge, and therefore may result in additional time and effort to understand and communicate that nonconvergence. All of these situations have implications for potential publication of the results. Therefore, the benefits of multimethod research are large, but so are the potential costs that go along with those benefits.

CONCLUSIONS

As indicated, there is a growing interest in multimethods inquiry. This interest is, in part, related to an increasing discontent with the adequacy of using single methods in a research area. Turner and Meyer (1999) summed it up when discussing the use of multiple methods in motivation research:

> Using multiple methods is one way to test theoretical notions in classroom contexts. Because findings from multiple methods must be reconciled, they provide a more stringent test of motivation theories in classrooms. For example, Marshall and Weinstein (1986) found that theoretical models of differential teacher treatments were often unsupported by classroom observations of instructional practices. Similarly, McCaslin and Good (1996) observed that researchers frequently report that students mediate classroom goals in unexpected ways, but cautioned that such findings are "unexpected" only if we assume that students react the same in all situations. (p. 90)

In other words, it is clear that the complexities of the problems that face education are not always best understood or dealt with in a useful manner with inquiry that employs a single method. It is hoped that the use of multiple methods will help with the problem-solving potential of inquiry.

> What might a research plan look like using multimethods? Is this approach
> to research an idea worth pursuing? What would be the challenges of using
> multimethods? Would you like to conduct this kind of research? Why or why
> not?

However, it must also be cautioned that venturing into multimethods inquiry
also brings with it some potential problems. As indicated, there are practical as
well as potential philosophical issues that make the use of multimethods more
complicated. Thus, for those training to become researchers, there is a need to
take advantage of opportunities in graduate school by taking as many quantitative
and qualitative courses as possible and, if possible, to seek out mentors who have
developed experience combining various methodologies. However, keep in mind
that these mentors currently may not be on their campuses

A paramount goal for all researchers in the social sciences should be to employ
the methods that best answer their proposed research questions. Because the people we study often have different worldview assumptions that are sociohistorical
constructed, it is only fitting that we use more than one method to attempt to capture experiences. This means that researchers should be receptive to using both
qualitative and quantitative approaches. We do realize, however, that complete
acceptance of multimethods research will be a lengthy process. Until then, the
future of multimethods research is, in part, dependent on the continued examination and evaluation of the worldview assumptions and the difficulties that arise
when the methods are combined, as well as researchers' willingness to approach
inquiry using multiple methods.

ACKNOWLEDGMENTS

Special thanks go to Kirsten Crowder Tisdale, Heather Davis, Sonja Lanehart,
Debra Meyer, the students in our spring 2001 Multimethods Research course, and
the editors of this volume for their comments on earlier versions of this chapter.
Their comments were very useful, and the chapter is better because of their time
and effort.

17

Survey Research

Susan R. Hutchinson
University of Northern Colorado

MEET THE AUTHOR

Susan R. Hutchinson received her doctorate in applied measurement from the University of Georgia in 1994 and is currently an associate professor of applied statistics and research methods at the University of Northern Colorado. Her research interests include applied measurement issues, particularly with respect to test bias and cross-cultural measurement, methodological topics related to structural equation modeling, curriculum design issues for doctoral training in research methods and statistics, and survey research methodology. Recent research projects have included examination of racial and ethnic invariance of a campus climate measure, measurement equivalence of a clinical measure across gender and race, and translation equivalence of a consumer buying behavior scale across three languages.

Undoubtedly, everyone reading this chapter has at some time or other participated in a form of survey research. Whether your previous experience with surveys has been favorable or otherwise will certainly color your view of survey research. Unfortunately, examples of poorly constructed surveys are plentiful, leading many to believe that survey research is simplistic, relatively easy to conduct, and perhaps somewhat limited in its utility. However, good survey research requires considerable thought and planning. To the extent that the principles of good design outlined in this chapter are followed, surveys can provide a valuable source of data for use in a variety of situations, including program planning, decision making, and theory building.

A detailed "cookbook" approach to designing and conducting survey research is beyond the scope of this single chapter. My hope instead is to sensitize you to the myriad decisions and potential pitfalls involved in the research process. Specifically, a primary goal of this chapter is to raise issues and to prompt questions that you as a researcher should ask yourself while designing, implementing, and analyzing any survey. The specific methods to address these issues will be left to other books that cover these topics in greater detail. I will begin the chapter with an introduction to the potential uses of surveys, followed by a discussion of the assumptions underlying valid survey research. The chapter continues with issues associated with the various stages in a survey study and concludes with some final thoughts regarding overall cautions and limitations related to survey research. At the end of the chapter, I will pose questions that you as the researcher should ask yourself as you progress through any survey-based study. It is hoped that by reading this chapter you will have a better appreciation for the value of, as well as difficulty in, designing and conducting a good survey study.

SURVEY RESEARCH?

. most simply as a means of gathering informa-
. using questionnaires or interviews. However, this
complex nature of this type of research given the
urveys are conducted, the array of settings in which
riety of modes by which they can be disseminated,
ons to which survey results are applied.

design, per se; instead, surveys are more commonly
considered the .   ed for data collection. However, most survey research
falls within the frame..   ι of nonexperimental or correlational research designs
in which no independent variable is experimentally manipulated. When used in
this context, information gathered from surveys is typically used either for purely
descriptive purposes or for examining relationships between variables. Though
not as common, surveys can also be included as part of an experimental study, for
example, where participants are surveyed about attitudes or opinions following
some type of experimental intervention. Surveys can also be used as a method of
data collection in qualitative research, although they tend to be employed less
frequently for this purpose, given the generally prescriptive structure of survey
questions. In addition, when surveys are used in qualitative studies, they usually
comprise only one of many sources of data, whereas in quantitative survey studies,
the survey is the primary, if not sole, method of data collection. Often subsumed
within the definition of survey research is the requirement of some type of rigorous sampling procedure (Miller, 1983). Some authors even make the distinction
between a survey as data collected from a sample and a census as data based on all
units of a given population (Jolliffe, 1986; Schwarz, Groves, & Schuman, 1998).

Survey research can also be defined in terms of the type of information gathered
or the purposes for which the information is collected. Alreck and Settle (1995)
contended that the reasons for conducting surveys include influencing a selected
audience, modifying a service or product, and understanding or predicting human
behavior. Rea and Parker (1997) added understanding people's interests and concerns as motives for using surveys, with data reflecting the descriptive, behavioral,
or preferential characteristics of respondents. Weisberg and Bowen (1977) categorized the types of information gathered from surveys into opinions, attitudes,
and facts.

What is your definition of *survey research* at this point?

Although survey research may seem like a relatively recent phenomenon, examples of early surveys can be traced back more than 2,000 years, to efforts used
in obtaining accurate population counts for purposes of tax collection and the

mustering of soldiers (Converse, 1987). Collection of data on epidemics and vital statistics in Europe during the 1600s and census and population surveys in the 1700s and 1800s can also be considered forerunners of the modern survey method. However, a landmark study by Charles Booth on social conditions in London in the late 1800s is cited by many as the first large-scale social survey (Converse, 1987). Although Booth's study lacked the technical sophistication of current survey designs, it was considered a pioneering effort to apply "scientific" methods for the purpose of effecting social change. Surveys in the early 1900s continued in the spirit of Booth's work by serving as instruments used by social activists to raise public consciousness about living and working conditions. But by the end of the 1920s, survey research was beginning to lose its activist focus and was becoming largely the domain of social scientists. In 1936, survey methods in general and sample surveys in particular achieved widespread acceptance as a result of George Gallup's accurate prediction of Franklin Delano Roosevelt's presidential election based on an opinion poll of only a few thousand respondents (Rea & Parker, 1997). Gallup's methods gave credence to notions of survey sampling still used today. Contemporary survey methods not only reflect the cumulative influences of social scientists such as Booth and opinion researchers such as Gallup, but also contributions by attitude researchers in the field of psychology. Development of scaling techniques by researchers including Likert, Osgood, and Thurstone has also influenced the format and nature of current surveys.

Today, in many social science disciplines, the use of self-reports has emerged as the method of choice for obtaining data on both attitudes and behaviors (Schwarz, Park, Knäuper, & Sudman, 1999), with surveys constituting the primary method for collecting self-report data (Isaac & Michael, 1984). In a study of the research methods reported in the published higher education literature during 3 recent years, Hutchinson and Lovell (1999) found that surveys were by far the most frequently used method of data collection among 209 studies reported in three leading higher education journals. Eighty-two percent of the studies relied on survey data either from primary (51%) or secondary (31%) sources.

The popularity of survey research is due in large part to its utility in countless research situations. Surveys are used for such diverse purposes as needs assessment, program evaluation, attitude measurement, political opinion polling, and policy analysis, as well as for simple descriptions of behaviors, activities, and population characteristics. The scope of surveys can range from large-scale national surveys such as the U.S. Census, the National Assessment of Educational Progress, and High School and Beyond, to smaller surveys confined to a single neighborhood, classroom, or organization. In some cases, surveys are used merely to assess the status quo; in others, they are used to test complex theoretical relationships among various constructs.

A second reason for the attractiveness of survey research is its applicability in situations where direct manipulation of variables is either unfeasible or unethical.

Assumptions Underlying Survey Research

Although there is no single theoretical framework underlying the use of surveys, there are several assumptions and guiding principles that drive survey research. The overriding assumption, derived from the reliance on self-report data, is that survey responses reflect the reality of the respondent to the greatest extent possible. Specifically, survey researchers assume that "if we ask someone about his world we can expect that, under normal conditions, he will 'tell it as it is'" (Bateson, 1984, p. 11). Further, survey responses are thought to mirror "the nature of the social world under investigation at the moment of investigation" (p. 32). Subsumed within this fundamental assumption are notions of accuracy and honesty. To have any confidence in the results, survey researchers must believe (and must help ensure) that respondents report information both correctly and truthfully, within the constraints of their memory, comprehension, and level of trust.

> What are a few reasons to trust and not to trust survey findings?

Survey researchers further assume that all respondents interpret survey questions in the same way; that is, a given item has the same meaning for everyone. This suggests that differences in response among respondents, as indicated by level of agreement on a particular item, for example, reflect true differences on the attitude, opinion, or behavior being measured, and not differences in interpretation of the item. To the extent that respondents glean different meanings from the item because of ambiguous wording, culturally biased language, inappropriate reading level, or other factors, this assumption is violated and the validity of the responses is compromised.

In the same way that surveys are neither inherently quantitative nor qualitative as data collection devices, the theoretical foundation underlying survey research is neither intrinsically positivist nor constructivist in nature. The "truth" or "reality" assumed in survey responses is not definitively an objective reality. Even within the quantitative or positivist realm, the issue of whether or not there exists an objective reality in survey responses has been questioned. In his discussion of measurement error in surveys, Kruskal (1991) stated, "... and I expect that few statisticians would agree that reality is easily known. Indeed we earn our livelihoods because of difficulties in knowing reality, or whatever each of us accepts as a substitute for, or reflection of, reality" (p. xxiv).

Thus, the particular theoretical orientation applied to survey research will depend in part on the purpose of the survey and in part on the philosophical inclination of the researcher. For some survey situations and for some types of questions, there is assumed to be a "correct" and potentially verifiable response. For example, in surveys requesting information about specific behaviors, such as the frequency and type of exercise, use of health care services, or attendance at an educational event, the validity of the responses is predicated on accurate reporting of these behaviors. In other situations where surveys address issues of a more affective or perceptual nature, the issue is less about an objective reality, but about the truthfulness of a respondent in conveying their reality. In a survey used for evaluating a particular program, for example, some questions might be designed to elicit factual information regarding frequency of attendance, types of activities, behavioral changes, and so forth. On these items, respondents are expected, to the best of their ability, to report accurate and relatively objective responses. However, for questions used to assess participants' satisfaction with the program, the researcher hopes to obtain the participants' honest perceptions of the program, regardless of whether it was considered successful by some objective standard.

Perhaps it is the lack of a clearly delineated theoretical or philosophical framework underlying survey research that has led some quantitative researchers to question the verifiability and rigor of such research. Similarly, qualitative researchers might not fully embrace survey research, because they view surveys as too rigid a medium for adequately allowing respondents to convey their experiences and attitudes.

Design of a Good Research Study

Although many novice researchers see surveys as a quick and easy method for collecting data, in fact, good survey research involves extensive planning and attention to detail throughout the entire research process, beginning with the theoretical or conceptual framework and ending with the analysis and interpretation of results. The principal criterion for judging the worth of a survey study is, as mentioned above, the extent to which the responses and inferences we make based on those responses reflect truth or reality. This is also what should drive the decisions made throughout the survey process.

Bateson (1984) offered three respondent conditions necessary for useful data construction: their understanding, ability, and willingness. The respondent's understanding involves his being able to adequately decipher and interpret the items and response options on a survey, whereas ability includes not only familiarity ability, and even willingness are present among respondents.

> Why might respondents be reluctant or unwilling to answer a survey truthfully or not willing to answer at all?

Good survey research requires that the researcher has a clear picture of the entire research process; that is, short-sighted decisions made at an earlier phase have the potential for disastrous consequences at a later phase (Alreck & Settle, 1995). Failure to consider the entire process is often characteristic of novice researchers who seem content to "worry about that later." An experienced researcher sees the connection among the various aspects of the study, including the underlying conceptual framework, selection of respondents, choice of survey items, and data analysis procedures. Inexperienced researchers tend to compartmentalize each phase or aspect of the study without considering their interdependence. In addition, the successful researcher often succeeds by assuming "Murphy's law," asking what might possibly go wrong at each stage of the study and planning accordingly.

Finally, survey researchers consider the data gathered via survey to reflect the interaction between respondents and the survey instrument. In this regard, any factor that might affect that relationship has the potential for affecting the validity of the data gathered. Examples of such factors include characteristics of respondents, attributes of the survey, as well as the nature of the research being conducted. Respondent characteristics that can influence the quality of survey data include cultural background, primary language, reading level, interest in the content, or even attitudes concerning the value of research in general. Aspects of the survey that affect survey responses include length, format, and content or topic. In general, relatively short surveys, based on a salient topic, with culturally and developmentally appropriate content, presented in a clear, unambiguous format, are likely to yield the highest response rates and the most trustworthy data.

Errors Encountered in Survey Research

Prior to designing a survey study, it is important that you be aware of the potential sources of errors and the phases of the study during which each is most likely to occur. Errors in survey research can be thought of as the numerous factors that in one way or another corrupt survey responses. Errors can be introduced into the study during planning and construction from failure to appropriately match content to the target population, during sample selection in the form of sampling errors and low response rates, during survey administration because of respondents' inability or unwillingness to respond accurately, and during data processing through careless data entry and unsuitable data analysis procedures. The goal in designing a good survey study is to select the sample, construct and disseminate the survey, and analyze the data in such a way as to minimize these various types of errors in order to maximize the usable information.

Stages in Conducting a Survey Study

Stage 1: Preliminary Planning

A survey study begins like any other, with the formulation of a clearly stated purpose, delineation of a set of research questions, and identification of the target population(s). The researcher should spend much of the initial planning conducting a thorough review of the literature to help justify the need for the study, establish a theoretical or conceptual framework, and identify the variables that should be included in the study. In addition, planning should include decisions about how and by whom the results will be used. In a sense, the preliminary planning stage provides the compass to guide you through the rest of the study. Consequently, scant attention paid to initial planning can lead to a fragmented and poorly designed study.

Stage 2: Selecting the Respondents

The sample selection phase of a survey study essentially involves deciding who the respondents will be, how they will be selected, and how many are needed. All three decisions are contingent on the purpose of your study and the type of data analyses you plan to conduct.

In quantitative survey studies, the ability to generalize results from participants to a larger population is of utmost importance, in contrast to qualitative research where the criterion for good sample selection is not generalizability per se, but the usefulness of particular respondents in providing information about the phenomenon under investigation. As a result, the kinds of respondents selected, as well as the methods used to select them, will tend to differ in qualitative and quantitative studies. Moreover, determination of sample size is made a priori in quantitative studies based on the number needed to conduct specific statistical analyses. This means that before researchers distribute their surveys, they must consult relevant references regarding sample size requirements for the specific statistical and psychometric analyses they plan to conduct (see, e.g., Cohen, 1988; Green, 1991). In contrast, sample size determination in qualitative studies is generally made during data collection based on the sufficiency of the data in achieving "saturation."

or not. The specifics of these methods will be left to other sources (____ ____ 1995). The choice of sampling method for a given study will depend on a num___ of factors, including cost, convenience, purpose of the study, and the need to generalize findings.

> Why would sampling be different in quantitative versus qualitative studies?

In quantitative survey studies, the primary concern is to select respondents in such a way that their responses are representative of some defined population of interest. For this purpose, sampling methods based on randomness such as simple random sampling, systematic sampling, stratified random sampling, and so forth are preferred. Convenience samples (e.g., members of intact classrooms, pedestrians on a college campus, or patients in a health clinic waiting room) may not provide responses that would generalize to the larger population of interest and thus are less useful to survey researchers. Volunteers or other self-selected samples can also be problematic if their reasons for volunteering distinguish them from other members of the target population. And even when disseminating surveys to a randomly selected list of potential respondents, the potential for nonresponse bias is always present when less than 100% of surveys are returned, with the risk of bias increasing as response rate decreases. Ultimately, the question you must ask yourself is, Are those who responded to the survey different in some important way(s) from those who did not respond to the survey? If so, in what ways are respondents and nonrespondents different? Graves (1991) contended that if a researcher is unable to obtain measurements on certain segments of the target population for any reason, including unreturned surveys, use of volunteers or convenience samples, refusal to answer selected survey items, insufficient sample size, and so forth, the researcher will be seriously limited in her or his ability to draw meaningful conclusions from the responses at hand. With this in mind, you need to design the study to maximize response rates and obtain responses characteristic of the group to which results should be applied.

> Why would random sampling with sufficient return rates allow for generalization of the results?

Sample selection for qualitative surveys can also involve random sampling methods, but more often entails use of criterion-based selection (Goetz & LeCompte, 1984) in which the researcher attempts to select survey respondents possessing particular attributes of interest. Criterion-based selection methods relevant to survey research include comprehensive sampling, snowball sampling, and quota sampling. In comprehensive selection, all members of the relevant population are selected and thus are considered representative of the population (Goetz & LeCompte, 1984). However, this type of selection is only practical for situations in which populations are relatively small and circumscribed. Quota sampling is another criterion-based selection procedure aimed at achieving representativeness but is limited to specific population subsets. Respondents are selected on the basis of key demographic characteristics such as gender, race, and socioeconomic status in proportions believed to reflect the target population. Use of quota sampling requires access to population data, such as census reports and registrar's records, that provide information about relative proportions of the subgroups of interest. Snowball sampling, also referred to as network selection (Goetz & Lecompte, 1984), involves use of referral, "word of mouth," and other methods of identifying potential survey respondents through previously identified participants (Fink, 1995). This type of sampling is useful when a formal listing of population members is unavailable or when access to population members is restricted, such as when attempting to locate adolescents with eating disorders or members of a cult. Regardless of the specific sampling procedure used, for qualitative surveys the primary question you need to answer regarding appropriateness of your sample is, How relevant are these respondents to my purpose and research questions?

Stage 3: Survey Construction

The construction of the survey instrument is probably the most important and most time-consuming aspect of any survey study. During this phase, you must determine what questions to ask (and how to ask them) to elicit the desired information. Hastily constructed surveys characterized by superficial understanding of the potential survey participants and by carelessness in selecting the survey content and format can seriously compromise the value of the entire study. During survey construction, you will need to consider the purpose of the study, special characteristics of the potential respondents, reliability and validity of the survey content, format(s) of the items, and length of the survey.

Prior to constructing the survey, you should first identify salient characteristics of the target audience that might influence your decisions regarding survey content, item format and wording, mode of dissemination, and overall length. Relevant respondent characteristics include educational training, reading level, age, language proficiency, cultural background, and potential knowledge of or interest in the survey topic. For example, item wording and item formats that would be appropriate for college-educated adults might be inappropriate or difficult to answer for children or adults with little formal education. Similarly, use of colloquial English might be suitable for respondents who are native speakers of English but might prove misleading to nonnative speakers of English who are familiar only with formal English. Specificity versus breadth of audience also needs to be physicians versus to the general public. Long surveys will tend to work for more highly educated adults, particularly if they are interested in the topic. For respondents with lower reading levels and little interest in the topic, expect poor response rates, especially with longer surveys. In sum, failure to recognize the unique characteristics of potential respondents can lead to disappointing and minimally useful survey results. Thorough review of the literature, examination of the survey by experts, and pilot testing with members of the target group should help prevent a mismatch between the content and the respondents.

Survey construction includes writing items original to the current study, as well as incorporating existing scales and measures. Often, items used to measure basic demographic variables or other factual types of information are developed by the researcher, whereas items used to measure variables reflecting attitudes, opinions, and other types of affective traits are generally selected from existing measures. When attempting to select and locate existing measures to incorporate into your survey, you should consult such sources as *The Mental Measurements Yearbook* (Buros Institute of Mental Measures, 2001), journal articles reporting reliability and validity information on the scale(s) of interest, ERIC documents detailing scale development and validation studies, and books containing collections of scales and measures for particular applications. These sources will be helpful in providing psychometric evidence such as reliability and validity to support (or refute) the use of a particular measure with your target group. For those deciding to modify an existing measure or to select only a subset of items from an existing scale, you should do so with caution and only with well-supported justification, as modification will usually nullify any prior reliability and validity evidence. If you are unable to locate existing measures appropriate to your purpose and population, several useful resources are available that can guide you through the scale development process (see, e.g., Benson & Clark, 1982; DeVellis, 1991; Gable & Wolfe, 1982).

Are you familiar with *The Mental Measurements Yearbook?* Go to the Web site www.unl.edu/buros and see if you can track down an instrument and a review of it.

Survey items are of two broad types: free-response and forced-choice. Free-response or open-ended questions are those that require survey respondents to answer in their own words and are useful when the researcher does not know the range of possible answers, seeks elaboration and detail not possible with forced-choice questions, wishes to see or hear the respondents' actual words, or wants to determine why a respondent answered in a particular way. Despite their usefulness, free-response items should be used sparingly in surveys, given that they

usually require more time to administer, are more difficult to code, and often reduce response rates because of the greater demand they place on the respondent
(Sudman & Bradburn, 1987).

In contrast, forced-choice items present a question or statement followed by
a set of response alternatives from which the respondent must select an answer.
Advantages of forced-choice items include shorter administration time, ease of
coding, and ability to cover a wider range of topics. Practical advantages notwith-
standing, forced-choice items can lead to inaccurate findings if the researcher does
not carefully consider the appropriateness of the response alternatives. The use of
vague or "high-inference" response options, such as "frequently," "occasionally,"
and "somewhat satisfied," should be avoided, because they may connote different meanings among respondents (Schwarz et al., 1998). Thus, two respondents
who engage in a particular behavior with equal frequency might select different
response alternatives, or, conversely, two respondents might select the same answer even though their behaviors or attitudes differ. The assumption, mentioned
earlier in the chapter, that respondents interpret survey items in the same way ex-
tends to interpretation of the response alternatives. Moreover, even when clearly
defined response alternatives are given, studies have found that respondents may
view the range of options as a cue concerning what constitutes "normal" or
"average" behavior and will respond accordingly rather than accurately (Schwarz
et al., 1998). Other considerations regarding response alternatives include developmental appropriateness and the ordering of response options. For young children, responses should be limited to two or three options or to pictures (e.g., the
FACES scale). Similarly, research on the use of surveys with the elderly has suggested that choice of response formats and even the ordering of response options
can substantially affect how older respondents answer survey questions (Schwarz
et al., 1999). This underscores the general need to have a thorough understanding
of your target group and their possible response tendencies when selecting item
formats, as well as content.

The overall layout and organization of the survey also need to be considered during survey construction. In general, you should strive for an unclut-
tered appearance that appears easy to complete. In addition, when organizing
the survey, you should take into account possible context effects or effects based
on item ordering. Tourangeau and colleagues (Tourangeau & Rasinski, 1988;
Tourangeau, Rasinski, Bradburn, & D'Andrade, 1989) found that responses to
a given item can vary noticeably depending on the content of preceding items.
Further, research on age-related survey responses has shown dramatic age differences relative to context effects, with younger adults being more susceptible to
question order than older respondents (Schwarz et al., 1999). Other recommendations regarding survey format and organization include beginning with "easy,"
or less-threatening, questions and placing demographic questions at the end of the
survey.

include technological sophistication of the potential respondents, access to and compatibility of e-mail and Internet systems, and rapid obsolescence of many e-mail addresses. In two studies comparing response rates of postal versus e-mail surveys, it was observed that substantially more surveys were returned as undeliverable for e-mail recipients than for postal recipients (Hutchinson & Green, 1998; University of Maryland, 1997, as cited in Nesbary, 2000). In addition, research on response rates for electronic surveys has been mixed, with some studies finding higher (Parker, 1992), lower (University of Maryland, 1997, as cited in Nesbary, 2000), and comparable (Hutchinson & Green, 1998; Mehta & Sivadas, 1995) response rates for electronic surveys when compared with postal surveys. Until additional research resolves the dissemination issues related to electronic surveys, you would probably be wise to limit your use of such surveys to short questionnaires delivered to a college-educated audience.

A final dissemination concern involves the use of methods to enhance response rates. Although there are a number of procedures that can improve response rates, a meta-analysis by Green and Hutchinson (1996) revealed that the most consistently effective methods have included higher or more expensive postage class, incentives or "rewards" for responding, and follow-up postcards or letters. At issue for the survey researcher is the tradeoff between the potential increase in response rate and the cost associated with using more expensive postage, mailing reminder letters, purchasing items to enclose as incentives, or some combination of these approaches. For electronic surveys, questions regarding the relative effectiveness of response enhancers are still largely unanswered because of the paucity of methodological research in this area. Nevertheless, even with the advent of newer methods for disseminating surveys, nonresponse continues to plague survey researchers as one of the greatest problems encountered in conducting a survey study.

Stage 5: Survey Analysis

Survey results can be analyzed by a variety of statistical methods, from basic descriptive statistics such as frequencies and means, to fairly complex procedures, including multivariate analysis of variance, factor analysis, and structural equation modeling. Or, if used within a qualitative study, data will be analyzed verbally, through examination of themes and patterns in the responses. Although descriptions of specific statistical and qualitative data analysis procedures are beyond the scope of this chapter, there are several points you need to take into account as you select your analytic methods: the purpose of the study, the nature of the variables being measured by the survey, the research questions you intend to answer, as well as the available sample size. The types of analyses possible will also depend on the way the survey items were constructed. Therefore, it is imperative that you consider the desired data analyses during survey construction and design of your sampling procedures to ensure that you will have the information needed for data analysis.

Ethical Issues in Conducting Survey Research

Conducting survey research requires the same adherence to ethical principles as any other type of research involving human subjects. Most professional organizations provide ethical guidelines for conducting research within a particular discipline or profession, and most of these guidelines are now available on the Web. Such guidelines delineate what is considered appropriate and inappropriate during the design, implementation, and reporting of your study (see, e.g., American Educational Research Association [AERA], 2001).

> Do you know about the AERA and its many publications? Check out its ethics Web site: http://www.aera.net/about/ policy/ethics.htm.

If you will be conducting your research under the auspices of a college or university, you will be required to submit an application for approval of research with human subjects prior to conducting the study. Although the application forms will differ somewhat from institution to institution, the process involved and criteria for approval are fairly standardized, with greater scrutiny applied to studies portending greater risk to participants. The purpose of the approval process stems from a federal mandate to protect the rights of research participants, particularly those considered vulnerable, such as children or institutionalized individuals. The institutional review board (IRB) at your university will provide specific details on the procedures and forms required for approval.

In the case of survey research, "red flags" are usually raised when the potential respondents are minors; the content is of a potentially invasive, offensive, or incriminating nature; or either of these factors is involved. For example, asking high school students or college undergraduates about their drinking behavior may not be permitted, because it would require students to divulge illegal behavior. Similarly, questions that are insensitive or highly personal might not pass approval of an IRB unless the researcher demonstrates that the potential benefits of the study outweigh any potential embarrassment or discomfort to the participants. Another major ethical issue in survey research is the treatment of responses in a confidential or anonymous manner. One facet of the human subjects approval process will be your description of the means you will use to hide the identity of respondents and to treat their responses confidentially. Even if responses are not anonymous, as would be the case in telephone surveys, face-to-face interviews, or when identification codes are used in postal surveys, you must demonstrate that the responses cannot be traced back to the person providing them. You should also be forthright with potential respondents regarding whether or not their responses will be anonymous. For example, if you promise anonymity in a survey cover letter, do not secretly include a code on the surveys that could potentially identify a respondent.

Many would argue that although asking an excessive number of questions tangential to the study does not violate ethical standards, it does convey a lack of respect for your respondents. In general, try to limit the items on your survey to variables that are part of your research questions. Do not include survey questions simply out of curiosity. However, including additional questions that help you describe your sample or that provide context for the study is not only appropriate but desirable. Although these items do not contribute to the study itself, they do provide useful information that assists readers in their ability to interpret the results of your study.

Criticisms and Limitations of Survey Research

Despite the popularity of surveys, this type of research does have its critics. One criticism frequently leveled against survey research is its inappropriate application to research questions and hypotheses posing some type of causal relationship. As so aptly pointed out by Cross and Belli (Chapter 19, this volume), a researcher interested in making causal inferences should do so only within the confines of a true experiment. This criticism is not unique to survey research but is also directed toward any type of nonexperimental research, based on its inability to control for all possible extraneous factors. This is not to say that surveys do not provide a valuable research tool in many situations where experimental manipulation is either unfeasible or inappropriate, but surveys are simply not appropriate when the goal is to attempt to establish cause-and-effect relationships between variables. This is true even when using statistical techniques such as structural equation modeling, which has sometimes been referred to inappropriately as "causal" modeling.

Another criticism arises from the reliance on self-report. As noted earlier in the chapter, the validity of conclusions drawn from surveys is dependent on the integrity of the responses. But how can one be certain that respondents are answering truthfully or accurately? In particular, Alreck and Settle (1995) suggested that the use of threatening or sensitive questions may preclude responding by some people. Tourangeau (1987) and Tourangeau, Rip, and Rasinski (2000) discussed the potential for response effects from the perspective of cognitive psychology. They argued that there are four steps involved in answering attitude questions: comprehension, retrieval, judgment, and response selection, and that each phase presents opportunities for response effects to occur. Although this will always be a concern for anyone conducting a survey study, adherence to many of the design and analysis principles outlined in this chapter should help to minimize these problems.

Other potential limitations include the extensive time required to design and implement a survey study and the diversity of skills demanded of survey researchers (Alreck & Settle, 1995). Specifically, survey researchers need to have strong language skills not only for writing items but also for presenting results, considerable training in psychometrics or measurement theory, and competence in a variety of statistical procedures or in qualitative research methods.

CONCLUSIONS

Surveys enjoy tremendous popularity as a research tool in the social sciences because of their flexibility, practical utility, and applicability in numerous situations. Yet, good survey research requires a sizeable investment in time and effort on the part of the researcher. If you have learned little else from this chapter, you should now appreciate not only the time involved but also the importance of considering the interdependence of various elements within a survey study. Virtually every decision you make during the process will affect other aspects of the study to some extent. A thorough review of the literature at the beginning of the study will not only provide a strong basis for conducting the study but will also facilitate your ability to obtain an appropriate group of respondents, construct a valid survey, and conduct appropriate data analyses. In contrast, a cursory review of the literature will surely doom your study to failure. Similarly, consideration of the potential survey respondents forms the basis for subsequent decisions about survey content, format, and mode of delivery. By understanding the connections among each aspect of a survey study and the myriad decisions required, you have the conceptual foundation needed to design sound survey research across almost limitless topics, settings, and target populations.

Survey Research Discussion Questions

Below are discussion questions designed to highlight some of the major issues raised in this chapter:

1. In what ways does a review of literature assist a survey researcher? During what aspects of a survey study should a researcher consult the literature and why? Describe different types of sources that might be consulted in a literature review and the type of information each might provide relative to a given survey study.

2. Discuss the importance of considering your potential respondents when designing a survey study. Specifically, how would your decisions regarding content, item format, length, and method of dissemination differ depending on the nature

of the respondents, for example, young children, well-educated adults, poorly educated adults, members of various cultural and ethnic groups, and elderly adults?

3. Explain why reliability and validity need to be considered when constructing a survey. How are both reliability and validity affected by the respondents? In particular, explain why a measure designed and validated for one group of respondents might not be valid and reliable when used with a different group of respondents. Why should you exercise caution if modifying or selecting items from an existing scale even if the original scale appeared to be valid and reliable? Explain why a scale needs to be revalidated if translated into a different language.

4. Describe various methods for disseminating surveys and the relative pros and cons of each. Discuss how length, content, and the characteristics of respondents might affect your choice of dissemination method. What procedures could you apply to maximize response rate, and would these procedures differ depending on the method of dissemination?

5. If fewer than 100% of survey recipients returned their completed surveys, why would you need to determine if respondents differed from nonrespondents? How might your results be affected if they did differ? Discuss methods you could use to determine differences between respondents and nonrespondents.

6. Discuss the role of ethics in survey research. Locate the ethical guidelines for your professional organization and identify the specific guidelines that pertain to conducting research. Discuss the role these guidelines would play in designing a survey study.

7. Why should a survey researcher always conduct a pilot study prior to conducting the actual study? What type of information would a researcher hope to gain from a pilot study? What are the potential risks associated with failing to conduct a pilot study?

18

Single-Subject Experimental Research: An Overview for Practitioners

Karen A. Sealander
Northern Arizona University

MEET THE AUTHOR

Karen Sealander earned her doctorate degree in special education with an emphasis in assessment and data-based interventions from the University of Florida. She taught in the public schools as a special educator before returning to graduate school. Throughout her doctoral program, she worked as an educational diagnostician as part of a multidisciplinary team in pediatrics neurology.

Ms. Sealander has continued her interest in data-based decision making and has authored articles dealing with interventions for students with attention deficit disorder, learning problems, and behavioral problems. Ms. Sealander is also interested in effective instruction for children who are culturally and linguistically diverse and living in rural and remote areas. She has coauthored several federally funded grants and currently teaches assessment at Northern Arizona University in Flagstaff, Arizona, where she is an associate professor in special education.

In addition to her work with students and families, Ms. Sealander teaches her students and students in public schools about therapy and service dogs. She raised a dog for Canine Companions for Independence, an organization that provides dogs for individuals with disabilities. She takes her therapy-certified dog Rothman to local schools and to her classes at the university.

In today's educational arena, practitioners are often challenged to provide evidence that their efforts contribute to the realization of a gamut of desired educational or social outcomes in schools and classrooms. Inquiries pertaining to pedagogical issues of instructional effectiveness, interventions, and general best practice have become increasingly common. In addition, the call to respond to social issues (e.g., affective development of students and school safety) has administrators, counselors, teachers, school psychologists, and policy makers asking how we are to deal with what some are calling an epidemic of needs in our schools. As a profession, we are struggling with both the pragmatic and the moral decisions as to what can and ought to be done to increase the quality, consistency, and long-term effects of educational services. If practitioners are to identify and respond to complex instructional and social issues in a proactive fashion, then we as educators must determine what interventions are effective, pragmatic, and ethically sound.

The quest to identify efficacious solutions requires that practitioners at all levels strive to systematically collect information (data) to guide their efforts in answering such questions as: What can we do to increase student knowledge acquisition, parent and student participation, and collaboration between professionals? What can we do to address the effects of students with emotional problems, personality disorders, or even psychiatric disorders within school and community environments? To develop valid and useful answers for any of these, and related, questions, practitioners must be able to understand and reliably measure how their efforts are actually effecting changes in student academic and affective abilities and needs.

An essential first step in the quest for potential solutions is recognizing the need to adapt our experimental methods to the characteristics of the phenomenon, rather than forcing the subject matter to fit our favored methods of inquiry (Johnston & Pennypacker, 1993). School violence, for example, especially as it occurs in the classroom, is most often not a group phenomenon but a product of one, or a few, individuals who may present matchless profiles or unique mitigating circumstances. In this and many other instances, teachers, counselors, psychologists, and special educators often need to evaluate the effectiveness of an intervention on the behavior of a single individual before they address the concerns of larger groups (Best & Kahn, 1998). To answer questions regarding the relationship between an intervention (an independent variable) and a corresponding change in the behavior of the individual (a dependent variable), single-subject experiments or single-case research methodology is the most appropriate choice (Barlow & Hersen, 1984; Best & Kahn, 1998; Gall, Borg, & Gall, 1996).

THE ORIGINS OF SINGLE-SUBJECT RESEARCH

Single-subject research has its roots in the behaviorist movement, which is based on the notion that the environment influences behavior. The now classic work of Watson, Pavlov, and Skinner are mainstays in the behavioral literature and serve as the framework for this field.

It was Watson and Pavlov who set the stage for the behaviorist movement with their work in classical and respondent conditioning the 1920s. The now famous studies of Watson and Rayner (1920) showed that the pairing of stimuli influenced behavior. Watson and Rayner paired the presentation of a small, furry animal with a loud sound to a small child. Soon, the child demonstrated fear when she saw the small animal.

Pavlov's (1927) work in classical conditioning showed that repeatedly pairing two events causes them to become associated in the participant's mind. In 1927, Pavlov experimented with the pairing of food and the sound of a bell on the behavior of a dog. Pavlov soon discovered that after multiple pairings of food and the bell, the dog salivated only in the presence of the bell.

Skinner (1953), noted for his work in operant conditioning, expanded the work of Pavlov by observing the pecking behavior of pigeons when presented with food. Skinner found that he could increase the pecking behavior of the pigeons if he followed it with food and that he could decrease the pecking behavior of the pigeons if he withheld food or if the birds were punished. From Skinner's work, three very important principles of operant conditioning were exemplified: reinforcement, extinction, and punishment. Skinner noted that behavior is "a process, rather than a thing. . . . It is changing, fluid, and evanescent" (p. 14), suggesting that it is more important to describe a behavior than to explain it. To that end, the emphasis of the behaviorist should be on determining which environmental factors serve to increase, decrease, or maintain the occurrence of specific behaviors (Skinner, 1953).

THE AIM OF SINGLE-SUBJECT EXPERIMENTAL RESEARCH

The purpose of single-subject research, or any experimental research, is to establish the effectiveness of an intervention on an individual's distinct behavior(s) under specified or proscribed condition(s). In contrast, many controlled experiments involve comparisons of the dissimilarity in the behavior of different groups of individuals who may or may not have been exposed to a particular treatment (or intervention). Experimental (group) research attempts to investigate the relationship between the independent and dependent variables. For example, the relationship between a proscribed counseling technique to reduce test anxiety and the level of test anxiety in students. There is an assumption of connection between the two variables and that this connection can be characterized as a causal relationship. In the context of single-subject research, however, causality is not defined as a logical, or "hard," connection between a preceding event (a cause) and a consistently recurring postevent (the effect). Rather, a causal relationship is defined as a *functional* relationship. This might be considered a quasicausal relationship in which a fixed and precisely quantifiable account of the relationship cannot be given. Instead of saying, at the conclusion of an experiment, for example, that an intervention caused scores to improve, we would more properly say that a relationship of functionality exists. That is, certain functions of an individual (e.g., the degree of success solving math problems) are related to certain functions of another, preceding process (type of math instruction). It is common throughout the social sciences to speak of probable or functional relationships rather than causal relationships, which, in a general way, belong more to the physical sciences.

> In your estimate, what is the distinction between causal and functional relationships? Why might this distinction be an important one?

A functional relationship, then, is assumed if the dependent variable shows a change when (and only when) the independent variable is introduced (Alberto & Troutman, 1999). For example, verbal praise (independent variable or treatment) would be reported to be functionally related to an individual's behavior if the frequency of hand raising (dependent variable) consistently and reliably increased contingent on the presentation of verbal praise (Sulzer-Azaroff & Mayer, 1991). Essentially, single-subject experimental research aims at ensuring that the observed changes in performance are more likely the result of an applied intervention and are not due to chance or normal variations in behavior.

It is also important to note that the establishment of a functional relationship between the independent and dependent variables can be achieved with little or no interruption of their day-to-day practices and responsibilities of practitioners. For example, if a teacher wants to increase the number of basic addition facts a first-grader knows, he or she may intervene using a traditional trials-to-criterion (teach-and-practice) format. Shortly after the intervention, the teacher assesses the child's skills using a basic addition skills probe. If the intervention is followed with a probe in a timely fashion, then the teacher can make a highly confident inference that a functional relationship exists between his selected intervention (trials to criterion) and the child's corresponding response (score increases on the probe). This example further illustrates that single-subject research can serve as a systematic measurement system that allows for experimental control.

A conceptual compatibility also exists between special education, counseling, and school psychology practices and single-subject designs (Tawney & Gast, 1984). Practitioners in these areas focus on assessment of individual performance, careful specification of interventions, evaluation, and decision making based on student or client behavior. This practice of making data-based decisions provides the practitioner with intervention strategies that are objective, effectual, and a replicable document of individual progress. Moreover, the use of repeated measurement, a metric common to all single-subject experimental research, is a more accurate method of observing individual learning than the measures commonly associated with group designs that may mask the effectiveness of interventions with certain types of learners. (Haring, Lovitt, Eaton, & Hanson, 1978). Thus, one must be careful not to erroneously associate single-subject research with quasi-experimental research (Best & Kahn, 1998). Although there are similarities, quasi-experimental designs focus on a group of participants and are analyzed as such. In contrast, single-subject research focuses on the individual with careful attention to changes in behavior across repeated observations.

> How are single-subject and quasi-experimental designs alike and different? What purposes does each approach serve?

Although single-subject researchers are concerned with the threats to internal validity (alternative explanations for treatment results) associated with this kind of research, there are designs within the single-subject paradigm that control for these threats. This chapter will focus on the most common designs. For a more exhaustive study of single-subject research methodology, the reader is referred to the influential work of Barlow and Hersen (1984), the early work of Kazdin (1982), and the work of Tawney and Gast (1984). More recent works that explain single-subject research methods include Sulzer-Azaroff and Mayer (1991), Repp and Horner (1999), and Alberto and Troutman (1999). *The Journal of Applied Behavior Analysis* is an excellent periodical resource.

COMPONENTS AND PROCEDURES OF SINGLE-SUBJECT EXPERIMENTAL RESEARCH

Single-subject methodology has four critical elements: (1) selection of the target behavior, (2) establishment of a baseline condition, (3) repeated measurement, and (4) intervention. These four elements are critical in helping the researcher or practitioner design a single-subject experiment that has high internal validity—a requirement if the researcher is to establish a clear functional relationship between the treatment (independent variable) as the potential reason for change in the behavior of interest (dependent variable).

> What are dependent and independent variables? Why do you think these names are used?

Selecting the Target Behavior and Reliable Observation

Selecting the target behavior is critical in any experiment. A target behavior is simply a performance or response of an individual that the researcher is interested in modifying. The target behavior may be an act of bullying. In this case, the behavior may be targeted for reduction or elimination. Conversely, the target behavior may be correct responses to word pronunciation cues, and in this case, the objective would be increasing the frequency of correct responses. In single-subject research, it is critical that the target behavior is defined in objective, observable, and measurable terms. Target behaviors must be rendered as unambiguous as possible, so that there is minimal disagreement between observers assigned to record such behaviors. The process of structuring precise definitions of behavioral outputs is often referred to as developing an operational definition.

The Importance of Operationalizing Our Measured Constructs

When we have an operational or behavior-specific definition of a construct, such as "aggressiveness," for example, we reduce the number and complexity of inferences that observers have to make. To assist with the operationalization or definition of target behavior(s), the practitioner may opt to describe how the target behavior is performed (topography) or the outcome of the behavior (function; Barlow & Hersen, 1984). Developing such "low inference" definitions makes recording easier and generally increases the reliability of the observations.

By and large, the target behaviors encountered in single-subject research are *constructs*, such as reading proficiency, knowledge of geometry, learning disorder, and prosocial behavior. We must be careful not to exchange or trade psychological constructs in our professional, research-based conversations, as if they were a kind of fixed verbal currency. In our everyday discourse, we often use our constructs like coins, as if they were minted from the same semantic press, as it were, wherein it is assumed that everyone knows the worth and application of such terms. And so we talk of anxiety, or attention deficit disorder in a shorthand way, assuming that our meaning is adequately understood.

However much we may agree on the general components of a psychological construct, it is nevertheless a construct, used to categorize behavior, and is not a directly observable entity. Aggression, or aggressiveness, is an example of a construct that references a cluster of behaviors. The behaviors in turn are thought to index an underlying, stable trait or disposition, such as aggressiveness. But rarely in normal discourse is the mental abstraction, or construct, ever operationalized or transcribed into a set of specific behaviors that can be observed, measured, and quantified. For research purposes, constructs such as aggressiveness, anxiety, attention deficit, or self-esteem must be distilled into specific, defining, behavioral acts, which *are* capable of being quantified. In short, the target behavior of interest must be *operationalized* if reliable and valid data are to be obtained.

The process of operationalizing a concept such as "adequate math performance," or "emotional disturbance," is actually a specific way of defining such a concept. For example, in defining *emotional disturbance*, the concept is talked about in terms of its observable behavioral components. The *operations* that go into making up the thing we call an emotional disturbance may be, for example, defined as (1) facial displays characteristic of heightened emotionality, which may include widened eyes, raised brow, and mouth drawn back at the corners; (2) loud vocalizations; and (3) intrusions into the personal space of others (which may need further specification). When collecting data in a single-subject experiment, one of the variables we may wish to measure, for example, is emotional disturbance. The data points we graph will be the overt behavioral components of emotional disturbance, such as loud vocalizations or violations of personal space. Or the data points comprising our measurement of adequate math performance may be rather straightforward behaviors, such as a correct solution of an addition problem, a subtraction problem, a multiplication problem, and a division problem. The point to keep in mind about obtaining reliable observations is that the thing we are attempting to observe and measure must be specified by naming the behaviors that make it up and that provide evidence for the construct.

In your words, define an operational target behavior. Why is it important to understand this concept in single-subject research?

Observation Systems

Although generating operational definitions of target behaviors is a central first step in the implementation of any experiment, it is equally important to design a systematic procedure for recording behavioral observations. The investigator must use an observation system that produces reliable data in order to ensure accurate and valid assessments of the intervention. Observer training is usually conducted prior to the data collection process. This involves practice in identifying the behavioral components of whatever activity or construct the investigator wishes to evaluate. If the researcher wishes to identify the level of literacy (the construct) in an individual who has certain language difficulties, then one of the behavioral components, or target behaviors, may be the number of correct responses to a word recognition probe (test). Or, if the researcher were trying to identify a student's level of aggression, observers may be instructed to recognize and count the number of specific behavioral indicators of aggression (e.g., slapping, kicking, and hitting), which occur in a given period of time, and then plot the frequency of such behaviors on a graph. The principle researcher will also conduct periodic checks on observer's recognition and recording of target behaviors to ensure continued interobserver agreement during the data collection process.

Although there may be multiple behaviors of interest that have been operationally defined and selected for observation (e.g., slapping, kicking, and hitting), such behaviors may be singled out and plotted individually. Gall, Borg, and Gall (1996) noted that the simplest procedure is to target one behavior for observation during the experiment (intervention). Although it is possible to monitor additional behaviors, Gall et al. cautioned that each additional behavior adds to the level of complexity of the research design. This is because single-subject research utilizes multiple observations or repeated measurement to determine whether significant changes in the performance of the participant have occurred. In contrast, group experimental designs typically collect data only twice—at the pretest and the posttest.

Establishing a Stable Baseline Condition

The baseline condition is to single-subject research what pretests are to group research. In the baseline condition, the researcher collects data on the target behavior prior to the implementation of any intervention (independent variable). Data on the target behavior are recorded according to the protocol established by the researchers. The purpose of establishing a baseline is to allow the researcher to see the frequency, intensity, or duration of the target behavior in its "natural state," as it were, in the absence of any intervention. This *baseline data* is then used as the basis of comparison to determine the degree of change that may occur during the treatment or intervention phase.

When establishing baseline conditions, enough data must be collected so the investigator is certain that the behavior observed is indeed representative of the behavior of concern. Because the baseline condition is used to determine the status of the participant's behavior in the absence of intervention, the investigator must collect data with enough frequency and adequate periodicity to be able to identify a stable trend or pattern in the data. Establishing a stable baseline will help control for intraparticipant variability, that is, response variability within a given participant.

It should be noted that no clear-cut rules have been laid down to determine just when data stability has been attained. Typically, the data will be collected for 3 to 5 days or three to five separate observations (Tawney & Gast, 1984). Although it is not uncommon for more observations to be taken, it is important to ensure that ethical considerations are not at issue. For example, withholding an intervention in the presence of self-injurious behavior just to establish a satisfactory baseline would violate a basic "do no harm" principle and be unethical.

As to the question of just how many trials or data points need to be collected in any given experimental condition, the answer is that it depends on the stability or lack of variance in the data phase. Some authors apply a formula approach (e.g., Tawney & Gast, 1984), whereas other authors take a more flexible approach and simply recommend that evidence of stability exists when most of the data points fall within an obviously narrow range (Heward, 1987). Although this is generally true, the actual number of data points needed will be greater when there is more intraparticipant variability, and less when there is minimal variability. Assurance of stability is more difficult to obtain when dealing with participant responses that are "all over the map." Thus, the ideal participant for the single-subject researcher is one who consistently produces a *flat profile* of responses.

In establishing the baseline, three data patterns or trends are generally noted: (1) stable trends, (2) increasing trends, and (3) decreasing trends (Figure 18.1). These trends, or patterns, help guide the practitioner's decision to move to the treatment phase or identify a different behavior for intervention.

Stable Baseline

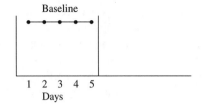

Increasing Baseline

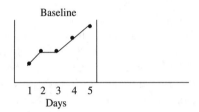

Decreasing Baseline

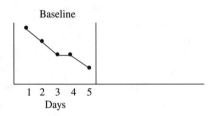

FIG. 18.1. Baselines.

To illustrate how data trends can guide the decision-making process, we will again revisit the example of the teacher wishing to teach basic addition facts. First, baseline data using a probe containing basic addition facts is given for 3 to 5 days. If the baseline data show continued increases in performance (increasing of correct responses) over the course of the baseline condition, an *improving trend* is indicated. In this case, it would be difficult for the teacher to discern the impact of drill and practice as a treatment, should the decision be made to move to the intervention phase. If, however, the child demonstrates a continued pattern of random correct and incorrect responses in the baseline, this would indicate a stable pattern, or stability in the data. The teacher can proceed to the intervention phase and use the baseline data to contrast with the data collected in the treatment phase.

In summary, the baseline condition provides a description or series of snapshots of the target behavior as it would naturally occur prior to or in the absence of any treatment. Because there is not an intervention or treatment provided during the baseline condition, it serves as the basis of comparison in evaluating the effectiveness of the treatment.

> What do you consider a baseline in single-subject research and how and why is it established?

Repeated Measurement

More than being a specific phase of single-subject experimental research, repeated measurement is a central principle of the single-subject methodology. Repeated measurement is a logic that applies equally to both baseline and intervention conditions. The role of repeated measurement is to establish a stable baseline condition, and in the intervention phase, repeated measures serve to identify when the relationship between the baseline and intervention condition is stable. It is only when this relationship has been stabilized that the researcher can accurately assess the degree of effectiveness of the intervention.

Repeated observation or measurement in single-subject methodology helps the researcher determine if specific interventions or treatments (the independent variable) applied in the experimental condition effects change in the participant's *target behavior* (the dependent variable). As previously noted, researchers who utilize single-subject experiments are typically working with an individual or a few individuals rather than a group of participants, and are interested in individual change and not collective change. Again, the use of repeated measures under these conditions are necessary to ascertain the impact of the intervention on the participant. In a sense, repeated measures of a single subject can act as a behavioral averaging device. Although not the same as a mean typically available to the investigator of group performances, repeated measures serve a similar function in capturing an individual's normal or average behavior under various phases of treatment implementation. Moreover, repeated measures allow the researcher to see both subtle and not so subtle changes in the data across time.

To illustrate the utility of repeated measurement, consider the earlier example of the teacher wishing to teach basic addition facts. If the child's ability to compute the basic addition facts were measured only twice in the experiment, say at the beginning of a semester (pretest) and at the end (posttest), it would be impossible to determine just what specific effect the intervention had, because it would not be possible to rule out alternative explanations of the child's acquisition of addition facts. All we would know is that sometime during the course of the intervention, the child learned addition facts. We could not say with confidence that the change in the child's performance was due to the intervention. Extensive time intervals between measures can introduce contamination by uncontrolled variables, such as a new tutor hired by the parents, an episode of *Sesame Street*, or a shopping trip with learning-relevant math problems to solve. Taking data across time, that is, using repeated measurement, allows us to view the change and develop hypotheses as we go, so to speak, concerning the source of behavior change.

When completing repeated measurements of a participant's behavior, it is important to ensure that the inferences regarding behavior change are clearly and solely the result of the intervention. Hence, procedural issues related to *standardization* merit discussion. It is important, first of all, that each replication (repeated measure) is conducted under the same, or standardized, conditions. Best and Kahn (1998) suggested that the setting of the experiment (e.g., the time of day and room conditions) be held constant, both when taking measurements in the baseline and treatment conditions. Thought must also be given to standardizing the unit of measurement (e.g., frequency of Behavior X, observed across Y units of time).

> How does the idea of repeated measures work in practice? In your judgment, how might it be important in this kind of research?

Basic Designs

In single-subject methodology, the participant is alternately exposed to a series of measurements in the nontreatment, or baseline, phase, referred to as A, and the same series of measurements again during the treatment or intervention phase, referred to as B. Single-subject designs are typically categorized into three fundamental types: the A-B, the A-B-A, and *multiple baseline*. Although other designs exist, they are complex and inappropriate for this introductory discussion.

A-B Designs

The A-B design is the least complicated of the single-subject designs. Although the conclusions that can be drawn from an A-B experiment are not as powerful as those associated with more complex designs, it nevertheless offers practitioners a quick, uncomplicated means of comparing a participant's behavior before and after some intervention. Each of the more complex and stronger single-subject designs is an expansion of this simple A-B format.

As the title of this design suggests, two phases are implemented: the baseline (A) and the treatment (B). Baseline data are collected and recorded until stability is established, after which the treatment is introduced. Treatment data are collected and recorded, and then differences between the A and B phases can be evaluated.

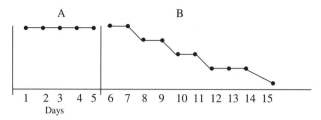

FIG. 18.2. A-B design—simplest design—baseline phase then treatment phase.

How are differences (changes) determined?   In all single-subject research designs, the relative success of any intervention is determined by visual inspection
of the graphed data points. This process simply consists of comparing the data
points on the graphs displaying baseline scores or responses with the data points
representing scores or responses recorded during the intervention phase. For example, in Figure 18.2 we see a stable baseline, or A, phase. In the B phase we see
a decrease in the data.

To determine whether a real or significant change has occurred, the researcher
or practitioner would first compare the level of the data points in the baseline
condition with those recorded in the treatment condition, across the repeated
measuring sessions. If there is a consistent pattern of abrupt changes or a different
trend (i.e., increasing or decreasing) in the data from the baseline to the treatment
phase, we may be justified in assuming that the treatment was responsible for the
change. When we as researchers study our graphs that show differences between
baseline and treatment phases, indicating that our treatment was successful, we
may want to cheer, but our elation must be tempered by other considerations.

Simple A-B designs cannot entirely rule out the possibility that other, extraneous variables have crept in to the individual's experiences, such as neurological
maturation, or changes in the environment that had the effect of contaminating
your experiment. In any case, we cannot be entirely confident in our determination that a functional relationship exists between the treatment and a change in
the performance of the individual.

Let's say our intervention is designed to decrease disruptive behavior in a child
with attention deficit hyperactivity disorder (ADHD). The child's doctor and
parents want to find out if medication will reduce his or her symptoms. First, the
severity of the target behavior (e.g., getting out of seat or talking out) is quantified with measurement (dependent variable) during the baseline condition (Phase
A). A trial of Ritalin medication (independent variable) is introduced (Phase B)
with the continued measure of the target behavior. A comparison of the A and
B phases will help the doctor, parents, and teacher determine if Ritalin is an effective treatment for the child. If there is a change when the medication is given,
it may be concluded that the treatment effected the change, and a functional

relationship exists between the independent and dependent variable. However, what if some unknown intervention or perhaps chance made the difference?

To rule out coincidence or other variables, we might remove the treatment and return to baseline and observe what happens. This process is referred to as a reversal, or withdrawal design (A-B-A)

A-B-A Designs

A-B-A is the most common single-subject experimental design in the social sciences (Slavin, 1992) and has high internal validity (Gall et al., 1996). This design uses the steps of the A-B design but adds an additional phase: withdrawal of the treatment with a return to baseline conditions. When using an A-B-A design, the researcher systematically introduces and removes the treatment (Schloss & Smith, 1999). The sequential application and removal (withdrawal) of the treatment allows the researcher to verify the effect of the treatment on behavior. By withdrawing the treatment and returning to the A phase, the investigator is able to note changes between the conditions and determine if a functional relationship exits between the independent and dependent variable. If changes occur in each condition, the researcher is able to conclude that the changes were due to the treatment variable. In many cases, the researcher will reintroduce the withdrawn treatment (B). If treatment effects return, this will serve as verification of the treatment as the principal source of change. The resulting design is depicted as A-B-A-B and is represented in Figure 18.3.

Consider our earlier example of the child with ADHD. Baseline data was collected (Phase A), and then a trial of Ritalin medication (independent variable) was introduced (Phase B), with the continued measure of the target behavior. The treatment is withdrawn (back to Phase A) for a period of time while measurement continues. The treatment is then reintroduced (Phase B), again with continued measurement.

A comparison of both the A and B phases will help the doctor, parents, and teacher determine if Ritalin is an effective treatment for the child. If there is a

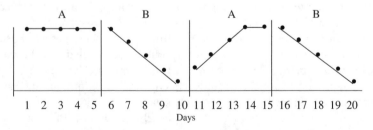

FIG. 18.3. A-B-A-B design—go back to baseline to show behavior under control of variable. Stronger design than A-B. This is sometimes referred to as a reversal design.

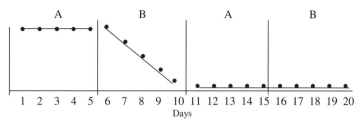

FIG. 18.4. The problem you sometimes get with withdrawal, especially with information that cannot be unlearned.

change when the medication is given and then another change when it is withdrawn, it may be concluded that the treatment effected the change, and a functional relationship exists between the independent and dependent variable.

There are two major limitations to the withdrawal or reversal designs: (1) cases where the withdrawal of treatment can pose ethical or safety problems to the person receiving treatment, or to the health and safety of other persons; and (2) situations when it is impossible to return to baseline (i.e., "unlearning" information). For example, in the case of learning the addition facts, the students would not unlearn the facts in a return to the A phase. In this case and cases like it, the investigator would be advised to use a multiple baseline design, as they do not require the withdrawal or reversal of treatment. Figure 18.4 exemplifies this pattern.

What do the symbols A and B stand for in single-subject designs? When would you not use it and why?

Multiple-Baseline Designs

There are three basic forms of multiple-baseline research. These essentially involve observations across (1) behaviors, (2) participants, and (3) settings.

Multiple-baseline designs can be considered replication designs (Alberto & Troutman, 1999; Best & Kahn, 1998; Kazdin, 1982). These designs are used as an alternative to collecting baseline data for a single target behavior, for a single participant, or within one specific setting. The researcher can design a study in a way that will analyze the effectiveness of multiple behaviors for one participant, one behavior for several participants, or a single participant in several settings. The researcher continues to systematically apply a treatment or intervention to the baselines (e.g., behavior, participant, or setting) systematically, at different points in time (Kazdin, 1982). By systematically applying a treatment or intervention to the baselines, the researcher is able to establish a causal or functional

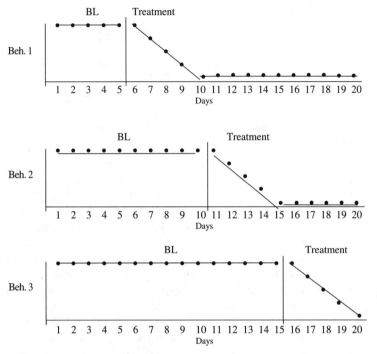

FIG. 18.5. **Multiple-baseline designs**. This design demonstrates the effect of an intervention by showing that behavior change accompanies introduction of the intervention at different points in time. Target one thing for treatment at a time. BL, baseline.

relationship between the independent variable (treatment) and the dependent variable (behavior of individuals) if the introduction of the dependent variable causes a stable change in the target behavior. Multiple-baseline designs enable researchers or practitioners to investigate the systematic introduction of treatment across (1) groups of individuals in same setting, (2) multiple behaviors of one individual, or (3) one individual and behavior across different settings. Figure 18.5 shows a multiple baseline across behaviors.

In a multiple-baseline *across participants design*, for example, data are collected on three or more participants with just one dependent variable (e.g., addition facts). The multiple-baseline *across behaviors* utilizes the collection of baseline data for three or more responses at the same time with the same individual (e.g., hitting, kicking, and screaming). A multiple baseline across settings follows the same pattern, except that the response of a single individual is observed in three or more settings. (e.g., classroom, gym, and study hall).

As with all single-subject designs, observations of baseline behaviors are taken until the investigator is satisfied that the observed behaviors present a stable pattern. Once stability is achieved in all the baselines, the treatment is introduced to the first subject (or in the first setting, or on the first behavior) while holding the other two in the baseline condition. When participant 1 has responded to the treatment and a stable pattern is noted, the treatment is introduced to participant 2. This pattern follows for the remaining subjects.

By systematically introducing the treatment, threats to validity such as history and maturation are controlled for, and the researcher is able to discern if a functional relationship exists between the independent and dependent variable. The functional relationship is said to exist if, and only if, a change in the dependent variable is noted following the introduction of the independent variable (Alberto & Troutman, 1999; Best & Kahn, 1998; Sulzer-Azaroff & Mayer, 1991).

Consider three students who have been identified by their therapist as being school phobic. All three are exhibiting increased anxiety regarding the starting of school in 2 weeks. The therapist decides to try a new therapy with these students and begins to collect baseline data at the same time for each of them. Student 1 is introduced to the therapy first, whereas Students 2 and 3 are kept in the baseline phase until Student 1 shows some change following the treatment phase. At that time, Student 2 is given the same therapy, whereas Student 3 stays in baseline. As with Student 1, when Student 2 shows a change in behavior following the treatment phase, Student 3 will be exposed to the treatment therapy.

What example of your own can you give for a multiple-baseline design?

ANALYSIS AND INTERPRETATION OF THE DATA

Within single-subject methodology, data are typically analyzed and interpreted by visual inspection of the graphed data points. Single-subject researchers want intervention results that demonstrate potent effects obvious from merely inspecting the data. If the researcher is confident that the design used in the experiment is adequate, conclusions regarding whether the data has reached a predetermined experimental criterion or has become stable can be made. Moreover, the treatment may be analyzed in terms of whether it had an effect, and to some degree, what kind of effect (i.e., increasing or decreasing the target behavior).

Visual Inspection of Data

The visual inspection of graphed data, in contrast to statistical analysis, has several advantages, as pointed out by Tawney and Gast (1984). For example, visual inspection allows for the evaluation of data gathered from individuals or small groups of individuals without collapsing the results. This enables the researcher to determine the effectiveness of the intervention with the individuals, thus reducing potential overestimation (or underestimation) of treatment effects. Graphic display of the data permits independent analysis and interpretation of the results, allowing others to discern for themselves the treatment effects, reliability (consistency), and social validity (value to society) of the treatment.

Visual inspection is a dynamic process, because the data are collected and evaluated continually. Visual inspection of the graphed data allows the researcher to make data-based decisions in an ongoing fashion rather than at the end of an experiment. This is important when individualizing instruction or interventions.

Although the graphing of data is considered relatively unrefined and insensitive by some, especially when compared with statistical analyses, and indeed has limitations (as do all methods of analysis), this unrefinement can be regarded as a virtue—only the obvious effects will be considered. For example, only those interventions that produce marked effects on behavior are judged by the scientific community as having produced a change, which in turn should lead to only clear and potent interventions being interpreted as reliable. Consider the treatment of a student participating in a program to reduce self-injurious behavior. The treatment resulted in a reduction of self-injurious behavior by 6%, which may be statistically significant, that decrease, however, is not clinically significant, that is, we want to see a more dramatic drop in this dangerous behavior, which is harmful to the student and potentially those around him. The researcher cannot settle for an intervention that produces statistically significant but clinically insignificant effects. Although statistical analyses are available to and used by some single-subject researchers (e.g., t and F tests), their use is debated (Gay & Airasian, 2000).

Despite the pragmatic appeal of visual inspection, there are some problems that merit discussion. The process of visual inspection encourages subjectivity and may lead to inconsistency in evaluations of intervention effects. Studies have been done that show that judges, even when experts in the field, often disagree about particular data patterns. This is especially true when the intervention effects are not dramatic. Similarly, others have criticized visual inspection, because only marked effects are likely to be regarded as significant. There may be consistent, but weak, effects that could be important but may be overlooked when using visual inspection.

Looking at the data in several ways then becomes important. Tawney and Gast (1984) noted three properties of data that need to be considered when engaging in data analysis: (1) the number of data points within a condition or phase, (2) the number of variables changed between the adjacent conditions or phases, and (3) trend direction, trend stability, and changes in trend.

How does the researcher or practitioner use visual inspection to analyze single-subject study results?

The following provides a brief overview regarding the different methods or techniques used to guide the examination and discussion of the data. Patterns of the data, changes in magnitude (means and level), trend, and latency are presented. Interpretation of nonoverlapping data points is also discussed.

Pattern of Data

In general, the researcher is looking for is a systematic pattern of behavior across phases. In an A-B-A-B design, for example, the researcher wants to show that the intervention effect is replicated over time. Similarly, for a multiple-baseline design, the intervention effect is replicated across the dimension for which the multiple-baseline data have been gathered.

Changes in Magnitude

One way to help elaborate on the visual inspection of the data is through reporting changes in magnitude (or strength). These may or may not help, but they are one of the first things the researcher examines. Changes in magnitude can be evaluated by *changes in the means* for the phases or *changes in the levels* across phases.

A change in means refers to changes in the average rate of performance across phases (Schloss & Smith, 1994) Let's use the following A-B-A-B design, illustrated in Figure 18.6.

In this example, you can use the mean of each phase to help illustrate the changing level of performance. We see that the first A phase has a mean of 2.6, which increases to a mean of 5.8 in the first intervention phase, drops to a mean of 4.2 in the second baseline phase, and increases to a mean of 7.6 in the second intervention phase.

Changes in level help to illustrate the changing nature of performance from phase to phase. The term *level* refers to the magnitude of the data as depicted on ordinate scale value. The researcher looks for a shift or discontinuity of performance from the end of one phase to the beginning of the next phase. This is independent of the mean. What you are looking for is what happened immediately after the intervention was implemented or withdrawn (Alberto & Troutman, 1999; Kazdin, 1982; Schloss & Smith, 1994; Tawney & Gast 1984). Figure 18.7 illustrates a change in level.

The last data point in A_1 is a 2; the first point in B_1 is a 6. The last point in B_1 is an 8, and the first point in A_2 is a 5. Finally, the last data point in A_2 is a 4; the first point in B_2 is an 8. This example would also be accompanied by a change in mean (2.4, 7, 4.6, & 8); however, level and mean do not always go together.

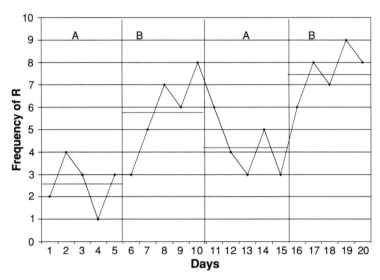

FIG. 18.6. **Changes in means**. This refers to changes in the average rate of performance across phases. Let's use an example from an A-B-A-B design. In this example, you can use the mean of each phase to help illustrate the changing level of performance.

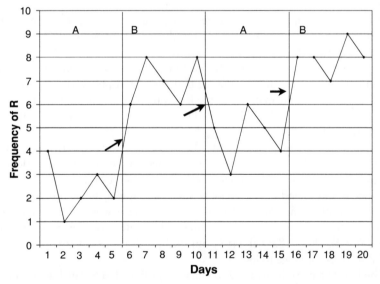

FIG. 18.7. Changes in level help to illustrate the changing nature of performance from phase to phase by looking for a shift or discontinuity of performance from the end of one phase to the beginning of the next phase. The arrows indicate the changes immediately after the intervention was implemented or withdrawn.

Changes in Trend

Changes in trend refers to the tendency of the data to show systematic increases or decreases over time as depicted by trend direction or slope (the steepness of the data across time) and can provide a prediction of future direction change (Alberto & Troutman, 1999; Schloss & Smith 1994; White & Haring, 1980). Trend is usually discussed in terms of celeration. Increasing in ordinate value over time is acceleration, whereas deceleration is decreasing ordinate value over time. No change, or zero celeration, is a line parallel to the abscissa. In addition to acceleration and deceleration, the researcher must note the trend in terms of improvement or decay in the target behavior.

Figure 18.8 illustrates changes in trend. If a researcher looks at the means (2.4, 5.6, 5.4, 6.0), she or he would miss the pattern for all except the change from A_1 to B_1, because the means are all very close. Similarly, if the researcher looked for a change in level, she or he would find absolutely nothing, as the last data point in each phase is equal to the first data point in the next phase. A change in trend allows one to see the differences over the phases that might not otherwise be noted.

Changes in Latency

Changes in latency simply refers to observing the period of time that elapses between the onset or termination of one condition and changes in performance (Alberto & Troutman 1994; Schloss & Smith, 1994; Tawney & Gast, 1984). The

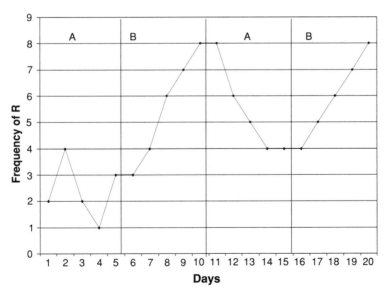

FIG. 18.8. Changes in trend refers to the tendency of the data to show systematic increases or decreases over time.

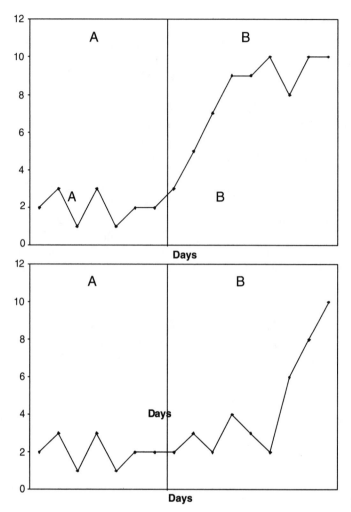

FIG. 18.9. **Changes in latency**. Latency is simply the period of time that elapses between the onset or termination of one condition and changes in performance. The upper graph shown a case where a rapid changes in behavior occured. The lower graph shows that behavior change did not occur immediately after the phase changes.

more closely in time the changes occur after the change in condition, the clearer the effect of the intervention. The graph examples in Figure 18.9 show us the change from phase A to B (or baseline to intervention).

The upper graph in Figure 18.9 illustrates a case where a rapid change in behavior occurred shortly after the change in phases was implemented, whereas the lower graph shows that behavior change did not occur immediately after the phase change. Both graphs show a change in behavior, but there is more certainty with the first one that the change was the result of intervention. The longer the latency, or time passed, between the phase change and change in behavior, the more questions that can be raised about whether the intervention or some extraneous fact accounted for the change.

Nonoverlapping Data Points

Nonoverlapping data points refers to the percentage of data points in the baseline and intervention phases that do not have overlapping ranges. Many people use the percentage of nonoverlapping data points to help document the effectiveness of their intervention. Let's look at the upper graph in Figure 18.9 as our first example. We can see that here are 7 data points during baseline, with a range from 1 to 3. There are 9 data points during the intervention; 8 of the 9 do not overlap the range of the baseline scores, yielding a percentage of nonoverlapping data points of 89%. Now let's look at the lower graph in Figure 18.9. We see that there are 5 data points in the B or intervention phase that overlap with baseline scores, for a percentage of only 44%. Looking at the overlap is not a foolproof method, however. Take the example illustrated in Figure 18.10.

In this case, we see that no data points overlap from Phase A to Phase B; that is, we have 100% nonoverlapping data points. But can we really say there is

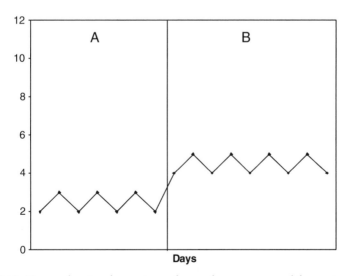

FIG. 18.10. Nonoverlapping data points refers to the percentage of data points in the baseline and intervention phase that do not have overlapping ranges. In this example, there are no overlapping data points.

meaningful change in behavior? The pattern remains the same in both the A and B phases, with the only difference being an increase in frequency of responses.

SUPPLEMENTAL DATA EVALUATION—STATISTICAL EVALUATION

Visual inspection is by far the method most frequently used to evaluate single-subject and small data sets. Some have proposed statistical analyses to supplement or even replace visual inspection. Not everyone agrees, however. The major objection is that statistical tests are likely to detect subtle and minor changes and will identify as significant effects that would be rejected via visual inspection. If the goal of single-subject research is to produce potent changes, the more stringent criterion, namely visual inspection, is needed. Statistical evaluation should be used to supplement, not replace, visual inspection. Some basic statistical methods are outlined below.

t and *F* Tests

The *t* and *F* Tests help the researcher determine whether differences between means are statistically reliable between, or among, the different phases. You do need to have several participants in each phase to perform these tests, however. They cannot be done with one participant, because one of the assumptions of *t* and *F* is that data points are independent of one another. With one participant, adjacent data points are significantly correlated; they are considered to be serially dependent. This is tested by pairing adjacent data points (i.e., Days 2 and 3, 3 and 4, 4 and 5, etc.) and computing a correlation coefficient. This correlation is referred to as an autocorrelation, and it is a measure of serial dependency. If serial dependency exists, *t* and *F* tests should not be used.

Time-Series Analysis

This is a statistical method that compares data over time for separate phases for individual participants or groups of participants. It tests whether there is a statistically significant change in level and trend from one phase to another. The actual analysis is not simple, and there are many variations on it, but it does involve computing separate *t* tests to evaluate changes in level and trend. Our searcher must have a sufficient number of data points to do time-series analysis, however, to determine the existence and pattern of serial dependency and derive the appropriate time-series analysis model for the data. Estimates range from 20 to 100 points per phase, and in many, if not most, cases there will simply be too few data points for time-series analysis.

Under what circumstances would one employ various single-subject designs?

ACKNOWLEDGMENTS

The author wishes to thank Martin Eigenberger (University of Wisconsin–Parkside), Suzanne Shellady (Central Michigan University), and Steven G. Little (State University of New York–Albany), for their thoughtful and insightful comments and contributions to earlier drafts of this chapter.

19

Experimental Research to Inform Educational Policy

Lawrence H. Cross and Gabriella M. Belli
Virginia Polytechnic Institute and State University

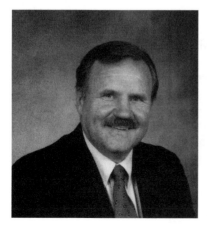

MEET THE AUTHORS

Lawrence H. Cross received his doctorate in 1973 from the University of Pennsylvania with a major in educational measurement, evaluation, and techniques of experimental research. He is a retired professor from Virginia Polytechnic Institute and State University, where he has taught graduate classes in research methods, statistics, and measurement since 1974. Most of his research and publications have been concerned with educational measurement. His early investigations focused on enhancing the reliability and validity of multiple-choice tests by means of choice-weighted scoring methods. In the 1980s, he published several studies comparing standards-setting techniques as part of his pioneering validation studies of the National Teachers Examination in Virginia, which were the first to be conducted by an agency other than the Educational Testing Service. He has also conducted investigations into grading practices and beliefs of teachers at both the public school and college level. In recent years, he has been a critic of the high-stakes testing program mandated for public schools in Virginia. His most recent publications and invited presentations document his concerns about the psychometric adequacy of these tests and the unethical uses made of the test scores for both student and school accountability. Although his personal research has focused largely on measurement, he has long been an advocate of experimental research methods in his teaching and writings.

Gabriella M. Belli is an associate professor in the Educational Research and Evaluation Program of the Department of Educational Leadership and Policy Studies at Virginia Polytechnic Institute and State University. She holds a doctorate in statistics and research design and a master of arts in measurement and evaluation from Michigan State University, and a bachelor of science in mathematics from St. Bonaventure University. A former math teacher, she has taught graduate-level core courses in statistics and behavioral science methods and advanced courses in experimental design, survey research, regression, and multivariate statistics since coming to Virginia Tech's Northern Virginia Center, which is located near Washington, DC.

Currently, one of her main research focuses is on statistical consulting and the two-way teaching–learning process in consultation. Her ongoing interest in teaching and communicating statistical concepts to nontechnical audiences is evidenced through scholarly papers, student guides to statistics and computer applications, and chapters such as the one in this book. She has worked with students on theses and dissertations in such diverse areas as adult learning, human resource development, community college studies, counseling, distance learning, educational administration, geography education,

> marriage and family therapy, mathematics achievement, nutrition education, and special education.

This chapter is concerned with quantitative research designs wherein the objective is to compare competing educational practices or treatments. Although the emphasis is on randomized experimental research where the researcher actively manipulates the treatments, it also addresses a special class of nonexperimental research in which a naturally occurring "treatment" has already occurred. Not addressed are research studies that explore causal relationships between variables that cannot be manipulated, such as between socioeconomic status and educational attainment. The chapter is written in the belief that experimental research in education too often takes a back seat to less adequate quantitative research designs out of expedience or failure to recognize its ability to provide far stronger evidence as to the relative effectiveness of competing practices.

The elegance by which an experiment can resolve a long-standing issue is captured well in a book the first author read as a child, entitled *Microbe Hunters*. It was published in 1926 and was written by Paul de Kruif, who, in writing about science for the common person, was the Carl Sagan of his day. He described how a simple experiment debunked the long-standing belief in the spontaneous generation of life. To quote from the book, "Even the scientists were on this side of the question. The English naturalist Ross announced learnedly that: 'To question that beetles and wasps were generated in cow dung is to question reason, sense, and experience'" (de Kruif, 1926, p. 29). The experiment, attributed to a person named Redi, is described as follows:

> See how easy he settles it. He takes two jars and puts some meat in each one. He leaves one open and then puts a light veil over the other one. He watches—and sees flies go down to the meat in the open pot—and in a little while there are maggots there and then new flies. He looks at the jar that has the veil over it—and there are no maggots or flies in that one at all. How easy! It is just a matter of the veil keeping the mother flies from getting to the meat. . . . But how clever, because for a thousand years people have been getting out of breath arguing about the question—and not one of them thought of doing this simple experiment that settles it in a minute. (p. 30)

Not only does this vignette illustrate the essential nature of an experiment, but it also has implications for many educational policy issues that people get out of breath arguing about today. By way of example, the national standards and accountability reform sweeping the United States has rekindled debate about many educational practices, such as social promotion, class size, and tracking, to name just three. Rather than resolve educational issues, educational research often contributes to the debate, with advocates on both sides of an issue citing research to support their position. Although no single experiment is likely to resolve any educational issue "in a minute," experimental research has greater potential to do so than other research methods. Some educational issues, such as whether private schools are superior to public schools, simply cannot be addressed using experimental methods. Extensive research has been reported on the effect of class size, but only a handful of these studies have been experimental. Other important issues, such as social promotion and grade retention, Head Start, and inclusion and mainstreaming for special education students, have been subject to a plethora of investigations, but rarely, if ever, have they been addressed using experimental designs. The paucity of experimental research in such debates is understandable but regrettable. Regrettable because experimental research has the greatest potential to provide unambiguous evidence as to the effectiveness of competing educational practices.

WHAT IS AN EXPERIMENT?

An experiment requires the researcher to manipulate something and observe the effect of that manipulation on something else. In the above example, Redi manipulated access of flies to the meat by placing a veil over one jar and not the other. The effect of that manipulation was gauged by comparing the presence or absence of maggots on the samples of meat. What he manipulated and what he observed are called variables.

Types of Variables

A *variable* is a characteristic or condition that can take on different values or levels. Variables may be classified in several ways. For the purpose of this chapter, the most important distinction is between independent, dependent, and extraneous variables. The independent variable is that which is thought to have an effect on the dependent variable. In experimental research, the independent variable is the manipulated variable and the effect of that manipulation is observed or measured on one or more dependent variables. Extraneous variables, also called nuisance or confounding variables, are variables that may also have an effect on the dependent variable but are not of primary interest. An extraneous variable that is not controlled is said to be confounded with the independent variable, meaning that it is not possible to say with confidence whether the treatment or the extraneous variable is responsible for the observed outcome.

Returning briefly to the Redi experiment, the manipulated independent variable was the presence or absence of the veil over the jars. Notice that this is one variable with two levels, or categories. The dependent variable was the observation of the presence or absence of maggots and flies on the pieces of meat so treated. Can you think of an extraneous variable that might be responsible for the observed outcome other than the independent variable? Of course, we assume that Redi sliced a single slab of meat into two equal portions for the two jars. Had Redi placed fish in one jar and beef in the other, the type of meat would constitute an uncontrolled extraneous variable, confounded with the treatment.

At this point, how would you define independent, dependent, and extraneous variables? Are these the same as explained in the previous chapter on single-subject design?

Theories, Hypotheses, and Proof

Linking the independent and the dependent variable is a hypothesis. A hypothesis is simply a conjecture or a hunch about the relationship between two variables, usually limited to the independent and dependent variables. Redi undertook this experiment because he believed that all living things had mothers, and if mother flies could not reach the meat to lay their eggs, no maggots would appear. Notice that his experiment was inspired by his belief in "motherhood for all," which constituted his theory. However, the experiment he conducted represented a test of a deduction drawn from his theory. The hypothesis he tested was that veiled meat would have no maggots and that unveiled meat would. Was Redi successful in proving that all living things have mothers? Of course not, but did he demonstrate that placing a veil over exposed meat eliminates infestation by flies? In general, experiments do not provide a direct test of a theory, but rather test hypotheses deduced from theories. No research is capable of proving a theory is true, even if the research findings are consistent with the theory. By contrast, theories can be undermined in part, if not altogether, if the research findings are inconsistent with theory.

What are theories? What are hypotheses? How are they different? How are they used in experimental research?

Criteria for Drawing Casual Inferences

Although many would agree that Redi's experiment demonstrated a causal relationship, others may disagree. Indeed, the philosophers of science have long debated the very meaning of cause and whether it is ever possible to draw a causal inference between two or more variables. However, those who engage in experimental research generally take a more pragmatic view and assert that a causal relationship can be inferred if three conditions are met (Porter, 1997). First, changes in the independent variable must be associated (correlated) with changes in the dependent variable. Second, changes in the independent variable must occur before changes in the dependent variable. Third, no other extraneous variables can be offered as rival explanations for the observed relationship. These three conditions preclude drawing a causal inference between two variables simply because there is a strong relationship (correlation) between them. In simple language, correlation does not imply causality.

An example may serve to illuminate the implications of these three conditions. It is well documented that a strong relationship exists between grade retention and dropping out of school. Moreover, grade retention occurs prior to dropping out of school, and thus the first two conditions for drawing a causal conclusion are satisfied. However, before concluding that grade retention contributes to dropping out of school, the third condition must be satisfied. Among many potential rival explanations for the observed relationship is the possibility that low academic ability is responsible for both being retained and dropping out of school. To establish that a causal relationship exists between X and Y, all other extraneous variables that might be considered a common cause of both X and Y must be controlled. This requirement is most fully satisfied in a true experimental design, and for this reason Kerlinger (1986) suggested that "the ideal of science is the controlled experiment" (p. 293).

What is your own definition for causal inference thus far? Why are correlation, chronological order, and no rival explanations essential to making causal inferences?

How would you compare and contrast this with the causal and functional references presented in Chapter 18?

Methods for Controlling Extraneous Variables

For the experimental comparison to be valid, it is essential that the treatment conditions be applied to comparable samples, just as we assumed that Redi used comparable pieces of meat in his two jars. The only surefire way to ensure that experimental samples are comparable at the outset is to *randomly assign* the experimental units to treatment conditions. In educational research, the experimental units usually consist of students, but they could consist of classes, schools, teachers, or some other entity. Randomly formed groups will differ only by chance amounts on any variable you wish to consider. The larger the samples are, the smaller these chance amounts will be. These chance differences can be reduced further if participants are first matched on one or more extraneous variables, and then the experimental groups are formed by randomly assigning match mates to the treatment conditions. Matching used in the absence of random assignment cannot, by itself, be counted on to yield comparable groups. The primary reason is that groups formed by simple matching may differ on many other important but unmeasured variables that may impact the effectiveness of the treatment. Attempts to match on more than one variable will result in considerable loss of participants for whom match mates cannot be found.

It is also possible to control an extraneous variable in several other ways. One way is to classify participants by levels of the extraneous variable and treat it as another independent variable. Another way is to include only participants representing one level of the extraneous variable. For example, sex either could be introduced as another independent variable, or sex could be controlled by including only males or only females in the sample. The former would permit comparisons between males and females, whereas the latter would limit the generalizability of the findings to only males or only females. Finally, statistical procedures have been used in an attempt to control extraneous variables. However, as will be discussed below, there is reason to question whether statistical procedures adequately control for group differences on extraneous variables.

EXPERIMENTAL DESIGNS AND THEIR VALIDITY

In a now classic publication, Campbell and Stanley (1963) provided an integrated framework for discussing various types of experimental research used in education. Three broad categories were used to classify a large number of designs. These categories are preexperimental, quasi-experimental, and true experimental. Perhaps more important was their identification of potential threats to the internal and external validity of these designs. Internal validity addresses the question, "Did in fact the experimental treatments make a difference in this specific experimental instance?" (p 5). External validity addresses the question, "To what populations, settings, treatment variables, and measurement variables can this effect be generalized?" (p. 5).

Cook and Campbell (1979) expanded on the work of Campbell and Stanley in the area of quasi-experimental research with another major contribution. Among the most visible contributions of their work was the special attention given to what they refer to as *statistical conclusion validity* and *construct validity of putative causes and effects*. Statistical conclusion validity, as the term implies, is concerned with whether the statistical analysis leads to valid conclusions. Construct validity is concerned with the interpretation of the manipulated and measured variables as constructs.

These two seminal publications have shaped the discussion of experimental research in education for more than a generation. References to these two publications are made in virtually every textbook treatment of the topic, as well as in published studies using experimental methods in education and related fields.

Excellent textbook treatments on the basic designs of experiments and threats to their validity can be found in Kerlinger (1986); Gall, Borg, and Gall (2003); Pedhazur and Schmelkin (1991); and Krathwohl (1998). Readers interested more in the analysis of experimental data, or more advanced designs, are referred to textbooks by Kirk (1995), Maxwell and Delaney (1990), and Keppel (1991).

The purpose here is not to present all of the design variations and threats to design validity, but to provide a foundation of understanding and appreciation of the concepts involved. Accordingly, we present only a single exemplar of each of the three designs and draw attention to only the major threats to the validity of these exemplars.

> What exactly are "threats to validity," and can they be related in some way to causal inferences in experiments? How might a researcher reduce these threats (also known as rival hypotheses)?

Preexperimental designs are those in which a treatment is applied but the basis for judging the effectiveness of the treatment is inadequate. Such designs either have no control group for comparison or an intact "static group" for which no pretest is available. Using the convention and terminology introduced by Campbell and Stanley (1963), a one-group pretest–posttest design is illustrated below:

$$O \quad X \quad O$$

The X represents the treatment and the Os represent pre- and posttest observations. More specifically, the Os represent mean scores for the participants exposed to the experimental condition. Although this design is appealing because of its simplicity and may have practical utility in some settings, it has little scientific value (Kerlinger, 1986, p. 295). Even if there is dramatic improvement in mean scores from pretest to posttest, any number of uncontrolled extraneous variables may be responsible for this change. Said differently, there are many potential threats to the internal validity of such research.

Perhaps the most obvious threat to internal validity is that factors or events other than the treatment are responsible for the observed change from pretest to posttest. Campbell and Stanley (1963) used the term *history* to refer to this threat. The term *maturation* is used to describe changes in the participants associated with the passage of time that may have nothing to do with the treatment. *Testing* represents another potential threat if taking the pretest can be expected to have an effect on the posttest that might enhance or mask the treatment effect. A more subtle threat is that associated with *statistical regression*. This threat is a statistical artifact and is of concern whenever participants are selected on the basis of extremely high or extremely low scores on a pretest measure. Suppose students scoring in the lowest, say, 10% of a score distribution on a reading test are selected for a remedial reading program. If this subgroup is retested even before remedial services are provided, you can expect the average score for this subgroup to regress toward the mean of the original score distribution. The less reliable the test, the greater this effect will be. In such situations, it is essential that students selected on the basis of their high or low pretest performance be retested on a parallel form of the selection test. Scores from the retest should be used as the basis for comparison with the posttest scores.

> Why are history, maturation, and regression considered threats to the internal validity of experiments?

True experimental designs are those in which alternative treatments are applied to groups that have been randomly formed. Illustrated below is what Campbell and Stanley (1963) described as the pretest–posttest control-group design:

$$R \quad O \quad X_1 \quad O$$
$$R \quad O \quad X_2 \quad O$$

As before, the Os represent pre- and posttest observations, and the Xs represent the experimental conditions applied to the two groups. The subscripts 1 and 2 could designate experimental and control conditions or two different treatments to be compared. Of course, this design can be extended to include more than two treatment conditions. The Rs represent random assignment of experimental units to the treatment conditions. As noted by Cook and Campbell (1979), "Random assignment is the great *ceteris paribus*—that is, other things being equal—of causal inference" (p. 5). If this requirement is met, and if the sample sizes are of sufficient size to yield a statistically significant difference on the posttest means, a causal inference regarding the effect of the treatment on the dependent variable can be made with a high level of confidence. Said differently, internal validity is largely assured, at least in theory. Formation of the experimental groups by random assignment is the hallmark of a true experiment.

It is important not to confuse *random assignment* of participants to experimental conditions with *random sampling* of participants from a population. Random sampling provides the basis for generalizing a study's findings from the sample at hand to the population of interest. Although random sampling is desirable in all forms of research, it is often impractical to do so in experimental research, because the participants must be within close proximity to each other and the researcher in order for the educational intervention to be administered. The absence of random sampling in most experimental studies precludes generalizing the findings to a well-defined population, and thus external validity suffers. However, internal validity is a higher priority for experimental research, and random assignment of participants to treatment conditions plays a crucial role in this regard. An experimenter's responsibility is first to demonstrate a treatment effect and second to describe the sample and procedures in sufficient detail that others may decide to what populations and settings the findings apply.

> What is the difference between random sampling and random assignment? What do you think, at this point, is the difference between internal and external validity of an experiment?

The use of a pretest in the above design is a desirable, but not an essential, feature of a true experimental design. As before, the use of a pretest may sensitize participants to the treatments, but it will not pose a threat to internal validity because the effect, if any, would apply equally to both groups. However, generalization of the study findings to settings in which a pretest is not given may not be valid. For this design, the use of a pretest poses a potential threat to external validity.

Pretests should be incorporated, not to check to make sure that the random assignment works, but rather to increase the chances of detecting treatment effects if they exist. In most instances, this consideration will outweigh any concern about the threat of testing on external validity. The ability to detect treatment effects, if they exist, is referred to as *statistical power*. The two most effective ways to increase statistical power are to increase the sample size or to include in the analysis additional information provided by the pretests. Administering a pretest is generally preferred to increasing the sample size. Increasing statistical power will enhance the statistical conclusion validity emphasized by Cook and Campbell (1979). For this reason, the use of a pretest is recommended, especially for studies involving modest-sized samples.

Quasi-experimental designs are "compromise designs" (Kerlinger, 1986, p. 315) that are recommended "*where better designs are not feasible*" (Campbell & Stanley, 1963, p. 34, emphasis in original). As our exemplar of quasi-experimental designs, we have selected what Campbell and Stanley (1963) referred to as the nonequivalent control-group design, illustrated below:

$$\frac{O \quad X_1 \quad O}{O \quad X_2 \quad O}$$

Except for the absence of random assignment of experimental units to treatment conditions, this design is identical to the true experimental design previously described. However, the absence of random assignment represents a major limitation and opens a door through which rival explanations to the treatments can march.

It should be noted that random assignment of participants to groups should not be confused with randomly assigning treatments to groups. A true experiment requires both random assignment of participants to groups *and* random assignment of treatments to groups thus formed. If any randomization is used in quasi-experiments, it is limited to the random assignment of treatments to groups. What may appear to some to be a minor semantic difference represents a major distinction between designs. In our experience, many graduate students are misled by statements like the following that appeared in the abstract and text of a published article: "A total of 406 heterogeneously grouped students in grades 3, 4, 6, 7, and 8 in three K through 8 Chicago public schools were assigned randomly to two conditions..." (Brown & Walberg, 1993). A careful reading of the article makes clear that intact classes, rather than 406 students, were randomly assigned to the treatment conditions.

To be classified as a true experiment, a large number of intact groups have to be randomly assigned to treatment conditions. Then, the intact groups are the experimental units and must also serve as the unit of analysis. This is to say, group means are to be used for the analysis rather than scores or observations of individual participants. Generally, this requirement calls for a large-scale study for the number of intact groups per treatment to yield adequate statistical power, thereby allowing true differences to actually show up in the statistical results. However, because group means tend to be less varied than performance measures for individuals, the number of groups needed will not be as great as when individuals serve as the unit of analysis. Too often, quasi-experimental research involves only one or two intact groups per treatment, and individual scores rather than group means are used inappropriately as the unit of analysis.

Whereas the pretest is optional in the true experimental design, it is essential in the nonequivalent control-group design. If a pretest were not available, the above design would reduce to a preexperimental design. Cook and Campbell (1979) pointed out that the interpretability of findings from this design depends, in part, on the particular pattern of findings. Moreover, they note that "... there are many, many ways in which two or more groups can differ from each other over time in the absence of a treatment effect..." (p. 107). The reader is encouraged to read Cook's and Campbell's description of the five patterns and the associated threats to internal validity for this design. However, we invite the reader to consider perhaps the most problematic situation.

Consider a case where the comparison groups differ significantly and substantially on the pretest measures. A quasi-experimental study reported in the literature is used here to illustrate the interpretative problems that can arise. The study, which shall remain anonymous, was conducted to investigate the effect of a series of six interactive computer assignments on a construct called *locus of control*.[1] Ostensibly, the interactive computer assignments would allow the "entering college freshman to operate the computer in an environment of personal control and

---

[1]Locus of control is a construct that represents the extent to which people perceive their fate is under their control (internal) or the result of luck or chance (external).

TABLE 19.1
Illustration of Misleading Results Due to Wrong Analysis

				Posttest			
Group	n	Pretest Mean	SD	Obtained Mean	SD	Adjusted Mean	F
Treatment	18	2.94	1.26	2.83	.86	3.04	5.4
Control	17	4.18	1.19	4.00	1.00	3.79	

autonomy." The research hypothesis was that this experience would yield lower "external" scores on the Norwicki–Strickland Internal–External Control scale for the experimental group over the control group that were not given computer assignments. The only scale that ostensibly yielded a significant difference was the Luck scale. Reproduced here is Table 19.1 from the article that shows these results.

A comparison of the pretest means across groups indicates that the experimental group placed less emphasis on luck than the control group. This mean difference is approximately a full standard deviation and, although not mentioned, it is statistically significant ($t = 2.98$, $p < .01$) by our calculations. This suggests that these two intact groups represented different populations at the outset with respect to locus of control, thus preempting any possibility of a valid experimental comparison on the luck factor. Moreover, these two groups may have differed with respect to other important variables that have gone unmeasured (e.g., prior computer experience), but which may impact the effectiveness of the treatments.

Inspection of the pre- to posttest scores shows only a very slight reduction in mean scores for both groups. On this basis, one might conclude that the computer assignments had no discernable effect. However, the author analyzed these data with a technique called analysis of covariance (ANCOVA), which indicated that the adjusted posttest means differed significantly ($F = 5.4$, $p < .025$). The author interpreted the statistically significant outcome as indicating that the students in the experimental class "changed their perception...from what it had been prior to the study." Clearly, this interpretation is erroneous in as much as the change for both groups was trivial, but the fact that the adjusted means were found to be significant using ANCOVA represents a paradox. The question of how to analyze data from a study wherein two intact groups differ significantly on the pretest was addressed by Lord (1967), and the situation has become known as Lord's paradox. Lord concluded his article by stating, "In the writer's opinion, the explanation is that with the data usually available for such studies, there is simply no logical or statistical procedure that can be counted on to make proper allowances for uncontrolled pre-existing differences between groups" (p. 305). Essentially, the same point was made a bit more whimsically by Anderson (1963), when he stated, "One may well wonder exactly what it means to ask what the data would be like if they were not what they are" (p. 70). These quotes should not be interpreted to mean than ANCOVA is without value. All agree that ANCOVA should be used to increase statistical power when comparing posttest means of groups that have been *randomly* formed.

Another strategy that has been suggested for dealing with groups that differ significantly on the pretest is to use matching. That is, identify participants across treatment groups that have the same, or nearly the same, scores on the pretest or on some other extraneous variables that might be desirable to control. The problem with this strategy is that the individuals within the comparison groups represent different populations (as evident by the significantly different pretest scores). On retest, the scores of individuals can be expected to regress to the means of their respective populations. Thus, the threat of *regression to the mean* jeopardizes the validity of the posttest comparisons. In light of the considerations noted here, it is understandable why Pedhazur and Schmelkin (1991) suggested "that quasi-experimental designs have acquired respectability far beyond what they deserve" (p. 277).

> From what you have read in this chapter, what seem to be the most important shortcomings of quasi-experiments, such as the nonequivalent control-group design?
> Why would anyone use these "compromise designs"?

THREATS NOT CONTROLLED BY RANDOM ASSIGNMENT

As Cook and Campbell (1979) noted, "Though random assignment conveniently rules out most threats to internal validity, it does not rule out all of them" (p. 56). Random assignment simply ensures that the experimental groups are comparable at the outset. As important as this contribution is, random assignment does not eliminate threats to internal validity that may arise during the treatment phase. The more common threats that may arise during the treatment are described in the literature using largely self-explanatory terms. *Resentful demoralization* would pose a threat in a class size experiment, if teachers assigned to the larger classes were to slack off due to being resentful or demoralized. *Compensatory rivalry*, also called the *John Henry effect*, would pose a threat in a study designed to compare a new reading program with the current program, if teachers assigned to the current program worked especially hard to show that it was just as good as the new. *Diffusion of treatments* will pose a threat in a study comparing two or more instructional strategies if the students within each instructional group study together during the treatment phase or, worse, study together for the examination that is used to evaluate the instructional methods. The extent to which these and other potential factors may bias the results is never known, but, if anticipated, steps can be taken in the design of the study to minimize their effects.

To illustrate how this might be done, we briefly describe a study that investigated the effect of two methods of teaching calculus at the Air Force Academy (Thompson, 1980). Although conducted in a military academy having a highly centralized authority structure, the study employed exemplary design features that can be adapted to less-structured educational settings. Entering freshmen ($n = 840$) were classified into four aptitude groups and, within aptitude groupings, cadets were randomly assigned to one of two calculus groups. One group was exposed to an individualized mastery (IM) strategy, the other to the traditional lecture–discussion–recitation (LDR) mode. Each instructional group was divided into 22 class sections. Instructors were randomly assigned to teach using either IM or LDR, with three experienced and three inexperienced instructors assigned to each condition.[2] Course loads, schedules, extracurricular activities, and living arrangements did not differ systematically between the two groups.

The "diffusion of treatments" threat was minimized in two ways. First, the two groups of cadets were housed "in different but identical dorm areas [in order] to reduce their interaction and awareness of the experiment" (Thompson, 1980, p. 363). Second, "the two instructor cadres maintained offices in separate areas to reduce interaction and sensitivity to the experiment" (p. 363). Threats described above as "compensatory rivalry" and "resentful demoralization" were minimized among the instructors by conducting 12-day training programs designed to "motivate the instructors and to improve their effectiveness in the respective treatments" (p. 363).

At the end of the semester, a standardized test and a department examination were administered. No significant differences were found between methods on these measures. The discussion explores possible reasons for the absence of a treatment effect, but this outcome cannot readily be attributable to the validity threats described above.

> What is your definition of threats that may arise during the treatment phase of an experiment (i.e., resentful demoralization, compensatory rivalry, and diffusion of treatment)? How might a researcher reduce these threats?

THE ETHICS OF EDUCATIONAL EXPERIMENTS

Anyone wishing to conduct research in the public schools must attend to the ethics of using human participants. The generally accepted ethical standard is

---

[2]The article makes explicit the random assignment of inexperienced instructors to teaching modes but does not indicate if this was done with the experienced instructors.

that the risk to the participants must be offset by the knowledge gained. Until the 1970s, the responsibility for upholding this ethical standard was often left to the professional judgment of those conducting the research. However, in 1972, the general public was outraged by newspaper accounts of a U.S. Public Health Service study that had been ongoing for 40 years. The study, initiated in 1932, known as the Tuskegee experiment was not actually an experiment but rather an investigation into the effects of untreated syphilis on 399 Black men in Macon County, Alabama. The study, and how it came to light, is described by Jones (1981) in his book *Bad Blood*. Failure to administer penicillin to these men when it became recognized as a cure in the 1940s represented perhaps the most serious and obvious ethical violation. However, as Jones noted, the initial decision to withhold less effective and painful treatments in the 1930s differed only in the severity of consequences for the men, but was no less unethical. The fact that all of the participants were poor illiterate Black men and were not advised of their condition only compounded the ethical problems. Remarkably, the physicians in charge defended the ethics of the study and failed to acknowledge any parallels between the Tuskegee study and the medical ethics that were the subject of the Nuremberg trials. Although the U.S. surgeon general had promulgated ethical guidelines for medical research in 1966, new, more stringent federal guidelines were adopted in response to the government hearings that looked into the "Tuskegee experiment." The guidelines call for an institutional review board (IRB) to review the ethics of all research proposals submitted to the U.S. Department of Health and Human Services (DHHS). The guidelines also specify that a nonresearch person (humanist) must serve on the IRB. Today virtually all U.S. agencies and universities engaged in research involving human participants voluntarily adhere to the federal guidelines, not just research funded by the DHHS. The legal basis under which IRBs operate is detailed in Title 45 Code of Federal Regulations, Section 46, and succeeding regulations.

A cornerstone to the federal regulations is informed written consent from those who might participate as participants in the research. Special consideration is given to protecting the welfare of special classes of people, for whom written consent may not imply informed consent.[3] Classes of special interest to educational researchers are children under the age of 18, prisoners, and people who are mentally or economically disabled. For these people, informed written consent is required of their parents or guardians. An informative overview of ethics in relation to participants of experiments, as well as to research ethics in relation to customers, colleagues, and the community, may be found in Dockrell (1988).

---

[3]What constitutes informed consent has become the center of controversy in a medical experiment investigating the effect of placing embryo cells in the brains of people with Parkinson's disease. The "double-blind" experiment calls for both the treatment and the placebo participants to have holes drilled in their skulls. Dissenters argue that it is unethical to ask consent from people who are desperately ill because they will consent to anything (Thompson, 1999, p. 66).

Are you familiar with IRBs? Is there one in place at your college or university? Have you or will you be required to request their review of your research proposals? (Refer to the discussion of IRBs in Chapter 1.)

To conduct a randomized experiment of any duration in schools using only students whose parents provide informed consent poses an almost insurmountable problem. The problem is what to do with students for whom parental consent is not obtained. If a randomized experiment is to be conducted, it is essential for all students to participate so as not to disrupt the normal course of educational activities. It is possible, however, to seek an exemption from IRB review if proper assurances can be made that there is minimal risk[4] to the participants. It can be argued that the minimum-risk criterion is satisfied if the purpose of the research is to compare two viable educational alternatives that fall within the range of acceptable, if debatable, educational practices.

Perhaps the bigger challenge is to persuade the school administration of the need for experimentation. Even if the competing educational practices to be subjected to experimentation are all viable, they may differ in perceived value. Given a choice, most students and their parents would prefer the more attractive alternative, such as smaller classes instead of larger ones. School administrators may have difficulty convincing stakeholders to accept the lesser valued alternative and so might shy away from allowing randomized experiments in their schools. Cook and Campbell (1979, p. 57) suggested that the degree of reluctance to undertake randomized experiments is related to an administrator's perception of the difference in value attached to the competing treatments and the prospect that students, teachers, or parents will learn of and resent the differential treatment.

This reluctance is understandable, but often the alternative is for a school system to adopt a new educational practice or curriculum, only to drop it sometime later in favor of the latest fad to capture the attention of the educational community. If research enters the deliberations at all, it is likely to be from nonexperimental studies, and both proponents and antagonists to an innovation can usually find nonexperimental research to support their positions. In essence, this approach to innovation is a form of experimentation, with competing treatments administered sequentially, rather than simultaneously. Thus, random assignment of students to treatments is avoided in favor of haphazard assignment, depending on where students are in their school career when the innovation is adopted. What is missing is any control or valid means for comparing the competing practices. If any evaluation of the adopted program is undertaken at all, it may consist

---

[4]Minimum risk is defined as situations wherein the risk of harm or discomfort is no greater than that encountered in daily life or during the performance of routine physical or psychological tests.

of nothing more formal than a survey of stakeholders about its effectiveness or a site visit by a recognized authority figure in the field. A randomized experiment with proper controls can provide a far more definitive basis for choosing between competing practices, if only those in charge would have the fortitude to do so. Rather than base policy decisions on the perceived value of competing practices, the ethical basis for such decisions, we assert, is to base them on the demonstrated effectiveness of the competing practices.

RANDOMIZED EXPERIMENTS AND EDUCATIONAL POLICY

We hope that our treatment of experimental research thus far has convinced you of the distinct advantage of using randomized experiments to investigate causal relationships and to inform educational policy. However, we recognize that other forms of research are far more in vogue today than experimental research methods. Qualitative modes of inquiry, which were hardly in evidence 25 years ago, have exploded on the scene of educational research and have become an integral part of nearly all educational research training programs. The availability of large-scale databases, such as High School and Beyond and the National Educational Longitudinal Study, has spawned a myriad of interesting correlational studies. Many of these studies have employed structural equation modeling in an effort to test theoretical causal models within the limits associated with correlational data. In light of these developments, it is easy to understand why experimental research has played a less prominent role in the quantitative educational research literature of the past 20 years.[5] Nonetheless, as advocates for experimental research, we feel it is important to illustrate by example how experimental research can resolve certain policy questions for which other modes of inquiry can provide only tentative answers. We recognize, however, that few readers of this book are likely to be devotees of experimental research. Indeed, we feel like Fred Astaire might have felt if, during the disco era, he tried to interest John Travolta in ballroom dancing. However, ballroom dancing is making somewhat of a comeback today, and in that spirit we hope to rekindle interest in experimental research. In what follows, we describe two excellent studies, one experimental and the other nonexperimental, that address two important and timely educational issues. The issues are the effects of class size and grade retention. Our intent is to illustrate the unique contribution of experimental research and the limitations

---

[5]This assertion is based on an informal review we undertook of articles published in *The Journal of Experimental Education* for the years 1998 and 1999 and on methodological reviews of published research done by others (Elmore & Woehlke, 1998; Goodwin & Goodwin, 1985; Hutchinson & Lovell, 1999). Although the first two reviews did not specifically code for methodology, both reported a marked decrease in the use of statistical methods typically employed in experimental research.

of nonexperimental research to resolving policy issues that people today "get out of breath arguing about." See Porter (1997) for additional discussion of strengths and limitations of experiments and the range of educational questions that they can address.

The Question of Class Size

Class size is a major educational issue, not because anyone believes small classes are undesirable, but because small classes are expensive. To justify the expense of providing smaller classes, it would seem prudent to have convincing evidence that smaller classes promote learning. Unfortunately, most of the evidence on this issue is nonexperimental and less than definitive. An exception is a large-scale experimental study reported by Finn and Achilles (1990), which is described later.

In their introduction, Finn and Achilles (1990) commented on a review of research on class size conducted by Glass and Smith (1978) using analytical procedures referred to as a meta-analysis. The meta-analysis, which included only five experimental studies, was meant to resolve the issue once and for all, but as Finn and Achilles (1990) noted, that was not the case. "Instead of settling the issue, the [Glass and Smith] report was met with criticism (some of it compelling) and extensive debate about the very existence, not to mention magnitude, of the 'class-size effect' [ensued]" (p. 558). They also noted "Correlational studies, and studies that match children after they have been assigned to small or large classes, are confounded" (p. 558), and they suggested that definitive answers can only come from randomized experiments.

> What do you conclude is the meaning of the term *meta-analysis*? For what reasons might this be an important technique in research?

The experiment they report was authorized and funded by a bill passed by the Tennessee legislature. All school systems in the state of Tennessee were invited to participate in a longitudinal study involving kindergarten and first-grade classes. From among those school systems that agreed to participate, 76 elementary schools were selected that met the enrollment criterion. To be included, the schools had to have at least three kindergarten classes. Within each school, children entering kindergarten were randomly assigned to one of three class-size conditions: small (13–17 students) with no teacher aide, large (22–25 students) with no teacher aide, or large (22–25 students) with a teacher aide. Students who entered the second year of the study as first graders were also randomly assigned to the same three class-size conditions. For both years of the study, teachers were randomly assigned to the classes as a separate step. During the spring of each study year, achievement in reading and mathematics was measured using a norm-referenced and a criterion-referenced test battery. Academic self-concept and motivation were also assessed.

As might be expected, the random assignment of pupils to the three class-size conditions was not popular among all parents. In response to this parental concern, project staff made a concession during the second year of the study, but only among those assigned to the regular-sized kindergarten class conditions. A random half of those who had been in a class without an aide were assigned to a first-grade class with an aide, and half that had been in a class with an aide were reassigned to a first-grade class without an aide. However, no concession was made to reassign kindergarten students from small classes to larger classes for first grade.

A cross-sectional analysis of all first-grade classes was undertaken using data from 6,570 students in 331 classrooms. A longitudinal analysis was conducted using the subset of 2,291 students who were in the study for both kindergarten and first grade (301 classes). The analyses used classroom means and the means of White and minority students within classrooms as the units of analysis.

The results of the study are forcefully and succinctly described in the abstract of the study: "The results are definitive: (a) a significant benefit accrues to students in reduced-size classes in both subject areas [reading and math] and (b) there is evidence that minority students in particular benefit from the smaller class environment, especially when curriculum based tests are used as learning criteria" (Finn & Achilles, 1990, p. 557). Regular-sized classes with teacher aides also scored somewhat higher than regular-sized classes without teacher aides. However, this difference was not statistically significant in the cross-sectional analysis and was most evident in the longitudinal data during the second year among first graders. No effect for class size was observed for academic self-concept or motivation.

As the authors note, this study provides definitive evidence of the effect of class size for the kindergarten and first-grade pupils who participated in this study. No attempt is made to generalize these findings to upper grade levels or to schools in other geographic regions of the United States. Strictly speaking, the results apply only to elementary schools in Tennessee whose school systems agreed to participate in the study and whose enrollment was large enough to have three kindergarten classes. That is to say that these factors limit the external validity of the findings somewhat, but the reader can decide whether the findings are applicable to his or her situation. However, the internal validity is excellent, meaning that there can be little doubt that the class-size conditions were responsible for the differences in measured achievement in this case.[6]

---

[6]A recent article by the same authors (Finn & Achilles, 1999) reports on the follow-up findings for the students in this study and discusses the current controversy surrounding class size. They stated that Tennessee's Project STAR "produced answers to questions that educators have long been asking" (p. 106), and that it has been cited as a model for future educational experiments.

The Question of Grade Retention and Social Promotion

The issue of whether students should be retained or promoted is much more emotionally charged than the issue of class size. Only out of fiscal concern would anyone argue in favor of larger classes. However, there are advocates for both sides
of the issue when it comes to grade retention versus social promotion. Although
there have been a few randomized experiments regarding class size, there have
been none in this area. All of the research conducted on this issue is nonexperimental but seeks to determine what effect grade retention has on subsequent
achievement or school dropout. As explained by Krathwohl (1998), various terms
have been used to describe such research, including "causal comparative," "ex post
facto," or "after-the-fact natural experiments" (p. 537). Regardless of the term
used, the preponderance of evidence from such studies suggests that retention in
grade does not benefit students and likely has a negative effect (Shepard & Smith,
1989). Nonetheless, the call for "no more social promotions" was made by President Bill Clinton in his 1999 State of the Union Address and has become a cen-
terpiece of the new educational reform movement in the United States. Perhaps
the time has come to address this issue by providing a "definitive answer" using a
randomized experiment. To make our case, we wish to report on an excellent study
that exemplifies the contributions and limitations of causal-comparative research.

What would your argument be for and against the authors' contention that
true randomized experiments are a good method for determining educational
policy?

Roderick (1994) undertook a very extensive and detailed analysis of transcript data for all of the 1,052 seventh-grade students enrolled in the Fall River,
Massachusetts, public schools during the 1980–1981 school year. She classified
these students as graduates (38%), dropouts (35%), or transfers (22%). The status for the remaining 5% could not be determined. The analysis was limited to
707 students representing 90% of the dropouts and 95% of the graduates.

Roderick (1994) considered only retentions that occurred in Grade 6 or before.
She did not consider seventh- and eighth-grade retentions, because these might
simply reflect the decisions of older students to give up on school as they awaited
the legal dropout age of 16. Consistent with other research, the dropout rate was
much higher among those who had repeated a grade (70%) than among those who
had not (27%). Moreover, retained students were far more likely to drop out at
age 16, rather than 17 or 18, compared with dropouts who had not been retained.

It has long been known that dropout rates are higher among those retained in
grade, but this research represented an attempt to isolate the effect of retention
from other variables that are also thought to be related to both grade retention
and dropping out. To this end, in her analyses, the author included measured

background characteristics, such as gender, number of siblings, father's occupation, number of school changes, and two socioeconomic status indicators associated with the communities served by the schools the students attended in fourth grade. Also available were attendance and grade records averaged for each school year. Clearly, this study represented a massive archival data collection effort. These school performance and background variables were included as control variables in a series of logistic regression models. The results indicate that even when these measured differences are statistically controlled, students who were retained were significantly more likely to drop out of school. This was true regardless of whether the retention was in the early grades (K–3) or the latter grades (4–6).

Also addressed by this study was the effect of being overage on dropping out. The sample included 61 students who had not repeated a grade but were overage at the start of seventh grade. Among these students, the dropout rate was an alarming 58%. When age was introduced as an additional control variable, the effect of grade retention was no longer statistically significant. This finding was interpreted to mean that "a large proportion of the impact of grade retention may operate through an effect of being overage for grade" (Roderick, 1994, p. 744).

As interesting and compelling as the findings of this study are, the author is careful to point out a major limitation. Specifically, retained and promoted students may differ in terms of motivation or ability or some other background or performance variables that were not measured or controlled statistically. Indeed, there are an infinite number of ways in which retained children might differ from those who are promoted. Only if you can be sure that you have included in the model all variables that could conceivably be a "common cause" of both grade retention and dropping out can you have confidence in what the true relationship is between being retained and dropping out of school. The situation confronted in this type of study is analogous to the problem one confronts when ANCOVA is used to equate nonequivalent groups. Roderick (1994) used logistic regression in an attempt to control systematic measured differences between retained and promoted students. Had she been successful, the only systematic difference between the two groups would have been that one group had been promoted and the other had not. But, unless retention decisions are completely arbitrary, the two groups are inherently unequal. Attempting to equate the two groups statistically is tricky business. To paraphrase Anderson (1963, p. 70), one may well wonder exactly what it means to ask what is the effect of grade retention if those retained were not who they were.

CONCLUSIONS

As noted by Fraenkle and Wallen (1998), it is "unfortunate [that] the field of education, unlike medicine, business, law, agriculture, pharmacology, or the military, has never had an ongoing research effort tied closely to practice" (p. 31). Before the Food and Drug Administration approves any new drug or surgical procedure, research must be conducted to demonstrate the effectiveness of the new treatment. In contrast, many school systems are embracing the call for no more social promotions despite evidence from a large number of nonexperimental studies that suggest that retention in grade benefits no one. We believe this situation is unfortunate and has the potential to cause irreparable harm to many students. Rather than embrace this movement, we would like to see a superintendent address the issue head-on by conducting an experiment. From a research design perspective, it would be a simple matter for a school superintendent to resolve this issue experimentally. All that would be required is to secure a list of all of the children in the school system that had been recommended for retention and promote a randomly selected half of them. The effect of the placement could then be judged unambiguously on the basis of measured differences subsequently observed between the randomly formed equivalent groups. The reluctance of administrators to undertake experiments is understandable, but there also is risk associated with adopting a policy advocated by a vocal minority. As a case in point, the promotion policy of the Pittsylvania County, Virginia, school division was the subject of a class action suit (*Sandlin v. Johnson*, 1981). Although the court upheld the school's right to deny promotion for failure to complete requisite levels in a reading series, the superintendent lost his job over the brouhaha attendant to the case.

Although the precedence of this court case may ward off future legal challenges to promotion policies, the fact remains that no one can say with confidence what effect retention in grade has on school dropout or on subsequent academic performance. As Roderick (1994, p. 731) noted, retention policies have shifted over the decades, often reflecting the attitudes of teachers and principals or swings of the political pendulum.[7] We would argue that to base promotion policies on the idiosyncratic philosophies of teachers, principals, or politicians poses a far greater ethical concern than does conducting a well-designed randomized experiment.

On the positive side, it should be noted that there is increasing enthusiasm at the national level for experimental research. In response to the growing debate about school vouchers, *Education Week* reported that the National Research Council (NRC) recommended a multidistrict, 10-year voucher experiment in its report to the National Academy of Sciences. As an advisory committee, it has no authority to act, but the hope is that an outside research group will hear the call (White, 1999).

---

[7]As an example, in an article about changes in promotion policies, the superintendent of the District of Columbia, Arlene Ackerman, reported to *The Washington Post* recently (Wilgoren, 1999, p. B1) that while the District schools base promotion decisions on more than standardized tests, they have not developed transitional programs to help students. She said, "In the last two years ... we've gone from promoting everybody to holding 3,000 kids back" (p. B1).

Although we have used the issues of class size and social promotion or retention to advocate the use of experimentation in education, we trust that our readers have come to recognize the potential of experimental research to resolve other educational issues as well. We hope that the NRC's proposed experiment gets support and funding, and expands into other reform areas so that educational decisions can be made with valid experimental evidence. Issues such as the elimination of tracking and the requiring of algebra for all eighth graders would benefit from such studies. Even with "definitive" answers from well-designed experiments, people will continue to "get out of breath arguing the question," but it will be more difficult for politicians to ignore these definitive findings as they advocate for one policy over another. We conclude with the fact that randomized experiments, even if well done, are not completely foolproof. However, they are the best mechanism for providing a valid way of choosing between competing alternatives. We hope that we have stimulated the reader to read further on the subject and, perhaps, to promote experiments that will help resolve educational questions. Just as Redi reversed a long-standing belief by simply placing meat in two different jars, so too may we resolve ongoing educational questions.

> What is your position on the role of randomized experiments versus other approaches outlined in this text? Under what conditions would you advocate for randomized experiments to determine educational policy? When would you not?

ACKNOWLEDGMENTS

The authors of the chapter are indebted to Dr. Andrew Porter and Dr. Liora Pedhazur Schmelkin for their insightful comments and critiques. In addition, an earlier draft of the chapter was read and critiqued by students in introductory and advanced statistics classes. Their comments lead to improvements in the chapter and discussions on how different research methods answer different types of research questions.

20

Using Multiple Methodologies:
The Case of Retention in Chicago

Ernest R. House
University of Colorado, Boulder

MEET THE AUTHOR

Ernest R. House is a professor in the School of Education at the University of Colorado at Boulder. Previously, he was at the Center for Instructional Research and Curriculum Evaluation at the University of Illinois in Urbana. He has been a visiting scholar at University of California at Los Angeles, Harvard, and the University of New Mexico, as well as in England, Australia, Spain, Sweden, Austria, and Chile.

His primary interests are evaluation and policy analysis. Books include *The Politics of Educational Innovation* (1974), *Survival in the Classroom* (with S. Lapan, 1978), *Evaluating With Validity* (1980), *Jesse Jackson and the Politics of Charisma* (1988), *Professional Evaluation: Social Impact and Political Consequences* (1993), *Schools for Sale* (1998), and *Values in Evaluation and Social Research* (with K. Howe, 1999). He is the 1989 recipient (with W. Madura) of the Harold E. Lasswell Prize in the policy sciences and the 1990 recipient of the Paul F. Lazarsfeld Award for Evaluation Theory, presented by the American Evaluation Association. He was editor of *New Directions in Program Evaluation* (1982–1985), a featured columnist for *Evaluation Practice* (1984–1989), and a fellow at the Center for Advanced Study in the Behavioral Sciences at Stanford University (1999–2000). Selected studies include evaluation of the Illinois Gifted Program for the Illinois legislature (1968–1972), assessment of the Michigan Accountability Program for the National Education Association (1974), critique of the National Follow-Through Evaluation for the Ford Foundation (1977), audit of the Promotional Gates Program evaluation for the mayor's office in New York City (1981), assessment of environmental education policies in Europe for the Organization for Economic Cooperation and Development (1992), a 5-year study of the evaluation office of the National Science Foundation (1991–1996), and participation in an evaluation of science, engineering, and technology education programs of federal departments for the Federal Coordinating Council for Science, Engineering, and Technology in Washington, DC (1993). Currently, he is monitor for the federal court in the English Acquisition legal settlement in the Denver schools.

PROLOGUE TO RETENTION IN CHICAGO

Throughout this text, authors have presented explanations about many possible approaches for conducting research. Each approach is usually selected because of the nature of the research questions asked, although mixed approaches are possible. Ernest House takes this decision process to a pragmatic

> level by demonstrating how many research studies representing vastly different
> paradigms offer answers to the practical question: Is the retention of students
> an effective means to improve their education? We ask that the reader attend
> closely to how House has combined findings from multiple methodologies in
> creative ways to address the important policy issue of retention. We include
> this chapter to illustrate the many avenues that lead to understanding, and
> when combined can make a significant contribution in influencing policy.
>
> The Editors

AUTHOR'S INTRODUCTION

In the fall of 1998, I received a phone call from Sue Davenport at Designs for
Change, the educational activist group that has been responsible for many of the
ideas on which the Chicago decentralization of schools was based. She told me
that Mayor Richard M. Daley had retaken centralized control of the schools and
had installed his aide as head of schools. The major reform policy was retention—
failing students who did not attain a specific score on a standardized achievement
test. She asked me to give a speech at a Chicago conference aimed at challenging
this policy. The purpose was to rally support against the retention policy and to
encourage other academics in the Chicago area to speak out. Few had been bold
enough to challenge the mayor.

Reluctantly, I decided the issue was too important to ignore and began to prepare the paper. I had helped evaluate a similar program in New York City in
the 1980s—which had failed—and I was familiar with the research on retention.
Initially, I started with the research literature, as academics are likely to do. However, Don Moore, founder of Designs for Change, suggested that a Chicago audience would pay little attention to the academic research in general but it would
pay a great deal of attention to what had happened in New York City. Also, costs
would be something such an audience would be concerned about. So I wrote a second draft of the paper focused on what had happened in New York, how similar the
New York and Chicago programs were, and how much the Chicago program cost.

When I gave the speech at the conference in Chicago, the conference sponsors
had arranged interviews with a newspaper and radio station. The publicity was
enough to elicit a reaction from the head of schools. The sponsors had also hired
a public relations firm that provided a contact with an editor of *The New York
Times*. After many revisions, I published an op-ed piece in the newspaper about
retention and social promotion, which received considerable national attention.
(The *Times* editors had their own opinions, which resulted in making President
Bill Clinton look better, eliminated statements about race, and reduced mention
of Chicago significantly.)

In January 1999, in his State of the Union address, President Bill Clinton attacked "social promotion"and lauded the Chicago retention program in particular as being a program that "worked,"in spite of there being no evaluation of the program. I was interviewed on radio programs, CNN, the *Lehrer Newshour*, and by several newspapers and journals. Social promotion had become national news. Each of these news organizations had its own interests and spin on events, but I used the basic ideas from the original paper as the content of my discussions. Some wanted the original document and read it avidly; some did not.

Typically, the media set the problem as an adversarial one—these people on this side, those on that side. No doubt, this arrangement fueled interest as the drama unfolded, even if it did not allow for nuanced discussion of complex issues. Some reporters included the race aspect; many wanted nothing to do with it. Although contesting such a strong ideology and confronting such powerful adversaries as the president and the mayor are not likely to carry the day, policy researchers owe it to the students, the public, and their own consciences to tell the truth, even when those in power will accept it.

RETENTION IN CHICAGO

Once again, we are faced with a massive program for flunking kids, retaining them in their current grades for another year. This time the program is in Chicago's public schools, though Chicago is not the first to employ retention. In fact, the research about the negative effects of retention is so overwhelming that Chicago's retention program should never have been carried out. Retention has consistently failed to boost student achievement, and it makes students much more likely to drop out of school. As I will explain, there is nothing unique about the Chicago retention program that suggests that the ultimate results here will be any different.

At first glance, retention is a practice that seems to make good sense. If kids don't master the knowledge and skills they are supposed to, they will fall further behind their classmates. Why not hold them back for a year to catch up on the material they have not learned? Then they can make good academic progress. Retaining students will be beneficial, even if it costs the school district extra money.

This argument is especially persuasive when retention is contrasted to "social promotion," passing students on when they have not learned much, or watering down the curriculum to something they can pass. The president of the United States, the mayor of Chicago, and the Illinois Board of Education oppose social promotion. Although there are effective alternative strategies, other than social promotion or retention for educating students, retention is often justified as the only alternative to social promotion, a false choice.

During the past few decades, another, often unspoken, justification for retention has had a major impact. Students were seen by some as being out of control.

One way to discipline them was to flunk them, put them on notice. This attitude has become especially strong in large cities, where the students are mostly
African American and Latino. Embattled officials, frustrated with poor student
performance (and operating with declining resources) turned to tough love. Well,
maybe it wasn't love, but it was meant to be tough—perform or flunk.

Unfortunately, flunking doesn't work. Whatever might be said for flunking students as an outlet for frustration, retention is a punitive policy that has the oppo-
site effects of what it intends. The evidence against retention is unequivocal and
overwhelming. The conclusion that retention does not improve student achievement over the long run and leads to a much higher dropout rate is one of the
clearest findings from research. I will illustrate this finding by describing the history of New York City's massive retention program, which is strikingly similar to
Chicago's and which I helped to evaluate.

The New York City Retention Program

In 1981, Frank Macchiarola, chancellor of the New York City schools, launched
a large-scale retention program that held back 25,000 students the first year, one
fifth of the students in fourth and seventh grades, because they could not meet
the cutoff scores on the citywide reading tests. New York City's program was
called Promotional Gates. Macchiarola himself came from a tough part of the city
and figured that teachers and students were not trying hard enough. Tough standards would shape them up, he thought. Both students and teachers needed more
discipline to improve their performances.

Once identified as being behind on the tests, students were sent to summer
school. If they did not attain the required cutoff scores there, they were put in
special classes with teachers who had been trained to use one of four compensatory
education strategies that had previously been employed in New York. At that
time, New York City elementary classes averaged 43 students, 80% of whom were
minority. Teaching students to read in classes of 43 was not easy. The retained
students were placed in classes of no more than 18. The first year, more than
1,100 additional teachers were required, at a cost between $40 and $70 million.
From what I could tell, the compensatory components of the Promotional Gates
plan were carried out (New York City Schools, Office of Educational Evaluation,
1982, 1983).

Some city officials, especially Deputy Mayor Wagner, did not think the program would work. However, Chancellor Macchiarola was a friend of Mayor Koch,
and he prevailed on the mayor for support. As a compromise, the mayor's office,
which supplied half the funding for the schools, insisted that an evaluation be
done. The next year the program was to be expanded to math, then to other subject areas and grade levels. The city hired me and two colleagues to oversee the
evaluation (House, Linn, & Raths, 1981–1982).

When we arrived in New York, the district was proclaiming large test gains from their summer sessions, heralded as proof that the retention program was working. Several months test gain for a few weeks in summer school seemed too good to be true. Indeed, it was too good to be true. The district had made serious statistical errors in their analysis of the summer test data. When the proper calculations were done, the average student had made no gains at all.

After 2 years, the test scores of the students who had been retained were compared with those of similar low-achieving students from previous years who had not been retained. It was found that there were no substantial differences between the students who had been retained and similar low-achieving students who had been passed in the years before the program. In other words, students did just as well if they were passed and received the education provided before Promotional Gates existed.

Further, many students were failing to meet the cutoff scores even after a year of retention. Some were being retained in fourth and seventh grades for 2 or 3 years. The school district faced the prospect of having to promote these students or have students shaving in fourth grade. The Promotional Gates program began to look like the Boulder Dam program, with tens of thousands of students backed up at fourth and seventh grades.

About this time, Chancellor Macchiarola was offered a job by billionaire David Rockefeller (which serves as a rebuttal to those who think nothing good comes from school reform). A succeeding head of the schools quietly put the Promotional Gates program to sleep without fanfare. Several years later, evaluations by the New York school system indicated that the retained students dropped out at much higher rates than similar low-achieving students who had not been retained. Forty percent of those retained dropped out of school, compared with 25% of those of a similar group who had not (Pick, 1998). The Promotional Gates program had retained tens of thousands of students at huge dollar and human costs without benefits.

The Chicago Retention Program

In 1996, 20 years after New York's failure, Chicago launched a very similar program. Chicago is also identifying tens of thousands of low-achieving students based on test scores and sending them to summer school. If they don't achieve minimum cutoff scores on the standardized tests after summer school, they are retained. The Chicago program is amazingly similar to the New York City program of the early 1980s. Let me point out some similarities, as well as a few differences.

The Chicago plan operates at Grades 3, 6, 8, and 9, whereas the New York plan focused on Grades 4 and 7, with the intention of expanding. In Chicago, students in the transitional bilingual programs are excluded (one of six students), and most special education students are included (Chicago Public Schools, 1997).

in addition. The manual for the ITBS specifically states that using this test as the primary basis for retaining or promoting students is an "inappropriate purpose" for using the test (Hoover et al., 1996). The head of Iowa testing, H. D. Hoover, has been quoted as saying the following:

> A single test should never be used as the sole basis to make a decision such as promotion and retention. That's because you have other information available from what the teacher knows. . . . The teacher has been with the kids all year, and that should be taken into account.

Presumably, the school district is in violation of the agreement it signed with Riverside Press, the publisher of the ITBS, which states that test purchasers must "avoid labeling students based on a single score" and "administer, score, interpret, and use tests exactly as specified in the manual" (Riverside Press, n.d.). As Hoover stated, one needs several pieces of information when considering retention, and the decision should be made with strong professional and parent involvement.

Claims About Summer Progress

Having the identified students attend summer school is a good idea used by both cities. Extra attention helps. However, the gains reported during the summer sessions are too large to be taken at face value. For example, in summer 1997, Chicago claimed reading gains of 4.4 months for third graders, 7.0 months for sixth graders, and 9.9 months for eighth graders who failed to meet the cutoff score on the Iowa reading test in spring 1997, and then retook the test after the 1997 summer school. Yet these claimed results were not presented in an independent evaluation, but rather in a school system press release 1997. How seriously can we take these claimed gains?

One possibility is that the data have been misanalyzed. A statistical phenomenon called regression toward the mean is a frequent problem in evaluating the progress of low-scoring students. If you separate out a lower scoring portion of students and then give them the same test again, they will score higher on the average without receiving any instruction at all. This artifact can be corrected for, but often it is not. This error explained the summer test gains initially claimed for the New York retention program. Whether the same problem exists in Chicago depends on their test use and data analysis. This is only one of many such technical pitfalls that must be guarded against when tests are used in this fashion.

A second possibility is that the summer curriculum is so narrowly focused that it is preparing students to pass one particular test with a certain format, without really helping students master general academic skills. What is wrong with this? Let's take an example from language arts. In the early grades, the Iowa Test in reading consists of short paragraphs, usually followed by two questions (River-side Press). Students are not required to write essays as part of the Iowa Test. A curriculum focused on preparing students for short reading passages with multiple-choice questions may not have a lasting effect on students' basic reading competence (e.g., a student's ability to understand a short story several pages long or an instruction manual). And the fact that the Iowa Test does not require students to write will mean that writing is deemphasized in the test-preparation curriculum. Research indicates that students exposed to such a test-focused curriculum may not perform better on other kinds of tests 1 or 2 years later (Linn, 1998). Linn's research shows that students performed better and better on the Kentucky tests while failing to perform much better on the National Assessment of Educational Progress Tests. As Bob Linn, the leading test expert in the United States, said

> [R]eliance on a single test for repeated testing can distort instruction and lead to in-flated and non-generalizable estimates of student gains in achievement. Assessment systems that are useful monitors lose much of their dependability and credibility for that purpose when high-stakes accountability uses are attached to them. . . . Don't put all the weight on a single test. (pp. 7, 28–29)

In the extreme, teachers may obtain copies of the exact tests being used and teach children the specific answers to test questions. Although Chicago has used different versions of the ITBS, the versions used to judge summer school progress have all been used before in Chicago. Chicago has made some effort to guard against outright cheating by using alternative forms, so I have focused more on the problem of teaching to the test format. However, I can cite many examples of such practices elsewhere in the United States. A good evaluation must take such possibilities into account.

A third problem with Chicago's claims about test gains is that a substantial number of students who failed to make the cutoff in the spring did not complete summer school and retake the test. In spring 1997, for example, *Education Week* used Chicago school system data to estimate that about 9,000 of the 41,000 students who failed the spring reading or math test at third, sixth, eighth, and ninth grades did not retake the tests in the summer (Hendrie, 1997). It is quite plausible that the students who were not retested were less motivated and had more severe learning problems than the students who completed summer school and were retested. This would inflate results. An impartial evaluation of the retention program must take into account all students who did not pass the test in the spring, including those who dropped out of the summer school process.

I might add that it is astonishing that a program that is so controversial and that costs so much money has not been independently evaluated after 3 years, and that only press releases and conflicting data in newspapers constitute the available information about such a massive retention effort. The need for an independent evaluation of Chicago's summer school program becomes even more critical because the claimed test score gains are being used to justify a systemwide curriculum of 9,360 daily lesson plans in every academic subject for the regular school year (Duffrin, 1998). The head of the Chicago school system responded to a study of elementary schools by using the alleged summer school gains to justify this lockstep curriculum:

> Vallas said efforts are under way to make sure teachers in all schools are provided with lesson plans and curriculum standards that will put schools "on the same page." That's why the eighth graders the last two summers have shown one year's growth in reading because of the improving quality of our curriculum. (Metsch, 1998)

THE PROGRAM OFFERED TO RETAINED STUDENTS

As I pointed out earlier, both New York and Chicago have placed retained students into special separate classes with reduced class sizes. A lower teacher–student ratio is certainly highly desirable. However, placing low-achieving students in separate classes is not good practice. Students in separate schools and classes often become stigmatized and marginalized (Oakes, 1985). For example, special educators have increasingly insisted that special education students be mainstreamed into regular classes. It seems strange that just as Chicago is abolishing separate classes for special education, it is setting up separate classes for retainees (Martinez & Poe, 1997). Chicago's Transition Centers carry separation to yet another degree. It is critical that an independent evaluation be conducted that focuses on how many students from these Transition Centers ever master academic skills and graduate from high school. I would predict enormous dropout rates.

The Costs of Retention Programs

Both the Chicago and New York retention programs incurred huge extra costs. Holding kids back means that Chicago students will spend an extra year in school at $4,641 per year per student ($6,941 per year counting categorical programs). If we use the smaller per pupil figure, retaining 10,000 elementary students in Chicago is costing $46 million this year alone. In addition, there are the costs of summer school and additional teachers for smaller classes during the regular school year. In New York, the cost was $40 to $70 million the first year for additional teachers (depending on who was estimating).

In Chicago, the summer schools cost $25 million in 1996, $34 million in 1997, and $42 million in 1998. Chicago's extra teachers and afterschool programs for retained elementary students cost at least $12 million. A conservative estimate is that Chicago's retention initiative is costing in excess of $100 million per year. These are heavy extra costs, indeed.

National Research About Retention

If we move away from New York and Chicago, what does the research say about retention? This research indicates that few practices have such negative effects. Researchers use a technique called meta-analysis to combine data from a number of studies on a particular topic, like retention. Meta-analysis indicates that retention is either harmful or ineffective (Holmes, 1989). Students retained are one fourth of a standard deviation worse off on educational outcome measures than comparable students who are promoted. These negative effects are even stronger for academic achievement alone. When children of the same age were compared, the retained group lost 0.45 standard deviation in achievement on average.

Evidence indicates that failing a grade is strongly tied to dropping out of school later. Being retained is as strong as low achievement in determining whether a student drops out or graduates. For example, in Austin, Texas, repeating a grade increased the chances of a White female dropping out by 17% and increased an African American male's chances of dropping out by 38% (Grissom & Shepard, 1989). This is a very powerful negative effect.

In fact, previous research in Chicago's schools indicated the same thing: The level of reading achievement and the student being overage (an indicator of flunking) were the best predictors that the student would drop out (Hess & Lauber, 1985). The dropout rate was 37% for those not retained, 59% for those retained once, and 69% for those retained twice. This study also concluded that students who were retained in elementary school were more likely to drop out, even when the retained student was reading significantly better than a student who entered high school at the normal age.

Research about the effects of retention on personal adjustment also shows negative results. In some cases, the stigmatizing effects on the children are striking. In one study, girls who had been retained refused to identify themselves as having been held back, even though they could name others who had been. Not only did students conceal that they had flunked, they were ridiculed by peers. Fully 84% reported feeling "sad, bad, or upset." Children said their parents were "mad" (48%) and "sad" (28%), and half reported being punished. Flunking evokes ridicule and punishment, shame and humiliation (Byrnes, 1989). In fact, Yamamoto found that the only things more stressful for children than flunking a grade are loss of a parent and going blind (cited in Shepard & Smith, 1990).

Not every study reports negative effects. Of 63 studies in the meta-analysis, 9 reported some positive results. However, these retention practices were in suburban settings in which retained students were put in special classes, given lots of help, and mainstreamed. It might be the case that retention helps some students sometimes under some circumstances. In a review of 21 studies between 1982 and 1992, 2 showed positive effects, 9 showed no effects, and 10 showed negative effects.

There is a recent challenge to the consistent conclusion that retention is ineffective or harmful for urban low-income students. Alexander, Entwistle, and Dunbar (1994) followed a sample of students in the Baltimore schools for 8 years, 53% of whom were retained at some point. They claim that their study shows that students who were retained gained academically and showed no ill effects in other ways. Unfortunately, the authors' own data do not support such claims. They became confused analyzing gain scores (a tricky business) and derived conclusions contrary to their own data.

Shepard, Smith, and Marion (1996) subsequently converted the Baltimore data to national percentile ranks and within-grade standard scores. Their analysis showed that retainees did improve their test scores during the repeated year itself. For example, first-grade retainees went from the 18th percentile in reading comprehension at the end of their first year to the 59th percentile at the end of their retained year (taking the same curriculum and tests). This looks good at first. Such short-term gains are the reason that architects of retention programs can point to higher test scores in the first year or two.

However, the important question is whether the students maintained such an advantage later. Alas, they did not. They were back at their same lower percentile level by second grade. Shepard et al. (1996) concluded that there is no effect from retention one way or the other in the Baltimore study. (Alexander's response to this critique was to acknowledge that their reanalysis was "fair and accurate" but that Shepard and her colleagues exaggerated his enthusiasm for retention.)

Why would scholars arrive at conclusions about retention contrary to their own data? Alexander and his colleagues (1994) supplied one clue:

> We wonder whether the studies now in the literature overrepresent children who are especially susceptible to retention's damaging effects. Retention no doubt is harder on children in some circumstances . . . and it could work differently in schools where just a handful of retainees stand out in comparison with a large majority of successful students. Little retention research has been conducted on children like those in [the Baltimore study], that is, minority and disadvantaged student populations in urban school systems where retention rates are high overall, and where many students fit the so-called risk profile . . . it seems plausible that social stigma would not be as much of a problem. (p. 6–21 7)

Indeed, 63% of the students retained in Baltimore were African American. But is it not particularly dangerous to conclude that African American children have such different sensibilities that they won't feel stigmatized or that retention won't harm them as it does others?

RETENTION IN OTHER DEVELOPED COUNTRIES

Views in the United States about retention contrast sharply with those in other countries. Few other countries tolerate flunking students. A British educator says

> I've been thinking about the issue of holding students back a grade. I've talked to some people here about it but we simply have no experience of the practice. As far as I can tell, it doesn't happen here. As far as possible, there is a strong preference for keeping children in their age cohort, not least because of friendship groups. Some primary schools are vertically grouped (very common in rural schools), which is to say that a class will have children across the age range for that phase of education, e.g., 5–8 or 8–12. There are also occasions when children are moved up a year because they are too advanced for their age group and this is causing problems. Holding back, however, is very rare.

An Australian educator suggested why Australian teachers do not endorse retention:

> Because they have this view that any targets are going to be too simplistic, that they are never going to measure the full extent of a kid's capacity, that different kids learn at different rates and eventually catch up. We know there is strong evidence that girls perform better up to a certain age, then boys catch up and sometimes overtake them. Kids from working class backgrounds respond better to different styles so having simplistic targets doesn't help, doesn't give you a true picture. And, of course, the bottom line is it would cost a fortune to hold kids back. We would prefer to have remedial teachers than keep half a cohort back.

THE CLIMATE OF THE TIMES

If the evidence about retention is so overwhelmingly negative, why does this practice persist? We might learn from the 19th-century science of "craniometry." Scientists who were convinced that Whites had superior intelligence and that men were smarter than women cast about for evidence to support their biases. They found that Whites had larger brains than other races and that men had larger brains than women. Based on these findings, they developed a pseudo-scientific theory. Larger brains meant more intelligence, they argued—after all, that relationship seemed to hold from one species to another among animals. The scientists then developed methods to measure the brain sizes of humans, with the connection to intelligence that they thought this entailed (Gould, 1981). These findings appeared in technical journals and the popular press, much like Herrnstein's and Murray's *The Bell Curve* (1994).

Stephen Jay Gould (1981) studied these craniometric methods and concluded that precision of measurement could never overcome the inherent racism and sexism implicit in the beginning assumptions. The scientists started with the assumption that the human races could be ranked on a linear scale of mental worth and explored any method they thought might yield the proper ranking. They explained away any exceptions they found contrary to their own beliefs. Although craniometry seems ludicrous now, gross injustices were perpetrated on vast numbers of people. From this history, we might draw two conclusions: First, the precision of methods is no guarantee of impartiality; second, the ideological climate of the age can seriously affect the conclusions reached.

The prevailing climate regarding retention is enthusiastic, from the president to a mayor to the public, and even to many educators. In one large city, 74% of the principals, 65% of the teachers, and 59% of the parents thought students should "always"or "usually"be retained for lack of basic skills. Teachers worried, but reassured themselves that it would be to the children's ultimate advantage. Teachers have deep-seated beliefs about child development. Half in one study believed that children develop in a linear fashion, "unfolding"through set stages when they are ready, and that this unfolding occurs outside the control of teachers and parents. Schools with teachers of this view held back 30% of their students, whereas teachers who believed that they could influence children's academic progress held back less than 1% or 2% (Smith, 1989).

Many teachers endorsed retention, though not all practiced it. Many expressed the belief that the next year the retained child would move from the bottom of the class to the top. Retention would save the child from becoming frustrated and failing in the future. Most teachers could not recall a single negative example of harmful repercussions and recited stories about children who had suffered after being socially promoted. They routinely misjudged retained children's feelings and the resistance of their parents. They located the child's inability to perform or behave properly in the child's psychological makeup rather than in the school (Smith, 1989).

There is another issue buried here. Sociologist William Julius Wilson contends that Americans will not support public policies that are seen to benefit minorities primarily. For example, Americans will support social security because it is seen as benefiting all people, not just minorities. But they will not support programs like welfare thought to benefit minorities primarily.

I have a corollary to Wilson's thesis. Americans will support programs and policies that are harmful to minorities, especially African Americans, that they would not support if these same policies were applied to the general population. New York would never have had the Promotional Gates program if minorities had not constituted 80% of the school population. Baltimore would not have carried out its retention program if its student population were not 55% African American. And Chicago would not have its retention program if Chicago's students were not 89% minority. By contrast, a survey of 15 Chicago suburban school districts indicated that those districts retained fewer than 1% of their students (Ryndar, 1997). It is the inner city with large minority populations where these harmful programs are implemented en masse.

CRITICAL NEXT STEPS

Given this research and these political realities, Chicago's educators, parents, and advocates for urban students should take a series of immediate steps.

First, they should publicize the negative research evidence about retention as it has been carried out over decades. The harm that it has caused nationally has been consistently documented by researchers, and nothing is being done in the Chicago retention program that shows promise of leading to any different results than the strikingly similar retention program that was carried out in New York City.

Second, they should insist that basic data about the process and impact of Chicago's retention program be made public immediately, so that any interested researchers can analyze it. Given the overwhelming negative evidence about retention, it is astonishing that this program has progressed for 3 years with no more than contradictory and inconsistent data contained in school district press releases as the basis for judging its impact. Further, you should insist that a truly independent evaluation of the Chicago program be carried out. The Consortium on Chicago School Research is conducting a study of Chicago retention, and it has shared some initial data. However, key data should be made generally available, so that many researchers can analyze Chicago's program, which has stimulated a national mania for flunking urban students.

Third, they should focus not only on the impact of retention at the grades where students are being retained as a matter of school system policy, but also on the ripple effect of increased retention at other grade levels. Side effects are often the most important outcomes of programs even when unanticipated.

Fourth, they should demand that the school system stop using the ITBS as the sole basis for making retention decisions in ways that are judged inappropriate by the company that publishes the test and by the head of the testing program. And Riverside Press should be asked to terminate Chicago's use of this test if Chicago does not agree to stop misusing it.

Fifth, they should identify better uses for the more than $100 million that is now being spent on retention. The focus of this chapter has not been on alternatives to retention, but there are a number of research-based strategies that are effective alternatives to both retention and social promotion. These effective strategies include fundamental restructuring of schools based on research about the practices of successful urban schools where few students score in the bottom quartile on tests (Designs for Change, 1998); high-quality early childhood education (Epstein, Schweinhart, & McAdoo, 1996); and promoting low-achieving students but providing them with extra help, such as tutors, reading recovery, before and afterschool programs, summer school, instructional aides, and peer tutoring (Shepard & Smith, 1990). All of these have proven positive research records. Educators, parents, and advocates should fight for redirecting the huge amount of money that is being spent on retention toward strategies that will really improve the achievement of Chicago's children.

How did House use different approaches and sources to contribute to policy? Can real-life decisions be made in this way? What examples do you know where this has been the case? Do you believe that state and federal policy makers rely on sound research to make policies? Discuss your views with your colleagues.

References

Adams, D. W. (1995). *Education for extinction: American Indians and the boarding school experience.* Lawrence: University of Kansas Press.

Adkins, A., & Gunzanheuser, M. (1999). Knowledge in critical ethnography. *Educational Foundations, 13*(1), 61–76.

Adler, P. A., & Adler, P. (1987). *Membership roles in field research.* Thousand Oaks, CA: Sage.

Agar, M. H. (1996). *The professional stranger: An informal introduction to ethnography* (2nd ed.). New York: Academic.

Alberto, P. A., & Troutman, A. C. (1999). *Applied behavior analysis for teachers.* Columbus, OH: Merrill, Prentice Hall.

Alexander, K. L., Entwistle, D. R., & Daubar, S. L. (1994). *On the success of failure.* New York: Cambridge University Press.

Allison, C. (1995). *Present and past: Essays for teachers in the history of education.* New York: Peter Lang.

Alreck, P. L., & Settle, R. B. (1995). *The survey research handbook: Guidelines and strategies for conducting a survey* (2nd ed.). Burr Ridge, IL: Irwin.

Altenbaugh, R. (1997). Oral history, American teachers and a social history of schooling: An emerging agenda. *Cambridge Journal of Education, 27,* 313–330.

Altork, K. (1998). You never know when you might want to be a redhead in Belize. In K. B. deMarrais (Ed.), *Inside stories: Qualitative research reflections* (pp. 111–126). Mahwah, NJ: Lawrence Erlbaum Associates.

Alvarez, C. (1996). The multiple and transformatory identities of Puerto Rican women in the U.S.: Reconstructing the discourse on national identity. In G. Etter-Lewis & M. Foster (Eds.), *Unrelated kin: Race and gender in women's personal narratives* (pp. 87–102). New York: Routledge.

Alvesson, M., & Skoldbert, K. (2000). *Reflexive methodology: New vistas for qualitative research.* London: Sage.

American Evaluation Association. Available: http://www.eval.org

American Educational Research Association. Available: http://www.aera.net

American Educational Research Association. (2001). *Ethical standards of AERA.* Available: http://www.aera.net/about/policy/ethics.htm. *American Journal of Evaluation* (formerly *Evaluation Practice*) published by AEA.

Anderson, E. (1978). *A place on the corner.* Chicago: University of Chicago Press.

Anderson, G. (1989). Critical ethnography in education: Origins, current status, and new directions, *Review of Educational Research, 59*(3), 249–270.

Anderson, G. L. (1989). Critical ethnography: Origins, current status, and new directions. *Review of Educational Research, 59*, 249–270.

Anderson, J. D. (1988). *The education of Blacks in the south, 1860–1935.* Chapel Hill: University of North Carolina Press.

Anderson, L. & Wilson, S. (1997). Critical incident technique. In D. L. Whetzel & G. R. Wheaton (Eds.), *Applied measurement methods in industrial psychology* (pp. 89–112). Palo Alto, CA: Davies-Black.

Anderson, N. H. (1963). Comparison of different populations: Resistance to Extinction and transfer. *Psychological Review, 70*, 162–179.

Andersson, B. E., & Nilsson, S. G. (1964). Studies in the reliability and validity of the critical incident technique. *Journal of Applied Pyschology, 48*, 398–403.

Angus, D. L., & Mirel J. E. (1999). *The failed promise of the American high school, 1890–1995.* New York: Teachers College Press.

Aristotle. (1947). (*Ethica Nicomachean*). In R. McKeon (Ed.), *Introduction to Aristotle.* New York: Modern Library. (Translated by W. D. Ross).

Armour, L. (2000). Socio-logic and the "use of colour." In S. Hester & D. Francis (Eds.), *Local ethnomethodological order: Ethnomethodological studies of knowledge in action* (pp. 163–196). Amsterdam & Philadelphia: Benjamins.

Atkin, J. M. (1991, April). *Teaching as research.* Paper presented at the meeting of the American Educational Research Association, San Francisco.

Atkinson, P. (1988). Ethnomethodology: A critical review. *Annual Review of Sociology, 14*, 441–465.

Atkinson, J. M., & Drew: (1979). *Order in court: The organization of verbal interaction in judicial settings.* London: Macmillan.

Atkinson, J. M., & Heritage, J. (1999). Jefferson's transcript notation. In A. Jaworski & N. Coupland (Eds.), *The discourse reader* (pp. 158–166). London & New York: Routledge.

Azevedo, J. (1997). *Mapping reality: An evolutionary realist methodology for the natural and social sciences.* Albany: State University of New York Press.

Bailyn, B. (1960). *Education in the forming of American society: Needs and opportunities for study.* Chapel Hill: University of North Carolina Press.

Baker, C. D. (1983). A "second look" at interviews with adolescents. *Journal of Youth and Adolescence, 12*(6), 501–519.

Baker, C. (1997a). Ethnomethodological studies of talk in educational settings. In B. Davies & D. Corson (Eds.), *Encyclopedia of language and education* (Vol. 3: Oral Discourse and Education, pp. 43–52). Dordrecht, the Netherlands: Kluwer.

Baker, C. D. (1997b). Membership categorisation and interview accounts. In D. Silverman (Ed.), *Qualitative research: Theory, method and practice* (pp. 130–143). London: Sage.

Baker, C. D. (1997c). Ticketing rules: Categorisation and moral ordering in a school staff meeting. In S. Hester & P. Eglin (Eds.), *Culture in action: Studies in membership categorization analysis* (Vol. 4, pp. 77–98). Washington, DC: International Institute for Ethnomethodology and Conversation Analysis and University Press of America.

Baker, C. D. (1997d). Transcription and representation in literacy research. In J. Flood, S. B. Heath, & D. Lapp (Eds.), *Handbook of research on teaching literacy through the communicative and visual arts* (pp. 110–120). New York: Simon & Schuster/Macmillan.

Baker, C. D. (2000). Locating culture in action: Membership categorisation in texts and talk. In A. Lee & C. Poynton (Eds.), *Culture and text: Discourse and methodology in social research and cultural studies* (pp. 99–113). St. Leonards, NSW Australia: Allen & Unwin.

Baker, C. D. (2002). Ethnomethodological analyses of interviews. In J. Gubrium & Holstein (Eds.), *Handbook of interviewing: Context and method* (pp. 777–795). Thousand Oaks, CA: Sage.

Baker, C. D., & Freebody, P. (1987). "Constituting the child" in beginning school reading books. *British Journal of Sociology of Education, 8*(1), 55–76.

Baker, C. D., & Johnson, G. (1998). Interview talk as professional practice. *Language and Education, 12*(4), 229–242.

Baker, C. D., & Keogh, J. (1995). Accounting for achievement in parent–teacher interviews. *Human Studies, 18,* 263–300.

Ball, S. J. (1990). Self-doubt and soft data: Social and technical trajectories in ethnographic fieldwork. *International Journal of Qualitative Studies in Education, 3*(2), 157–171.

Banks, J. A. (1998). The lives and values of researchers: Implications for education citizens in a multicultural society. *Educational Researcher, 27*(7), 4–17.

Barbour, R. S., & Kitzinger, J. (1999). *Developing focus group research: Politics, theory and practice.* Thousand Oaks, CA: Sage.

Barker, G., & Loewenstein, I. (1997). Where the boys are: Attitudes related to masculinity, fatherhood, and violence toward women among low-income adolescent and young adult males in Rio de Janeiro, Brazil. *Youth & Society, 29*(2), 166–219.

Barlow, D. H., & Hersen, M. (1984). *Single case experimental design: Strategies for studying behavior change* (2nd ed.). New York: Pergamon Press.

Barzun, J., & Graff, H. F. (1985). *The modern researcher.* New York: Harcourt, Brace, Jovanovich.

Bateson, N. (1984). *Data construction in social surveys.* Boston: Allen & Unwin.

Baudrillard, J. (1988). *Selected works* (M. Poster, Ed.). Cambridge, England: Polity.

Baxter-Magolda, M. (1992). *Knowing and reasoning in college.* San Francisco: Jossey-Bass.

Beauvoir, S. de. (1968). *The second sex.* (H. M. Parshley, Ed. and Trans.). New York: Modern Library. (Original work published 1949)

Becker, H. S. (1963). *Outsiders: Studies in the sociology of deviance.* London: Free Press.

Becker, H. S. (1964). *The other side: Perspectives on deviance.* New York: Free Press of Glencoe.

Becker, H. S. (1967). Whose side are we on? *Social Problems, 14,* 239–247.

Becker, H. S. (1970). *Sociological work: Method and substance.* Chicago: Aldine.

Becker, H. S., Geer, B., Hughes, E. C., & Strauss, A. L. (1961). *Boys in white: Student culture in medical school.* Chicago: University of Chicago Press.

Becker, L. C. (1995). Situation ethics. In R. Audi (Ed.), *The Cambridge dictionary of philosophy* (p. 738). Cambridge, UK: Cambridge University Press.

Behar, R. (1993). *Translated woman: Crossing the border with Esperanza's story.* Boston: Beacon.

Behar, R. (1996). *The vulnerable observer: Anthropology that breaks your heart.* Boston: Beacon.

Benard, H. R., & Pedruza, J. S. (1989). *Native ethnography: A Mexican Indian describes his culture.* Newbury Park, CA: Sage.

Bennett, K. (1986). *Study of reading ability grouping and its consequences for urban Appalachian first graders.* Unpublished doctoral dissertation, University of Cincinnati, OH.

Bennett, K. (1990). Doing school in an urban Appalachian first grade. In C. Sleeter (Ed.), *Empowerment through multicultural education.* NY: State University of New York Press.

Bennett, K., & LeCompte, M. D. (1990). *The way schools work.* New York: Longman.

Benson, J., & Clark, F. (1992). A guide for instrument development and validation. *The American Journal of Occupational Therapy, 36,* 789–800.

Beoku-Betts, J. (1994). When Black is not enough: Doing field research among Gullah women. *National Women's Studies Association Journal, 6,* 413–433.

Berger, P., & Luckmann, T. (1967). *The social construction of reality.* Garden City, NY: Anchor.

Bernstein, C., & Woodward, B. (1974). *All the president's men.* New York: Simon & Schuster.

Best, J. H. (1983). *Historical inquiry in education: A research agenda.* Washington, DC: American Educational Research Association.

Best, W., & Kahn, J. V. (1998). *Research in education* (8th ed.) Boston: Allyn & Bacon.

Bilmes, J. (1991). *Toward a theory of argument in conversation: The preference for disagreement.* In F. H. van Eemeren, R. Grootendorst, J. A. Blair, C. A. Willard (eds.), Proceedings of the Second International Conference on Argumentation. Amsterdam: SISCAT: International Centre For The Study Of Argumentation: 462–69.

Binet, A., & Simon, T. (1905). Methods nouvelles pour le diagnostic niveau intellectuel des anormaux. *L'Anne Psychologigue, 11,* 191–244.

Blount, J. (1998). *Destined to rule the schools: Women and the superintendency, 1873–1995.* Albany: State University of New York Press.

Blumer, H. (1969). *Symbolic interactionism: Perspective and method.* Englewood Cliffs, NJ: Prentice Hall.

Boas, F. (1940). *Race, language, and culture.* Chicago: University of Chicago Press.

Bogdan, R., & Biklen, S. (1982). *Qualitative research for education: An introduction to theory and methods.* Boston: Allyn & Bacon.

Bowles, S., & Gintis, H. (1976). *Schooling in capitalist America: Educational reform and the contradictions of economic life.* New York: Basic Books.

Bradlee, B. C. (1995). *A good life: Newspapering and other adventures.* New York: Simon & Schuster.

Bresler, L. (1996). Towards the creation of a new ethical code in qualitative research. *Bulletin of the Council for Research in Music Education, 130,* 17–29.

Brewer, J., & Hunter A. (1989). *Multimethod research: A synthesis of styles.* Newbury Park, CA: Sage.

Bromley, D. G., & Shupe, A. (1995). Anti-cultism in the United States. *Social Compass, 42,* 331–336.

Brown, K. M. (1992, April 15). Writing about "the Other." *Chronicle of Higher Education,* p. A56.

Brown, S. M., & Walberg, H. J. (1993). Motivational effects on test scores of elementary students. *The Journal of Educational Research, 86,* 133–136.

Bruner, J. (1986). *Actual minds, possible worlds.* Cambridge, MA: Harvard University Press.

Bruner, J. (1989). Life as narrative. *Social Research 54*(1), 11–32.

Bruner, J. (1990). *Acts of meaning.* Cambridge, MA: Harvard University Press.

Bruner, J. (1991). The narrative construction of reality. *Critical Inquiry, 18*(1), 1–22.

Bruner, J. (1996). *The culture of education.* Cambridge, MA: Harvard University Press.

Brunner, I., & Guzman, A. (1989). Participatory evaluation: A tool to assess projects and empower people. In R. F. Conner & M. Hendricks (Eds.), *International innovations in evaluation methodology* (pp. 9–18). San Francisco: Jossey-Bass.

Bryk, A. S. & Associates (1998). *Examining the academic productivity of Chicago public elementary schools.* Chicago: Consortium on Chicago School Research. Retrieved from http://www.designforchange.org

Bryman, A. (1984). The debate about quantitative and qualitative methods: A question of method or epistemology? *British Journal of Sociology, 35*, 75–92.

Budd, F. (1997). Helping the helpers after the bombing in Dhahran: Critical-incident stress services for an air rescue squadron. *Military Medicine, 162*, 515–520.

Buros Institute of Mental Measures. (2001). *Mental Measurements Yearbook* [Online]. Available: www.unl.edu/buros

Butchart, R. E. (1988). Outthinking and outflanking the owners of the world: A historiography of the African American struggle for education. *History of Education Quarterly 28*, 333–366.

Button, G. (1990). On varieties of closings. In G. Psathas (Ed.), *Interactional competence* (pp. 93–147). Washington, DC: University Press of America.

Byrnes, D. A. (1989). Attitudes of students, parents, and educators toward repeating a grade. In L. A. Shepard & M. L. Smith (Eds.), *Flunking grades: Research and policies on retention* (pp. 108–131). London: Falmer.

Cambell, D. T., & Fiske, D. W. (1959). Convergent and discriminate validation by the multitrait-multimethod matrix. *Psychological Bulletin, 56*, 81–105.

Campbell, D. T., & Stanley, J. C. (1963). *Experimental and quasi-experimental designs for research.* Chicago: Rand McNally.

Code of Federal Regulations, Title 45 Section 46. (1999). Washington DC: Government Printing Office.

Carr, D. (1985). Life and narrator's art. In *Hermeneutics and Deconstruction: Selected studies in phenomenology and existential philosophy* (pp. 108–121). Albany: State University of New York Press.

Carr, D. (1986). *Time, narrative, and history.* Bloomington: Indiana University Press.

Carspecken, P. (1996). *Critical ethnography in educational research.* New York: Routledge.

Cassell, J. (1977). *A group called women: Sisterhood and symbolism in the feminist movement.* New York: McKay.

Cassell, J. (1978). Risk and benefit to subjects of fieldwork. *The American Sociologist, 13*, 134–143.

Cherryholmes, C. (1988). *Power and criticism: Poststructural investigations in education.* New York: Teachers College Press.

Chicago Public Schools. (1997). *1997–1998 guidelines for promotion in the Chicago public schools.* Chicago: Author.

Chicago Public Schools. (1997). *Eighth graders master promotion criteria: Students at all levels show growth.* Chicago: Author.

Chicago Public Schools, Office of Management and Budget. (1998). *Personal communication to Jessica Clarke, Designs for Change.*

Cizek, G. (1995). Crunchy granola and the hegemony of narrative. *Educational Researcher,* *24*(3), 26–28.

Clayman, S. E., & Maynard, D. W. (1995). Ethnomethodology and conversation analysis. In P. ten Have & G. Psathas (Eds.), *Situated order: Studies in the social organization of talk and embodied activities* (pp. 1–30). Washington, DC: International Institute for Ethnomethodology and Conversation Analysis & University Press of America.

Clifford, G. J. (1989). Man/woman/teacher: Gender, family, and career in American educational history. In D. Warren (Ed.), *American teachers: Histories of a profession at work* (pp. 293–343). New York: MacMillan.

Clifford, J., & Marcus, G. (Eds.). (1986). *Writing culture: The poetics and politics of ethnography.* Berkeley, CA: University of California Press.

Cohen, A. M., & Smith, R. D. (1976). *The critical incident in growth groups: Theory and technique* (Vol. 1). La Jolla, CA: University Associates.

Cohen, J. (1988). *Statistical power analysis for the behavioral sciences.* Hillsdale, NJ: Lawrence Erlbaum Associates.

Cohen, J. H. (2000). Problems in the field: Participant observation and the assumption of neutrality. *Field Methods, 12*(4), 316–333.

Cohen, R. M., & Scheer, S. (1997). *The work of teachers in America: A social history through stories.* Mahwah, NJ: Lawrence Erlbaum Associates.

Cohen, S., & DePaepe, M. (1996). History of education in the postmodern era: Introduction *Paedagogica Historica 32,* 301–305.

Coles, R. (1989). *The call of stories: Teaching and the moral imagination.* Boston: Houghton Mifflin.

Collins, P. H. (1990). *Black feminist thought: Knowledge, consciousness, and the politics of empowerment.* London: HarperCollins Academic.

Collins, P. H. (1991). *Black feminist thought: Knowledge, consciousness, and the politics of empowerment.* New York: Routledge.

Collins, P. H. (1998). *Fighting words: Black women and the search for justice.* Minneapolis: University of Minnesota Press.

Collins, P. H. (1999). Learning from the outsider within: The sociological significance of Black feminist thought. In S. Hesse-Biber, C. Gilmartin, & R. Lydenberg (Eds.), *Feminist approaches to theory and methodology: An interdisciplinary reader* (pp. 155–178). New York: Oxford University Press.

Collins, T., Noblit, G., & Ciscel, D. (1978). Retail socialization: The preparation of Black high school students for employment in business. *Integrated Education, 14*(2), 12–16.

Collins, T., Noblit, G., & Ciscel, D. (1980). High school preparation for employment in a segmented labor market. In M. Sugar (Ed.). *Responding to adolescent needs* (pp. 235–249). New York: Spectrum.

Comaroff, J., & Comaroff, J. (1992). *Ethnography and the historical imagination.* Boulder, CO: Westview.

Connelly, F. M., & Clandinin, D. J. (1987). *Narrative experience and the study of curriculum.* Washington, DC: American Association of Colleges for Teacher Education.

Connelly, F. M., & Clandinin, D. J. (1990). Stories of experience and narrative inquiry. *Educational Researcher 19*(4), 2–15.

Connelly, F. M., & Clandinin, D. J. (1994). Personal experience methods. In N. K. Denzin & Y. S. Lincoln (Eds.), *Handbook of qualitative research* (pp. 413–427). Newbury Park, CA: Sage.

Consortium on Chicago School Research. (1998). *Preliminary data from study of Chicago retention policies*. Chicago: Author.

Converse, J. M. (1987). *Survey research in the United States: Roots and emergence 1890–1960*. Berkeley, CA: University of California Press.

Cook, T. D. (1991). Clarifying the warrant for generalized causal inferences in quasi-experimentation. In M. W. McLaughlin & D. C. Phillips (Eds.), *Evaluation and education: At quarter century* (115–144). Chicago: National Society for the Study of Education.

Cook, T. D., & Campbell, D. T. (1979). *Quasi-experimentation: Design and analysis issues for field settings*. Chicago: Rand McNally.

Cookingham, F. (1992). Defining evaluation. *Together, 3,* 21.

Cookingham, F. (1993). Free evaluation articles, Part 2. *Together, 2,* 30.

Cooper, D. D. (1998). Reading, writing, and reflection. In R. A. Rhoads & J. P. F. Howard (Eds.), *New directions for teaching and learning: Academic service learning: A pedagogy of action and reflection* (pp. 47–56). San Fransisco: Jossey-Bass.

Copelman, D. (1996). *London's women teachers: Gender, class, and feminism, 1870–1930*. London: Routledge.

Cotterill, P., & Letherby, G. (1993). Weaving stories: Personal autobiographies in feminist research. *Sociology, 7*(1), 67–79.

Coughlim, E. (1992, June 10). Mother love and infant death in a Brazilian shantytown. *Chronicle of Higher Education,* pp. A7–A9.

Coulter, J. (Ed.). (1990). *Ethnomethodological sociology*. Aldershot, England: Elgar.

Cousins, J. B., & Earl, L. M. (1992). The case for participatory evaluation. *Educational Evaluation and Policy Analysis, 14,* 397–418.

Cousins, J. B., & Leithwood, K. A. (1986). Current empirical research on evaluation utilization. *Review of Educational Research, 56,* 331–335.

Cremin, L. A. (1977). *Traditions of American education*. New York: Basic Books.

Cronbach, L. J. (1957). The two disciplines of scientific psychology. *American Psychologist, 12,* 671–684.

Cronbach, L. J. (1975). Beyond the two disciplines of scientific psychology. *American Psychologist, 30,* 116–127.

Cronbach, L. J., Ambron, S. R., Dombusch, S. M., Hess, R. D., Hornik, R. C., Phillips, D. C., Walker, D. F., & Weiner, S. S. (1980). *Toward reform of program evaluation*. San Francisco: Jossey-Bass.

Cronbach, L. J. (1982). *Designing evaluations of educational and social programs*. San Francisco: Jossey-Bass.

Cross, L. H., & Belli, G. M. (chapter in this volume). Experimental research to inform educational policy. In K. B. deMarrais and S. D. Lapan (Eds.), *Foundation of research: Methods of inquiry in education and the social sciences*. Hillsdale, NJ: Lawrence Erlbaum Associates.

Crotty, M. (1999). *The foundations of social research: Meaning and perspective in the research process*. London: Sage.

Crowder, K. (in press). In K. B. deMarrais & S. D. Lapan (Eds.), *Research methods in the social sciences: Frameworks for knowing and doing*. Hillsdale, NJ: Lawrence Erlbaum Associates.

Csikszentmihalyi, M. (1985). Emergent motivation and the evolution of the self. In D. A. Kleiber & M. Maehr (Eds.), *Advances in motivation and achievement, 4,* 93–119. Greenwich, CT: JAI.

Cubberly, E. (1919). *Public education in the United States: A study and interpretation of American educational history.* Boston: Houghton Mifflin.

Cuff, E. C., Sharrock, W. W., & Francis, D. W. (1998). *Perspectives in sociology.* New York: Routledge.

Cutler, W. W. (1989). Cathedral of culture: The schoolhouse in American educational thought and practice since 1820. *History of Education Quarterly 29,* 1–40.

Daiker, D. A., & Morenberg, M. (1990). *The writing teacher as researcher.* Portsmouth, NH: Boynton/Cook.

Danby, S., & Baker, C. D. (2000). Unravelling the fabric of social order in block area. In S. Hester & D. Francis (Eds.), *Local educational order: Ethnomethodological studies of knowledge in action* (pp. 91–140). Amsterdam & Philadelphia: Benjamins.

Daniels, A. K. (1983). Self-deception and self-discovery in fieldwork. *Qualitative Sociology, 6*(3), 195–214.

Dant, T. (1991). *Knowledge, ideology, and discourse: A sociological perspective.* London: Routledge.

Data, L. (1994). Paradigm wars: A basis for peaceful coexistence and beyond. In C. S. Reichardt & S. F. Rallis (Eds.), *The qualitative–quantitative debate: New perspectives* (pp. 53–70). San Francisco: Jossey-Bass.

Davies, B. (1992). Women's subjectivities and feminist stories. In C. Ellis & M. G. Flaherty (Eds.), *Investigating subjectivity: Research on lived experience* (pp. 53–76). Newbury Park, CA: Sage.

Davis, J. E. (2000). Accounts of false memory syndrome: Parents, "retractors," and the role of institutions in account making. *Qualitative Sociology, 23*(1), 29–56.

Dawson, J. A., & D'Amico, J. J. (1985). Involving program staff in evaluation studies: A strategy for increasing information use and enriching the data base. *Evaluation Review, 9,* 284–295.

de Beauvoir, S. (1968). *The second sex.* (H. M. Parshley Ed. and Trans.) New York: The Modern Library. (Original work published 1949).

Deegan, M. J. (1988). *Jane Addams and the men of the Chicago School, 1892–1918.* New Brunswick, NJ: Transaction.

Deegan, M. J., & Hill, M. R. (Eds.). (1987). *Women and symbolic interaction.* Boston: Allen & Unwin.

Degérando, J.-M. (1969). *The observation of savage peoples.* (F. C. T. Moore, Trans.). Berkeley, CA: University of California Press. (Original work published 1800)

Deigh, J. (1995). Ethics. In R. Audi (Ed.), *The Cambridge dictionary of philosophy* (pp. 244–249). Cambridge, UK: Cambridge University Press.

De Kruif, P. (1926). *Microbe hunters.* New York: Harcourt Brace.

Delamont, S. (1989). *Knowledgeable women: Structuralism and the reproduction of elites.* New York: Routledge.

Delamont, S. (1992). *Fieldwork in educational settings: Methods, pitfalls and perspectives.* London: Falmer.

Deleuze, G. (1992). What is a dispotif? In T. Armstrong (Ed. and Trans.), *Michel Foucault, philosopher* (pp. 159–168). New York: Routledge.

Deleuze, G., & Ghutari, F. (1983). *On the line* (J. Johnson, Trans.). New York:Seminonext(e).

Deloria, E. C. (1933). *Dakota texts* (Vol. 14 of the Publications of the American Ethnological Society). Leiden, the Netherlands: Brill.

Deloria, E. C. (1988). *Waterlily*. Lincoln: University of Nebraska Press.

deMarrais, K. (1998). Mucking around in the mud: Doing ethnography with Yup'ik Eskimo girls. In K. deMarrais (Ed.), *Inside stories: Qualitative research reflections* (pp. 87–96). Mahwah, NJ: Lawrence Erlbaum Associates.

Denzin, N. K. (1978). *The research act: An introduction to sociological actions*. New York: McGraw-Hill.

Denzin, N. K. (1987a). *The alcoholic self*. Beverly Hills, CA: Sage.

Denzin, N. K. (1987b). *The recovering alcoholic*. Beverly Hills, CA: Sage.

Denzin, N. K. (1994). The art and politics of interpretation. In N. K. Denzin & Y. S. Lincoln (Eds.), *Handbook of qualitative research* (pp. 500–515). Thousand Oaks, CA: Sage.

Depaepe, M., & Simon, F. (1995). Is there any place in the history of "education" in the "history of education"? A plea for the history of everyday educational reality in and outside schools. *Paedagogica Historica 31*, 9–16.

Depaepe, M., & Henkens, B. (Eds.). (2000). The challenge of the visual in the history of education. *Paedagogica Historica, 36*, 11–17.

Derrida, J. (1978). *Writing and difference*. London: Routledge & Kegan Paul.

Derrida, J. (1997). *Of grammatology* (G. C. Spivak, Trans.) (Corrected Edition ed.). Baltimore: Johns Hopkins University Press.

De Saussure, F., (1959). Course in general linguistics. In C. Bally & A. Sechehaye (Ed.), New York: McGraw-Hill.

Designs for Change. (1988). *What makes these schools stand out: Chicago elementary schools with a seven-year trend of improved reading achievement*. Chicago: Author.

Designs for Change. (1998). *Characteristics of Chicago elementary schools with varying percentages of spring 1997 Iowa test failures*. Chicago: Author.

DeVellis, R. F. (1991). *Scale development: Theory and applications*. Newbury Park, CA: Sage.

Dexter, L. A. (1970). *Elite and specialized interviewing*. Evanston, II: Northwestern University Press.

Deyhle, D. (1998). The role of the applied anthropologist: Between schools and the Navajo nation. In K. B. deMarrais (Ed.), *Inside stories: Qualitative research reflections* (pp. 35–48). Mahwah, NJ: Lawrence Erlbaum Associates.

Didion, J. (1961). On keeping a notebook. In *Slouching toward Bethlehem*. New York: Dell.

Doble, J. (1987, Winter). "Interpreting Public Opinion: Five Common Fallacies." In R. Kingston (Ed.), *Kettering Review*, 7–17.

Doble, J. (1993, Winter) personal communications.

Dockrell, W. B. (1988). Ethical considerations in research. In J. P. Keeves (Ed.), *Educational research, methodology, and measurement: An international handbook* (pp. 180–185). New York: Pergamon.

Dollard, J. (1935). *Criteria for the life history, with analyses of six notable documents*. New Haven, CT: Yale University Press.

Dougherty, J. (1999). From anecdote to analysis: Oral interviews and new scholarship in educational history. *Journal of American History, 86*, 712–723.

Drew, P. (1992). Contested evidence in courtroom cross-examination: The case of a trial for rape. In P. Drew & J. Heritage (Eds.), *Talk at work: Interaction in institutional settings* (pp. 470–520). Cambridge, UK: Cambridge University Press.

Drew, & Heritage, J. (1992). *Talk at work: Interaction in institutional settings.* Cambridge, UK: Cambridge University Press.

DuBois, W. E. B. (1899). *The Philadelphia negro: A social study.* Philadelphia: University of Pennsylvania Press.

Duffrin, E. (1998). 9,360 lesson plans on the way. Catalyst in The Designs for Schools Journal, *10*(1), 6–7. Regrieved from http://www.designforchange.org

Ebert, T. (1991). Political semiosis in/of American cultural studies. *The American Journal of Semiotics, 8*(1/2), 113–135.

Eder, D., & Corsaro, W. (1999). Ethnographic studies of children and youth: Theoretical and ethical issues. *Journal of Contemporary Ethnography, 28*(5), 520–531.

Educational Evaluation and Policy Analysis published by AERA.

Edwards, R. (1996). White woman researcher—Black women subjects. In S. Wilkinson & C. Kitzinger (Eds.), *Representing the other: A feminism and psychology reader* (pp. 83–88). Thousand Oaks, CA: Sage.

Eglin, P., & Hester, S. (1992). Category, predicate and task: The pragmatics of practical action. *Semiotica, 88,* 243–268.

Eicher, J. B., Baizerman, S., & Michelman, J. (1991). Adolescent dress. Part 2: A qualitative study of suburban high school students. *Adolescence, 26,* 679–686.

Eisner, E. (1976). Educational connoisseurship and criticism: Their form and functions in educational evaluation. *Journal of Aesthetic Education, 10,* 135–150.

Eisner, E. W. (1991a). *The enlightened eye.* New York: Macmillan.

Eisner, E. W. (1991b). Forms of understanding and the future of educational research. *Educational Researcher 22*(7), 5–11.

Eisner, E. W., & Peshkin, A. (1990). Introduction. In E. W. Eisner & A. Peshkin (Eds.). *Qualitative inquiry in education: The continuing debate.* Teachers College Press: NY, pp. 1–14.

Elliott, J. (1991). *Action research for educational change.* Philadelphia: Keynes.

Ellis, C. (1991). Sociological introspection and emotional experience. *Symbolic Interaction, 14,* 23–50.

Ellis, C. (1995). *Final negotiations: A story of love, loss, and chronic illness.* Philadelphia: Temple University Press.

Ellis, C., & Bochner, A.P. (1992). Telling and performing personal stories: The constraints of choice in abortion. In C. Ellis & M. G. Flaherty (Eds.), *Investigating subjectivity: Research on lived experience* (pp. 79–101). Newbury Park, CA: Sage.

Ellis, C., & Bochner, A. (Eds.). (1996). *Composing ethnography: Alternative forms of qualitative writing.* London: Altamira.

Ellis, R. (1990). *Instructed second language acquisition.* Oxford, UK: Oxford University Press.

Ellsworth, E. (1989). Why doesn't this feel empowering? Working through the repressive myths of critical pedagogy. *Harvard Educational Review, 59,* 297–324.

Elmore, P. B., & Woehlke, P. L. (1998, April). Twenty years of research methods employed in *American Educational Research Journal, Educational Researcher,* and *Review of Educational Research.* Paper presented at the annual meeting of the American Educational Research Association, San Diego, CA. (ERIC Document Reproduction Service No. ED 420701).

Emmison, M., & Smith, P. (2000). *Researching the visual: Images, objects, contexts and interactions in social and cultural inquiry.* London: Sage.

Engel, J., & Noblit, G. (1989). Organization development, critical theory, and purposive inquiry: An alternative for healthcare educators. *Journal of Healthcare Education and Training, 4*(2), 28–31.

Engelking, J. L. (1986). *Teacher job satisfaction and dissatisfaction. Spectrum, 4* (1), 33–38.

Epstein, A. S., Schweinhart, L. J., & McAdoo L. (1996). *Models of early childhood education.* Ypsilanti, MI: High/Scope.

Erickson, D. J., & Tewksbury, R. (2000). The "gentlemen" in the club: A typology of strip club patrons. *Deviant Behavior: An Interdisciplinary Journal, 21,* 271–293.

Etter-Lewis, G. (1993). *My soul is my own: Oral narratives of African American women in the professions.* New York: Routledge.

Etter-Lewis, G., & Foster, M. (Eds.). (1996). *Unrelated kin: Race and gender in women's personal narratives.* New York: Routledge.

Evaluation published by Sage in London and Thousand Oaks, California in association with The Tavistock Institute (London, UK).

Everhart, R. (1983). *Reading, writing, and resistance: Adolescence and labor in a junior high school* (Critical Thought Series). Boston: Routledge & Kegan Paul.

Eyre, S. L. (1997). The vernacular term interview: Eliciting social knowledge related to sex among adolescents. *Journal of Adolescence, 20,* 9–27.

Fay, B. (1987). *Critical social science.* Ithaca, NY: Cornell University Press.

Feuerstein, M. T. (1986). *Partners in evaluation: Evaluating development and community programmes with participants.* London: Macmillan.

Fielding, N., & Fielding J. (1986). *Linking data.* Beverly Hills, CA: Sage.

Fields, M. (1997). Students try to catch up in transition centers. *Catalyst* VIII (9), pp. 23–24.

Fields, G. A. (1993). Ten lies of ethnography: Moral dilemmas of field research. *Journal of Contemporary Ethnography, 22,* 267–294.

Fine, A. (1986). *The shaky game: Einstein, realism and the quantum theory.* Chicago: University of Chicago Press.

Fine, G. A. (Ed.). (1995). *A second Chicago school? The development of a postwar American sociology.* Chicago: University of Chicago Press.

Fine, M. (1992). *Disruptive voices: The possibilities of feminist research.* Ann Arbor: University of Michigan Press.

Fine, M. (1994). Distance and other stances: Negotiations of power inside feminist research. In A. Gitlin (Ed.), *Power and method: Political activism and educational research* (pp. 13–35). New York: Routledge.

Fine, M. (1994). Working the hyphens: Reinventing self and other in qualitative research. In N. Denzin & Y. Lincoln (Eds.). *Handbook of qualitative research* (pp. 70–82). London: Sage.

Fine, M., & Weiss, L. (2000). *Speed bumps: A student-friendly guide to qualitative research.* New York: Teachers College Press.

Fink, A. (1995). *How to sample in surveys.* Thousand Oaks, CA: Sage Publications.

Finkelstein, B. (1974) *Regulated children/liberated children: Education in psychohistorical perspective.* New York: Psychohistory.

Finkelstein, B. (1989). *Governing the young: Teacher behaviour in popular primary schools in the 19th-century United States.* New York: Falmer Press.

Finkelstein, B. (1992). Educational historians as mythmakers. In G. Grant (Ed.), *Review of research in education* (pp. 255–297). Washington, DC: American Educational Research Association.

Finn, J. D., & Achilles, C. M. (1990). Answers and questions about class size: A statewide experiment. *American Educational Research Journal, 27*, 557–577.

Finn, J. D., & Achilles, C. M. (1999). Tennessee's class size study: Findings, implications, misconceptions. *Educational Evaluation and Policy Analysis, 21*(2), 97–109.

Fiske, D., & Shweder, R. (Eds.). (1986). *Metatheory in social science: Pluralisms and subjectivities.* Chicago: University of Chicago Press.

Fitzgerald, F. (1979). *America revised: History schoolbooks in the twentieth century.* Boston: Little, Brown.

Flanagan, J. C. (1954). The critical incident technique. *Psychological Bulletin, 51*, 327–358.

Fly, B. J., van Bark, W. P., Weinman, L., Kitchener, K. S., & Lang, P. R. (1997). Ethical transgressions of psychology graduate students: Critical incidents with implications for training. *Professional Psychology: Research and Practice, 28*, 492–495.

Fosnot, C. T. (Ed.). (1996). *Constructivism: Theory, perspectives, and practice.* New York: Teachers College Press.

Foster, M. (1996). Like us but not one of us: Reflections on a life history study of African American teachers. In G. Etter-Lewis & M. Foster (Eds.), *Unrelated kin: Race and gender in women's personal narratives* (pp. 215–224). New York: Routledge.

Foucault, M. (1980). *Power and knowledge.* (C. Gordon, Ed.). New York: Pantheon.

Foucault, M. (1980). *Power/knowledge: Selected interviews and other writings, 1972–1977* (C. Gordon, Ed.; C. Gordon, L. Marshall, J. Mepham, & K. Soper, Trans.). New York: Pantheon.

Fraenkle, J. R., & Wallen, N. E. (1998). *How to design and evaluate research in education* (4th ed.). Boston: McGraw-Hill.

Frankel, R. (1990). Talking in interviews: A dispreference for patient-initiated questions in physician–patient encounters. In G. Psathas (Ed.), *Interactional competence* (pp. 231–262). Washington, DC: University Press of America.

Franklin, B. (1994). *From "backwardness" to "at risk": Childhood learning difficulties and the contradictions of school reform.* Albany: State University of New York Press.

Freeman, J., Weitzenfeld, J., Klein, G., Riedl, T., & Musa, J. (1991). *A knowledge elicitation technique for educational development: The critical decision method.* (ERIC Reproduction Services Document No. ED334223). Paper presented at the annual meeting of the American Educational Research Association, Chicago.

Fris, J. (1992). Principals' encounters with conflict: Tactics they and others use. *Alberta Journal of Educational Research, 38*(1), 65–78.

Fuller, W. E. (1982). *The old country school: The story of rural education in the Middle West.* Chicago: University of Chicago Press.

Gable, R. K., & Wolf, M. B. (1993). *Instrument development in the affective domain* (2nd ed.). Boston: Kluwer.

Gadamer, H. (1976). *Philosophical hermeneutics.* (E. L. David, Trans.). Berkeley, CA: University of California Press.

Gage, N. (1989). The paradigm wars and their aftermath: A "historical" sketch of research and teaching since 1989. *Educational Researcher, 18*, 4–10.

Gall, M. D., Borg, W. R., & Gall, J. P. (1996). *Educational research: An introduction* (6th ed.). New York: Longman.

Galliher, J. F. (1991). The protection of human subjects: A reexamination of the professional code of ethics. In J. F. Galliher (Ed.), *Deviant behavior and human rights* (pp. 344–352). Englewood Cliffs, NJ: Prentice Hall.

Game, A. (1991). *Undoing the social: Towards a deconstructive sociology.* Toronto: University of Toronto Press.

Gardner, P., & Cunningham P. (1997). Oral history and teachers' professional practice: A wartime turning point? *Cambridge Journal of Education 27,* 331–342.

Garfinkel, H. (1967). *Studies in ethnomethodology.* Englewood Cliffs, NJ: Prentice Hall.

Garfinkel, H. (1974). The origins of the term "ethnomethodology." In R. Turner (Ed.), *Ethnomethodology* (pp. 15–18). Middlesex, England: Penguin.

Garfinkel, H. (1991). Respecification: Evidence for locally produced, naturally accountable phenomena of order, logic, reason, meaning, method, etc. in and as of the essential haecceity of immortal ordinary society: (I) An announcement of studies. In G. Button (Ed.), *Ethnomethodology and the human sciences* (pp. 10–19). Cambridge, England: Cambridge University Press.

Garfinkel, H., Lynch, M., & Livingston, E. (1981). The work of a discovering science construed with materials from the optically discovered pulsar. *Philosophy of the Social Sciences, 11*(2), 131–158.

Garrick, J. (1999). Doubting the philosophical assumptions of interpretive research. *International Journal of Qualitative Studies in Education, 12*(2), 147–156.

Gay, L. R., & Airasian, P. (2000). *Educational research: Competencies for analysis and application.* (6th ed.) Columbus, OH: Merrill-Prentice Hall.

Geertz, C. (1973). *The interpretation of cultures.* New York: Basic Books.

Geertz, C. (1988). *Works and lives: The anthropologist as author.* Stanford, CA: Stanford University Press.

Geisinger, K. F. (1994). Cross-cultural normative assessment: Translation and adaptation issues influencing the normative interpretation of assessment instruments. *Psychological Assessment, 6,* 304–312.

Gergen, K. J., & Gergen, M. M. (1986). Narrative form and the construction of psychological science. In T. R. Sarbin (Ed.), *Narrative psychology: The storied nature of human conduct* (pp. 22–44). New York: Praeger.

Giddens, A. (1979). *Central problems in social theory: Action, structure and contradiction in social analysis.* Berkley: University of California Press.

Gilbert, J., & Priest, M. (1997). Models and discourse: A primary school science class visit to a museum. *Science Education, 81,* 749–762.

Gilligan, C. (1982). *In a different voice: Psychological theory and women's development.* Cambridge, MA: Harvard University Press.

Giorgi, A. (1970). *Psychology as human science: A phenomenology-base approach.* New York: Harper & Row.

Giorgi, A. (1975). An application of phenomenological method in psychology. In A. Giorgi, C. Fischer, & E. Murray (Eds.), *Duquesne studies in phenomenological psychology* (Vol. 2). Pittsburgh, PA: Duquesne University Press.

Giorgi, A. (1983). Concerning the possibility of phenomenological research. *Journal of Phenomenological Psychology, 14,* 129–170.

Giroux, H. (1983). Theories of reproduction and resistance in the new sociology of education: A critical analysis. *Harvard Educational Review, 53*(3), 257–293.

Giroux, H., Lankshear, C., McLaren, P., & Peters, M. (1996). *Counternarratives: Cultural studies and critical pedagogies in postmodern spaces*. New York: Routledge.

Glaser, G. B., & Strauss, A. L. (1967). *The discovery of grounded theory: Strategies for qualitative research*. Chicago: Aldine.

Glass, G. V., & Smith, M. L. (1978). *Meta-analysis of research on the relationship of class size and achievement*. San Francisco: Far West Laboratory for Educational Research and Development.

Glassner, B., & Hertz, R. (Eds.). (1999). *Qualitative sociology as everyday life*. Thousand Oaks, CA: Sage.

Glesne, C. (1997). That rare feeling: Re-presenting research through poetic transcription. *Qualitative Inquiry, 3*(2), 202–221.

Glesne, C. (1999). *Becoming qualitative researchers: An introduction*. New York: Longman.

Gluck, S. B. (1991). Advocacy oral history: Palestinian women in resistance. In S. B. Gluck & D. Patai (Eds.), *Women's words: The feminist practice of oral history* (pp. 205–219). New York: Routledge.

Gluck, S. B., & Patai, D. (Eds.). (1991). *Women's words: The feminist practice of oral history*. New York: Routledge.

Goetz, J. P., & LeCompte, M. D. (1984). *Ethnography and qualitative design in educational research*. Orlando, FL: Academic.

Gold, R. L. (1958). Roles in sociological field observations. *Social Forces, 36*, 217–233.

Goldman, A., & McDonald, S. (1987). *The group depth interview: Principles and practice*. New York: Prentice Hall.

Goldsmith, D. J. (1999). Content-based resources for giving face sensitive advice in troubles talk episodes. *Research on Language and Social Interaction, 32*, 303–336.

Goodson, I. F. (1988). Teachers' life histories and studies of curriculum and schooling. In I. Goodson (Ed.), *The making of curriculum: Collected essays* (pp. 71–92). Philadelphia: Falmer.

Goodwin, L. D., & Goodwin, W. L. (1985). Statistical techniques in AERJ articles, 1979–1983: The preparation of graduate students to read the educational research literature. *Educational Researcher, 14*(2), 5–11.

Goodson, I. F. (1995). The story so far: Personal knowledge and the political. In J. A. Hatch & R. Wisniewski (Eds.), *Life history and narrative* (pp. 89–98). London: Falmer.

Goodwin, C., & Heritage, J. (1990). Conversation analysis. *Annual Review of Anthropology, 19*, 283–307.

Goodwin, L. D. & Goodwin, W. L. (1985). Statistical techniques in AERJ articles, 1979–1983: The preparation of graduate students to read the educational research literature. *Educational Researcher, 14*(2), 5–11.

Gordon, A. D. (1979). The young ladies' academy of Philadelphia. In C. R. Berkin, & M. B. Norton (Eds.), *Women of America: A history*. Boston: Houghton Mifflin.

Gorman, T. (1998). Social class and parental attitudes toward education: Resistance and conformity to schooling in the family. *Journal of Contemporary Ethnography, 27*(1), 10–44.

Goswami, D., & Stillman, P. R. (Eds.). (1987). *Reclaiming the classroom: Teacher research as an agency for change*. Upper Montclair, NJ: Boynton/Cook.

Gould, S. J. (1981). *The mismeasure of man*. New York: Norton.

Gouldner, A. (1970). *The coming crisis of Western sociology*. New York: Basic Books.

Graham, P. A. (1978). Expansion and exclusion: A history of women in American higher education. *Signs 3*, 759–773.

Gramsci, A. (1971). *Selections from the Prison Notebooks of Antonio Gramsci*. (Q. Hoare & G. Smith, Ed. & Trans.). New York: International Publishers.

Granada, A. J. (1997). *Getting gifted: A comparative case study*. Unpublished doctoral dissertation, Northern Arizona University, Flagstaff.

Granada, J., & Lapan, S. D. (n. d.). *Implementing a gifted program: A case study*. Unpublished manuscript, Northern Arizona University, Flagstaff.

Granada, J., & Lapan, S. D. (2001). Teaming and collaborating for change. In K. T. Henson (Ed.), *Curriculum planning* (2nd ed., pp. 297–306). Boston: McGraw-Hill.

Graves, R. M. (1991). *Measurement error across the disciplines*. In P. P. Biemer, R. M. Groves, L. E. Lyberg, N. A. Mathiowetz, & S. Sudman (Eds.), *Measurement errors in surveys*. New York: Wiley.

Greatbatch, D. (1992). On the management of disagreement between news interviewers. In P. Drew & J. Heritage (Eds.), *Talk at work: Interaction in institutional settings* (pp. 268–301). Cambridge, UK: Cambridge University Press.

Green, A. (1994). Postmodernism and state education. *Journal of Educational Policy 9*, 67–83.

Green, K. E., & Hutchinson, S. R. (1996, April). Reviewing the research on mail survey response rates: Meta-analysis. In *Reviewing the research on survey response rates: Alternative approaches*. Symposium presented at the annual meeting of the American Educational Research Association, New York.

Green, K. E., & Kvidahl, R. F. (1990, April). *Research methods courses and post-bachelor education: Effects on teachers' research use and opinions*. Paper presented at the annual meeting of the American Educational Research Association, Boston.

Green, S. B. (1991). How many subjects does it take to do a regression analysis? *Multivariate Behavioral Research, 26*, 299–310.

Greenbaum, T. L. (1993). *The handbook of focus group research*. New York: Lexington.

Greenbaum, T. L. (1987). *The practical handbook and guide to focus group research*. Lexington, MA: Heath.

Greene, J. (1994). Qualitative program evaluation: Practice and promise. In N. K. Denzin, & Y. S. Lincoln (Eds.), *Handbook of qualitative research* (pp. 530–544). Thousand Oaks, CA: Sage.

Greene, J. C. (1986, April). *Participatory evaluation and the evaluation of social programs: Lessons learned from the field*. Paper presented at the annual meeting of the American Educational Research Association, San Francisco.

Greene, J. C. (1988). Communication of results and utilization in participatory program evaluation. *Evaluation and Program Planning, 11*, 341–351.

Greene, J. C. (1990). Technical quality versus user responsiveness in evaluation practice. *Evaluation and Program Planning, 13*, 267–274.

Greene, J. C., Caracelli, V. J., & Graham, W. F. (1989). Toward a conceptual framework for mixed-method evaluation designs. *Educational Evaluation and Policy Analysis, 11*, 255–274.

Greene, M. (1991). Foreword. In C. Witherell & N. Noddings (Eds.), *Stories lives tell: Narrative and dialogue in education* (pp. ix–xi). New York: Teachers College Press.

Gregoriou, Z. (1995). Derrida's responsibility: Autobiography, the teaching of vulnerability, diary fragments. *Educational Theory, 45*, 311–335.

Grissom, J. B., & Shepard, L. A. (1989). Repeating and dropping out of school. In L. A. Shepard & M. L. Smith (Eds.), *Flunking grades: Research and policies on retention* (pp. 34–63). London: Falmer.

Groce, N. E. (1985). *Everyone here spoke sign language: Hereditary deafness on Martha's Vineyard.* Cambridge, MA: Harvard University Press.

Grossberg, L., Nelson, C., & Treichler, P. (Eds.). (1992). *Cultural studies.* New York: Routledge.

Grosvenor, I., Lawn, M., & Rousmaniere, K. (Eds.). (1999). *Silences and images: The social history of the classroom.* New York: Lang.

Grumet, M. (1988). *Bitter milk: Women and teaching.* Amherst, MA: University of Massachusetts Press.

Grumet, M. (1991). The politics of personal knowledge. In C. Witherell & N. Noddings (Eds.), *Stories lives tell: Narrative and dialogue in education* (pp. 67–77). New York: Teachers College Press.

Guba, E. G. (1990). *The paradigm dialog.* Newbury Park, CA: Sage.

Guba, E. G. (1981). Criteria for assessing the trustworthiness of naturalistic inquiries. *Educational Communication and Technology Journal, 29,* 75–2.

Guba, E. G. (Ed.). (1990). *The paradigm dialog.* Newbury Park, CA: Sage.

Guba, E. G., & Lincoln, Y. S. (1981). *Effective evaluation.* San Francisco: Jossey-Bass.

Guba, E. G., & Lincoln, Y. S. (1989). *Fourth generation evaluation.* Newbury Park, CA: Sage.

Guba, E. G., & Lincoln, Y. S. (1994). Competing paradigms in qualitative methods. In N. Denzin & Y. Lincoln (Eds.), *Handbook of qualitative research* (pp. 105–117). Thousand Oaks, CA: Sage.

Gubrium, J. F., & Holstein, J. A. (1997). *The new language of qualitative method.* New York: Oxford University Press.

Gumperz, J. J. (1982). *Discourse strategies.* Cambridge, England: Cambridge University Press.

Habermas, J. (1971a). *Knowledge and human interests.* Boston: Beacon.

Habermas, J. (1971b). *Theory and practice* (J. Biertel, Trans.). Boston: Viking.

Habermas, J. (1975). *Legitimation crisis* (T. McCarthy, Trans.). Boston: Beacon.

Hall, S. (1986). The problem of ideology—Marxism without guarantees. *Journal of Communication Inquiry, 10*(2), 28–43.

Hammersley, M. (1992). *The dilemma of qualitative method: Herbert Blumer and the Chicago tradition.* London: Routledge & Kegan Paul.

Hammersley, M. (1992). Some reflections on ethnography and validity. *International Journal of Qualitative Studies in Education, 5*(3), 195–203.

Hansen, J. F. (1976). The anthropologist in the field: Scientist, friend, voyeur. In M. A. Rynkiewich & J. P. Spradley (Eds.), *Ethics and anthropology: Dilemmas in fieldwork* (pp. 123–134). New York: Wiley.

Harding, S. (1987). Is there a feminist method? In S. Harding (Ed.), *Feminism and methodology:* Bloomington: Indiana University Press.

Hargreaves, D. (1967). *Social relations in a secondary school.* London: Routledge & Kegan Paul.

Haring, N. G., Lovitt, T. C., Eaton, M. D., & Hansen, M. D., Hansen, C. L. (1978). *The fourth R: Research in the classroom.* Columbus, OH: Merrill.

Hatch, J. A., & Wisniewski, R. (Eds.). (1995). *Life history and narrative.* London: Falmer.

Heap, J. L. (1980). What counts as reading: Limits to certainty in assessment. *Curriculum Inquiry, 10,* 265–292.

Heap, J. L. (1990). Applied ethnomethodology: Looking for the local rationality of reading activities. *Human Studies, 13*, 39–72.

Heap, J. L. (1997). Conversation analysis methods in researching language and education. In N. H. Hornberger & D. Corson (Eds.), *Encyclopedia of language and education* (Vol. 8, pp. 217–225). Dordrecht, the Netherlands: Kluwer.

Heath, C., Knoblauch, H., & Luff. (2000). Technology and social interaction: The emergence of "workplace studies." *British Journal of Sociology, 51*, 299–320.

Heidegger, M. (1962). *Being and time* (J. Macquarrie & E. Robinson, Trans.). New York: Harper & Row. (Original work published 1927)

Hendrie, C. (1997, Sept. 10). Chicago data show mixed summer gain. *Education Week* XVII (3), p. 1.

Hennessey, R. (1995). Queer visibility in commodity culture. In L. Nicholson & S. Seidman (Eds.), *Social postmodernism: Beyond identity politics* (pp. 142–186). Cambridge, UK: Cambridge University Press.

Heritage, J. (1984). *Garfinkel and Ethnomethodology*. Cambridge, UK: Polity.

Heritage, J. (1987). Ethnomethodology. In A. Giddens & J. H. Turner (Eds.), *Social theory today* (pp. 224–272). Stanford, CA: Stanford University Press.

Heritage, J. (1997). Conversation analysis and institutional talk: Analysing data. In D. Silverman (Ed.), *Qualitative research: Theory, method and practice* (pp. 161–182). London: Sage.

Herrnstein, R. J., & Murray, C. (1994). *The bell curve: Intelligence and class structure in American life*. New York: Free Press.

Hertz, R. (Ed.). (1997). *Reflexivity and voice*. Thousand Oaks, CA: Sage.

Hess, G. A., & Lauber, D. (1985). *Dropouts from the Chicago public schools: Chicago Panel on Public School Finances*. Chicago Public Schools retrieved from http://www.chipubsch.org

Hesse-Biber, S., Gilmartin, C., & Lydenberg, R. (Eds.). (1999). *Feminist approaches to theory and methodology: An interdisciplinary reader*. New York: Oxford University Press.

Hester, S. (2000). The local order of deviance in school: Membership categorisation, motives and morality in referral talk. In S. Hester & D. Francis (Eds.), *Local educational order: Ethnomethodological studies of knowledge in action* (pp. 197–222). Amsterdam: Benjamins.

Hester, S., & Francis, D. W. (2000a). Ethnomethodology and local educational order. In S. Hester & D. W. Francis (Eds.), *Local educational order: Ethnomethodological studies of knowledge in action* (pp. 1–20). Amsterdam: Benjamins.

Hester, S., & Francis, D. (Eds.). (2000b). *Local educational order: Ethnomethodological studies of knowledge in action*. Amsterdam: Benjamins.

Heward, W. L. (1987). Production and interpretation of graphic data displays. In J. O. Cooper, T. E. Heron, & W. L. Heward (eds.), *Applied behavior analysis* (pp. 106–141). Columbus, OH: Merrill.

Hirsch, P. M. (1999). Qualitative sociology and good journalism as demystifiers. In B. Glassner & R. Hertz (Eds.), *Qualitative sociology as everyday life* (pp. 251–258). Thousand Oaks, CA: Sage.

Hollinger, R. (1994). *Postmodernism and the social sciences* (Social Theory Series). Thousand Oaks, CA: Sage.

Holmes, C. T. (1989). Grade-level retention effects: A metaanalysis of research studies. In Shepard, & Smith, (pp. 16–33).

Holstein, J. A., & Gubrium, J. F. (1998). Phenomenology, ethnomethodology, and interpretive practice. In N. K. Denzin & Y. S. Lincoln (Eds.), *Strategies of qualitative inquiry* (pp. 137–157). Thousand Oaks, CA: Sage.

hooks, b. (1989). *Talking back: Thinking feminist, thinking Black*. Boston: South End Press.

hooks, b. (1999). Eating the other: Desire and resistance. In S. Hesse-Biber, C. Gilmartin, & R. Lydenberg (Eds.), *Feminist approaches to theory and methodology: An interdisciplinary reader* (pp. 179–194). New York: Oxford University Press.

Hoover, H. D., Associates (1996). *ITBS: A message to parents*. Itasca, IL: Riverside Press.

Hoover, H. D., Associates (1996). *Iowa Tests of Basic Skills: Interpretive guide for school administrators* (Levels 5–14, Form M). Itasca, IL: Riverside Press. Riverside Press. Test purchaser qualification form. Itasca, IL: Author.

Horowitz, I. L. (Ed.). (1967). *The rise and fall of Project Camelot*. Cambridge, MA: MIT Press.

House, E. R. (1977). *The logic of evaluative argument*. Los Angeles: University of California, Center for the Study of Evaluation.

House, E. R. (1980). *Evaluating with validity*. Beverley Hills, CA: Sage.

House, E. R. (1983). Assumptions underlying evaluation models. In G. F. Madaus, M. Scriven, & D. L. Stufflebeam (Eds.), *Evaluation models* (pp. 45–65). Hingham, MA: Kluwer-Nijhoff.

House, E. R. (1993). *Professional evaluation*. Newbury Park, CA: Sage.

House, E. R. (1994). Integrating the quantitative and qualitative. In C. S. Reichardt & S. F. Rallis (Eds.), *The qualitative–quantitative debate: New perspectives* (pp. 13–22). San Francisco: Jossey-Bass.

House, E. R., & Howe, K. R. (1999). *Values in evaluation and social research*. Thousand Oaks, CA: Sage.

House, E. R., Linn, R., & Raths, J. (1981–1982). An audit of the evaluation of New York City's Promotional Gates Program. (Four reports, October 1981, February 1982, April 1982, October 1982). Urbana, IL: University of Illinois. Center for Instructional Research and Curriculum Evaluation.

Howe, E., & Eisenhart, M. (1990). Standards for qualitative (and quantitative) research: A prolegomenon. *Educational Researcher, 19*, 2–9.

Howell, J. T. (1972). *Hard living on Clay Street: Portraits of blue-collar families*. Prospect Heights, IL: Waveland.

Huberman, M. (1987). Steps toward an integrated model of research utilization. *Knowledge: Creation, diffusion, utilization, 8*, 586–611.

Huberman, M. (1990). Linkage between researchers and practitioners: A qualitative study. *American Educational Research Journal, 27*, 363–391.

Humphreys, L. (1975). *Tearoom trade: Impersonal sex in public places*. New York: de Gruyter.

Hurston, Z. N. (1935). *Mules and men*. New York: Negro Universities Press.

Hurston, Z. N. (1937). *Their eyes were watching God: A novel*. New York: Negro Universities Press.

Husserl, E. (1931). *Ideas: General introduction to pure phenomenology* (W. Gibson, Trans.). New York: Collier. (Original work published 1913)

Husserl, E. (1970). *The idea of phenomenology*. The Hague, the Netherlands: Martinus Nijhoff.

Hutchby, I. (2001). *Conversation and technology: From the telephone to the Internet*. Cambridge, UK: Polity.

Hutchby, I., & Wooffitt, R. (1998). *Conversation analysis: Principles, practices and applications*. Cambridge, UK: Polity.

Hutcheon, L. (1988). *A poetics of postmodernism: History, theory, fiction*. New York: Routledge.

Hutchinson, J. (1986). Of mirrors and dragons. *Together, 4*, 24–28.

Hutchinson, S. R., & Green, K. E. (1998, April). *Survey response rates for postal mail, electronic mail, and fax returns among educational researchers*. Paper presented at the annual meeting of the American Educational Research Association, San Diego, CA.

Hutchinson, S. R., & Lovell, C. D. (1999, April). A review of methodological characteristics of research published in *The Journal of Higher Education, The Review of Higher Education, and Research in Higher Education: Implications for graduate research training*. Paper presented at the annual meeting of the American Educational Research Association, Montreal, Canada.

Hymes, D. (1967). Models of the interaction of language and social setting. *Journal of Social Issues, 22*(2), 8–28.

Hymes, D. (Ed.). (1972). *Reinventing anthropology*. New York: Pantheon.

Irvine, L. (1998). Organizational ethics and fieldwork realities: Negotiating ethical boundaries in Codependents Anonymous. In S. Grills (Ed.), *Ethnographic research: Fieldwork settings* (pp. 167–183). Thousand Oaks, CA: Sage.

Isaac, S., & Michaels, W. B. (1984). *Handbook in research and evaluation* (2nd ed.). San Diego: Edits.

Jackson, B. (1987). *Fieldwork*. Urbana: University of Illinois Press.

Jacob, E. (1987). Qualitative research traditions: A review. *Review of educational research, 57*(1), 1–50.

Jacobs, S. E. (1980). Where have we come? *Social Problems, 27*, 371–378.

Janesick, V. J. (1999). A journal about journal writing as a qualitative research technique: History, issues, and reflections. *Qualitative Inquiry, 5*, 505–524.

Jayyusi, L. (1984). *Categorization and the moral order*. Boston: Routledge & Kegan Paul.

Jayyusi, L. (1991). The equivocal text and the objective world: An ethnomethodological analysis of a news report. *Continuum, 5*(1), 166–190.

Jefferson, G. (1984). On the organisation of laughter in talk about troubles. In J. M. Atkinson & J. Heritage (Eds.), *Structures of social action: Studies in conversation analysis* (pp. 346–369). Cambridge, UK: Cambridge University Press.

Jefferson, G. (1988). On the sequential organization of troubles-talk in ordinary conversation. *Social Problems, 35*(4), 418–441.

Jefferson, G. (1993). Caveat speaker: Preliminary notes on recipient topic-shift implicature. *Research on Language and Social Interaction, 26*, 1–30.

Jennings, M. (1999). Social theory and transformation in the pedagogy of Dr. Huey P. Newton: A nativist reclamation of the critical ethnographic project. *Educational Foundations, 13*(1), 77–94.

Jick, T. (1983). Mixing qualitative and quantitative methods: Triangulation in action. In J. Van Maanen (Ed.), *Qualitative methodology* (pp. 135–148). Beverly Hills, CA: Sage.

Johnson, G. C. (1999). Telling tales: A complicated narrative about courtship. *Narrative Inquiry, 9*(1), 1–23.

Johnson-Bailey, J. (1998). Black reentry women in the academy: Making a way out of no way. *Initiatives, 58*(4), 37–48.

Johnson-Bailey, J. (1999). The ties that bind and the shackles that separate: Race, gender, class, and color in a research process. *Qualitative Studies in Education, 12,* 659–670.

Johnson-Bailey, J. (2000). *Everyday perspectives on feminism: Black women speak out.* Unpublished manuscript.

Johnston, J. M., & Pennypacker, H. S. (1993). *Readings for strategies and tactics of behavioral research* (2nd ed.). Hillsdale, NJ: Lawrence Erlbaum Associates.

Jolliffe, F. R. (1986). *Survey design and analysis.* Chichester, UK: Horwood.

Jones, J. H. (1981). *Bad blood.* New York: Free Press.

Joseph, P. B., & Burnaford, G. E. (1994). *Images of schoolteachers in twentieth-century America: Paragons, polarities, complexities.* New York: St. Martin's.

Juhnke, G. A. (1997). After school violence: An adapted critical incident stress debriefing model for student survivors and their parents. *Elementary School Guidance & Counseling, 31*(3), 163–179.

Kaestle C. F., & Vinovskis, M. A. (1980). *Education and social change in nineteenth-century Massachusetts.* Cambridge, MA: Harvard University Press.

Kain, D. L. (1997). Teacher collaboration on interdisciplinary teams. *Research in Middle Level Education Quarterly, 21*(1), 1–29.

Kain, D. L., Tanner, M., & Raines, P. (1997). Integrated Secondary Teacher Education Program: On the edge of partnership. In S. D. Lapan & S. Minner (Eds.), *Monograph series: Perspectives: School–university partnerships* (pp. 39–72). Flagstaff, AZ: Center for Excellence in Education.

Karp, D. A. (1980). Observing behavior in public places: Problems and strategies. In W. B. Shaffir, R. A. Stebbins, & A. Turowetz (Eds.), *Fieldwork experience: Qualitative approaches to social research* (pp. 82–97). New York: St. Martin's.

Katz, M. (1968). *The irony of early school reform: Educational innovation in mid-nineteenth-century Massachusetts.* Cambridge, MA: Harvard University Press.

Kazdin, A. (1982). *Single-case research designs: Methods for clinical and Applied settings.* New York, NY: Oxford University Press.

Keppel, G. (1991). *Design and analysis: A researchers handbook* (3rd ed.). Englewood Cliffs, NJ: Prentice Hall.

Kerby, A. P. (1991). *Narrative and the self.* Bloomington: Indiana University Press.

Kerlinger, F. N. (1986). *Foundations of behavioral research* (2nd ed.). New York: Holt, Rinehart & Winston.

Kierkegaard, S. (1936). *Philosophical fragments* (D. Swenson, Trans.). Princeton, NJ: Princeton University Press. (Original work published 1844)

Kierkegaard, S. (1941). *Concluding unscientific postscript* (D. Swenson & W. Lowrie, Trans.). Princeton, NJ: Princeton University Press. (Original work published 1846)

Kierkegaard, S. (1980). *Concept of anxiety* (W. Lowire, Trans.). Princeton, NJ: Princeton University Press. (Original work published 1844)

Kincheloe, J., & McLaren, P. (1994). Rethinking critical theory and qualitative research. In N. K. Denzin & Y. S. Lincoln (Eds.), *Handbook of qualitative research* (pp. 138–157). London: Sage.

Kincheloe, J. S., Rodriguez, S., & Chennault, R. (1998). *White reign: Deploying Whiteness in America.* New York: St. Martin's.

Kirk, R. E. (1995). *Experimental design: Procedures for the behavioral sciences* (3rd ed.). Pacific Grove, CA: Brooks/Cole.

Kleiber, P. B. (1993). *Trajectories of opinions in focus group research: A comparative analysis.* Unpublished doctoral dissertation, University of Georgia, Athens.

Kliebard, H. (1986). *The struggle for the American curriculum, 1893–1958.* Boston: Routledge & Kegan Paul.

Knafl, K. A., & Breitmayer, B. J. (1989). Triangulation in qualitative research: Issues of conceptual clarity and purpose. In J. M. Morse (Ed.), *Qualitative nursing research: A contemporary dialogue* (pp. 209–220). Rockville, MD: Aspen.

Koppelman, K. L. (1983). The explication model: An anthropological approach to program evaluation. In G. Madaus, M. Scriven, & D. L. Stufflebeam (Eds.), *Evaluation models* (pp. 349–356). Boston: Kluwer-Nijhoff.

Kozol, J. (1967). *Death at an early age: The destruction of the hearts and minds of Negro children in the Boston public schools.* New York: New American Library.

Kramp, M. K. (1995). *Dropping a line into a creek and pulling out a whale: A phenomenological study of six teachers' experiences of their students' stories of learning.* Unpublished doctoral dissertation, University of Tennessee, Knoxville.

Kramp, M. K., & Humphreys, W. L. (1993). Narrative, self-assessment and the reflective learner. *College Teaching 41,* 83–88.

Krathwohl, D. R. (1998). *Methods of educational social science research.* New York: Longman.

Kreuger, R. A. (1994). *Focus groups: A practical guide for applied research,* (2nd ed.). Newbury Park, CA: Sage.

Kridel, C. (1998). *Writing educational biography: Explorations in qualitative research.* New York: Garland.

Krieger, S. (1985). Beyond "subjectivity": The use of self in social science. *Qualitative Sociology, 8,* 309–324.

Krueger, R. A. (1988). *Focus groups: A practical guide for applied research.* Newbury Park, CA: Sage.

Krueger, R. A., & Casey, M. A. (2000). *Focus groups: A practical guide for applied research.* Newbury Park, CA: Sage.

Krug, E. A. (1969). *The shaping of the American high school, 1880–1920.* Madison: University of Wisconsin Press.

Krug, E. A. (1972). *The shaping of the American high school, 1920–1941.* Madison: University of Wisconsin Press.

Kruskal, W. (1991). Introduction. In P. P. Biemer, R. M. Groves, L. E. Lyberg, N. A. Mathiowetz, & S. Sudman (Eds.), *Measurement errors in surveys.* New York: Wiley.

Kuhn, T. (1970). *The structure of scientific revolutions.* Chicago: University of Chicago Press.

Kvale, S. (1983). The qualitative interview: A phenomenological and a hermeneutical mode of understanding. *Journal of Phenomenological Psychology 25*(2), 147–173.

Kvale, S. (1995). The social construction of validity. *Qualitative Inquiry, 1*(1), 19–40.

Kvale, S. (1996). *Interviews: An introduction to qualitative research interviewing.* Thousand Oaks, CA: Sage.

Labaree, D. F. (1988). *The making of an American high school: The credentials market and the central high school of Philadelphia, 1838–1939.* New Haven, CT: Yale University Press.

Ladner, J. A. (1971). *Tomorrow's tomorrow: The Black woman.* Garden City, NY: Doubleday.

Ladwig, J. (1996). *Academic distinctions: Theory and methodology in the sociology of school knowledge.* New York: Routledge.

Lagemann, E. C. (1979). *Generations of women: Education in the lives of progressive reformers.* Cambridge, MA: Harvard University Press.

Lakoff, G., & Johnson, M. (1980). *Metaphors we live by.* Chicago: University of Chicago Press.

Lal, J. (1999). Situating locations: The politics of self, identity, and "Other" in living and writing the text. In S. Hesse-Biber, C. Gilmartin, & R. Lydenberg (Eds.), *Feminist approaches to theory and methodology: An interdisciplinary reader* (pp. 100–137). New York: Oxford University Press.

Langel, L. B. (1998). Researching the "Other," transforming ourselves: Methodological considerations of feminist ethnography. *Journal of Communication Inquiry, 22*(3), 229–250.

Langness, L. L., & Frank, G. (1986). *Lives: An anthropological approach to biography.* Novato, CA: Chandler & Sharp.

Lankeneau, S. E. (1999). Stronger than dirt: Public humiliation and status enhancement among panhandlers. *Journal of Contemporary Ethnography, 28*(3), 288–318.

Lareau, A., & Shultz, J. (Eds.). (1996). *Journeys through ethnography: Realistic accounts of fieldwork.* New York: Westview.

LaRossa, R., Bennett, L. A., & Gelles, R. J. (1981). Ethical dilemmas in qualitative research. *Journal of Marriage and the Family, 43*(2), 303–313.

Lather, P. (1986). Research as praxis. *Harvard Educational Review, 56,* 257–277.

Lather, P. (1986a). Issues of validity in openly ideological research: Between a rock and a soft place. *Interchange, 17*(4), 63–84.

Lather, P. (1986b). Research as praxis. *Harvard Educational Review, 56*(3), 257–277.

Lather, P. (1991). *Getting smart: Feminist research and pedagogy with/in the postmodern.* New York: Routledge.

Lather, P. (1992, October). *Feminism, methodology and the crisis of representation: Researching the lives of women with HIV/AIDS.* Paper presented at the Annual Conference of the Journal of Curriculum Theorizing, Dayton, OH.

Lather, P., & Smithies, C. (1997). *Troubling the angels: Women living with HIV/AIDS.* Boulder, CO: Westview.

Lawrence, J. (1992). Literacy and human resources development. *Annals of the American Academy of Political and Social Sciences, 520,* 42–53.

Lazerson, M. (1987). The origin of special education. In J. Chambers & W. Hartman (Eds.), *Special education policies: Their history, implementation, and finance.* Philadelphia, Temple University Press.

LeCompte, M. D. (1995). Some notes on power, agenda, and voice: A researcher's personal evolution toward critical collaborative research. In P. McLaren & J. Giarelli (Eds.), *Critical theory and educational research* (pp. 91–112). Albany: State University of New York Press.

LeCompte, M. D., & Geotz, J. P. (1982). Problems of reliability and validity in ethnographic research. *Review of Educational Research, 52,* 31–60.

LeCompte, M. D., & Preissle, J. (1993). *Ethnography and qualitative design in educational research* (2nd ed.). San Diego, CA: Academic.

LeCourt, D. (1975). *Marxism and epistemology.* London: National Labor Board.

Lee, C., & Jackson, R (1992). *Faking it: A look into the mind of a creative learner.* Portsmouth, NH: Heinemann.

Lemert, C. (1991). The end of ideology, really. *Sociological Theory, 9*(2), 164–172.

Lepper, G. (2000). *Categories in text and talk: Practical introduction to categorization analysis.* Thousand Oaks, CA: Sage.

Levine, L. W. (1996). *The opening of the American mind.* Boston: Beacon.

Lengel, L. B. (1998). Researching the "Other," transforming ourselves: Methodological considerations of feminist ethnography. *Journal of Communication Inquiry, 22*(3), 229–250.

Lincoln, Y. S. (1995). Emerging criteria for quality in qualitative and interpretive research. *Qualitative Inquiry, 1,* 275–289.

Lincoln, Y. S., & Guba, E. G. (1985). *Naturalistic inquiry.* Beverly Hills, CA: Sage.

Lincoln, Y. S., & Guba, E. G. (1989). Ethics: The failure of positivist science. *The Review of Higher Education, 12*(3), 221–240.

Lincoln, Y. S., & Guba, E. G. (1994). Competing paradigms in qualitative research. In K. D. Norman & S. L. Yvonna (Eds.), *Handbook of qualitative research* (pp. 105–117). Newbury Park, CA: Sage.

Linn, R. L. (1998). *Assessments and accountability.* Boulder: University of Colorado, Center for Research on Evaluation, Standards, and Student Testing.

Livingston, E. (1986). *The ethnomethodological foundations of mathematics.* London: Routledge & Kegan Paul.

Livingston, E. (1987). *Making sense of ethnomethodology.* London: Routledge & Kegan Paul.

Livingston, E. (2000). The availability of mathematics as an inspectable domain of practice through the use of origami. In S. Hester & D. Francis (Eds.), *Local educational order: Ethnomethodological studies of knowledge in action* (pp. 245–270). Amsterdam: Benjamins.

Lofland, J. H., & Lofland, L. H. (1994). *Analyzing social settings: A guide to qualitative observation and analysis* (3rd ed.). Belmont, CA: Wadsworth.

Lofland, J. H., & Lofland, L. H. (1995). *Analyzing social settings: A guide to qualitative observation and analysis* (3rd ed.). Belmont, CA: Wadsworth.

Lord, F. M. (1967). A paradox in the interpretation of group comparisons. *Psychological Bulletin, 72,* 336–337.

Lowe, R. (1996). Postmodernity and historians of education: A view from Britain. *Paedagogica Historica 32,* 307–324.

Lynch, M. (1993). *Scientific practice and ordinary action.* Cambridge, UK: Cambridge University Press.

Lynch, M., & Macbeth, D. (1998). Demonstrating physics lessons. In J. Greeno, & S. Goldman (Eds.), *Thinking Practices in Mathematics and Science Learning.* Mahwah, NJ: Lawrence Erlbaum Associates: 269–97.

Lyotard, J. (1984). The postmodern condition: A report on knowledge (G. Bennington & B. Massumi, Trans.). Minneapolis: University of Minnesota Press.

Madaus, G., Kellaghan, T., & Stufflebeam, D. L. (Eds.). (2000). *Evaluation models.* Boston: Kluwer.

Malinowsky, B. (1922). *Argonauts of the western Pacific: An account of native enterprise and adventure in the archipelagoes of Melanesian New Guinea.* New York: Dutton.

Mannheim, K. (1952). *Essays on the sociology of knowledge.* London: Routledge & Kegan Paul.

Marcus, G. (1995). The redesign of ethnography after the critique of its rhetoric. In R. Goodman & W. Fisher, (Eds.), *Rethinking knowledge: Reflections across the disciplines* (pp. 103–121). Albany: State University of New York Press.

Marcus, G., & Fisher, M. (1986). *Anthropology as cultural critique: An experimental moment in the human sciences*. Chicago: University of Chicago Press.

Mark, M. M., & Shotland, R. L. (1985). Stakeholder-based evaluation and value judgements. *Evaluation Review, 9*, 605–626.

Markowitz, R. (1993). *My daughter, the teacher: Jewish teachers in New York City schools*. New Brunswick, NJ: Rutgers University Press.

Marshall, C. M. (1997). *Feminist critical policy analysis I*. Washington, DC: Falmer.

Marshall, H. H., & Weinstein, R. S. (1986). Classroom context of student-perceived differential teacher treatment. *Journal of Educational Psychology, 78*, 441–453.

Martinez, M., & Poe, J. (1997, November 7). Doors open to disabled students: Court deal to boost mainstreaming in city's classrooms. *The Chicago Tribune*.

Maxwell, S. E., & Delaney, H. D. (1990). *Designing Experiments and Analyzing Data: A Model Comparison Perspective*. Belmont CA: Wadsworth Publishing Company.

May, R. A. B. (2001). The Sid Cartwright incident: An African American male's interpretive narrative of interracial encounters at the University of Chicago. *Studies in Symbolic Interaction, 24*, 75–100.

May, R. A. B., & Patillo-McCoy, M. (2000). Do you see what I see? Examining a collaborative ethnography. *Qualitative Inquiry, 6*(1), 65–87.

May, W. F. (1980). Doing ethics: The bearing of ethical theories on fieldwork. *Social Problems, 27*, 358–370.

Maynard, D. W. (1991). Bearing bad news in clinical settings. In B. Dervin (Ed.), *Progress in communication sciences* (pp. 143–172). Norwood, NJ: Ablex.

Maynard, D. W. (1992). On clinicians co-implicating recipients' perspective in the delivery of diagnostic news. In P. Drew & J. Heritage (Eds.), *Talk at work: Interaction in institutional settings* (pp. 331–358). Cambridge, UK: Cambridge University Press.

Maynard, D. W. (1996). On "realization" in everyday life: The forecasting of bad news as a social relation. *American Sociological Review, 61*, 109–131.

Mazeland, H., & ten Have, P. (1998). Essential tensions in (semi-)open research interviews. In I. Maso & F. Wester (Eds.), *The deliberate dialogue: Qualitative perspectives on the interview* (pp. 87–113). Brussels: VUB University Press.

McCadden, B., Dempsey, V., & Adkins, A. (1999). Critical research and narrative omniscience: Looking for researcher voice in the crisis of objectification. *Educational Foundation, 13*(1), 31–40.

McCall, M. M., & Becker, H. S. (1990). Performance science. *Problems, 37*(1), 117–132.

McCarthy, C., & Apple, M. (1988). Race, class, and gender in American educational research. Toward a nonsynchronous parallelist position. In L. Weis (Ed.), *Class race and gender in American education*. (pp. 9–39). Albany: State University of New York Press.

McCarthy, E. D. (1996). *Knowledge as culture: The new sociology of knowledge*. London: Routledge.

McCaslin, M., & Good, T. L. (1996). *Listening in classrooms*. New York: HarperCollins.

McClure, C. R., & Bertot, J. C. (1998). *Public library use in Pennsylvania: Identifying uses, benefits, and impacts. Final report*. (ERIC Reproduction Services Document No. ED419548). Harrisburg, PA: Pennsylvania State Department of Education.

McColskey, W. H., Altshuld, J. W., & Lawton, R. W. (1985). Predictors of principals' reliance on formal and informal sources of information. *Educational Evaluation and Policy Analysis, 7,* 427–436.

McCracken, G. (1988). *The long interview.* Beverly Hills, CA: Sage.

McEwan, H., & Egan, K. (Eds.). (1995). *Narrative in teaching, learning and research.* New York: Teachers College Press.

McHoul, A. (1978). The organization of turns at formal talk in the classroom. *Language in Society, 7,* 183–213.

McHoul, A. (1990). The organization of repair in classroom talk. *Language in Society, 19,* 349–377.

McHoul, A., & Watson, D. R. (1982). Two axes for the analysis of "comonsense" and " formal" geographical knowledge in the classroom. *British Journal of the Sociology of Education, 5,* 281–302.

McIntosh, P. (2000). White privilege and male privilege: A personal account of coming to see correspondences through working in women's studies. In L. Richardson, V. Taylor, & N. Whittier (Eds.), *Feminist frontier* (5th ed., pp. 29–36). Boston: McGraw-Hill.

McLaren, P. (1986). *Schooling as a ritual performance: Towards a political economy of educational symbols and gestures.* London: Routledge & Kegan Paul.

McNee, P., & Wood, B. (1993). Empowerment: Process still has problems. *Together, 38,* 26–27.

McRobbie, A. (1978). Working-class girls and the culture of femininity. In Centre for Contemporary Culture Studies (Ed.), *Women take issue: Aspects of women's subordination* (pp. 96–108). (Women Studies Group, University of Birmingham). London: Hutchinson.

McWilliam, E. (1992a). *Educative research in pre-service teacher education: Postpositivist possibilities.* Unpublished manuscript.

McWilliam, E. (1992b). *In broken images: A postpositivist analysis of student needs talk in pre-service teacher education.* Unpublished doctoral dissertation, University of Queensland, Australia.

Mead, G. H. (1934). *Mind, self, and society from the standpoint of a social behaviorist.* Chicago: University of Chicago Press.

Mead, M. (1949). *Male and female: A study of the sexes in a changing world.* New York: Morrow.

Mehan, H. (1979). *Learning lessons: Social organization in the classroom.* Cambridge, MA: Harvard University Press.

Mehan, H. (1991). The school's work of sorting students. In D. Boden & D. H. Zimmerman (Eds.), *Talk and social structure: Studies in ethnomethodology and conversation analysis* (pp. 71–90). Berkeley: University of California Press.

Mehan, H., & Wood, H. (1975). *The reality of ethnomethodology.* Malabar, FL: Krieger.

Mehta, R., & Sivadas, E. (1995). Comparing response rates and response content in mail versus electronic mail survey. *Journal of the Market Research Society, 37,* 429–439.

Mental Measurements Yearbook The, (14th ed.). (2001). Lincoln, NE: Buros Institute of Mental Measurements.

Mercier, L., & Murphy, M. (1991). Confronting the demons of feminist public history: Scholarly collaboration and community outreach. In S. B. Gluck & D. Patai (Eds.), *Women's words: The feminist practice of oral history* (pp. 175–187). New York: Routledge.

Merleau-Ponty, M. (1962). *The phenomenology of perception* (C. Smith, Trans.). London: Routledge & Kegan Paul. (Original work published 1945)

Merriam, S. (1998). *Qualitative research and case study applications in education.* San Francisco: Jossey-Bass.

Merton, R. K. (1972). Insiders and outsiders. *American Journal of Sociology, 77,* 9–47.

Merton, R. K. (1994). Insiders and outsiders: A chapter in the sociology of knowledge. In R. C. Monk (Ed.), *Taking sides: Clashing views on controversial issues in race and ethnicity* (pp. 4–14). Guilford, CT: Dushkin.

Merton, R. K., Fiske, M., & Kendall, P. L. (1990).*The focused interview: A manual of problems and procedures.* New York: Free Press. (Original work published 1956)

Merton, R. K., & Kendall, P. L. (1946). The focused interview. *American Journal of Sociology, 51,* 542–557.

Metsch, S. (1998). Chicago schools criticized: Unchallenging work and repetition seen. *Daily Southtown,* (p. 1).

Middleton, S. (1993). *Educating feminists: Life histories and pedagogy.* New York: Teachers College Press.

Miles, M., & Huberman, A. M. (1994). *Qualitative data analysis.* London: Sage.

Miller, W. L. (1983). *The survey method in the social and political sciences: Achievements, failures, prospects.* New York: St. Martin's.

Miron, L. (1996). *The social construction of urban schooling.* Cresskill, NJ: Hampton.

Mish, F. C. (1984). *Webster's ninth new collegiate dictionary.* Springfield, MA: Merriam-Webster.

Mishler, E. G. (1986). *Research interviewing: Context and narrative.* Cambridge, Hampton.

Mishler, E. G. (1979). Meaning in context. Is there any other kind? *Harvard Educational Review, 49*(1), 1–19.

Mitchell, J. T., & Everly, G. S. (1995). *Critical incident stress debriefing: An operations manual for the prevention of traumatic stress among emergency services and disaster workers* (2nd ed.). Baltimore, MD: Chevron.

Mitnick, D. G. (1996). *Critical incident stress debriefing.* Available: http:www.trauma-tir.com/cisd.htm

Mongia, P. (Ed.). (1996). *Contemporary postcolonial theory: A reader.* London: Arnold.

Monroe, P. (1940). *Founding of the American public school system: A history of education in the United States from the early settlements to the close of the Civil War period* New York: Macmillan.

Morgan, B. B., Jr., Glickman, A. S., Woodard, E. A., Blaiwes, A., & Salas, E. (1986). *Measurement of team behaviors in a navy environment* (NTSC Tech. Rep. No. 86–014). Orlando, FL: Naval Training Systems Center.

Morgan, D. L. (1988). *Focus groups as qualitative research.* Newbury Park, CA: Sage.

Morgan, D. L. (1993). *Successful focus groups: Advancing the state of the art.* Newbury Park, CA: Sage.

Morgan, D. L., & Spanish, M. T. (1984). Focus groups: A new tool for qualitative research. *Qualitative Sociology, 7,* 253–270.

Morrow, R., & Torres, C. (1998). Education and the reproduction of class, gender, and race: Responding to the postmodern challenge. In C. Torres & T. Mitchell (Eds.), *Sociology of education: Emerging perspectives* (pp. 19–46). Albany: State University of New York Press.

Moustakas, C. (1994). *Phenomenological research methods.* Thousand Oaks, CA: Sage.

Mullings, L. (1994). Images, ideology, and women of color. In M. B. Zinn & B. T. Dill (Eds.), *Women of color in U.S. society* (pp. 265–290). Philadelphia: Temple University Press.

Munro, P., & Bloom, L. R. (1995). Conflicts of selves: Nonunitary subjectivity in women administrators' life history narratives. In J. A. Hatch & R. Wisniewski (Eds.), *Life history and narrative* (pp. 99–112). London: Falmer Press.

Murillo, E. Jr. (1999). Mojado crossings along neoliberal borderlands. *Educational Foundations, 13*(1), 7–30.

Myerhoff, B. (Producer), & Littman, L. (Director). (1983). *Number our days.* [Video]. (Available from Direct Cinema Limited, P.O. Box 10003, Santa Monica, CA 90410-1003).

Myers, G. (2000). Analysis of conversation and talk. In M. W. Bauer & G. Gaskell (Eds.), *Qualitative researching with text, image and sound: A practical handbook* (pp. 191–206). London: Sage.

Nack, A. (2000). Damaged goods: Women managing the stigma of STDs. *Deviant behavior: An Interdisciplinary Journal, 21,* 95–121.

Nash, G., Crabtree, C., & Dunn, R. (1997). *History on trial: Culture wars and the teaching of the American past.* New York: Knopf.

National Commission for the Protection of Human Subjects of Biomedical and Behavioral Research (1978). *The Belmont Report: Ethical Principles and Guidelines for the Protection of Human Subjects of Research* (U.S. Department of Health, Education, and Welfare Publication No. [OS] 78-0012). Washington, DC: U.S. Department of Health, Education, and Welfare.

Naylor, G. (1988). *Mama day.* New York: Ticknor & Field.

Neale, J. (2000). Suicidal intent in non-fatal illicit drug overdose. *Addiction, 95*(1), 85–93. (*New Directions for Evaluation,* published by the American Evaluation Association).

Nelson, L. W. (1996). Hands in the chit'lins: Notes on native anthropological research among African American women. In G. Etter-Lewis & M. Foster (Eds.), *Unrelated kin: Race and gender in women's personal narratives* (pp. 183–200). New York: Routledge.

Nesbary, D. K. (2000). *Survey research and the World Wide Web.* Boston: Allyn & Bacon.

Nevo, D. (1983). The conceptualization of educational evaluation: An analytical review of the literature. *Review of Educational Research, 53*(1), 117–128.

New York City Schools, Office of Educational Evaluation. (1982). *The Promotional Gates Program: Mid-year assessment and analysis of January 1982, test results.* New York: Author.

New York City Schools, Office of Educational Evaluation. (1983). *The 1982–1983 Promotional Gates program: Mid-year assessment and analysis of August 1982 and January 1983, test results.* New York: Author.

Nias, J., & Groundwater-Smith, S. (1988). *The enquiring teacher.* London: Falmer.

Noblit, G. (1993). Power and caring. *American Educational Research Journal, 30*(1), 23–38.

Noblit, G. (1999). *Particularities: Collected essays one ethnography and education.* New York: Lang.

Noblit, G., & Eaker, D. (1989). Evaluation designs as political strategies. In J. Hannaway, & R. Crowson, (Eds), *The politics of reforming school administration* (pp. 127–138). New York: Falmer.

Noblit, G., & Hare, R. D. (1988). *Meta-ethnography: Synthesizing qualitative studies.* (Qualitative Research Methods Series). Newbury Park, CA: Sage.

Noddings, N. (1995). *Philosophy of education.* Boulder, CO: Westview.

Oakes, J. (1985). *Keeping track: How schools structure inequality.* New Haven, CT: Yale University Press.

Oakley, A. (1981). Interviewing women: A contradiction in terms. In H. Roberts (Ed.), *Doing feminist research* (pp. 30–61). New York: Routledge.

Ochs, E. (1979). Transcription as theory. In E. Ochs & B. Shieffelin (Eds.), *Developmental pragmatics* (pp. 43–72). New York: Academic.

O'Connor, F. W. (1979). The ethical demands of the Belmont Report. In C. B. Klockars & F. W. O'Connor (Eds.), *Deviance and decency: The ethics of research with human subjects* (pp. 225–260). Thousand Oaks, CA: Sage.

Oja, S. N., & Smulyan, L. (1989). *Collaborative action research: A developmental approach.* London: Falmer.

Oldfather, P., & Thomas, S. (1996a). *The changer and the changed: Student-initiated research on literacy motivation and schooling* (Reading Research Rep. No. 61). Athens, GA: National Reading Research Center.

Oldfather, P., & Thomas, S. (1996b). What does it mean when teachers participate in collaborative research with high school students on literacy notivations? (Reading Research Rep.). Athens, GA: National Reading Research Center.

Olson, K., & Shopes, L. (1991). Crossing boundaries, building bridges: Doing oral history among working-class women and men. In S. B. Gluck & D. Patai (Eds.), *Women's words: The feminist practice of oral history* (pp. 189–204). New York: Routledge.

Ormiston, G. (1990). Postmodern differends. In A. Dallery & C. Scott (Eds.), *Crisis in continental philosophy* (pp. 235–283). Albany: State University of New York Press.

Padillo, R. V. (1993). *HyperQual2* [Computer program]. Chandler, AZ: Author.

Palmieri, P. A. (1995). *In Adamless Eden: The community of women faculty at Wellesley.* New Haven, CT: Yale University Press.

Parker, L. (1992). Collecting data the e-mail way. *Training and Development, 46*, 52–54.

Patai, D. (1991). U.S. academics and third world women: Is ethical research possible? In S. B. Gluck & D. Patai (Eds.), *Women's words: The feminist practice of oral history* (pp. 137–153). New York: Routledge.

Patton, M. Q. (1990). *Qualitative evaluation and research methods* (2nd ed.). Newbury Park, CA: Sage.

Patton, M. Q. (2000). *Utilization-focused evaluation* (3rd ed.). Thousand Oaks, CA: Sage.

Patton, M. Q. (2002). *Qualitative research and evaluation methods.* (3rd ed.). Newbury Park, CA: Sage.

Patton, M., & Westby, C. (1992). Ethnography and research: A qualitative view. *Topics in Language Disorders, 12*(3), 1–14.

Paul J. L., & Marfo, K. (2001, Winter). Preparation of educational researchers in philosophical foundations of inquiry. *Review of Educational Research, 71*, 525–547.

Pavlov, I. P. (1927). Conditioned reflexes: An investigation of the psychological activity of the cerebral cortex. New York: Dover.

Payne, G. (1976). Making a lesson happen. In M. Hammersley & P. Woods (Eds.), *The process of schooling.* London: Routledge & Kegan Paul.

Pearl, A., & Knight, T. (1999). *The democratic classroom: Theory to inform practice.* Cresskill, NJ: Hampton.

Pedhazur, E. J., & Schmelkin, L. P. (1991). *Measurement, design, and analysis: An integrated approach.* Hillsdale, NJ: Lawrence Erlbaum Associates.

Pelto, P. J. (1970). *Anthropological research: The structure of inquiry.* New York: Harper & Row.

Perlmann, J. (1988). *Ethnic differences, schooling and social structure among the Irish, Italians, Jews, and Blacks in an American city, 1880–1935.* Cambridge, MA: Harvard University Press.

Perlstein, D. (1997). Community and democracy in American schools: Arthurdale and the fate of progressive education. *Teachers College Record, 97*, 625–650.

Perlstein, D. (2000). Imagined authority: *Blackboard Jungle* and the project of educational liberalism, *Paedagogica Historica, 36,* 407–426.

Peshkin, A. (1988). In search of subjectivity—one's own. *Educational Researcher, 17*(7), 17–22.

Phillips, D. C. (1990). Post-positivistic science: Myths and realities. In E. Guba (Ed.), *The paradigm dialog* (pp. 31–45). Newbury Park, CA: Sage.

Pick, G. (1998, April). Strict retention comes, goes, LA, NYC wary. *Catalyst* IX (7), pp. 8–9.

Platt, J. (1995). Research methods and the second Chicago school. In G. A. Fine (Ed.), *A second Chicago school? The development of postwar American sociology* (pp. 82–107). Chicago: University of Chicago Press.

Polkinghorne, D. E. (1983). *Methodology for the human sciences: Systems of inquiry.* Albany: State University of New York Press.

Polkinghorne, D. E. (1988). *Narrative knowing and the human sciences.* Albany: State University of New York Press.

Polkinghorne, D. E. (1989). Phenomenological research methods. In R. S. Valle & S. Halling (Eds.), *Existential–phenomenological perspectives in psychology* (pp. 41–60). New York: Plenum.

Polkinghorne, D. E. (1995). Narrative configuration in qualitative analysis. In J. A. Hatch & R. Wisniewski (Eds.), *Life history and narrative* (pp. 3–25). London: Falmer.

Pollio, H. R., Henley, T., & Thompson, C. B. (1997). *The phenomenology of everyday life.* New York: Cambridge University Press.

Pomerantz, A. (1984). Agreeing and disagreeing with assessments: Some features of preferred/dispreferred turn shapes. In J. M. Atkinson & J. Heritage (Eds.), *Structures of social action: Studies in conversation analysis* (pp. 57–101). Cambridge, UK: Cambridge University Press.

Pomerantz, A., & Fehr, B. J. (1997). Conversation analysis: An approach to the study of social action as sense making practices. In T. A. van Dijk (Ed.), *Discourse as social interaction* (pp. 64–91). London: Sage.

Popham, W. J. (1988). *Educational evaluation* (2nd ed.). Englewood Cliffs, NJ: Prentice Hall.

Popkewitz, T. (1995). Foreword. In P. McLaren & J. Giarelli, (Eds.), *Critical theory and educational research.* Albany: State University of New York Press.

Popkewitz, T. (1998). The sociology of knowledge and the sociology of education: Michel Foucault and critical traditions. In C. A., Torres, & T. Mitchell, (Eds.), *Sociology of education: Emerging perspectives* (pp. 47–90). Albany: State University of New York Press.

Popper, K. (1972). *Objective knowledge.* Oxford, UK: Oxford University Press.

Porter, A. C. (1997). Comparative experiments in educational research. In R. Jaeger (Ed.), *Complementary methods for research in education* (2nd ed., pp. 523–551). Washington, DC: American Educational Research Association.

Poster, M. (1989). *Critical theory and poststructuralism: In search of a context.* Ithaca, NY: Cornell University Press.

Poster, M. (1990). *The mode of information: Poststructuralism and social context.* Chicago: University of Chicago Press.

Provenzo, E. (1999). *Culture as curriculum: Education and the international expositions, 1876–1940.* New York: Lang.

Provus, M. M. (1971). *Discrepancy evaluation.* Berkeley, CA: McCutchan.

Prus, R. (1996). *Symbolic interaction and ethnographic research: Intersubjectivity and the study of human lived experience.* Albany: State University of New York Press.

Psathas, G. (1995). *Conversation analysis: The study of talk-in-interaction*. Thousand Oaks, CA: Sage.

Psathas, G., & Anderson, T. (1990). The "practices" of transcription in conversation analysis. *Semiotica, 78*, 75–99.

Punch, M. (1994). Politics and ethics in qualitative research. In N. K. Denzin & Y. S. Lincoln (Eds.), *Handbook of qualitative research* (pp. 83–97). Thousand Oaks, CA: Sage.

Quantz, R. (1992). Interpretive method in historical research: Ethnohistory reconsidered. In R. Altenbaugh (Ed.), *The teacher's voice: A social history of teaching* (pp. 174–190). London: Falmer.

Quantz, R. (1992). On critical ethnography (with some postmodern considerations). In *The handbook of qualitative research* (pp. 447–505). New York: Academic.

Quinby, L. (1991). *Freedom, Foucault, and the subject of America*. Boston: Northeastern University Press.

Rahilly, T. J., & Saroyan, A. (1997, March). *Characterizing poor and exemplary teaching in higher education: Implications for faculty development* (ERIC Reproduction Services Document No. ED410806). Paper presented at the annual meeting of the American Educational Research Association, Chicago.

Rapley, M., & Antaki, C. (1998). "What do you think about . . . ?" Generating views in an interview. *Text, 18*, 587–608.

Rapley, T. J. (2001). The art(fulness) of open-ended interviewing: Some considerations on analysing interviews. *Qualitative Research, 1*, 303–323.

Rawls, A. W. (2002). Editor's introduction. In H. Garfinkel. *Ethnomethodology's program: Working out Durkheim's aphorism* (pp. 1–64). Lanham, MD: Rowman & Littlefield.

Rea, L. M., & Parker, R. A. (1997). *Designing and conducting survey research: A comprehensive guide* (2nd ed.). San Francisco: Jossey-Bass.

Reichardt, C. S., & Rallis, S. F. (1994). *The qualitative–quantitative debate: New perspectives*. San Francisco: Jossey-Bass.

Reinharz, S. (1979). *On becoming a social scientist: From survey research and participant observation to experiential analysis*. San Francisco: Jossey-Bass.

Reinharz, S. (1986). The social psychology of a miscarriage: An application of symbolic interaction theory and method. In M. J. Deegan & M. R. Hill (Eds.), *Women and symbolic interaction* (pp. 229–249). New York: Allen & Unwin.

Reinharz, S. (1992). *Feminist methods in social research*. New York: Oxford University Press.

Repp, A. C., & Horner, R. H. (1999). *Functional analysis of problem behavior: From effective assessment to effective support*. Belmont, CA: Wadsworth.

Richardson, L. (1992). The consequences of poetic representation: Writing the other, rewriting the self. In C. Ellis & M. Flasherty (Eds.), *Windows on lived experience* (pp. 125–140). Newbury Park, CA: Sage.

Richardson, L. (1993). Poetics, dramatics, and transgressive validity: The case of the skipped line. *Sociological Quarterly, 35*, 695–710.

Richardson, L., & Lockridge, E. (1998). Fiction and ethnography: A conversation. *Qualitative Inquiry, 4*(3), 328–336.

Richardson, M. (1990). *Cry lonesome and other accounts of the anthropologist's project*. Albany: State University of New York Press.

Richardson, T. (1996). Ambiguities in the lives of children: Postmodern views on the history and historiography of childhood in English Canada. *Paedagogica Historica, 32*, 363–394.

Ricouer, P. (1988). *Time and narrative*, (Vol. 3, K. B. Pellauer & D. Pellauer, Trans.). Chicago: University of Chicago Press.

Riessman, C. K. (1987, June). When gender is not enough: Women interviewing women. *Gender & Society, 2*, 172–207.

Riessman, C. K. (1993). *Narrative Analysis*. Newbury Park, CA: Sage.

Riley, D. (1988). *"Am I that name?" Feminism and the category of "women" in history*. Minneapolis: University of Minnesota Press.

Rimmon-Kenan, S. (1983). *Narrative fiction: Contemporary poetics*. London: Methuen.

Riverside Press. *Test purchaser qualification form*. Itasca, IL: Author.

Roderick, M. (1994). Grade retention and school dropout: Investigating the association. *American Educational Research Journal, 31*(4), 729–759.

Ronai, C. R. (1992). The reflexive self through narrative: A night in the life of an erotic dancer/researcher. In C. Ellis & M. G. Flaherty (Eds.), *Investigating subjectivity: Research on lived experience* (pp. 102–124). Newbury Park, CA: Sage.

Rorty, R. (1979). *Philosophy and the mirror of nature*. Princeton, NJ: Princeton University Press.

Rorty, R. (Ed.). (1967). *The linguistic turn: Recent essays in philosophical method*. Chicago: University of Chicago Press.

Rosaldo, R. (1989). *Culture and truth: The remaking of social analysis*. Boston: Beacon.

Rosenberg, R. (1982). *Beyond separate spheres: Intellectual roots of modern feminism*. New Haven: Yale University Press.

Rosenau, P. (1992). *Post-modernism and the social sciences: Insights, inroads, and intrusions*. Princeton, NJ: Princeton University Press.

Rosenblatt, P. C. (1995). Ethics of qualitative interviewing with grieving families. *Death Studies, 19*, 139–155.

Ross, E. W., Cornett, J. W., & McCutcheon, G. (Eds.). (1992). *Teacher personal theorizing*. Albany: State University of New York Press.

Rossi, P. H. (1994). The war between the quals and the quants: Is a lasting peace possible? In C. S. Reichardt, & S. F. Rallis (Eds.), *The qualitative–quantitative debate: New perspectives* (pp. 23–36). San Francisco: Jossey-Bass.

Rossi, P. H., & Freeman, H. E. (1993). *Evaluation: A systematic approach* (5th ed.). Newbury Park, CA: Sage.

Rossman, G. B., & Rallis, S. F. (1998). *Learning in the field: An introduction to qualitative research*. Thousand Oaks, CA: Sage.

Rossman, G. B., & Wilson, B. L. (1985). Numbers and words: Combining quantitative and qualitative methods in a single large-scale evaluation. *Evaluation Review, 9*, 627–643.

Rossman, G. B., & Wilson, B. L. (1994). Numbers and words revisited: Being shamelessly eclectic. *Quality & Quantity, 28*, 317–327.

Roulston, K. (2000a). *Itinerant music teachers' work in Queensland*. Unpublished doctoral dissertation, University of Queensland, Brisbane, Australia.

Roulston, K. (2000b). The management of "safe" and "unsafe" complaint sequences in research interviews. *Text, 20*(3), 1–39.

Rousmaniere, K. (1997). *City teachers: Teaching and school reform in historical perspective*. New York: Teachers College Press.

Rousmaniere, K., Dehli, K., & deConinck-Smith, N. (Eds.) (1997). *Discipline, moral regulation and schooling: A social history*. New York: Garland Press.

Rousmaniere, K. (2000). From Memory to Curriculum. *Teaching Education*, *11*, 87–98.

Rowland, S. (1988). My body of knowledge. In J. Nias & S. Groundwater-Smith (Eds.), *The enquiring teacher*. London: Falmer.

Rubin, H. J., & Rubin, I. S. (1995). *Qualitative interviewing: The art of hearing data*. Thousand Oaks, CA: Sage.

Rubin, L. B. (1976). *Worlds of pain: Life in the working-class family*. New York: Basic Books.

Rugh, J. (1986). *Self evaluation: Ideas for participatory evaluation of rural community development projects*. Oklahoma City, OK: World Neighbors.

Russell, D. E. H. (1996). Between a rock and a hard place: The politics of White feminists conducting research on Black women in South Africa. In S. Wilkinson & C. Kitzinger (Eds.), *Representing the other: A feminism & psychology reader* (pp. 89–93). Thousand Oaks, CA: Sage.

Ryan, J. (1992). Literacy research, policy, and practice. *Annals of the American Academy of Political and Social Sciences*, *520*, 36–41.

Rymes, B., & Pash, D. (2001). Questioning identity: The case of one second-language learner. *Anthropology and Education Quarterly*. *32* (3), 276–300.

Ryndar, R. (1997, August 25). Suburban schools are leery of making kids repeat grade. *The Chicago Tribune*, p. 1.

Sacks, H. (1972). An initial investigation of the usability of conversation data for doing sociology. In D. Sudnow (Ed.), *Studies in social interaction* (pp. 31–74). New York: The Free Press.

Sacks, H. (1992). *Lectures on conversation*. Oxford, UK: Blackwell.

Sacks, H., Schegloff, E. A., & Jefferson, G. (1974). A simplest systematics for the organization of turn-taking for conversation. *Language*, *50*, 696–735.

Sandlin v. Johnson, 643 F.2d 1027 (4th Cir. 1981). Argued Nov. 14, 1980. Decided March 11, 1981.

Sarbin, T. R. (Ed.). (1986). *Narrative psychology: The storied nature of human conduct*. New York: Praeger.

Saussure, Ferdinand de. (1959). Nature of the linguistic sign. (W. Baskin, Trans.) In Charles Bally & Albert Sechehaye (Eds.), Course in general linguistics (pp. 65–70). New York: Philosophical Library.

Schatzman, L., & Strauss, A. L. (1973). *Field research: Strategies for a natural sociology*. Englewood Cliffs, NJ: Prentice Hall.

Schegloff, E. A., & Sacks, H. (1973). Opening up closings. *Semiotica*, *8*, 289–327.

Schensul, S. L. (1980). Anthropological fieldwork and sociopolitical change. *Social Problems*, *27*, 309–319.

Scheper-Hughes, N. (1992). *Death without weeping: The violence of everyday life in Brazil*. Berkeley: University of California Press.

Scheurich, J. (1997). *Research method in the postmodern*. London: Falmer.

Scheurich, J., & Young, M. (1997). Coloring epistemologies: Are our research epistemologies racially biased? *Educational Researcher*, *26*(4), 4–16.

Schubert, W. H., & Ayers, W. C. (Eds.). (1992). *Teacher lore: Learning from our own experience*. New York: Longman.

Schutz, A., & Luckmann, T. (1973). *The structures of the life-world*. Evanston, IL: Northwestern University Press.

Schwandt, T. A. (1996). Farewell to criteriology. *Qualitative Inquiry*, *2*(1), 58–72.

Schwartz, N. (1999). Self-reports: How the questions shape the answers. *American Psychologist, 54*(2), 93–105.

Schwarz, N., Groves, R. M., & Schuman, H. (1998). Survey methods. In D. T. Gilbert, S. T. Fiske, & G. Lindzey (Eds.), *The handbook of social psychology* (Vol. 1). New York: McGraw-Hill.

Scharwz, N., Park, D. C., Knäuper, B., & Sudman, S. (1999). Cognition, aging, and self-reports: Editors' introduction. In N. Schwarz, D. Park, B. Knäuper, & S. Sudman (Eds.), *Cognition, aging, and self-reports*. Philadelphia: Psychology Press.

Schloss, P. J., & Smith, M. A. (1994). *Applied behavior analysis in the classroom*. Boston, MA: Allyn & Bacon.

Scott, J. (1999). The evidence of experience. In S. Hesse-Biber, C. Gilmartin, & R. Lydenberg (Eds.), *Feminist approaches to theory and methodology: An interdisciplinary reader* (pp. 79–99). New York: Oxford University Press.

Scriven, M. (1967). The methodology of evaluation. *AERA Monograph Series in Curriculum Evaluation, 1*, 39–83.

Scriven, M. (1969). An introduction to meta-evaluation. *Education Product Report, 2*(5), 36–38.

Scriven, M. (1973). Goal-free evaluation. In E. R. House (Ed.), *School evaluation: The politics and process* (pp. 319–328). Berkley, CA: McCutchan.

Scriven, M. (1974). Evaluation perspectives and procedures. In J. W. Popham (Ed.), *Evaluation in education* (pp. 1–95). Berkeley, CA: McCutchan.

Scriven, M. (1983). Evaluation ideologies. In G. F. Madaus, M. Scriven, & D. L. Stufflebeam (Eds.), *Evaluation models* (pp. 229–260). Boston: Kluwer-Nijhoff.

Seale, C. (1999). *The quality of qualitative research*. London: Sage.

Seidman, S. (1995). Deconstructing queer theory or the under-theorization of the social and the ethical. In L. Nicholson, & S. Seidman, (Eds.), *Social postmodernism: Beyond identity politics* (pp. 116–141). Cambridge, UK: Cambridge University Press.

Senge, P. (1990). *The fifth discipline: The art and practice of the learning organization*. New York: Doubleday.

Seretny, M. L., & Dean, R. S. (1986) Interspersed post passage questions and reading comprehension achievement. *Journal of Educational Psychology, 78*, 228–229.

Shadish, W., Cook, T., & Leviton, L. (1995). *Foundations of program evaluation*. Thousand Oaks, CA: Sage.

Shani, D. O., & Perkins, M. (1991). *Participation in development* (World Vision Working Paper No. 12).

Sharrock, W. W., & Anderson, B. (1986). *The ethnomethodologists*. Chichester, UK: Horwood.

Sharrock, W. W., & Ikeya, N. (2000). Instructional matter: Readable properties of an introductory text in matrix algebra. In S. Hester & D. Francis (Eds.), *Local educational order: Ethnomethodological studies of knowledge in action* (pp. 271–288). Amsterdam: Benjamins.

Shepard, L. A., & Smith, M. L. (1989). *Flunking grades*. London: Falmer Press.

Shepard, L. A., & Smith, M. L. (1990). Synthesis of research on grade retention. In *Educational Leadership, 48*, 84–88.

Shepard, L. A., Smith, M. L., & Marion, S. F. (1996). Failed evidence on grade retention. *Psychology in the Schools, 33*, 251–261.

Silverman, D. (1997). Towards an aesthetics of research. In D. Silverman (Ed.), *Qualitative research: Theory, method and practice* (pp. 239–253). London: Sage.

Silverman, D. (1998). *Harvey Sacks: Social science and conversation analysis*. Cambridge, UK: Polity.

Silverman, D., & Gubrium, J. F. (1994). Competing strategies for analyzing the contexts of social interaction. *Sociological Inquiry, 64*(2), 179–198.

Simon, R., & Dippo, D. (1986). On critical ethnographic work. *Anthropology and Education Quarterly, 17*, 195–202.

Skinner, B. F. (1953). Science and human behavior. New York: Macmillian.

Slavin, R. E. (1989). PET and the pendulum: Faddism in education and how to stop it. *Phi Delta Kappan, 70*, 752–758.

Slavin, R. E. (1992). *Research methods in education*. (2nd ed.) Boston: Allyn & Bacon.

Sleeter, C. (1998). Activist or ethnographer? Researchers, teachers, and voice in ethnographies that critique. In K. B. deMarrais (Ed.), *Inside stories: Qualitative research reflections* (pp. 49–58). Mahwah, NJ: Lawrence Erlbaum Associates.

Smith, D. E. (1987). *The everyday world as problematic: A feminist sociology*. Boston: Northeastern University Press.

Smith, F. (1998). Behind the lines: Lives of loss. *Journal for a Just and Caring Education, 4*, 253–283.

Smith, J. K. (1983). Quantitative versus qualitative research: An attempt to clarify the issue. *Educational Researcher, 12*, 6–13.

Smith, J. K., & Heshusius, L. (1986). Closing down the conversation: The end of the quantitative–qualitative debate among educational researchers. *Educational Researcher, 15*, 4–12.

Smith, M. L. (1989). Teachers' beliefs about retention. In L. A. Shepard, & M. L. Smith (Eds.), *Flunking grades: Research and policies on retention* (pp. 132–150). London: Falmer.

Spindler, G. (Ed.). (1982). *Doing the ethnography of schooling: Educational anthropology in action*. New York: Holt, Rinehart & Winston.

Spradley, J. P. (1980). *Participant observation*. New York: Holt, Rinehart & Winston.

Srinivasan, L. (1992). *Options for educators: A monograph for decision makers on alternative participatory strategies*. New York: PACT/CDS.

Stacey, J. M., & Thorne, B. (1985). The missing feminist revolution in sociology. *Social Problems, 32*, 301–316.

Stake, R. (1976). *Evaluating educational programmes*. Washington, DC: OECD Publications Center.

Stake, R. (1983). Program evaluation, particularly responsive evaluation. In G. F. Madaus, M. Scriven, & D. L. Stufflebeam (Eds.), *Evaluation models* (pp. 287–310). Boston: Kluwer-Nijhoff.

Stake, R. E. (1995). *The art of case study research*. Thousand Oaks, CA: Sage.

Stake, R. E. (2000). Case Studies. In N. Denzin, & Y. Lincoln (Eds.), *The Handbook of Qualitative Research*. Thousand Oaks: Sage.

Stano, M. (1983, April 7–9). *The critical incident technique: A description of the method* (ERIC Reproduction Services Document No. ED232219). Paper presented at the annual meeting of the Southern Speech Communication Association, Lincoln, NE.

Stenhouse, L. (1971). Humanities curriculum project: The rationale. *Theory Into Practice, 10*(3), 154–162.

Stewart, D. S., & Shamdasani, P. N. (1990). Focus groups: Theory and practice. *Applied Social Research Methods Series*. Newbury Park CA: Sage.

Stewart, D. W., & Shamdasani, P. N. (1990). *Focus groups: Theory and practice*. Newbury Park, CA: Sage.

Stone, L. (1995). Feminist educational research and the issue of critical sufficiency. In P. McLaren, & J. Giarelli, (Eds.), *Critical theory and educational research* (pp. 145–162). Albany: State University of New York Press.

St. Pierre, E. A. (1997). Methodology in the fold and the irruption of transgressive data. *Qualitative Studies in Education, 10*(2), 175–189.

Stufflebeam, D. L. (1966). A depth study of the evaluation requirement. *Theory Into Practice, 5*, 121–134.

Stufflebeam, D. L., & Webster, W. J. (1980). An analysis of evaluation. *Educational Evaluation and Policy Analysis, 3*(2), 5–19.

Suchman, L. (1987). *Plans and situated actions*. Cambridge, England: Cambridge University Press.

Sudman, S., & Bradburn, N. M. (1987). *Asking questions: A practical guide to questionnaire design*. San Francisco: Jossey-Bass.

Sulzer-Azaroff, B., & Mayer, G. R. (1991). *Behavior Analysis for lasting change*. Fort Worth, TX: Harcourt Brace.

Sustainable Agriculture Programme. (1988–1991). *RRA notes*. London: IIED.

Swenson, J., W. G., & Kleiber, P. (1992, November). Focus groups: A qualitative method of inquiry/intervention. *Small Group Research, 23*, 459–474.

Tappan, M. B., & Brown, L. M. (1991). Stories told and lessons learned: Toward a narrative approach to moral development and moral education. In C. Witherell & N. Noddings, (Ed.) *Stories lives tell: Narrative and dialogue in education* (pp. 171–192). New York: Teachers College Press.

Tashakkori, A., & Teddlie, C. (1998). *Mixed methodology: Combining qualitative and quantitative approaches*. Thousand Oaks, CA: Sage.

Tawney, J. W., & Gast, D. L. (1984). *Single-subject research in special education*. Columbus, OH: Merrill.

Templeton, J. T. (1988). *Focus groups: A guide for marketing and advertising professionals*. Chicago: Probus.

ten Have, P. (1999). *Doing conversation analysis: A practical guide*. London: Sage.

Theobald, M. (1996). *Call school: Rural education in the Midwest to 1918*. Carbondale: Southern Illinois University Press.

Thomas, J. (1993). *Doing critical ethnography* (Qualitative Research Methods Series). London: Sage.

Thompson, C. J., Locander, W. B., & Pollio, H. R. (1989). Putting consumer experience back into consumer research: The philosophy and method of existential phenomenology. *Journal of Consumer Research 16*(2), 133–146.

Thompson, D. (1999, February 22). Real knife, fake surgery, *Time*, 66.

Thompson, S. B. (1980). Do individualized mastery and traditional instructional systems yield different course effects in college calculus? *American Educational Research Journal, 17*(3), 361–375.

Thorne, B. (1978). Political activist as participant observer: Conflicts of commitment in a study of the draft resistance movement of the 1960s. *Symbolic Interaction, 2*, 73–88.

Thorne, B. (1980). "You still takin' notes?" Fieldwork and problems of informed consent. *Social Problems, 27*, 284–297.

Toews, J. (1987). Intellectual history after the linguistic turn: The autonomy of meaning and the irreducibility of experience. *The American Historical Review, 92*, 879–907.

Tolley, K. (1996). Science for ladies, classics for gentlemen: A comparative analysis of scientific subjects in the curricula of boys' and girls' secondary schools in the United States, 1974–1850. *History of Education Quarterly, 36*, 129–154.

Torres, C., & Mitchell, T. (1998). *Sociology of education: Emerging perspectives.* Albany: State University of New York Press.

Tourangeau, R. (1987). Attitude measurement: A cognitive perspective. In H. J. Hippler, N. Schwarz, & S. Sudman (Eds.), *Social information processing and survey methodology* (pp. 149–162). New York: Springer-Verlag.

Tourangeau, R., & Rasinski, K. A. (1988). Cognitive processes underlying context effects in attitude measurement. *Psychological Bulletin, 103*, 299–314.

Tourangeau, R., Rasinski, K. A., Bradburn, N., & D'Andrade, R. (1989). Carryover effects in attitude surveys. *Public Opinion Quarterly, 53*, 495–524.

Tourangeau, R., Rip, L. J., & Rasinski, K. (2000). *The psychology of survey response.* New York: Cambridge University Press.

Trend, M. G. (1980). Applied social research and the government: Notes on the limits of confidentiality. *Social problems, 27*, 342–349.

Tripp, D. (1993). *Critical incidents in teaching: Developing professional judgment.* London: Routledge.

Tuchman, G. (1994). Historical social science: Methodologies, methods, and meanings. In N. K. Denzin & Y. S. Lincoln (Eds.), *Handbook of qualitative research* (pp. 306–323). Thousand Oaks, CA: Sage.

Tunnell, K. D. (1998). Interviewing the incarcerated: Personal notes on ethical and methodological issues. In K. B. deMarrais (Ed.), *Inside stories: Qualitative research reflections* (pp. 127–138). Mahwah, NJ: Lawrence Erlbaum Associates.

Turner, J. T., & Meyer, D. K. (1999). Integrating classroom context into motivation theory and research: Rationales, methods and implications. In M. L. Maehr & P. R. Pintrich (Eds.), *Advances in motivation and achievement* (pp. 87–121). Samford, CT: JAI.

Turner, V. W., & Bruner, E. M. (Eds.). (1986). *The anthropology of experience.* Urbana, IL: University of Chicago Press.

Tyack, D., & Cuban, L. (1995). *Tinkering toward utopia: A century of public school reform.* Cambridge, MA: Harvard University Press.

Tyler, R. (1949). *Basic principles of curriculum and instruction.* Chicago: University of Chicago Press.

Van de Vijver, F., & Hambleton, R. K. (1996). Translating tests: Some practical guidelines. *European Psychologist, 1*, 89–99.

Van Maanen, J. (1988). *Tales of the field: On writing ethnography.* Chicago: University of Chicago Press.

Van Manen, M. (1990). *Researching lived experience: Human science for an action-sensitive pedagogy.* Albany: State University of New York Press.

Vaughn-Roberson, C. (1992). Having a purpose in life: Western women teachers in the 20th century. In R. Altenbaugh (Ed.). *The teachers' voice: A social history of teaching.* London: The Falmer Press.

Vaz, K. M. (Ed.) (1997). *Oral narrative research with Black women.* Thousand Oaks, CA: Sage.

Velazquez, L. C. (1998). Personal reflections on the process: The role of the researcher and transformative research. In K. B. deMarrais (Ed.), *Inside stories: Qualitative research reflections* (pp. 59–66). Mahwah, NJ: Lawrence Erlbaum Associates.

Velody, I., & Williams, R. (Eds.). (1998). *The politics of constructionism.* London: Sage.

Voorhies, S. (1993). Development is participation. *Together, 38,* 14–15.

Warren, J. (1999). Whiteness and cultural theory: Perspectives on research and education. *The Urban Review, 31*(2), 185–203.

Watson, J. B., & Rayner, R. (1920). Conditioned emotional reactions. *Journal of Experimental Psychology, 3,* 1–14.

Wax, R. (1971). *Doing fieldwork: Warnings and advice.* Chicago: University of Chicago Press.

Webb, B. (1926). *My apprenticeship.* New York: Longmans, Green.

Weiler, J. D. (2000). *Codes and contradictions: Race, gender identity, and schooling.* Albany: State University of New York Press.

Weiler, K. (1992). Remembering and representing life choices: A critical perspective on teachers' oral history narratives. *Qualitative Studies in Education, 5*(1), 39–50.

Weiler, K. (1998). Country Schoolwomen: Teaching in Rural California, 1850–1950. Stanford, CA: Stanford University Press.

Weis, L. (1995). Constructing the "Other": Discursive renditions of White working-class males in high school. In P. McLaren, & M. Giarelli, (Eds.), *Critical theory and educational research* (pp. 203–222). Albany: State University of New York Press.

Weis, L., & Fine, M. (1993). *Beyond silenced voices: Class, race, and gender in U.S. schools.* Albany: State University of New York Press.

Weisberg, H. F., & Bowen, B. D. (1977). *An introduction to survey research and data analysis.* San Francisco: Freeman.

Weiss, C. H. (1983, April). *Curriculum commonplaces and the evaluation counterparts.* Paper presented at the annual meeting of the American Educational Research Association, Montreal.

Weiss, R. (1994). *Learning from strangers: The art and method of qualitative interview studies.* New York: Free Press.

Welter, R. (1962). *Popular education and democratic thought in America.* New York: Columbia University Press.

Wexler, P. (1987). *Social analysis of education: After the new sociology.* New York: Routledge.

White, H. (1981). The value of narrativity in the representation of reality. In W. J. T. Mitchell (Ed.), *On narrative* (pp. 1–23). Chicago: University of Chicago Press.

White, K. A. (1999). NRC report calls for voucher experiment. *Education Week, 17*(2), 3.

White, O. R. & Haring, N. G. (1980). Exceptional teaching (2nd ed.). Columbus, OH: Merrill.

Whitford, M. (1991). *Luce Irigaray: Philosophy in the feminine.* London: Routledge.

Whyte, W. (1984). *Learning from the field: A guide from experience.* Beverly Hills, CA: Sage.

Whyte, W. F. (1991). Introduction. In W. F. Whyte (Ed.), *Participatory action research* (pp. 7–19). Newbury Park, CA: Sage.

Wieder, A. (1992). One who left and one who stayed: Teacher recollections and reflections of school desegregation in New Orleans. In R. Altenbaugh (Ed.), *The teacher's voice: A social history of teaching* (pp. 107–120). London: Falmer.

Wieder, A. (1997). *Race and education: Narrative essays, oral histories, and documentary photography.* New York: Lang.

Wilgoren, D. (1999, Sept. 27). Taking a chance on promotion. *The Washington Post*, pp. B1, B5.

Wilkinson, S., & Kitzinger, C. (Eds.). (1996). *Representing the other: A feminism and psychology reader*. Thousand Oaks, CA: Sage.

Willinsky, J. (1998). *Learning to divide the world*. Minneapolis: University of Minnesota Press.

Willis, P. (1977). *Learning to labour: How working-class kids get working-class jobs*. Farnborough, England: Saxon House.

Wilson, W. J. (1987). *The truly disadvantaged*. Chicago: University of Chicago Press.

Witherell, C., & Noddings, N. (Eds.). (1991). *Stories lives tell: Narrative and dialogue in education*. New York: Teachers College Press.

Wodlinger, M. G. (1990). April: A case study in the use of guided reflection. *Alberta Journal of Educational Research, 36*(2), 115–131.

Wolcott, H. F. (1967). *A Kwakiutl village and school*. New York: Holt, Rinehart & Winston.

Wolcott, H. F. (1974). The teacher as an enemy. In G. D. Spindler (Ed.), *Education and cultural process: Toward an anthropology of education* (pp. 411–425). New York: Holt, Rinehart & Winston.

Wolcott, H. F. (1988). Ethnographic research in education. In R. M. Jaeger (Ed.), *Complementary methods for research in education* (pp. 185–249). Washington, DC: American Educational Research Association.

Wolcott, H. F. (1990a). On seeking—and rejecting—validity in qualitative research. In E. W. Eisner & A. Peshkin (Eds.), *Qualitative inquiry in education: The continuing debate* (pp. 121–152). New York: Teachers College Press.

Wolcott, H. F. (1990). *Writing up qualitative research*. Thousand Oaks, CA: Sage.

Wolcott, H. F. (1999). *Ethnography: A way of seeing*. Lanham, MD: Rowman & Littlefield.

Wolf, M. (1992). *A thrice-told tale: Feminism, postmodernism, and ethnographic responsibility*. Stanford, CA: Stanford University Press.

Woodbrooks, C. (1991). *The construction of identity through the presentation of self: Black women candidates interviewing for administrative positions at a research university*. Unpublished doctoral dissertation, Ohio State University.

Woody, T. (1929). *A history of women's education in the United States* (2 vols.) New York: Science Press.

Woolsey, L. K. (1986). The critical incident technique: An innovative qualitative method of research. *Canadian Journal of Counselling, 20*, 242–254.

World Vision. (1992). *Participatory planning and evaluation process*. Monrovia, CA: World Vision International Evaluation Department.

Worthen, B., Sanders, J. R., & Fitzpatrick, J. L. (1996). *Program evaluation* (2nd ed.). Reading, MA: Addison-Wesley.

Wrigley, J. (1982). *Class, politics, and public schools: Chicago, 1900–1950*. New Brunswick, NJ: Rutgers University Press.

Yin, R. K. (1994). *Case study research: Design and methods* (2nd ed.). Thousand Oaks, CA: Sage.

Yohn, S. (1991). An education in the validity of pluralism: The meeting between Presbyterian mission teachers and Hispanic Catholics in New Mexico, 1870–1912. *History of Education Quarterly* (pp. 343–364).

Yon, D. A. (2000). *Elusive culture: Schooling, race, and identity in global times*. Albany: State University of New York Press.

Young, M. (1971). *Knowledge and control: New directions for the sociology of education.* London: Collier MacMillan.

Zavella, P. (1996). Feminist insider dilemmas: Constructing ethnic identity with Chicana informants. In D. L. Wolf (Ed.), *Feminist dilemmas in fieldwork* (pp. 138–159). Boulder, CO: Westview.

Zimmerman, D. (1992). Achieving context: Openings in emergency calls. In G. Watson & R. M. Seiler (Eds.), *Text in context: Contributions to ethnomethodology* (pp. 3–51). London: Sage.

Zinn, H. (1989). Objections to objectivity. *Zeta Magazine 2,* 58–62.

Zinn, M. B. (1979). Field research in minority communities: Ethical, methodological and political observations by an insider. *Social Problems, 27*(2), 209–219.

Author Index

Subject Index